LIVIN

INTERNATIONAL

FOREIGN LANGUAGE GUIDE FOR HOTEL EMPLOYEES

LIVING LANGUAGE®

INTERNATIONAL FOREIGN LANGUAGE GUIDE FOR HOTEL EMPLOYEES

Written by
David D'Aprix
Cornell School of Hotel and Restaurant Management

Edited by
Ana Suffredini and Anthony Di Stefano

Living Language, A Random House Company
New York

ACKNOWLEDGMENTS

Many thanks to the Living Language® staff: Kathy Mintz, Helga Schier, Lisa Alpert, Christopher Warnasch, Germaine Ma, Olivia Valera, Eric Sommer, Liana Parry, Lenny Henderson, and Erin Bekowies. Special thanks to Marie-Claire Antoine, Erika Levy, Anthony Terrizzi, Fernanda Beccaglia-Unter, Wenston Zhou, and Beau Friedlander and Context for their expert translations.

Living Language books and packages are available at special discounts for bulk purchases for premiums and sales promotions, as well as for fund-raising or educational use. For more information, contact the Special Sales Manager at the address below.

Published by Living Language, A Random House Company,
201 East 50th Street, New York, New York, 10022.

Random House, Inc. New York, Toronto, London, Sydney, Auckland
www.livinglanguage.com

Living Language is a registered trademark of Crown Publishers, Inc.

Printed in the United States of America

Designed by Cynthia Dunne

Library of Congress Cataloging in Publication Data is available upon request.

ISBN 0-609-80283-6

10 9 8 7 6 5 4 3 2 1

First Edition

CONTENTS

INTRODUCTION

The *Living Language® International Foreign Language Guide for Hotel Employees* offers a fast, efficient, and cost-effective way to learn the language skills you'll need on the job. The program gives you *only* the vocabulary and phrases relevant to the hospitality industry in Chinese, French, German, Italian, Japanese, Korean, Portuguese, and Spanish. The phrasebook format lets you speak and understand the foreign language immediately, without hours of serious study. The tips you'll find throughout the book will help you use the language and interact with international clients more effectively.

The *International Foreign Language Guide for Hotel Employees* takes you through the most typical situations in which successful communication is a must. You'll learn how to take reservations, handle customer complaints, give directions in emergency situations, suggest activities and places of interest, accommodate business clients—all in the language of your choice. Unlike any other program, the *Living Language® International Foreign Language Guide for Hotel Employees* features *realistic* language that will help you handle almost any situation.

The complete program consists of this text and three hours of audio recordings.

Course Materials

• THE MANUAL •

The *Living Language® International Foreign Language Guide for Hotel Employees* comprises eight languages: Chinese, French, German, Italian, Japanese, Korean, Portuguese, and Spanish. They appear in alphabetical order in the manual, and there are seven sections for each language: *The Bare Essentials,*

Useful Expressions, Common Hospitality Scenarios, Checking In, Providing Assistance, Business Services and Clientele, and *Checking Out.*

The Bare Essentials and *Useful Expressions* sections provide a brief introduction to the sounds and structure of each language, together with a cultural note and useful expressions to get you started. The remaining sections are in the form of dialogues that branch out in several directions to account for the most likely outcomes of each situation. For example, *Common Hospitality Scenarios* covers *Greetings and Introductions, Reservations, Courtesy and Complaints,* and *Emergencies and Safety.*

Communication is not a one-way street. Therefore, speaking *and* comprehension skills are taught to guarantee that you can ask the questions *and* understand the responses. In addition, cultural tips address different customs in the various countries to help you do your job better and make your guests feel more comfortable. And vocabulary notes will improve your ability to speak. We have also included phonetic transcriptions of each phrase, making the manual easy to use even if you have no prior knowledge of a language.

• THE RECORDINGS (TWO NINETY-MINUTE CASSETTES) •

The recordings feature the *Common Hospitality Scenarios* section in each language. You'll hear each phrase in English first, followed by its equivalent in the target language. Pauses are provided for you to repeat the phrase in the foreign language. The phrases on the recordings appear in **boldface type** in the manual. The recordings can also be used without the manual—perfect for practicing and learning on the go.

SECTION A

CHINESE

1. The Bare Essentials

A. PRONUNCIATION CHART

CONSONANTS

CHINESE	ENGLISH EQUIVALENT	CHINESE	ENGLISH EQUIVALENT
b	boat	*p*	pass
m	mouse	*f*	flag
d	dock	*t*	tongue
n	nest	*l*	life
g	goat	*k*	keep
h	house	*j*	judge
q	chicken	*x*	short
zh	seeds+r*	*chi*	dots+r*
sh	pass+r*	*r**	read
z	seeds	*c*	dots
s	seed		

VOWELS

CHINESE	ENGLISH EQUIVALENT	CHINESE	ENGLISH EQUIVALENT
ü	you	*ia*	yard
üe	you+e	*ian*	yen

*There is no English sound that actually matches the Chinese "r" sound. However, you can manage to get a sound very close to that of the Chinese "r" by curling up the tip of your tongue when you pronounce the "r" in "read." As for the "r" in "seeds+r," "dots+r," and "pass+r," you need only to curl up the tip of your tongue when you pronounce the "ds," "ts," and "s" to achieve the sound represented by "zhi," "chi," and "shi," respectively.

a	father	*iang*	young
ai	kite	*ie*	yet
ao	now	*o*	all
e	earn	*ou*	go
ei	day	*u*	wood
er	curve	*ua*	waft
i	yield	*uo*	wall

B. THE CHINESE LANGUAGE

Word Order The basic Chinese sentence structure is the same as in English, following the pattern of subject-verb-object:

He took my pen.	*Tā ná le wǒ de bǐ.*
S V O	S V O

Nouns There are no articles in Chinese, although there are many "counters," which are used when a certain number of a given noun is specified. Various attributes of a noun, such as size, shape, or use, determine which counter is used with that noun. Chinese does not distinguish between singular and plural.

Verbs Chinese verbs are not conjugated, and they do not have tenses. Instead, a system of word order, word repetition, and the addition of a number of adverbs serves to indicate the tense of a verb, whether the verb is a suggestion or an order, or even whether the verb is part of a question. *Tā ná wǒ de bǐ.* (He is taking my pen.) *Tā ná le wǒ de bǐ.* (He took my pen.) *Tā yǒu méi yǒu ná wǒ de bǐ?* (Did he take my pen?) *Tā yào ná wǒ de bǐ.* (He will take my pen.)

Tones In English, intonation patterns can indicate whether a sentence is a statement (He's hungry.), a question (He's hungry?), or an exclamation (He's hungry!). Entire sentences carry particular "tones," but individual words do not. In Chinese, words have a particular tone value, and these tones are important in determining the meaning of a word. Observe the meanings of the following examples, each said with one of the four tones found in standard Chinese: *mā* (high, steady tone): mother, *má* (rising tone, like a question): fiber, *mǎ* (dipping tone): horse, and *mà* (dropping tone): swear.

C. THE CHINESE CULTURE

As the Chinese economy continues to grow, more guests from mainland China will have the opportunity to experience American hospitality. While they know about the handshake, most Chinese will also bow, out of habit. The Chinese are known for their good manners, and discussing negative aspects of China or its politics is considered to be in poor taste. Touching by strangers (other than a handshake) is perceived as extremely rude.

Tipping is traditionally an insult in China, so your best choice is to include a service charge on the check, if your restaurant policy allows that.

2. Useful Expressions

A. GENERAL

Hello.	*Nín hǎo.*
Good-bye.	*Zài-jiàn.*
Yes.	*Shì-de.*
No.	*Bù. (Bú-shì.)*
Maybe.	*Kě néng./Huò-xǔ.*
Please.	*Qǐng.*
Thank you (very much).	*Xiè-xiè. (Fēi-cháng gǎn-xiè.)*
You're welcome.	*Bù yòng xiè. (Bù-kè-qì.)*
Excuse me.	*Duì-bù-qǐ (apology). Mā-fán-nǐ (attention).*
I beg your pardon.	*Duì-bù-qǐ.*
I'm sorry.	*Hěn bào-qiàn.*

One moment, please.	*Qǐng, děng-yi-xià.*
Do you speak English?	*Nǐ shuō Yīng-yǔ ma?*
• Yes, I do.	• *Shì. Wǒ shuō Yīng-yǔ.*
• No, I don't.	• *Bù. Wǒ bù shuō Yīng-yǔ.*
• A little.	• *Shuō yì-diǎn Yīng-yǔ.*
• No, not at all.	• *Bù, yì-diǎn yě bú huì.*
That's okay.	*Nà ye méi guān-xì.*
It doesn't matter.	*Méi guān-xì.*
I don't speak Chinese.	*Wǒ bú-huì shuō Zhōng-wén.*
I can speak a little.	*Wǒ huì shuō yì-diǎn-diǎn.*
I understand a little.	*Wǒ dǒng yì-diǎn-diǎn.*
I don't understand.	*Wǒ bù dǒng.*
Please speak more slowly.	*Qǐng shuō màn yì-diǎn-diǎn.*
Would you repeat that, please?	*Qǐng chóng-fù yì-xià?*
Yes, sir/ma'am.	*Shì-de, xiān-sheng/tài-tài.*
No problem.	*Méi wèn-tí.*
It's my pleasure.	*Wǒ yě hěn gāo-xìng.*

B. NEEDS

I'd like _____.	*Wǒ xiǎng-yào _____.*
I need _____.	*Wǒ xū-yào _____.*
What would you like?	*Nǐ xiǎng-yào shén-me?*
Please bring me _____.	*Qǐng gěi wǒ _____.*
I'm looking for _____.	*Wǒ zài zhǎo _____.*
I'm hungry.	*Wǒ dù-zi è le.*
I'm thirsty.	*Wǒ kǒukě le.*
It's important.	*Hěn zhòng-yào.*
It's urgent.	*Hěn jǐn-jí.*

C. QUESTION WORDS

How?	*Zěn-me?*
How much?	*Duō-shǎo?*
How many?	*Duō-shǎo (gè)?*
Which?	*Nǎ yì-gè?*
What?	*Shén-me?*
What kind of?	*Shén-me yàng de?*
Who?	*Sheí?*
Where?	*Nǎ-lǐ?*
When?	*Shén-me shí-hòu?*
What does this mean?	*Zhè-shì shén-me yì-si?*
What does that mean?	*Nà-shì shén-me yì-si?*
How do you say _____ in Chinese?	*_____ yòng Zhōng-wen zěn-me shuō?*

D. COLORS

black	*hēi-sè*	pink	*táo-hóng-sè*
blue	*lán-sè*	purple	*zǐ-sè*
brown	*zōng-sè*	red	*hóng-sè*
gold	*jīn-sè*	silver	*yín-sè*
gray	*huī-sè*	violet	*lán-zǐ-sè*
green	*lǜ-sè*	white	*bái-sè*
orange	*chéng-huáng-sè*	yellow	*huáng-sè*

E. CARDINAL NUMBERS

1	*yī*	5	*wǔ*
2	*èr (counting), liǎng (quantity)*	6	*liù*
3	*sān*	7	*qī*
4	*sì*	8	*bā*

9	*jiŭ*	70	*qī-shí*
10	*shí*	80	*bā-shí*
11	*shí-yī*	90	*jiŭ-shí*
12	*shí-èr*	100	*yī-băi*
13	*shí-sān*	101	*yī-băi-líng-yī*
14	*shí-sì*	102	*yī-băi-líng-èr*
15	*shí-wŭ*	110	*yī-băi-yī-shí*
16	*shí-liù*	120	*yī-băi-èr-shí*
17	*shí-qī*	200	*èr-băi*
18	*shí-bā*	210	*èr-băi-yī-shí*
19	*shí-jiŭ*	300	*sān-băi*
20	*èr-shí*	400	*sì-băi*
21	*èr-shí-yī*	500	*wŭ-băi*
22	*èr-shí-èr*	600	*liù-băi*
23	*èr-shí-sān*	700	*qī-băi*
24	*èr-shí-sì*	800	*bā-băi*
25	*èr-shí-wŭ*	900	*jiŭ-băi*
26	*èr-shí-liù*	1,000	*yī-qiān*
27	*èr-shí-qī*	1,100	*yī-qiān-yī-băi*
28	*èr-shí-bā*	1,200	*yī-qiān-èr-băi*
29	*èr-shí-jiŭ*	2,000	*èr(liăng)qiān*
30	*sān-shí*	10,000	*yī-wàn*
31	*sān-shí-yī*	50,000	*wŭ-wàn*
32	*sān-shí-èr*	100,000	*(yī)shí-wàn*
40	*sì-shí*	1,000,000	*(yī)băiwàn*
50	*wŭ-shí*	1,000,000,000	*shíyì*
60	*liù-shí*		

F. ORDINAL NUMBERS

first	*dì-yī*	seventeenth	*dì-shí-qī*
second	*dì-èr*	eighteenth	*dì-shí-bā*
third	*dì-sān*	nineteenth	*dì-shí-jiǔ*
fourth	*dì-sì*	twentieth	*dì-èr-shí*
fifth	*dì-wǔ*	twenty-first	*dì-èr-shí-yī*
sixth	*dì-liù*	twenty-second	*dì-èr-shí-èr*
seventh	*dì-qī*	thirtieth	*dì-sān-shí*
eighth	*dì-bā*	fortieth	*dì-sì-shí*
ninth	*dì-jiǔ*	fiftieth	*dì-wǔ-shí*
tenth	*dì-shí*	sixtieth	*dì-liù-shí*
eleventh	*dì-shí-yī*	seventieth	*dì-qī-shí*
twelfth	*dì-shí-èr*	eightieth	*dì-bā-shí*
thirteenth	*dì-shí-sān*	ninetieth	*dì-jiǔ-shí*
fourteenth	*dì-shí-sì*	hundredth	*dì-yī-bǎi*
fifteenth	*dì-shí-wǔ*	thousandth	*dì-hī-qiān*
sixteenth	*dì-shí-liù*		

G. TIME OF DAY

1:00	*yī-diǎn*
2:00	*liǎng-diǎn*
3:00	*sān-diǎn*
4:00	*sì-diǎn*
5:00	*wǔ-diǎn*
6:00	*liù-diǎn*
7:00	*qī-diǎn*
8:00	*bā-diǎn*
9:00	*jiǔ-diǎn*
10:00	*shí-diǎn*
11:00	*shí-yī-diǎn*

12:00	*shí-èr-diǎn*
1:00 A.M.	*líng chén yī-diǎn*
3:00 P.M.	*xià-wǔ sān-diǎn*
noon	*zhōng-wǔ*
midnight	*wǔ-yè (bàn-yè)*
1:15	*yī-diǎn yí kè/yī-diǎn shí-wǔ fēn*
12:45	*shí-èr-diǎn sì-shí-wǔ fēn*
1:30	*yī-diǎn bàn/yī-diǎn sān-shí*
7:05	*qī-diǎn líng wǔ fēn*
4:55	*sì-diǎn wǔ-shí-wǔ fēn*

H. DAYS OF THE WEEK

Monday	*xīng-qī-yī*	Friday	*xīng-qī-wǔ*
Tuesday	*xīng-qī-èr*	Saturday	*xīng-qī-liù*
Wednesday	*xīng-qī-sān*	Sunday	*xīng-qī-rì/ xīng-qī-tiān*
Thursday	*xīng-qī-sì*		

I. MONTHS

January	*yī-yuè*	July	*qī-yuè*
February	*èr-yuè*	August	*bā-yuè*
March	*sān-yuè*	September	*jiǔ-yuè*
April	*sì-yuè*	October	*shí-yuè*
May	*wǔ-yuè*	November	*shí-yī-yuè*
June	*liù-yuè*	December	*shí-èr-yuè*

J. DATES

1998	*yī-jiǔ-jiǔ-bā-nián*
1999	*yī-jiǔ-jiǔ-jiǔ nián*
2000	*èr-líng-líng-líng nián*
2001	*èr-líng-líng-yī-nián*

2002	*èr-líng-líng-èr nián*
2003	*èr-líng-líng-sān nián*
2004	*èr-líng-líng-sì nián*
2005	*èr-líng-líng-wǔ nián*
Today is Thursday, September 22.	*Jīn-tiān shì jiǔ-yuè èr-shí-èr hào, xīng-qī-sì.*
Yesterday was Wednesday, September 21.	*Zuó-tiān shì jiǔ-yuè èr-shí-yī hào, xīng-qī-sān.*
The day before yesterday was Tuesday, September 20.	*Qián-tiān shì jiǔ-yuè èr-shí hào, xīng-qī-èr.*
Tomorrow is Friday, September 23.	*Míng-tiān shì jiǔ-yuè èr-shí sān hào, xīng-qī-wǔ.*
The day after tomorrow is Saturday, September 24.	*Hòu-tiān shì jiǔ-yuè èr-shí-sì hào, xīng-qī-liù.*
Next Friday is September 30.	*Xià-zhōu xīng-qī-wǔ shì jiǔ-yuè sān-shí hào.*
Last Friday was September 16.	*Shàng-zhōu xīng-qī-wǔ shì jiǔ-yuè shí-liù hào.*

K. MEASUREMENTS: DISTANCE

inch	*yīng-cùn*
foot	*yīng-chǐ*
yard	*mǎ*
mile	*yīng-lǐ*
millimeter	*háo-mǐ*
meter	*mǐ*
kilometer	*gōng-lǐ*

q=ch zh=ds+r sh=s+r z=ds x=sh chi=ts+r c=ts ü=yew üe=you+e
e=earn i=yield ia=yard ian=yen iang=young ie=yet ou=low u=wood

TIP! ••••

Most American employees are used to greeting guests jovially and asking them how they are. However, in any but the most informal settings, this behavior may actually be considered impolite. Asking guests how they are is stepping outside the bounds of your position and throws the burden onto the guest to answer you. Other cultures usually observe this principle to a much greater extent than we do.

3. Common Hospitality Scenarios

A. GREETINGS AND INTRODUCTIONS

GREETING THE GUEST

EMPLOYEE

Good morning,...	...*zǎo-ān.*
• Mr. _____.	• _____ *xiān-shēng*
• Mrs. _____.	• _____ *fū-ren*
• Miss _____.	• _____ *xiǎo-jiě*
• sir.	• *Xiān-shēng*
• ma'am.	• *Nǚ-shì*
• ladies and gentlemen.	• *Nǚ-shì-men, xiān-shēng-men*
• everyone.	• *Dà-jiā (gè-wèi)*
Good afternoon, Mr. _____.	_____ *xiān-shēng, nǐ hǎo.*
Good evening, Mr. _____.	_____ *xiān-shēng, wǎn-shàng hǎo.*
Hello, Mr. _____.	_____ *xiān-shēng, hǐ hǎo.*
Welcome to...	*Huān-yíng nǐ dào...*
• the hotel.	• *lǚ-guǎn.*

• the restaurant.	• *cān-guǎn.*
• our city.	• *wǒ-men de chéng-shì.*
• the United States.	• *Měi-guó.*
If there is anything I can do to make your stay more pleasant, please let me know.	*Rú yǒu shén-me kě-yǐ shǐ nǐ zài zhèr gùo de gèng-jiā shūshì, qǐng yī-dìng gào-sù wǒ-men.*
May I…	*Kě-yǐ ràng wǒ…*
• take your coat(s)?	• *jiē-xià nín de waì-yī ma?*
• carry your…for you?	• *gěi nín ná…ma?*
• bags	• *tí-bāo*
• suitcase	• *xīang-zi*
How are you today?	*Nín jīn-tiān gǎn-jué rú-hé?*

GUEST

I am…	*Wǒ…*
• fine, thank you.	• *hěn hǎo, xiè-xie.*
• okay.	• *hái kě-yǐ.*
• so-so.	• *rú-cǐ ér-yí.*
• very tired.	• *hěn lèi.*
• not feeling well.	• *bù hǎo.*
And you?	*Nǐ ne?*

INTRODUCTIONS

TIP! ••••

It is typical of American employees to introduce themselves to the guest. This practice allows the guest to call an employee by name when s/he needs something. This is not a common practice in other countries, however, so the international guest may simply ignore your introduction.

EMPLOYEE

My name is ____.	*Wǒ de míng-zì jiào ____.*
I am your…	*Wǒ shì nín de…*
• door attendant (doorman).	• *kān-mén-rén.*
• bell attendant (bellman).	• *shì-zhě.*
• driver.	• *sī-jī.*
• captain.	• *lǐng-duì.*
• concierge.	• *mén-fáng.*
• room attendant.	• *fáng-jiān guǎn-lǐ-yuán.*
• host.	• *zhǔ-rén.*
• hostess.	• *nǚ-zhǔ-rén.*
• manager.	• *jīng-lǐ.*
• server (waiter/waitress).	• *fú-wù-yuán.*
• chef.	• *dà-chú-shī.*
• activities director.	• *huó-dòng zhí-dǎo.*
Mr. (Mrs., Miss) ____, this is Mr. (Mrs., Miss) ____, the manager.	*____ xiān-shēng (tài-tài, xiǎo-jié), zhè-shì ____ xiān-shēng (tài-tài, xiǎo-jié), tā shì wǒ-men de jīng-lǐ.*
Mr. (Mrs., Miss) ____, may I introduce our manager, Mr. (Mrs., Miss) ____?	*____ xiān-shēng (tài-tài, xiǎo-jié), qǐng yǔn-xǔ wǒ jiè-shào wǒ-men de jīng-lǐ, ____ xiān-shēng (tài-tài, xiǎo-jié)?*

B. RESERVATIONS

HOTEL RESERVATIONS

OPERATOR

Good morning (afternoon, evening), ____ Hotel.	*Nín hǎo, zhè-shì ____ lǚ-guǎn.*
How may I direct your call?	*Qǐng-wèn nǐ yào zhǎo shéi?*

GUEST

Hello. Do you speak Chinese?	*Nín hǎo. Nǐ shuō Zhōng-wén ma?*

OPERATOR	
One moment, please.	*Qǐng děng yī-xià.*
I'll connect you with a bilingual operator.	*Wǒ yào gěi nǐ jiē yī-wèi shuāng-yǔ jiē-xiàn-yuán.*
I have a book here to help me.	*Wǒ yǒu yī-běn shū zuò zhí-dǎo.*
Please speak slowly.	*Qǐng màn-màn shuō.*
GUEST	
I would like to make a reservation, please.	*Wǒ yào yù-yuē.*
OPERATOR	
For a room or for one of the restaurants?	*Shi yù-yuē fáng-jiān hái-shì cān-guǎn?*
GUEST	
For a room, please.	*Yù-yuē fáng-jiān.*
For the _____ Restaurant, please.	*Yù-yuē _____ cān-guǎn.*
OPERATOR	
One moment, please. I will direct your call to Reservations.	*Qǐng děng yī-xià. Wǒ gěi nǐ jiē yù-yuē-bù.*
One moment, please. I will direct your call to the restaurant.	*Qǐng děng yī-xià. Wǒ gěi nǐ jiē cān-guǎn.*
CLERK	
Hello. This is Reservations.	*Nǐ hǎo. Zhè-shì yù-yuē-bù.*
What date would you like?	*Yù-yuē nǎ yī-tiān?*
GUEST	
May 27th.	*Wǔ-yuè èr-shí qī hào.*
CLERK	
For how many nights?	*Yào zhù jǐ-wǎn?*
GUEST	
For three nights, please.	*Zhù sān-gè wǎn-shàng.*

For a week.	*Zhù yī-gè xīng-qī.*
Just one night.	*Zhǐ zhù yī-yè.*
CLERK	
For how many people?	*Yǒu jǐ-wèi kè-rén?*
GUEST	
For two people.	*Liǎng-wèi.*
For one person.	*Yī-wèi.*
For two adults and a child.	*Liǎng-ge dà-rén, yī-ge xiǎo-hái(er).*
CLERK	
Do you have…	*Nín yǒu shén-me…*
• any special needs?	• *tè-bié xū-yào ma?*
• any special requests?	• *tè-bié yāo-qiú ma?*
GUEST	
No, thank you.	*Méi-yǒu, xiè-xie.*
Yes, I (we, my spouse) would like…	*Shì-de, wǒ (wǒ-men, wǒ de pèi-ǒu) xiǎng yào…*
• to be near the stairs.	• *kào-jìn lóu-tī.*
• to be near an exit.	• *kào-jìn chū-kǒu-chù.*
• a cot for our child.	• *yī-zhāng wá-wa-chuáng.*
• a handicapped-accessible room.	• *yī-jiān cán-fèi-rén de fáng-jiān.*
CLERK	
The rate is _____ per night.	*Měi zhù yī-wǎn shōu-fèi _____.*
Would you like to guarantee the reservation with a credit card?	*Nǐ xiǎng yòng xìn-yòng-kǎ lái bǎo-zhèng nǐ de yù-yuē ma?*
GUEST	
Yes, here is my card.	*Shì-de, zhè-shì wǒ de xìn-yòng-kǎ.*
My credit card number is _____.	*Wǒ de xìn-yòng-kǎ hào mǎ shì _____.*
CLERK	
What is the expiration date?	*Shén-me shí-jiān shī-xiào?*
Thank you.	*Xiè-xie.*

RESTAURANT RESERVATIONS

RESTAURANT HOST	
Good morning (afternoon, evening), _____ Restaurant.	*Nín hǎo, zhè-shì _____ cān-guǎn.*
GUEST	
I'd like to reserve a table for…	*Wǒ yào dìng zuò…*
• breakfast.	• *zǎo-cān.*
• lunch.	• *zhōng-cān.*
• dinner.	• *wǎn-cān.*
HOST	
For what time?	*Shén-me shí-jiān?*
GUEST	
For… o'clock.	*…diǎn zhōng.*
• seven	• *Qī-diǎn*
• eight	• *Bā-diǎn*
• nine	• *Jiǔ-diǎn*
For eight-thirty.	*Bā-diǎn sān-shí.*
HOST	
For how many people?	*Qǐng-wèn yǒu jǐgè rén?*
GUEST	
For one person.	*Yī-gè rén.*
For two people.	*Liǎng-gè rén.*
HOST	
And your name, please?	*Qǐng wèn nǐ de míng-zi?*
GUEST	
My name is _____.	*Wǒ jiào _____.*
HOST	
And is there a phone number where we can reach you?	*Qǐng-wèn nín de diàn-huà hào-mǎ shì duō-shǎo?*

GUEST

Yes, the number is _____.	*Wǒ de diàn-huà hào-mǎ shì _____.*
By the way, do you have any… items on the menu?	*Shùn-biàn wèn yī-xià, nín-men cài-dān shàng dōu yǒu shén-me…cài?*
• vegetarian	• *shū-cài*
• macrobiotic	• *wéi-shēng-wù shí-pǐn*
• low-fat	• *dī zhī-fáng*
• low-sodium	• *dī yán*

HOST

Would you like smoking or nonsmoking?	*Nǐ xī-yān hái-shì bù xī-yān?*

GUEST

We would like…	*Wǒ-men yào…*
• smoking.	• *xī-yān.*
• nonsmoking.	• *bù xī-yān.*

HOST

Thank you.	*Xiè-xiè.*
That will be two people at eight o'clock.	*Bā-diǎn, liǎng-gè rén, duì ma.*
That's a party of six at seven-thirty.	*Nǐ dìng de shì qī-diǎn-sān-shí, liù-gè rén.*

C. COURTESY AND COMPLAINTS

GENERAL EXPRESSIONS OF COURTESY

Please.	***Qǐng.***
Thank you.	***Xiè-xie.***
You're welcome.	***Huān-yíng.***
Excuse me.	***Duì-bù-qǐ.***
I beg your pardon.	***Qǐng yuán-liàng.***
I'm (terribly) sorry.	***Wǒ hěn bào-qiàn.***

That's okay.	*Méi shén-me.*
No problem.	*Méi wèn-tí.*
It doesn't matter.	*Méi guān-xì.*

COURTESY IN THE HOTEL

CONCIERGE

Good morning, sir, ma'am.	*Xiān-shēng hǎo, fū-rén hǎo.*
May I help you with something today?	*Wǒ kěyǐ bāng nǐ shén-me ma?*

GUEST

Yes, I need…	*Wǒ xū-yào…*
• my room made up between now and ____.	• *zài xiàn-zài yú ____ diǎn zhī-jiān zhěng-lǐ hǎo wǒ de fáng-jiān.*
• more towels, please.	• *gèng-duō de mǎo-jīn.*
• a rental car.	• *zū yī-liàng chē.*
• a taxi.	• *yī-liàng jì-chéng-chē (Taiwan)/ yī-liàng chū zū chē.*
• a fax sent.	• *fā chuán-zhēn.*
• some letters mailed.	• *fā jì-fēng xìn.*
• to make arrangements for a business meeting.	• *ān-pái yī-gè shēng-yì huì-tán.*
• tickets to a baseball game.	• *mǎi bàng-qiú piào.*
• tickets to a concert.	• *mǎi yīn-yuè-huì de piào.*

GUEST COMPLAINTS IN THE HOTEL

CONCIERGE

Is everything satisfactory?	*Yī-qiè dōu mǎn-yì ma?*

GUEST

No, there is a problem.	*Bù, yǒu wèn-tí.*
• The light	• *Diàn-dēng*
• The toilet	• *Cè-suǒ*

• The television	• *Diàn-shì*
• The radio	• *Shōu-yīn-jī*
• The air-conditioning	• *Kōng-tiáo*
• The alarm clock	• *Nào-zhōng*
• The heat	• *Nuǎn-qì*
• The key	• *Yào-shi*
• The lock	• *Suǒ*
• The fan	• *Diàn-shàn*
. . . doesn't work.	*. . . huài le.*

CLERK

I'll have Maintenance fix that right away.	*Wǒ mǎ-shàng jiào-rén xiū-lǐ.*
I apologize.	*Duì-bù-qǐ.*

GUEST

My room . . .	***Wǒ de fáng jiān . . .***
• wasn't clean.	***• méi-yǒu dǎ-sǎo gān-jìng.***
• was noisy.	***• tài chǎo le.***
• stinks (smells).	***• yǒu chòu-wèi.***
The bed was uncomfortable.	***Chuáng bù shū-fu.***
The water wasn't hot.	***Shuǐ bù rè.***
Room service was late.	***Fáng-jiān de fú-wù tài màn le.***
The service was very poor.	***Fú-wù tài chà.***
The employees were . . .	***Gōng-rén . . .***
• very good.	***• hěn hǎo.***
• excellent.	***• fēi-cháng-hǎo.***
• rude.	***• méi lǐ-mào.***
• incompetent.	***• bù chèng-zhí.***
• unfriendly.	***• bù yǒu-hǎo.***

The room attendant is rude and inattentive.	*Fáng-jiān guǎn-lǐ-yuán fú wú bù hǎo.*
I didn't receive my wake-up call.	*Méi-yǒu rén jiào-xǐng wǒ.*
I'm very disappointed with the level of service in this hotel.	*Zhè-ge lǚ-guǎn de fú-wù shuǐ-píng shǐ wǒ shí-fen shī-wàng.*
This is the worst hotel I've ever seen.	*Zhè-shì wǒ suǒ zhù-guò de zuì chà de yī-jiā lǚ-guǎn.*

CONCIERGE

Please let me make the situation right.	*Qǐng ràng wǒ mí-bǔ wǒmen de guò-shí.*
I'm certain we can straighten out the problem.	*Wǒ xiāng-xìn wǒ-men kě-yǐ jiě-jué zhè-gè wèn-tí.*
You won't pay for anything that wasn't completely up to your standards.	*Rú-guǒ méi-yǒu wán-quán dá-dào nín de biāo-zhǔn, nín bù yòng fù-qián.*
Please tell me what I can do to correct this terrible situation.	*Qǐng gào-sù wǒ zěn-yàng cái kě-yǐ míbǔ zhè-gè cuò-wù.*
We'll take ____ percent off your bill.	*Wǒ-men jiāng cóng nín de zhàng-dān zhōng jiǎn-qù bǎi-fēn-zhī ____.*
We're going to give you ____ night(s), compliments of the hotel.	*Wǒ-men jiāng ràng nín zài zhèr miǎn-fèi zhù ____ wǎn-shàng.*
Your entire bill is compliments of the house.	*Nín de quán-bù feì-yòng jiāng yóu wǒ-men lái fù.*

GUEST

Yes, that would be satisfactory.	*Hǎo, zhè-yàng kě-yǐ shǐ wǒ mǎn-yì.*
No, that would not be satisfactory.	*Bù, bù-huì sàng wǒ gǎn-dào mǎn-yì.*
I appreciate all your efforts.	*Wǒ-gǎn-ji nǐ zuò de yī-qiè.*
Thank you, that would be very nice.	*Nà tài hǎo le.*
I will never come here again.	*Wǒ jué-duì bù-huì zài-lái zhè-li.*

---

q=ch zh=ds+r sh=s+r z=ds x=sh chi=ts+r c=ts ü=yew üe=you+e
e=earn i=yield ia=yard ian=yen iang=young ie=yet ou=low u=wood

MANAGEMENT COMPLAINTS

MANAGER

We have had some complaints about the noise coming from your room. — *Yǒu-rén bào-yuàn nín fáng-jiān li de zào-yīn tài dà.*

You are disturbing… — *Nín zài rǎo-luàn…*

- the people in the room next door. — *gé-bì de kè-rén.*
- the people at the next table. — *lín-zuò de rén.*
- our other guests. — *de qí-tā fáng-kè.*

GUEST

We're sorry. — *Duì-bù-qǐ.*

We understand. — *Wǒ-men zhī-dào le.*

We'll take care of it. — *Wǒ-men huì zhù-yì de.*

We'll keep it down from now on. — *Wǒ-men huì bǎo-chí ān-jìng de.*

Who cares! — *Wǒ cái bù guǎn ne!*

Leave us alone! — *Nín bù-yào rě wǒ!*

MANAGER

If you don't cooperate, I'm afraid I'll have to… — *Rú guǒ bù-yú wǒ-men hé-zuò, wǒ zhǐ-hǎo…*

- ask you to leave the hotel (restaurant). — *qǐng nín lí-kāi (cānguǎn).*
- call security. — *jiào bǎo-ān rén-yuán.*
- call the police. — *jiào jǐng-chá.*

D. EMERGENCIES AND SAFETY

EMPLOYEE

Please note the emergency exits on this card. — *Qǐng zhù-yì kǎ-piàn shàng biāo-yǒu jǐn-jí chū-kǒu de wèi-zhì.*

Please note the emergency escape route on the door. — *Qǐng zhù-yì mén shàng biāo-yǒu jǐn-jí chè-tuì lù-xiàn.*

---

q=ch zh=ds+r sh=s+r z=ds x=sh chi=ts+r c=ts ü=yew üe=you+e e=earn i=yield ia=yard ian=yen iang=young ie=yet ou=low u=wood

Your room is equipped with smoke alarms.	*Nĭ de fáng-jiān bèi-yŏu fáng-yān jĭng-bào-qì.*
Here is the fire alarm.	*Zhè shì huŏ-jĭng.*
In an emergency, dial ____.	*Yŏu jĭn-jí qíng-kuàng, qĭng bō ____.*
GUEST	
Help!	*Jiù-rén-a!*
Fire!	*Shī-hŭo le!*
I need a doctor.	*Wŏ xū-yào yī-shēng.*
I'm…	*Wŏ…*
My husband (wife) is…	*Wŏ zàng-fū (qī-zĭ)…*
Someone is…	*Yŏu rén…*
• very sick.	• *shēn-bìng le.*
• having a heart attack.	• *xīn-zhàng-bìng fā le.*
• nauseated.	• *ŏu-tù.*
• choking.	• *chuăn-bù-guò-qì lái.*
• losing consciousness.	• *hūn-dăo le.*
• about to vomit.	• *yào ŏu-tù.*
• having a seizure.	• *fā-bìng le.*
• stuck.	• *bèi kùn-zhù le.*
I can't breathe.	*Wŏ bù-néng hū-xī.*
MANAGER	
I'll call an ambulance.	*Wŏ qù jiào jiù-hù-chē.*
Don't move.	*Bié dòng.*
The doctor will be here very soon.	*Yī-shēng mă-shàng jiù-yào dào le.*
Are you hurt?	*Hĕn tòng ma?*
What happened?	*Chū le shén-me máo-bìng?*
GUEST	
I tripped and fell.	*Wŏ bàn-dăo le.*
I cut myself.	*Wŏ gē-shāng le.*

I drank too much.	*Wǒ hē-de tài-duō le.*
I don't know.	*Wǒ bù zhī-dào.*
I've injured my…	*Wǒ shāng le wǒ de…*
• head.	• *tóu.*
• neck.	• *bó-zǐ.*
• back.	• *bèi.*
• arm.	• *gē-bi.*
• leg.	• *tuǐ.*
• foot.	• *jiǎo.*
• eye(s).	• *yǎn-jīng.*

DOCTOR (MEDICAL TECHNICIAN)

You'll be fine; try to relax.	*Nǐ méi-shì; bù-yào jǐn-zhāng.*
We're taking you to the hospital.	*Wǒ-men yào sòng nǐ qù yī-yuàn.*
Whom should we notify?	*Yào wǒ-men tōng-zhī shén-me rén ma?*

GUEST

I've been robbed.	***Wǒ bèi qiǎng le.***

MANAGER

What did they take?	***Tā-men ná-zǒu le shén-me dōng-xī?***
Let me call the police.	***Ràng wǒ bào jǐng-chá.***
Attention, ladies and gentlemen.	***Nǚ-shì-men, xiān-shēng-men, qǐng zhù-yì le.***
May I have your attention, please?	***Qǐng dà-jiā zhù-yì le.***
Please…	***Qǐng…***
• remain calm.	**• *bǎo chí lěng-jìng.***
• follow the instructions of the staff.	**• *zūn-cóng-gōng-zuò rén-yuán de zhí-shì.***
• wait in your rooms.	**• *zài fáng-jiān-lǐ děng-hòu.***
• get under a table or doorway.	**• *cáng-zài zhuō-zi dǐ xià huò mén kuāng lǐ.***

• follow the evacuation plan (route) printed on your door (in the hallways).	• *yī-zhào yìn zài mén-shàng (guò-dào-lǐ) de jì-huà (lù-xiàn) shū-sàn.*
We'll have the situation under control as soon as possible.	*Wǒ-men jiāng jìn-kuài kòng-zhì jú-miàn.*
Thank you for your patience.	*Xiè-xie nǐ-men de nài-xīn.*

4. Checking In

A. AT THE FRONT DESK

FRONT DESK CLERK

Good morning (afternoon, evening).	*Nín-zǎo (xià-wǔ hǎo, wǎn-shàng hǎo).*
How may I help you?	*Yǒu shén-me xū-yào wǒ bāng-máng ma?*

GUEST

I have a reservation under the name _____.	*Wǒ yòng _____ de míng-zì yù-yuē guò.*
Do you have a room for one (two)?	*Yǒu dān-rén (shuāng-rén) fáng-jiān ma?*

CLERK

Yes, we have your reservation.	*Shì-de, wǒ-men yǒu ní de yù-yūe.*
Yes, for how many nights?	*Nǐ dǎ-suàn zhù duō-shǎo tiān?*
No, I'm sorry, we're full.	*Duì-bù-qǐ, wǒ-men kè-mǎn le.*

GUEST

For _____ night(s), please.	*Zhù _____ tiān.*
What are your rates?	*Qǐng-wèn jià-gé rú-hé?*

CLERK

• For a single,	• *Dān-rén fáng-jiān,*
• For a double,	• *Shuāng-rén fáng-jiān,*
• For adjoining rooms,	• *Lín-jiē fáng-jiān,*

• For a suite,	• *Tào-jiān,*
...the rate is _____ per night.	*...měi-wǎn shōu-fèi _____.*
GUEST	
Are any meals included?	*Bāo-kuò chī-fàn ma?*
Is breakfast included?	*Zǎo-cān bāo-kuò zài-nèi ma?*
CLERK	
No, meals are extra.	*Bù, chī-fàn bù bāo-kuò zài-nèi.*
Yes, breakfast is included.	*Shì-de, zǎo-cān bāo-kuò zài-nèi.*
You can choose...	*Nǐ kě xuǎn-zé...*
• the American plan (all meals included).	• *Měi-guó jì-huà (bāo-kuò sān cān).*
• the modified American plan (breakfast and dinner).	• *xīu-zhèng de Měi-guó jì-huà (bāo-kuò zǎo-cān hé wǎn-cān).*
• the European plan (no meals included).	• *Ōu-zhōu jì-huà (bù bāo chī-fàn).*
GUEST	
I'd like a room...	*Wǒ yaò...de fáng-jiān.*
• that faces the back (front).	• *miàn-xiàng bèi-hòu (qián-miàn)*
• that faces the water (pool).	• *miàn-xiàng shuǐ (yóu-yǒng-chí)*
• with a private bath/toilet/shower.	• *yǒu sī-rén yù-shì/cèsǔo/lín-yù*
• with a handicapped-accessible bathroom.	• *yǒu cán-jī shè-shī yù-shì*
• with air-conditioning.	• *yǒu kōng-tiáo*
• with a TV.	• *yǒu diàn-shì*
• with cable.	• *yǒu yǒu-xiàn diàn-shì*
• with a fax machine.	• *yǒu chuán-zhēn-jī*
• with a phone.	• *yǒu diàn-huà*
• with a network hookup for my computer.	• *yǒu diàn-nǎo lián-jiē*
• with a view.	• *yǒu fēng-jíng*

• with a whirlpool bath/Jacuzzi.	• *yǒu xuàn-wō yù-shì/Jiā-kù-rè yù-shì*
• with two double beds.	• *yǒu liǎng-gè shuāng-rén-chuáng*
• with a king-size bed.	• *yǒu dà-chuáng*
• with an extra bed.	• *yǒu duō-yú de chuáng*
• with a baby crib.	• *yǒu yīng-ér-chuáng*
• with a balcony.	• *yǒu yáng-tái*
• with a sitting area.	• *yǒu qǐ-jū-shì*
• with a bar.	• *yǒu jiǔ-bā*
• with a kitchenette.	• *yǒu xiǎo-chú-fáng*
• away from the elevator.	• *lí diàn-tī yuǎn*
• with no meals.	• *bù bāo-kuò chī-fàn*

CLERK

No problem.	*Méi-wèn-tí.*
I'm sorry.	*Duì-bù-qǐ.*
There is none available.	*Xiàn-zài méi-yǒu.*
We don't offer that.	*Wǒ-men bù tí-gòng zhè-lèi dōng-xi.*

GUEST

Does the hotel have…	*Lǚ-guǎn yǒu…*
• a restaurant?	• *cān-guǎn ma?*
• a bar?	• *jiǔ-bā ma?*
• room service?	• *fáng-jiān fú-wù ma?*
• a gym/health club?	• *jiàn-shēn-fáng/jù-lè-bù ma?*
• a spa hot tub?	• *quán-shuǐ rè-zǎo-pén ma?*
• a swimming pool?	• *yóu-yǒng-chí ma?*
• baby-sitting?	• *yīng-ér kān-hù ma?*
• tennis courts?	• *wǎng-qiú-chǎng ma?*
• laundry (dry-cleaning) service?	• *xǐ-yī (gān-xǐ) fú-wù ma?*
• a garage?	• *tíng-chē-fáng ma?*
May I see the room?	*Kě-yǐ kàn yī-xià fáng-jiàn ma?*

---

q=ch zh=ds+r sh=s+r z=ds x=sh chi=ts+r c=ts ü=yew üe=you+e
e=earn i=yield ia=yard ian=yen iang=young ie=yet ou=low u=wood

CLERK

Yes, certainly. Here's the key.	*Dāng-rán kě-yǐ. Zhè-shì fáng-jiān de yào-shi.*
Would you like another room?	*Nǐ yào-bù-yào huàn yī-gè fáng-jiān?*

GUEST

I'd like something…	*Wǒ yào…*
• smaller.	• *xiǎo yī-diǎnr de.*
• larger.	• *dà yī-diǎnr de.*
• quieter.	• *ān-jìng yī-diǎnr de.*
• better.	• *hǎo yī-diǎnr de.*
• cheaper.	• *pián-yí yī-diǎnr de.*
• on another floor.	• *huàn-dào lìng yī-céng lóu qù.*
I'll take the room, please.	*Qǐng gěi wǒ zhè jiān fáng ba.*

CLERK

Very well, how will you be paying?	*Hǎo de, nín zěn-me fù-fèi?*

GUEST

I'll pay with…	*Wǒ yòng…zhī-fù.*
• cash.	• *xiàn-jīn*
• a credit card.	• *xìn-yòng-kǎ*
• traveler's checks.	• *lǚ-xíng zhī-piào*

CLERK

Thank you.	*Xiè-xie.*
To charge meals and services to your room, I'll need a credit card.	*Yào bǎ chī-fàn hé fú-wù-fèi jì-zaì nǐ de fáng-jiān zhàng-hào shang, nǐ xū-yào yǒu xìn yòng-kǎ.*
You may settle the bill with traveler's checks (cash).	*Nǐ kě-yǐ yòng lǚ-xíng zhī-piào (xiàn-jīn) lái fù-zhàng.*
If you would like to store valuables, we have a safe.	*Rú yǒu zhēn-guì wù-pǐn, wǒ-men yǒu bǎo-xiǎn-guì.*
Please note that…	*Qǐng zhù-yì…*
• quiet hours are between _____ and _____.	• *ān-jìng shí-jiān shì zài _____ yú _____ zhī-jiān.*

- there are no pets allowed. — • *bù yǔn-xǔ dài chǒng-wù.*
- children under _____ stay free. — • _____ *suì yǐ-xià de ér-tóng miǎn-feì jū-zhù.*
- smoking is allowed only in the bar. — • *zhǐ-yǒu jiǔ-bā yǔn-xǔ chōu-yān.*
- we do not allow cooking in the rooms. — • *bù yǔn-xǔ zaì fáng-jiān-lǐ zuò-fàn.*

GUEST

Do I (we) have any messages? — *Yǒu rén gěi wǒ (wǒ-men) liú-yán ma?*

I would like a wake-up call, please. — *Wǒ xū-yào yǒu-rén jiào-xǐng wǒ.*

May we have..., please? — *Qǐng zài gěi wǒ-men...kě-yǐ ma?*

- extra blankets — • *yī-xiē tǎn-zi*
- extra towels — • *yī-xiē máo-jīn*
- a hair dryer — • *yī-gè chuī-fēng-jī*
- an iron — • *yī-gē yùn-dǒu*
- ice — • *yī-xiē-bīng*

CLERK

I'll have that brought to your room right away. — *Wǒ mǎ-shàng gěi nín daì-dào fáng-jiān lái.*

GUEST

Where is... — *...zài nǎ-lí?*

- the room attendant? — • *Fáng-jiān fú-wù-yuán*
- the bellman (bell attendant)? — • *Lǚ-guǎn shì-zhě*
- the manager? — • *Jīng-lǐ*
- the dining room? — • *Cān-tīng*
- the gift shop? — • *Lǐ-pǐn-diàn*
- the newsstand? — • *Bào-tān*

CLERK

Just over there. — *Jiù-zài nà-biān.*

GUEST

How do I use the telephone?	*Gāi zěn-yàng shǐ-yòng diàn-huà?*

CLERK

The instructions are next to the phone.	*Shuō-míng jiù-zài diàn-huà páng-biān.*
Dial _____ for a local (long-distance) call,	*Dǎ běn-dì (cháng-tú) diàn-huà, qǐng bō _____,*
wait for the tone,	*zài děng xùn-hào,*
then dial the number.	*rán-hòu bō hào-mǎ.*
Dial _____ for an operator.	*Dǎ cha-hào-tái bō _____.*
To use a credit card, dial _____.	*Shǐ-yòng xìn-yòng-kǎ, bō _____.*

GUEST

Please have our luggage brought to our room.	*Qǐng-bǎ xíng-lǐ sòng-dào wǒ-men fáng-jiān lái.*
We'll need a wheelchair.	*Wǒ-men xū-yaò shǐ-yòng lún-yǐ.*

CLERK

Yes, right away.	*Mǎ-shàng jiù-lái.*

GUEST

We'd like to order a pizza, please.	*Wǒ-men xiǎng jiào yì-dà-lì cuì-bǐng.*

MANAGER

I'll be happy to call someone for you.	*Wǒ hěn lè-yì dài-nǐ dǎ diàn-huà.*
We have room service, but we don't allow outside vendors into the hotel.	*Wǒ-men tí-gòng fáng-jiān fú-wù, dàn bùyǔn-xǔ shāng-fàn dào lǚ-guǎn lái.*

GUEST

We'd like to entertain a few friends in our room.	*Wǒ-men xiǎng zài fáng-jiān lǐ qǐng-kè.*

MANAGER

We allow guests in the rooms until _____.	*Kè-rén kě-yǐ zài fáng-jiān lǐ dāi-dào _____ zhōng.*

B. SHOWING GUESTS TO THEIR ROOMS

BELLMAN (BELL ATTENDANT)

My name is _____, and I'm your bell attendant.	*Wǒ jiào _____, wǒ shì nín de jiē-daì-yuán.*
May I show you to your room?	*Qǐng ràng wǒ daì nǐ qù nín de fáng-jiān?*

GUEST

No, thanks. We'll find it ourselves.	*Bù, xiè-xie. Wǒ-men zì-jǐ zhǎo-de-dào.*
Yes, please.	*Kě-yǐ, qǐng ba.*

BELLMAN

This way, please.	*Qǐng zǒu zhè-biān.*
The elevator(s) is (are) over here.	*Diàn-tī zài zhè-biān.*
May I show you the features of your room?	*Qǐng ràng wǒ jiè-shào yī-xià nǐ de fáng-jián, hǎo ma?*
This is the key to the minibar.	*Zhè-shì xiǎo-jiǔ-bā de yào-shi.*
• Any movie you select	• *Nǐ kàn-de diàn-yǐng*
• Any long-distance calls you make	• *Nǐ dǎ-de cháng-tú diàn-huà*
• Any snack or beverage you take from the refrigerator	• *Nǐ shǐ-yòng bīng-xiāng lǐ de diǎn-xīn huò yǐn-liào*
...will be charged to your room.	*...dōu huì jì-zài nǐ fáng-jiān de zhàng-hào shàng.*

TIP! ••••

International guests in particular may have questions about using the telephone and will appreciate seeing how the television and pay movies work.

Here is the control for the heating (air-conditioning).	*Zhè-shì nuǎn-qì (kōng-tiáo) de kòng-zhì.*
GUEST	
How do I call Room Service?	*Zěn-yàng jiào fáng-jiān fú-wù?*
BELLMAN	
Dial ____.	*Bō ____.*
GUEST	
This room…	*Zhè-gè fáng-jiān…*
• is too close to the elevator(s).	• *lí diàn-tī taì jìn le.*
• hasn't been made up.	• *méi-yǒu zhěng-lǐ hǎo.*
• doesn't get enough sun.	• *méi-yǒu zú-gòu de yáng-guāng.*
• smells (like cigarettes).	• *yǒu (xiāng-yān) wèir.*
The toilet (bathtub, sink) is clogged.	*Cè-suǒ (yù-pén, xǐ-shoǔ-chí) dǔ-zhù le.*
May I (we) change rooms, please?	*Wǒ (wǒ-men) kě-yǐ huàn-gè fáng-jiàn ma?*
BELLMAN	
Please let me check our availability with the front desk.	*Qǐng ràng wǒ yú qián-tái dǎ-tīng yī-xià shì-fǒu hái-yǒu fáng-jiān.*
Sure, I'll be happy to assist you.	*Dāng-rán, wǒ hěn yuàn-yì bāng-zhù nǐ.*
Please call if I can help you with anything else.	*Yǒu shì qǐng dǎ diàn-huà gěi wǒ.*

VOCABULARY ••••

THE GUEST ROOM

air-conditioning	*kōng-tiaó*
balcony	*yáng-tái*
bath mat	*yù-shì diàn-zǐ*
bathtub	*yù-gāng*
bed	*chuáng*
bedspread	*chuáng-dān*
blanket	*máo-tǎn*
blinds	*chuāng-lián*
carpet	*dì-tǎn*
ceiling	*tiān-huā-bǎn*
chair	*yǐ-zi*
closet	*yī-chú*
conditioner	*tiáo-jié-qì*
couch	*cháng-shā-fā*
crib	*ér-tóng-chuáng*
desk	*xiě-zì-tái*
Do Not Disturb sign	*bù-yào-dǎ-rǎo-biāo-zhì*
door	*mén*
drapes	*chuāng-lián*
dresser	*shū-zhuāng-taí*
fan	*shàn*
floor	*dì-bǎn*
glass(es)	*bēi zi*
hair dryer	*diàn-chuī-fēng*
(coat) hanger	*(yī)jiàr*
heat	*nuǎn-qì*

(cont'd.)

The Guest Room *(cont'd.)*

heater	*qǔ-nuǎn-jī*
ice bucket	*bīng-tǒng*
iron	*tiě*
lamp	*dēng*
light	*diàn-dēng*
lock	*suǒ*
minibar	*mǐ-nǐ-jiǔ-bā*
mirror	*jìng-zi*
nightstand	*chuáng-tou-guì*
pillow	*zhěn-tóu*
radio	*shōu-yīn-jī*
razor	*guā-hú-dāo*
sewing kit	*féng-rèn-baō*
shampoo	*xǐ-fà-jīng*
sheets	*chuáng-dān*
shower	*lín-yù*
shower cap	*lín-yù-zhào*
sink	*xǐ-shoǔ-chí*
soap	*féi-zào*
telephone	*diàn-huà*
television	*diàn-shì*
thermostat	*héng-wēn-jī*
toilet	*chōu-shuǐ mǎ-tǒng*
toilet paper	*wèi-shēng-zhǐ*
toothbrush	*yá-shuā*
toothpaste	*yá-gāo*
towel	*máo-jīn*
VCR	*lù-yǐng-jī*
wall	*qiáng*
window	*chuāng-hù*

5. Providing Assistance

A. GIVING DIRECTIONS

CONCIERGE

Good morning. May I help you?	*Nín hǎo. Yǒu shén-me xū-yào wǒ bāng-máng ma?*

GUEST

Yes, where is (are) the...	*Shì-de,...zài nǎr?*
• bathrooms?	• *cè-suǒ*
• lounge/bar?	• *xiū-xī-shì/jiǔ-bā*
• coffee shop/restaurant?	• *kā-fēi-diàn/cān-guǎn*
• barbershop/hairdresser's?	• *lǐ-fā-diàn/měi-róng-diàn*
• gift shop?	• *lǐ-pǐn-diàn*
• health club/gym?	• *jiàn-shēn jù-lè-bù/liàn-shēn-fáng*
• ballroom?	• *tiào-wǔ-tīng*
• elevator?	• *diàn-tī*
• pay phones?	• *zì-fù diàn-huà*
• ice machine?	• *zhì-bīng-jī*

CONCIERGE

Take...	*Nǐ kě shǐ-yòng...*
• the escalator.	• *shēng-jiàng-tī.*
• the elevator.	• *diàn-tī.*
• the stairs.	• *lóu-tī.*
Go...	*Wàng...zǒu.*
• up.	• *shàng*
• down.	• *xià*
• left.	• *zuǒ*
• right.	• *yòu*
• straight ahead.	• *qián*
• around the corner.	• *zhuǎn-gùo jiē-jiǎo*

• left, then right.	• *xiān wàng zuǒ, zài wàng yòu*
• past the elevators.	• *chuān-gùo diàn-tī*
• to the first (second, third, fourth) floor.	• *dào dì-yī (dì-èr, dì-sān, dì-sì) céng*
• left (right) when you exit the elevator.	• *chū dìan-tī hòu wàng zuǒ (yòu) zòu*
• in through the second set of doors.	• *chuān-guò dì-èr shàn mén*
It will be…	*Jiù-zài…*
• on your right.	• *nǐ de yòu-biān.*
• on your left.	• *nǐ de zuǒ-biān.*
• right in front of you.	• *nǐ de miàn-qián.*
GUEST	
How do I get…	*Dào…zěn-me zǒu?*
• to the hospital?	• *yī-yuàn*
• to city hall?	• *shì-zhèng-tīng*
• to the _____ restaurant/hotel?	• _____ *cān-tīng/lǚ-guǎn*

TIP! ••••

You can simply explain many directions, but when they're more complex, you should use either a map or written instructions (or both). Hotels should keep preprinted directions to major sites on hand. Also, many cultures don't speak of distance in terms of city blocks but will understand if you use the word "streets" instead. And remember that most international guests use the metric system and may have difficulties figuring a distance given in miles, yards, or feet.

q=ch zh=ds+r sh=s+r z=ds x=sh chi=ts+r c=ts ü=yew üe=you+e
e=earn i=yield ia=yard ian=yen iang=young ie=yet ou=low u=wood

• to the train station?	• *huǒ-chē-zhàn*
• to the bus station?	• *qì-chē-zhàn*
• to the nearest bus stop?	• *zuì-jìn de qì-chē-zhàn*
• to the mall?	• *shāng-cháng*
• to the post office?	• *yóu-jú*
• to the airport?	• *feī-jī-cháng*
• downtown?	• *shì-qú*
• to the car rental agency?	• *zū-chē-diàn*
• to _____ Street/Avenue?	• _____ *jiē/dà-jiē*

CONCIERGE

When you exit the hotel, go…	*Chū lǚ-guǎn hòu, wàng…zǒu.*
• left.	• *zuǒ*
• right.	• *yòu*
• straight ahead.	• *qián*
• north.	• *běi*
• south.	• *nán*
• east.	• *dōng*
• west.	• *xī*

GUEST

How far is it?	*Yǒu duō-yuǎn?*

CONCIERGE

It's about _____…	*Dà-gài yǒu* _____…
• blocks (streets).	• *tiaó-jiē.*
• miles.	• *yīng-lǐ.*
• kilometers.	• *gōng-lǐ.*
• minutes…	• *fēn-zhōng…*
• on foot.	• *zǒu-lù.*
• by car.	• *zuò qì-chē.*
• by bus.	• *zuò gōng-gòng qì-chē.*
• by metro (subway).	• *zuò dì-tiě.*

GUEST

Can you show me on the map?	*Nǐ néng gào-sù wǒ zài dì-tǔ shàng de wèi-zhì ma?*

CONCIERGE

Sure, it's right here.	*Dāng-rán kě-yǐ, jiù-zài zhèr.*
Let me draw you a little map.	*Ràng wǒ gěi nǐ huà gè tú.*

GUEST

Can you tell me where I can… around here?	*Qǐng-wèn, wǒ kě-yǐ zài shén-me dì-fāng…*
• take a walk	• *sàn-bù?*
• ride a bike	• *qí dān-chē?*
• jog	• *pǎo-bù?*

CONCIERGE

Yes, we have maps of…trails right here.	*Wǒ-men zhèr yǒu…lù-xiàn de dì-tǔ.*
• jogging	• *pǎo-bù*
• walking	• *sàn-bù*
• bike	• *dān-chē*

B. RECOMMENDING PLACES OF INTEREST

GUEST

Can you recommend any places to visit?	*Néng gěi wǒ-men tuī-jiàn jǐ-gè yóu-lǎn de dì-fāng ma?*

CONCIERGE

There are lots. Are you interested in…	*Dì-fāng hěn duō. Nín gǎn xìng-qù de shì…*
• art?	• *yì-shù ma?*
• theater?	• *xì-jù ma?*
• shopping?	• *gòu-wù ma?*
• museums?	• *bó-wù-guǎn ma?*
• sports?	• *yùn-dòng ma?*

• sight-seeing?	• *guān-guāng ma?*
• music?	• *yīn-yuè ma?*
• outdoor activities?	• *shì-wài huó-dòng ma?*
• children's activities?	• *ér-tóng huó-dòng ma?*
GUEST	
What do you recommend?	*Nín tuī-jiàn shén-me ne?*
CONCIERGE	
If you're interested in art, I'd suggest…	*Nín rú-guǒ duì yì-shù gǎn-xìng-qù, wǒ jiàn-yì…*
• the _____ gallery.	• *nín qù _____ měi-shù-guǎn.*
• the _____ art museum.	• *nín qù _____ yì-shù-guǎn.*
If you're interested in theater, I can get you tickets to…	*Nǐ rú-guǒ duì xì-jù gǎn-xìng-qù, wǒ kě-yǐ gěi nǐ mǎi…de piaò.*
• a show.	• *yī-chǎng yǎn-chū*
• an opera.	• *yī-chǎng gē-jù*
• a movie.	• *yī-chǎng diàn-yǐng*
For shopping, I'd recommend…	*Rú-yào gòu-wù, wǒ tuī-jiàn…*
• downtown.	• *qù-shì-qū.*
• the mall.	• *qù shāng-chǎng.*
• the discount outlets.	• *qù lián-jià shāng-diàn.*
GUEST	
Do they have…there?	*Nàr yǒu…ma?*
• clothes	• *fú-zhuāng*
• furniture	• *jiā-jù*
• rugs (carpets)	• *tǎn-zi (dì-tǎn)*
• souvenirs	• *jì-niàn-pǐn*
• books	• *shū*
• sporting goods	• *yùn-dòng yòng-pǐn*
• candy	• *táng-guǒ*
• antiques	• *gǔ-dǒng*

---

q=ch zh=ds+r sh=s+r z=ds x=sh chi=ts+r c=ts ü=yew üe=you+e
e=<u>ea</u>rn i=<u>yi</u>eld ia=<u>ya</u>rd ian=<u>ye</u>n iang=<u>young</u> ie=<u>ye</u>t ou=l<u>ow</u> u=w<u>oo</u>d

• electronics	• *diàn-qì*
• computers	• *diàn-nǎo*
• a farmers' market	• *nóng-fū shì-chǎng*
• a supermarket	• *chāo-jí shì-chǎng*
• a flea market	• *jiù-huò shì-chǎng*

CONCIERGE

Perhaps you'd like a museum.	*Huò-xǔ nǐ xiǎng qù bó-wù-guǎn.*
A local favorite is the… museum.	*Běn-dì de…bó-wù-guǎn hěn shòu-rén xǐ-huān.*
• natural history	• *zì-rán lì-shǐ*
• modern art	• *xiàn-dài yì-shù*
• science	• *kē-xué*
• local history	• *dì-fāng-lì-shǐ*

GUEST

We were thinking of sight-seeing.	*Wǒ-men xiǎng qù guān-guāng.*

CONCIERGE

I'd be happy to arrange a city tour.	*Ràng wǒ gěi nǐ-men ān-pái shì-qū yóu-lǎn ba.*

GUEST

How about…	*…zěn-me-yàng?*
• interesting architecture?	• *Yǒu-qù de jiàn-zhù*
• churches?	• *Jiào-táng*
• a vineyard?	• *Pú-tao-yuán*
• the business district?	• *Shāng-yè-qū*
• the government buildings?	• *Zhèng-fǔ jiàn-zhù*
• the university?	• *Dà-xué*
• monuments?	• *Jì-niàn-bēi*
• the countryside?	• *Nóng-cūn*

CONCIERGE

There are many sports events.	*Yǒu bù-shǎo yùn-dòng xiàng-mù.*

Would you like tickets to…	*Nǐ yào-bù-yào…piào?*
• a baseball game?	• *bàng-qiú*
• a basketball game?	• *lán-qiú*
• a football game?	• *zú-qiú*
• a hockey game?	• *bíng-qiú*
• a tennis match?	• *wǎng-qiú*
GUEST	
Are there any musical events?	*Yǒu méi-yǒu yīn-yuè huǒ-dòng?*
CONCIERGE	
There is a…concert tonight.	*Jīn-wǎn yǒu…yīn-yuè-huì.*
• rock-and-roll	• *yáo-gǔn*
• blues	• *bù-lù-shì yáo-gǔn*
• classical music	• *gǔ-diǎn*
• jazz	• *jué-shì-yuè*
There's musical entertainment at _____.	*Zài _____ yǒu yīn-yuè yú-lè huǒ-dòng.*
GUEST	
Is there anything else going on tonight?	*Jīn-wǎn hái-yǒu qí-tā huǒ-dòng ma?*
CONCIERGE	
Other than the movies, I'd suggest…	*Chú diàn-yǐng yǐ-wài, hái-yǒu…*
• bowling.	• *bǎo-líng-qiú.*
• a nightclub.	• *yè-zǒng-huì.*
• a video rental.	• *lù-yǐng-dài chū-zū.*
GUEST	
What do you suggest for outdoor activities?	*Kě-yǐ tuī-jiàn shén-me shì-wài huǒ-dòng ma?*
CONCIERGE	
How about…	*…zén-me-yàng?*
• hiking?	• *Tú-bù lǚ-xíng*

• fishing?	• *Diào-yú*
• skiing?	• *Huá-xuě*
• skating?	• *Liū-bīng*
• Rollerblading?	• *Lún-shì liū-bīng*
• swimming?	• *Yóu-yǒng*
• surfing?	• *Chōng-làng*
Or you might like to go...	*Nǐ yě kě-yǐ qù...*
• to the river.	• *hé-biān.*
• to the lake.	• *hú-biān.*
• to the mountains.	• *dēng-shān.*
• for a drive.	• *kāi-chē dōu-fēng.*
• to the beach.	• *hǎi-tān.*
• to the forest.	• *shù-lín.*
GUEST	
Is there anything for children?	*Ér-tóng yǒu shén-me huó-dòng ma?*
CONCIERGE	
Yes, there's...	*Shì-de, yǒu...*
• a zoo.	• *dòng-wù-yuán.*
• a children's museum.	• *ér-tóng bó-wù-guǎn.*
• an amusement park.	• *yóu-lè-yuán.*
• a water park.	• *shuǐ-shàng lè-yuán.*
Would you like to rent...	*Nǐ yào zū...*
• a bicycle?	• *yī-liàng dān-chē ma?*
• a car?	• *yī-liàng jiào-chē ma?*
• a boat?	• *yī-tiáo chuán ma?*
• some skis?	• *xuě-qiào ma?*
• some Rollerblades?	• *lún-shì liū-bīng-xié ma?*
Would you like a tour guide who speaks Chinese?	*Nǐ yào-bū-yào shuō Zhōng-wén ma yǔ de dǎo-yóu ma?*

---

q=ch zh=ds+r sh=s+r z=ds x=sh chi=ts+r c=ts ü=yew üe=you+e
e=earn i=yield ia=yard ian=yen iang=young ie=yet ou=low u=wood

May I make a reservation for you?	*Yào wǒ gěi nǐ yù-yuē ma?*
GUEST	
Can you recommend a good restaurant?	*Néng tuī-jiàn yī-gè hǎo de cān-guǎn ma?*
CONCIERGE	
What type of cuisine would you like?	*Nǐ xǐ-huān nǎ-zhǒng fàn-cài?*
GUEST	
We'd like a(n)…restaurant.	*Wǒ-men xǐ-huān…cān-guǎn.*
• casual	• *biàn-cān*
• elegant	• *yōu-yǎ de*
• fast-food	• *kuài-cān*
• inexpensive	• *lián-jià*
• seafood	• *hǎi-xiān*
• vegetarian	• *sù-shí*
We'd like an authentic American steakhouse.	*Wǒ-men xiǎng-qù zhèng-zōng Měi-guó níu-pái cān-guǎn.*
CONCIERGE	
You can get there by…	*Nǐ kě zuò…qù nàr.*
• bus.	• *gōng-gōng-qi-chē*
• train.	• *huǒ-chē*
• subway.	• *dì-tiě*
Take the…bound for _____.	*Chéng qù _____ de…*
• number _____ bus	• *_____ lù gōng-gōng-qi-chē.*
• train	• *huǒ-chē.*
• subway	• *dì-tiě.*
You'll need to transfer to…at _____.	*Nǐ xū-yào zài _____ huàn-chéng…*
• the _____ line	• *_____ xiàn chē.*
• the number _____ bus	• *_____ lù gōng-gōng-qi-chē.*

Get off at _____.	*Zài _____ xià-chē.*
May I call you a taxi?	*Yào wǒ gěi nín jiào chū-zū-chē ma?*
We have a free shuttle bus service available to _____.	*Wǒ-men tí-gòng qù _____ de miǎn-fèi háo-huá-chē fú-wù.*
It leaves every _____ minutes.	*Měi gé _____ fēn-zhōng fā yī-cì chē.*
It leaves every hour.	*Měi gé yī xiǎo-shí fā yī-cì chē.*

GUEST

What's the price range?	*Jià-gé duō-shǎo?*

6. Business Services and Clientele

A. BOOKING A BUSINESS MEETING

EMPLOYEE

Good morning.	*Nín zǎo.*
How may I help you today?	*Jīn-tiān yǒu shén-me xū-yào bāng-máng ma?*

GUEST

I'd like to make arrangements for a business meeting.	*Wǒ yào ān-pái yī-gè shēng-yì huì-tán.*

TIP! ••••

Clients who do business from the hotel need a great deal of service from you. They tend to be seasoned travelers who don't want a lot of explanation from hotel employees, just competent action. Attending to their every need often yields substantial financial rewards!

EMPLOYEE	
For how many people?	*Duō-shǎo rén?*
GUEST	
For _____ people on _____.	*Zài (date), yǒu (number) gè rén.*
EMPLOYEE	
Fine.	*Hǎo de.*
We have space available.	*Wǒ-men zhèng-hǎo yǒu kòng-xián chǎng-dì.*
We can provide all your meals, as well as your meeting needs.	*Wǒ-men bù-guāng kě-yǐ tí-gòng huì-tán chǎng-dì, hái kě tí-gōng suǒ-yǒu fàn-cài.*
GUEST	
That's good. We'd like...for each day.	*Nà hěn hǎo. Wǒ-men měi-tiān xū-yào...*
• a continental breakfast	• *ōu-shì zǎo-cān.*
• coffee breaks	• *kā-fēi.*
• a working lunch	• *gōng-zùo (zhōng)cān.*
• snacks	• *xiǎo-chī.*
• a cocktail reception	• *jī-wěi-jiǔ-huì.*
• dinner	• *wǎn-cān.*
Also, we'll require...for the meeting room.	*Cǐ-wài, huì-yì-shì xū-yào yǒu...*
• a VCR with a large-screen monitor	• *dà-diàn-shì hé lù-yǐng-jī.*
• an overhead projector with transparencies and markers	• *tóu-yǐng-jī, tòu-míng-zhǐ hé biāo shì-bǐ.*
• a chalkboard	• *hēi-bǎn.*
• a flip chart	• *fān-dòng tú-biǎo.*
• a slide projector	• *huàn-dēng-jī.*
• a computer with a large-screen monitor	• *dài dà-píng-mù de diàn-nǎo.*

And please be sure to provide… *Qǐng yī-dìng tí-gòng…*

- water. • *shuǐ.*
- pads with pencils. • *zhǐ hé bǐ.*
- ashtrays. • *yān-huī-gāng.*

EMPLOYEE

Let's decide on what time you'd like everything, and we'll be all set. *Ràng wǒ-men bǎ-shí-jiān jué dìng xià-laí, zhè-yàng nǐ jiù yī-qiè dōu bàn-hǎo le.*

GUEST

Okay. How will the room be set up? *Hǎo. Fáng-jiān gāi zěn-me bù-zhì?*

EMPLOYEE

We can set up the room… *Wǒ-men kě-yǐ bǎ fáng-jiān bù-zhì chéng…*

- theater style. • *jù-yùan fēng-gé.*
- in a square. • *fāng-zhèng.*
- horseshoe ("U") style. • *("U") zì-xíng.*
- classroom style. • *jiào-shì xíng-zhuàng.*
- boardroom style. • *huì-yì-shì fēng-gé.*

We're looking forward to having your group here. *Wǒ-men děng-hòu nín-men de guāng-lín.*

B. AT THE MEETING

ATTENDANT

I'm _____, the meeting-room attendant. *Wǒ jiào _____, shì huì-yì-shì de guǎn-lǐ-yuán.*

How is everything? *Yī-qiè dōu mǎn-yì ma?*

GUEST

Everything is fine, thank you. *Yī-qiè dōu hěn hǎo, xiè-xiè nǐ.*

We need… *Wǒ-men xū-yào…*

- more chairs. • *gèng-duō de yǐ-zi.*
- more coffee. • *zài lái-diǎn kā-feī.*

• the ashtrays emptied.	• *bǎ yān-huī dào-diào.*
• more water.	• *gèng-duō de shuǐ.*

ATTENDANT

I'll take care of it right away.	*Wǒ mǎ-shàng jiù-qù bàn-lǐ.*
Is everything else satisfactory?	*Qí-tā yī-qiè dōu mǎn-yì ma?*

GUEST

It's quite nice, but the room…	*Hái bù-cuò, dàn fáng-jiān…*
• needs more light.	• *guāng-xiàn bù zú.*
• is too bright.	• *guāng-xiàn tài qiáng le.*
• needs more ventilation.	• *xū-yào gèng-duō xīn-xiàn kōng-qì.*
• is too hot (cold).	• *tài rè (lěng).*
• is a little noisy.	• *yǒu-diǎn tài chǎo le.*
• is crowded.	• *tài yōng-jǐ le.*
Can you take care of it?	*Nǐ néng xiǎng-xiǎng bàn-fǎ ma?*
Can we get another room?	*Kě-yǐ zài gěi wǒ-men yī-gè fáng-jiān ma?*

ATTENDANT

Let me see what we can do.	*Ràng wǒ xiǎng-xiǎng bàn-fǎ ba.*

C. CATERING TO BUSINESS GUESTS

CONCIERGE

How may I help you?	*Yǒu shén-me shì-qíng ma?*

GUEST

Where is breakfast for the _____ group?	_____ *xiǎo-zǔ de zǎo-cān zài nǎr?*
Where is the exhibits hall?	*Zhǎn-shì-tīng zài nǎr?*

CONCIERGE

There's a buffet set up outside your meeting room.	*Huì-yì-shì wài-miàn yǒu zì-zhù-cān.*
Just down the hall.	*Jiù-zài nà-biān.*
In the dining room.	*Zài cān-tīng lǐ.*

---

q=ch zh=ds+r sh=s+r z=ds x=sh chi=ts+r c=ts ü=yew üe=you+e
e=earn i=yield ia=yard ian=yen iang=young ie=yet ou=low u=wood

GUEST

Thank you.	*Xiè-xie.*
I need…	*Wǒ xūyào…*
• a fax sent.	• *fā chuán-zhēn.*
• some typing done.	• *dǎ-zì.*
• a hookup to the Internet.	• *shàng diàn-nǎo wǎng-lù.*
• a computer.	• *yī-tái diàn-nǎo.*
• a package sent overnight.	• *gé-yè kuài-dì.*
• courier service.	• *xìn-chāi fú-wù.*
• some letters mailed.	• *jì-xìn.*
• some copies made.	• *fù-yìn dōng-xi.*

CONCIERGE

I'll take care of that right away.	*Wǒ mǎ-shàng jiù gěi nín bàn-lǐ.*

GUEST

Later, I'd like to host a small reception.	*Wǎn-yī-diǎnr, wǒ yào jǔ-xīng yī-gè zhāo-daì-huì.*
Can you arrange that?	*Nǐ kě-yǐ gěi wǒ ān-pái yī-xià ma?*

CONCIERGE

Certainly. What would you like?	*Dāng-rán kě-yǐ. Nǐ xū-yào xiē shén-me ne?*

GUEST

We need a full bar and some hors d'oeuvres.	*Wǒ-men xū-yào shè-zhì jiǔ-bā hé yī-xiē kāi-wèi-pǐn.*
Make sure there are plenty of chilled shrimp.	*Yī-dìng yào yǒu hěn-duō liáng-xiā.*
Lots of champagne, please.	*Qǐng fàng-shàng hěn-duō xiāng-bīn-jiǔ.*

CONCIERGE

I'll have Room Service put together a proposal right away, and get back to you.	*Wǒ mǎ-shàng jiào Fáng-jiān Fúwùbù zhǔn-bèi yī-fèn qīng-dān ràng nǐ guò-mù.*

---

q=ch zh=ds+r sh=s+r z=ds x=sh chi=ts+r c=ts ü=yew üe=you+e
e=earn i=yield ia=yard ian=yen iang=young ie=yet ou=low u=wood

7. Checking Out

GUEST

At what time is checkout? — *Shén-me shí-hòu jié-zhàng lí-kāi?*

FRONT DESK CLERK

Checkout is at… — *…jié-zhàng.*

- 10 A.M. — *Shàng-wǔ shí-diǎn*
- noon. — *Zhōng-wǔ*
- 3 P.M. — *Xià-wǔ sān-diǎn*

You may audit your bill on channel _____ on your television. — *Nín kě-yǐ zài diàn-shì _____ pín-dào chá-kàn nǐ de zhàng-mù.*

We provide an express checkout service. — *Wǒ-men tí-gòng kuài-sù jié-zhàng fú-wù.*

Your bill will be left outside your door the night before you check out. — *Jié-zhàng qián yī-tiān wǎn-shàng, wǒ-men huì bǎ zhàng-dān fàng zài nín de mén-wài.*

If you're satisfied with your bill, simply sign it, and leave your key in your room. — *Rú-guǒ zhàng-dān méi-yǒu wèn-tí, nín zhǐ-yào qiān-zì, bǎ yào-shi liú zài fáng-jiān-lǐ jiù xíng le.*

Any late charges such as breakfast or minibar will be added automatically. — *Zǎo-cān huò mǐ-nǐ-jiǔ-bā de fèi-yòng jiāng zì-dòng jì-zài nín de zhàng-dàn-shàng.*

GUEST

I'd like to check out, please. — *Qǐng jié-zhàng.*

CLERK

May I have your luggage brought down? — *Yào wǒ bǎ nǐ de xíng-lǐ ná xià-lái ma?*

GUEST

Yes, please. — *Shì-de.*

No, I brought (will bring) it myself. — *Bù, wǒ zì-jǐ yǐ-jīng (huì qù ná) ná-lái le.*

---

q=ch zh=ds+r sh=s+r z=ds x=sh chi=ts+r c=ts ü=yew üe=you+e
e=earn i=yield ia=yard ian=yen iang=young ie=yet ou=low u=wood

CLERK

How was everything?	*Yī-qiè dōu mǎn-yì ma?*

GUEST

It was very nice, thank you.	*Hěn hǎo, xiè-xiè.*
I want to speak with the manager.	*Wǒ yào jiàn jīng-lǐ.*

CLERK

Certainly. The manager on duty is _____. One moment, please.	*Kě-yǐ. Dāng-bān jīng-lǐ shì _____. Qǐng shāo-děng yī-huìr.*

GUEST

Our experience was…	*Wǒ-men de jīng-lì…*
• good.	• *hěn hǎo.*
• excellent.	• *fēi-cháng hǎo.*
• poor.	• *bù hǎo.*
• very bad.	• *feī-cháng bù hǎo.*

MANAGER ON DUTY

That's nice to hear.	*Tīng nín zhè-yàng shuō wǒ hěn gāo-xìng.*
I'm sorry to hear that.*	*Tīng nín zhè-yàng shuō wǒ hěn baò-qiàn.*
Thank you. Please come again.	*Xiè-xie. Qǐng zài-lái.*

*Please refer to "Guest Complaints in the Hotel" on page 19 for more on handling dissatisfied clients.

FRENCH

1. The Bare Essentials

A. THE FRENCH ALPHABET

a	ah	*o*	oh
b	beh	*p*	peh
c	seh	*q*	kew
d	deh	*r*	ehr
e	uh	*s*	ehss
f	ehf	*t*	teh
g	zhay	*u*	ew
h	ahsh	*v*	veh
i	ee	*w*	doo-bluh veh *(double v)*
j	zhee		
k	kah	*x*	eex
l	ehl	*y*	ee grayk *(i grec)*
m	ehm		
n	ehn	*z*	zehd

B. PRONUNCIATION CHART

VOWELS

FRENCH SOUND	TRANSCRIPTION/ APPROXIMATE SOUND IN ENGLISH	EXAMPLE
a	ah (f<u>a</u>ther)	*ananas* (pineapple)
e	uh (sof<u>a</u>)	*barbecue* (barbecue)
i, y	ee (b<u>ee</u>)	*merci* (thank you), *curry* (curry)

o	oh (not)	*carotte* (carrot)
u	ew (ü)	*mur* (wall)

In French, the vowels *a, e, i, o,* and *u* are sometimes written with an accent mark. The accent slightly alters the pronunciation of the vowel, making its sound longer or shorter. There are four types of accents:

- The acute accent (´) shortens the vowel sound: é is pronounced *eh* as in the English word *bet.*
  Example: béret *(beh-reh)* (beret)
- The grave accent (`) and the circumflex (^) accent make the vowel's sound longer: è, ê are pronounced *ay* as in the English word *day.*
  Example: mère *(mayr)* (mother); être *(aytr)* (to be)
  Also: à, â *(ah);* ô *(oh);* ù, û *(ew);* and î *(ee)*
- The umlaut (¨) indicates that the vowel it accents must be pronounced separately.
  Example: maïs *(mah-eess)* (corn)

French has some particular sounds, called nasal vowels, for which there is no equivalent in English.

NASAL VOWEL	TRANSCRIPTION/ APPROXIMATE SOUND IN ENGLISH	EXAMPLE
on, om	ohn (song)	*rond*—rohn (round)
en, em, an, am	ahn (bank)	*banque*—bahnk (bank)
un, in, ain	ehn (bent)	*pinte*—pehnt (pint)

The vowel before the consonant directs the sounds (as in "an," "on," and "un").

DIPHTHONGS

FRENCH SOUND	ENGLISH EQUIVALENT	EXAMPLE
ai	ay (day)	*mai* (may)
ail	ai (aye)	*ail* (garlic)
oi	wa (water)	*moi* (me)

ou	oo (moose)	*court* (short)
eu	uh	*deux* (two)

CONSONANTS

FRENCH CONSONANT	APPROXIMATE SOUND IN ENGLISH	EXAMPLE
b	*b* (boat)	*bon* (good)
c	*c* cat (before *a, o, u*); *ss* (before *e, i*)	*côté* (side); *ici* (here)
ç	*s* (sit)	*garçon* (boy)
ch	*ch* as in chicken; or *sh* as in short	*match* (game); *chapeau* (hat)
d	*d* (dock)	*dimanche* (Sunday)
f	*f* (flag)	*fatigue* (tiredness)
g	*g* goat (before *a, o, u*); *zh* (before *e, i*)	*gare* (station); *manger* (to eat)
gn	*ny* as in onion	*mignon* (cute)
h	*(silent)* honor	*haricot* (bean)
j	*zh* (pleasure)	*jaune* (yellow)
k	*k* (koala)	*kangourou* (kangaroo)
l	*l* (life)	*laboratoire* (laboratory)
lli	*ly* as in million	*milliard* (billion)
m	*m* (mouse)	*minute* (minute)
n	*n* (nest)	*navette* (shuttle)
p	*p* (pass)	*pizza* (pizza)
ph	*f* (telephone)	*éléphant* (elephant)
q	*c* as in coffee; or *k* as in koala	*Québec* (Quebec); *coq* (rooster)
r	*r* right *(or rolling r, or guttural r)*	*route* (route)
s	*ess* as in miss; or *z* as in rose	*mystère* (mystery); *rose* (rose)
t	*t* (tongue)	*téléphone* (telephone)
v	*v* (voice)	*vélo* (bicycle)

FRENCH

w	*w* as in whiskey; or *v* as in vary	*week-end* (weekend); *wagon* (car)
x	*x* (excellent)	*exemple* (example)
z	*z* (zest)	*zéro* (zero)

Note: A final consonant must be pronounced, except when it occurs in the nasal vowel *ehn, uhn, ohn,* or *ahn.* In the transcription that follows, when a final consonant has been doubled *(ehnn, ahnn),* it must be pronounced.

C. THE FRENCH LANGUAGE

Word Order The basic word order of French is the same as in English—subject-verb-object:

Le serveur	apporte	la pizza.	The waiter	brings	the pizza.
S	V	O	S	V	O

Nouns and Adjectives All nouns in French have gender. *Le* (the) and *un* (a/an) are used with masculine nouns, and *la* (the) and *une* (a/an) are used with feminine nouns. Most nouns take an *-s* to form the plural. *Les* (the) and *des* (some) are used with plural nouns. Adjectives in French change to agree with the nouns they modify. An *-e* is added for the feminine; an *-s* is added for masculine plural; and an *-es* is added for feminine plural: *le garçon intelligent* (the smart boy), *une fille intelligente* (a smart girl), *les garçons intelligents* (the smart boys), and *les filles intelligentes* (the smart girls). Notice that most adjectives in French come after the noun they modify.

Verbs French verbs undergo various changes to indicate subject, tense, or mood. *Le serveur apporte la pizza.* (The waiter brings the pizza.) *Nous apportons une bouteille.* (We bring a bottle.) *Ils apportaient des fleurs.* (They were bringing flowers.) *J'apporterais du fromage.* (I would bring some cheese.) *Apportez-moi une bièrre!* (Bring me a beer!) *Monsieur Duval apportera l'argent.* (Mr. Duval will bring the money.)

These simple rules will help you communicate on a basic level in French. The phrases and sentences in the French sections are written so that you can use them as printed. All you have to do is familiarize yourself with them, and you'll be ready to go. Good luck. *Bonne chance!*

D. THE FRENCH CULTURE

The French are among the most patriotic people in the world, and they are extremely proud of their culture. You'll find their dress fashionable and their behavior a bit less casual than that of Americans in dealing with strangers. Don't stand with your hands in your pockets, an irksome habit to the French, and don't ever chew gum in front of a French guest! Avoid personal questions, and don't acknowledge a sneeze.

Tipping is always a sticking point. In France, a service charge is always included in the bill, and they leave only a small amount of change in addition to that. You should have a policy in your restaurant for French guests, as they may not know to leave an adequate tip. Consider adding a 15 or 20 percent service charge to the bill, if your restaurant's cashiering and bookkeeping systems allow for that.

2. Useful Expressions

A. GENERAL

Hello.	*Bonjour.*	Bohn-ZHOOR.
Good-bye.	*Au revoir.*	Oh ruh-VWAHR.
Yes.	*Oui.*	WEE.
No.	*Non.*	NOHN.
Maybe.	*Peut-être.*	Puh-TEHTR.
Please.	*S'il vous plaît.*	Seel voo PLEH.
Thank you (very much).	*Merci (beaucoup).*	Mehr-SEE (boh-KOO).
You're welcome.	*De rien.*	Duh RYEHN.
Excuse me.	*Excusez-moi.*	Ehx-kew-zay MWAH.
I beg your pardon.	*Je vous demande pardon.*	Zhuh voo duh-mahnd pahr-DOHN.

I'm sorry.	*Je suis désolé(e).*	Zhuh swee day-zoh-LAY.
One moment, please.	*Un moment, s'il vous plaît.*	Ehn moh-MAHN, seel voo PLEH.
Do you speak English?	*Parlez-vous anglais?*	Pahr-lay voo ahn-GLEH?
• Yes, I do.	• *Oui.*	• WEE.
• No, I don't.	• *Non.*	• NOHN.
• A little.	• *Un peu.*	• Ehn PUH.
• No, not at all.	• *Non, pas du tout.*	• NOHN, pah dew TOO.
I don't speak French.	*Je ne parle pas français.*	Zhuh nuh pahrl pah frahnSEH.
I can speak a little.	*Je parle un petit peu.*	Zhuh pahrl ehn puh-tee PUH.
I understand a little.	*Je comprends un peu.*	Zhuh kohn-prahn ehn PUH.
I don't understand.	*Je ne comprends pas.*	Zhuh nuh kohn-prahn PAH.
Please speak more slowly.	*Parlez plus lentement, s'il vous plaît.*	Pahr-lay plew lahnt-MAHN, seel voo PLEH.
Would you repeat that, please?	*Pourriez-vous répéter, s'il vous plaît?*	Poo-ryay voo ray-pay TAY, seel voo PLEH?
Yes, sir/ma'am.	*Oui, monsieur/madame.*	WEE, muh-SYUH/mah-DAHM.
No problem.	*Il n'y a pas de problème.*	Eel nee ah pah duh proh-BLEHM.
It's my pleasure.	*Avec plaisir.*	Ah-vehk pleh-ZEER.

B. NEEDS

I'd like ____.	*J'aimerais ____.*	Zheh-muh-reh ____.
I need ____.	*J'ai besoin de ____.*	Zheh buh-zwehn duh ____.
What would you like?	*Qu'aimeriez-vous?*	Keh-muh-ryeh VOO?
Please bring me ____.	*S'il vous plaît, apportez-moi ____.*	Seel voo PLEH, ah-pohr-tay mwah ____.

I'm looking for _____.	*Je cherche _____.*	Zhuh shayrsh _____.
I'm hungry.	*J'ai faim.*	Zheh FEHN.
I'm thirsty.	*J'ai soif.*	Zheh SWAHF.
It's important.	*C'est important.*	Say tehn-pohr-TAHN.
It's urgent.	*C'est urgent.*	Say tewr-ZHAHN.

C. QUESTION WORDS

How?	*Comment?*	Koh-MAHN?
How much/many?	*Combien?*	Kohn-BYEHN?
Which?	*Lequel (laquelle/ lesquels/lesquelles)?*	Luh-KEHL (lah-KEHL/lay-KEHL/ lay-KEHL)?
What?	*Quel (quelle/quels/ quelles)?*	Kehl?
What kind of?	*Quelle sorte de?*	Kehl sohr-tuh duh?
Who?	*Qui?*	Kee?
Where?	*Où?*	Oo?
When?	*Quand?*	Kahn?
What does that mean?	*Qu'est-ce que cela veut dire?*	Kehss kuh suh-lah vuh DEER?
How do you say _____ in French?	*Comment dit-on _____ en français?*	Koh-mahn dee-tohn _____ ahn frahnSEH?

D. COLORS

black	*noir*	nwahr
blue	*bleu*	bluh
brown	*marron*	mah-ROHN
gold	*doré*	doh-RAY
gray	*gris*	gree
green	*vert*	vehr
orange	*orange*	oh-RAHNJ
pink	*rose*	rohz
purple	*pourpre*	POOR-pruh
red	*rouge*	ROOJ

silver	*argenté*	ahr-zhahn-TAY
violet	*violet*	vyoh-LEH
white	*blanc*	blahn
yellow	*jaune*	ZHOHNN

E. CARDINAL NUMBERS

1	*un*	ehn
2	*deux*	duh
3	*trois*	trwah
4	*quatre*	kahtr
5	*cinq*	sehnk
6	*six*	seess
7	*sept*	seht
8	*huit*	weet
9	*neuf*	nuhf
10	*dix*	deess
11	*onze*	ohnz
12	*douze*	dooz
13	*treize*	trehz
14	*quatorze*	kah-TOHRZ
15	*quinze*	kehnz
16	*seize*	sehz
17	*dix-sept*	dee-SEHT
18	*dix-huit*	dee-ZWEET
19	*dix-neuf*	deez-NUHF
20	*vingt*	vehnt
21	*vingt et un*	vehn teh EHN
22	*vingt-deux*	vehnt-DUH
23	*vingt-trois*	vehnt-TRWAH
24	*vingt-quatre*	vehnt-KAHTR
25	*vingt-cinq*	vehnt-SEHNK
26	*vingt-six*	vehnt-SEESS

27	*vingt-sept*	vehnt-SEHT
28	*vingt-huit*	vehnt-WEET
29	*vingt-neuf*	vehnt-NUHF
30	*trente*	trahnt
31	*trente et un*	trahnt ay EHN
32	*trente-deux*	trahnt-DUH
40	*quarante*	kah-RAHNT
50	*cinquante*	sehn-KAHNT
60	*soixante*	swah-SAHNT
70	*soixante-dix*	swah-sahnt-DEESS
80	*quatre-vingts*	kaht-ruh-VEHNT
90	*quatre-vingt-dix*	kaht-ruh-vehnt-DEESS
100	*cent*	sahn
101	*cent un*	sahn-EHN
102	*cent deux*	sahn-DUH
110	*cent dix*	sahn-DEESS
120	*cent vingt*	sahn-VEHNT
200	*deux cents*	duh-SAHN
210	*deux cent dix*	duh-sahn-DEESS
300	*trois cents*	trwah-SAHN
400	*quatre cents*	kahtr-SAHN
500	*cinq cents*	sehnk-SAHN
600	*six cents*	see-SAHN
700	*sept cents*	seht-SAHN
800	*huit cents*	wee-SAHN
900	*neuf cents*	nuhf-SAHN
1,000	*mille*	meel
1,100	*mille cent*	meel SAHN
1,200	*mille deux cents*	meel duh SAHN
2,000	*deux mille*	duh MEEL
10,000	*dix mille*	dee MEEL
50,000	*cinquante mille*	sedn-kahnt MEEL

100,000	*cent mille*	sahn MEEL
1,000,000	*un million*	ehn mee-LYOHN
1,000,000,000	*un milliard*	ehn mee-LYAHR

F. ORDINAL NUMBERS

first	*premier/première*	pruh-MYAY/pruh-MYEHR
second	*second/seconde*	suh-GOHN/suh-GOHND
third	*troisième*	trwah-ZYEHM
fourth	*quatrième*	kah-TRYEHM
fifth	*cinquième*	sehn-KYEHM
sixth	*sixième*	see-ZYEHM
seventh	*septième*	seh-TYEHM
eighth	*huitième*	wee-TYEHM
ninth	*neuvième*	nuh-VYEHM
tenth	*dixième*	dee-ZYEHM
eleventh	*onzième*	ohn-ZYEHM
twelfth	*douzième*	doo-ZYEHM
thirteenth	*treizième*	treh-ZYEHM
fourteenth	*quatorzième*	kah-tohr-ZYEHM
fifteenth	*quinzième*	kekn-ZYEHM
sixteenth	*seizième*	seh-ZYEHM
seventeenth	*dix-septième*	dee-seh-TYEHM
eighteenth	*dix-huitième*	dee-zwee-TYEHM
nineteenth	*dix-neuvième*	deez-nuh-VYEHM
twentieth	*vingtième*	vehn-TYEHM
twenty-first	*vingt et unième*	vehnt ay ew-NYEHM
twenty-second	*vingt-deuxième*	vehnt-duh-ZYEHM
thirtieth	*trentième*	trahn-TYEHM
fortieth	*quarantième*	kah-rahn-TYEHM
fiftieth	*cinquantième*	sehn-kahn-TYEHM
sixtieth	*soixantième*	swah-sahn-TYEHM

seventieth	*soixante-dixième*	swah-sahnt-dee-ZYEHM
eightieth	*quatre-vingtième*	kaht-ruh-vehn-TYEHM
ninetieth	*quatre-vingt-dixième*	kaht-ruh-vehn-dee ZYEHM
hundredth	*centième*	sahn-TYEHM
thousandth	*millième*	mee-LYEHM

G. TIME OF DAY

1:00	*une heure*	ewn uhr
2:00	*deux heures*	duhz UHR
3:00	*trois heures*	trwahz UHR
4:00	*quatre heures*	kahtr UHR
5:00	*cinq heures*	sehnk UHR
6:00	*six heures*	seez UHR
7:00	*sept heures*	seht UHR
8:00	*huit heures*	weet UHR
9:00	*neuf heures*	nuhv UHR
10:00	*dix heures*	deez UHR
11:00	*onze heures*	ohnz UHR
12:00	*douze heures*	dooz UHR
1:00 A.M.	*une heure du matin*	ewn uhr dew mah-TEHN
3:00 P.M.	*trois heures de l'après-midi*	trwahz uhr duh lah-preh mee-DEE
noon	*midi*	mee-DEE
midnight	*minuit*	mee-NWEE
1:15	*une heure quinze*	ewn uhr kehnz
12:45	*douze heures quarante-cinq*	dooz uhr kah-rahnt-SEHNK
1:30	*une heure trente*	ewn uhr TRAHNT
7:05	*sept heures cinq*	seht uhr SEHNK
4:55	*quatre heures cinquante-cinq*	kahtr uhr sehn-kahnt-SEHNK

H. DAYS OF THE WEEK

Monday	*lundi*	lehn-DEE
Tuesday	*mardi*	mahr-DEE
Wednesday	*mercredi*	mehr-kruh-DEE
Thursday	*jeudi*	zhuh-DEE
Friday	*vendredi*	vahn-druh-DEE
Saturday	*samedi*	sahm-DEE
Sunday	*dimanche*	dee-MAHNSH

I. MONTHS

January	*janvier*	zhahn-VYAY
February	*février*	feh-VRYAY
March	*mars*	mahrss
April	*avril*	ah-VREEL
May	*mai*	meh
June	*juin*	zhwehn
July	*juillet*	zhwee-YEH
August	*août*	oot
September	*septembre*	sehp-TAHN-bruh
October	*octobre*	ohk-TOH-bruh
November	*novembre*	noh-VAHN-bruh
December	*décembre*	day-SAHN-bruh

J. DATES

1998	*mille neuf cent quatre-vingt dix-huit*	meel nuhf SAHN kaht-ruh-vehnt deez-WEET
1999	*mille neuf cent quatre-vingt-dix-neuf*	meel nuhf SAHN kaht-ruh-vehnt-deez-NUHF
2000	*deux mille*	duh MEEL
2001	*deux mille un*	duh meel EHN
2002	*deux mille deux*	duh meel DUH
2003	*deux mille trois*	duh meel TRWAH
2004	*deux mille quatre*	duh meel KAHTR

2005	*deux mille cinq*	duh meel SEHNK
Today is Thursday, September 22.	*Aujourd'hui, on est jeudi, le vingt-deux septembre.*	Oh-zhoor-DWEE, ohn ay zhuh-DEE, luh vehnt-duh sehp-TAHN-bruh.
Yesterday was Wednesday, September 21.	*Hier, on était mercredi, le vingt et un septembre.*	YEHR, ohn ay-teh mehr-kruh-DEE, luh vehnt ay ehn sehp-TAHN-bruh.
The day before yesterday was Tuesday, September 20.	*Avant-hier, on était mardi, le vingt septembre.*	Ah-vahn-TYEHR, ohn ay-teh mahr-DEE, luh vehnt sehp-TAHN-bruh.
Tomorrow is Friday, September 23.	*Demain, on sera vendredi, le vingt-trois septembre.*	Duh-MEHN, ohn suh-rah vahn-druh-DEE, luh vehnt trwah sehp-TAHN-bruh.
The day after tomorrow is Saturday, September 24.	*Après-demain, on sera samedi, le vingt-quatre septembre.*	Ah-preh duh-MEHN, ohn suh-rah sahm-DEE, luh vehnt-kahtr sehp-TAHN-bruh.
Next Friday is September 30.	*Vendredi prochain on sera le trente septembre.*	Vahn-druh-dee proh-SHEHN, ohn suh-rah luh trahnt sehp-TAHN-bruh.
Last Friday was September 16.	*Vendredi dernier, on était le seize septembre.*	Vahn-druh-dee dayr-NYAY, ohn ay-teh luh sehz sehp-TAHN-bruh.

K. MEASUREMENTS: DISTANCE

inch	*un pouce*	ehn pooss
foot	*un pied*	ehn pyay
yard	*un yard*	ehn yahrd
mile	*un mile*	ehn meel
millimeter	*un millimètre*	ehn mee-lee-MEHTR
meter	*un mètre*	ehn MEHTR
kilometer	*un kilomètre*	ehn kee-loh-MEHTR

3. Common Hospitality Scenarios

A. GREETINGS AND INTRODUCTIONS

GREETING THE GUEST

EMPLOYEE

Good morning,...	***Bonjour,...***	Bohn-ZHOOR,...
• Mr. _____.	***• M. _____.***	• muh-SYUH _____.
• Mrs. _____.	***• Mme. _____.***	• mah-DAHM _____.
• Miss _____.	***• Mlle. _____.***	• mah-duh-mwah-ZEHL _____.
• sir.	***• Monsieur.***	• muh-SYUH.
• ma'am.	***• Madame.***	• mah-DAHM.
• ladies and gentlemen.	***• Mesdames et Messieurs.***	• may-DAHM zay may-SYUH.
• everyone.	***• à tous.***	• ah TOOSS.
Good afternoon, Mr. _____.	***Bonjour, M. _____.***	Bohn-ZHOOR, muh-syuh _____.
Good evening, Mr. _____.	***Bonsoir, M. _____.***	Bohn-SWAHR, muh-syuh _____.
Hello, Mr. _____.	***Bonjour, M. _____.***	Bohn-ZHOOR, muh-syuh _____.

TIP! ••••

Most American employees are used to greeting guests jovially and asking them how they are. However, in any but the most informal settings, this behavior may actually be considered impolite. Asking guests how they are is stepping outside the bounds of your position and throws the burden onto the guest to answer you. Other cultures usually observe this principle to a much greater extent than we do.

Welcome to…	*Bienvenue…*	Byehn-vuh-new…
• the hotel.	• *à l'hôtel.*	• ah loh-TEHL.
• the restaurant.	• *au restaurant.*	• oh rehss-toh-RAHN.
• our city.	• *dans notre ville.*	• dahn noh-truh VEEL.
• the United States.	• *aux États-Unis.*	• oh zay-tah-zew-NEE.
If there is anything I can do to make your stay more pleasant, please let me know.	*S'il y a quelque chose que je puisse faire pour rendre votre séjour plus agréable, faites-le-moi savoir.*	Seel ee ah kehl-kuh shoz kuh zhuh pweess FEHR poor rahn-druh voh-truh say-zhoor plew zah-gray-AH-bluh, feht-luh-mwah sah-VWAHR.
May I…	*Puis je…*	Pweej…
• take your coat?	• *vous débarrasser de votre manteau?*	• voo day-bah-rah-say duh voh-truh mahn-TOH?
• carry your…for you?	• *porter votre/vos… pour vous?*	• pohr-tay voh-truh/voh…poor VOO?
• bags	• *bagages*	• bah-gahj
• suitcase	• *valise*	• vah-leez
How are you today?	*Comment allez-vous aujourd'hui?*	koh-mahn tah-lay voo oh-zhoor-DWEE?
GUEST		
I am…	*Je vais…*	Zhuh veh…
• fine, thank you.	• *bien, merci.*	• BYEHN, mehr-SEE.
• okay.	• *assez bien.*	• ah-say BYEHN.
• so-so.	• *comme ci, comme ça.*	• kohm SEE, kohm SAH.
I am very tired.	*Je suis très fatigué(e).*	Zhuh swee treh fah-tee-GAY.
I am not feeling well.	*Je ne me sens pas bien.*	Zhuh nuh muh sahn pah BYEHN.
And you?	*Et vous?*	Ay VOO?

TIP! ••••

It is typical of American employees to introduce themselves to the guest. This practice allows the guest to call an employee by name when s/he needs something. This is not a common practice in other countries, however, so the international guest may simply ignore your introduction.

INTRODUCTIONS

EMPLOYEE

My name is ____.	***Je m'appelle ____.***	Zhuh mah-pehl ____.
I am your…	***Je suis votre…***	Zhuh swee voh-truh…
• **door attendant** (doorman).	• ***portier.***	• pohr-TYAY.
• **bell attendant** (bellman).	• ***chasseur** (groom).*	• shah-SUHR (GROOM).
• **driver.**	• ***chauffeur.***	• shoh-FUHR.
• **captain.**	• ***surveillant**(e).*	• suhr-vay-YAHN(T).
• **concierge.**	• ***concierge.***	• kohn-SYEHRJ.
• **room attendant.**	• ***employé**(e) **au service de votre chambre.***	• ahn-plwah-yay oh sayr-veess duh voh-truh SHAHN-bruh.
• **host.**	• ***hôte.***	• OH-tuh.
• **hostess.**	• ***hôtesse.***	• oh-TEHSS.
• **manager.**	• ***gérant (gérante).***	• zhay-RAHN (zhay-RAHNT).
• **server** (waiter/waitress).	• ***le serveur/ la serveuse.***	• luh sayr-VUHR/ lah sayr-VUHZ.
• **chef.**	• ***chef.***	• shehf.
• **activities director.**	• ***directeur** (directrice) **de l'animation.***	• dee-rehk-tuhr (dee-rehk-treess) duh lah nee-mah-SYOHN.

Mr. (Mrs., Miss) **_____, this is Mr.** (Mrs., Miss) **_____, the manager.**	***M.** (Mme., Mlle.) **_____, voici M.** (Mme., Mlle.) **_____, notre gérant** (gérante).*	Muh-syuh (mah-dahm, mah-duh-mwah-zehl) _____, vwah-see muh-syuh (mah-dahm, mah-duh-mwah-zehl) _____, noh-truh zhay-RAHN (zhay-RAHNT).
Mr. (Mrs., Miss) **_____, may I introduce our manager, Mr.** (Mrs., Miss) **_____?**	***M.** (Mme., Mlle.) **_____, permettez-moi de vous présenter notre gérant** (gérante)**, M.** (Mme., Mlle.) **_____?***	Muh-syuh (mah-dahm, mah-duh-mwah-zehl) _____, payr-may-tay mwah duh voo pray-sahn-tay noh-truh zhay-RAHN (zhay-RAHNT), muh-syuh (mah-dahm, mah-duh-mwah-zehl) _____?

B. RESERVATIONS

HOTEL RESERVATIONS

OPERATOR

Good morning (afternoon, evening), **_____ Hotel.**	***Bonjour** (Bonjour, Bonsoir)**, ici l'hôtel _____.***	Bohn-ZHOOR (bohn ZHOOR, bohn-SWAHR), ee-see loh-tehl _____.
How may I direct your call?	***Quel service désirez-vous?***	Kehl sayr-veess day-zee-ray-VOO?

GUEST

Hello. Do you speak French?	***Bonjour. Est-ce que vous parlez français?***	Bohn-ZHOOR. Ehss kuh voo pahr-lay frahn SEH?

OPERATOR

One moment, please.	***Un moment, s'il vous plaît.***	Ehn moh-MAHN, seel voo PLEH.
I'll connect you with a bilingual operator.	***Je vais vous passer un (une) standardiste bilingue.***	Zhuh veh voo pah-say ehn (ewn) stahn-dahr-deesst bee-LEHNG.
I have a book here to help me.	***J'ai un livre pour m'aider.***	Zheh ehn leevr poor meh-DAY.

Please speak slowly.	*Parlez lentement, s'il vous plaît.*	Pahr-lay lahn-tuh-MAHN, seel voo PLEH.
GUEST		
I would like to make a reservation, please.	*Je voudrais faire une réservation, s'il vous plaît.*	Zhuh voo-dreh fehr ewn ray-zayr-vah-SYOHN, seel voo PLEH.
OPERATOR		
For a room or for one of the restaurants?	*Pour une chambre ou pour un de nos restaurants?*	Poor ewn SHAHN-bruh oo poor ehn duh noh rehss-toh-RAHN?
GUEST		
For a room, please.	*Pour une chambre, s'il vous plaît.*	Poor ewn SHAHN-bruh, seel voo PLEH.
For the ____ Restaurant, please.	*Au restaurant ____, s'il vous plaît.*	Oh ress-toh-rahn ____, seel voo PLEH.
OPERATOR		
One moment, please. I will direct your call to Reservations.	*Un moment, s'il vous plaît. Je vous passe le service des réservations.*	Ehn moh-MAHN, seel voo PLEH. Zhuh voo pahss luh sayr-veess day ray-zayr-vah-SYOHN.
One moment, please. I will direct your call to the restaurant.	*Un moment, s'il vous plaît. Je vous passe le restaurant.*	Ehn moh-MAHN, seel voo PLEH. Zhuh voo pahss luh rehss-toh-RAHN.
CLERK		
Hello. This is Reservations.	*Bonjour. Ici le service des réservations.*	Bohn-ZHOOR. Ee-see luh sayr-veess day ray-zayr-vah-SYOHN.
What date would you like?	*Quelle date voulez-vous?*	Kehl daht voo-lay VOO?
GUEST		
May 27th.	*Le vingt-sept mai.*	Luh vehnt-seht MEH.
CLERK		
For how many nights?	*Pour combien de nuits?*	Poor kohn-byehn duh NWEE?

GUEST		
For three nights, please.	*Pour trois nuits, s'il vous plaît.*	Poor trwah NWEE, seel voo PLEH.
For a week.	*Pour une semaine.*	Poor ewn suh-MEHN.
Just one night.	*Pour une nuit.*	Poor ewn NWEE.
CLERK		
For how many people?	*Pour combien de personnes?*	Poor kohn-byehn duh payr-SOHNN?
GUEST		
For two people.	*Pour deux personnes.*	Poor duh payr-SOHNN.
For one person.	*Pour une personne.*	Poor ewn payr-SOHNN.
For two adults and a child.	*Pour deux adultes et un enfant.*	Poor duhz ah-DEWLT ay ehn ahn-FAHN.
CLERK		
Do you have…	*Avez-vous…*	Ah-vay-voo…
• any special needs?	• *besoin de quelque chose en particulier?*	• buh-zwehn duh kehl-kuh shohz ahn pahr-tee-kew-LYAY?
• any special requests?	• *des préférences?*	• day pray-fay-RAHNSS?
GUEST		
No, thank you.	*Non, je vous remercie.*	NOHN, zhuh voo ruh-mehr-SEE.
Yes, I (we, my spouse) would like…	*Oui, j'aimerais (nous aimerions/mon époux aimerait/mon épouse aimerait)…*	WEE, zheh-muh-reh (nooz eh-muh-ryohn/mohn ay-poo eh-muh-reh/mohn ay-pooz eh-muh-reh)…
• to be near the stairs.	• *être près des escaliers.*	• ehtr preh dayz ayss-kah-LYAY.
• to be near an exit.	• *être près d'une issue de secours.*	• ehtr preh dewn ee-sew duh suh-KOOR.
• a cot for our child.	• *un lit de camp pour notre enfant.*	• ehn lee duh KAHN poor nohtr ahn-FAHN.

• a handicapped-accessible room.	• *une chambre accessible aux personnes handicapées.*	• ewn shahn-bruh ak-seh-see-bluh oh pehr-sohnn ahn-dee-kah-PAY.

CLERK

The rate is _____ per night.	*Le tarif est de _____ la nuit.*	Luh tah-reef ay duh _____ lah NWEE.
Would you like to guarantee the reservation with a credit card?	*Aimeriez-vous garantir la réservation avec une carte de crédit?*	Eh-muh-ryay voo gah-rahn-teer lah ray-sehr-vah-syohn ah-vehk ewn kahrt duh kray-DEE?

GUEST

Yes, here is my _____ card.	*Oui, voici ma carte _____.*	WEE, vwah-see mah kahrt _____.
My credit card number is _____.	*Le numéro de ma carte de crédit est le _____.*	Luh new-may-rota duh mah kahrt duh kray-DEE ay luh _____.

CLERK

What is the expiration date?	*Quelle est la date d'expiration?*	Kehl ay lah daht dehx-pee-rah-SYOHN?
Thank you.	*Merci.*	Mehr-SEE.

RESTAURANT RESERVATIONS

RESTAURANT HOST

Good morning (afternoon, evening), _____ Restaurant.	*Bonjour (Bonjour, Bonsoir), ici le restaurant _____.*	Bohn-ZHOOR (bohn ZHOOR, bohn-SWAHR), ee-see luh rehss-toh-rahn _____.

GUEST

I'd like to reserve a table for…	*J'aimerais réserver une table pour…*	Zheh-muh-reh ray-zayr-vay ewn TAH-bluh poor…
• breakfast.	• *le petit déjeuner.*	• luh puh-tee-day-zhuh-NAY.
• lunch.	• *le déjeuner.*	• luh day-zhuh-NAY.
• dinner.	• *le dîner.*	• luh dee-NAY.

HOST

For what time?	*À quelle heure?*	Ah kehl UHR?

GUEST

For…o'clock.	*À…heures.*	Ah…UHR.
• seven	• *sept*	• seht
• eight	• *huit*	• weet
• nine	• *neuf*	• nuhv
For eight-thirty.	*À huit heures et demie.*	Ah weet uhr ay duh-MEE.

HOST

For how many people?	*Pour combien de personnes?*	poor kohn-byehn duh payr SOHNN?

GUEST

For one person.	*Pour une personne.*	Poor ewn payr-SOHNN.
For…people.	*Pour…personnes.*	Poor…payr-SOHNN.
• two	• *deux*	• duh
• four	• *quatre*	• kahtr
• six	• *six*	• see

HOST

And your name, please?	*Quel est votre nom, s'il vous plaît?*	Kehl ay voh-troh NOHN, seel voo PLEH?

GUEST

My name is _____.	*Mon nom est _____.*	Mohn nohn ay _____.

HOST

And is there a phone number where we can reach you?	*Y a-t-il un numéro de téléphone où on peut vous joindre?*	Ee ah-teel ehn new-may-roh duh tay-lay-FOHNN oo ohn puh voo JWEHN-druh?

GUEST

Yes, the number is _____.	*Oui, au _____.*	WEE, oh _____.
By the way, do you have any…items on the menu?	*À propos, avez-vous des plats…au menu?*	Ah proh-POH, ah-vay voo day plah…oh muh-NEW?

• vegetarian	• *végétariens*	• vay-zhay-tah-ryehn
• macrobiotic	• *macrobiotiques*	• mah-kroh-byoh-teek
• low-fat	• *allégés*	• ah-lay-zhay
• low-sodium	• *sans sel*	• sahn sehl
HOST		
Would you like smoking or nonsmoking?	*Préférez-vous la section fumeurs ou non-fumeurs?*	Pray-fay-ray-voo lah sehk-syohn few-MUHR oo nohn few-MUHR?
GUEST		
We would like…	*Nous aimerions…*	Nooz eh-muh-ryohn…
• smoking.	• *la section fumeurs.*	• lah sehk-syohn few-MUHR.
• nonsmoking.	• *la section non-fumeurs.*	• lah sehk-syohn NOHN few-MUHR.
HOST		
Thank you.	*Je vous remercie.*	Zhuh voo ruh-mehr-SEE.
That will be two people at eight o'clock.	*Ça sera donc deux personnes à huit heures.*	Sah suh-rah dohnk duh payr-SOHNN ah weet UHR.
That's a party of six at seven-thirty.	*Ça sera donc un groupe de six à sept heures et demie.*	Sah suh-rah dohnk ehn groop duh SEESS ah seht uhr ay duh-MEE.

C. COURTESY AND COMPLAINTS

GENERAL EXPRESSIONS OF COURTESY

Please.	***S'il vous plaît.***	Seel voo PLEH.
Thank you.	***Merci.***	Mehr-SEE.
You're welcome.	***De rien.***	Duh RYEHN.
Excuse me.	***Excusez-moi.***	Ehx-kew-zay MWAH.
I beg your pardon.	***Je vous demande pardon.***	Zhuh voo duh-mahnd pahr-DOHN.
I'm (terribly) sorry.	***Je suis (vraiment) désolé(e).***	Zhuh swee (vreh-mahn) day-zoh-LAY.
That's okay.	***Ce n'est rien.***	Suh nay RYEHN.

No problem.	*Il n'y a pas de problème.*	Eel nee ah pah duh proh-BLEHM.
It doesn't matter.	*Cela ne fait rien.*	Suh-lah nuh feh RYEHN.

COURTESY IN THE HOTEL

CONCIERGE

Good morning, sir, ma'am.	*Bonjour, monsieur, madame.*	Bohn-zhoor, muh-SYUH, mah-DAHM.
May I help you with something today?	*En quoi puis-je vous être utile aujourd'hui?*	Ahn qwah pweej vooz EH-truh oo-TEEL oh-zhoor-DWEE?

GUEST

I need…	*J'ai besoin…*	Zheh buh-ZWEHN…
• my room made up between now and ____.	• *qu'on fasse ma chambre entre maintenant et ____.*	• kohn fahss mah SHAHN-bruh ahn-truh mehn-tuh-NAHN ay ____.
• more towels, please.	• *de serviettes supplémentaires, s'il vous plaît.*	• duh sehr-vyeht sew-play-mahn-TEHR, seel voo PLEH.
• a rental car.	• *d'une voiture de location.*	• dewn vwah-tewr duh loh-kah-SYOHN.
• a taxi.	• *d'un taxi.*	• dehn tahx-SEE.
• a fax sent.	• *d'envoyer un fax.*	• dahn-vwah-yay ehn FAHX.
• some letters mailed.	• *qu'on poste mes lettres.*	• kohn pohsst may LEHTR.
• to make arrangements for a business meeting.	• *de prendre des dispositions pour une réunion d'affaires.*	• duh prahn-druh day deess-poh-zee-SYOHN poor ewn ray-ew-nyohn dah-FEHR.
• tickets to a show.	• *de billets pour un spectacle.*	• duh bee-yay poor ehn spayk-TAH-kluh.
• tickets to a game.	• *de billets pour un match.*	• de bee-yay poor ehn mahtch.
• tickets to a concert.	• *de billets pour un concert.*	• duh bee-yay poor ehn kohn-SAYR.

GUEST COMPLAINTS IN THE HOTEL

CONCIERGE

Is everything satisfactory?	***Êtes-vous satisfait(e)?***	Eht-voo sah-teess-FEH(T)?

GUEST

No, there is a problem.	***Non, il y a un problème.***	NOHN, eel ee ah ehn proh-BLEHM.
• The light	• *La lumière*	• Lah lew-MYEHR
• The toilet	• *Les toilettes*	• Lay twah-LEHT
• The television	• *La télévision*	• Lah tay-lay-vee-ZYOHN
• The radio	• *La radio*	• Lah rah-DYOH
• The air-conditioning	• *La climatisation*	• Lah klee-mah-tee-zah-SYOHN
• The alarm clock	• *Le réveil*	• Luh ray-VAY-yuh
• The heat	• *Le chauffage*	• Luh shoh-FAHJ
• The key	• *La clé*	• Lah klay
• The lock	• *La serrure*	• Lah seh-REWR
• The fan	• *Le ventilateur*	• Luh vahn-tee-lah-TUHR
…doesn't work.	*…ne marche pas.*	…nuh mahr-shuh PAH.

CLERK

I'll have Maintenance fix that right away.	*Je vais demander au service d'entretien de s'en occuper tout de suite.*	Zhuh veh duh-mahn-day oh sehr-veess dahn-truh-TYEHN duh sahn oh-kew-pay too duh SWEET.
I apologize.	*Je m'excuse.*	Zhuh mehx-KEWZ.

GUEST

My room…	***Ma chambre…***	Mah shahn-bruh…
• wasn't clean.	***• n'était pas propre.***	• nay-teh pah PROHPR.
• was noisy.	***• était bruyante.***	• ay-teh brwee-YAHNT.
• stinks (smells).	***• empeste (sent mauvais).***	• ahm-PEHSST (sahn moh-VEH).

The bed was uncomfortable.	*Le lit n'était pas confortable.*	Luh lee nay-teh pah kohn-fohr-TAH-bluh.
The water wasn't hot.	*L'eau n'était pas chaude.*	Loh nay-teh pah SHOHD.
Room service was late.	*Le service à l'étage était en retard.*	Luh sher-veess ah lay-tahj ay-teh ahn ruh-TAHR.
The service was very poor.	*Le service était médiocre.*	Luh sehr-veess ay-teh may-DYOH-kruh.
The employees were…	*Les employés étaient…*	Layz ahn-plwah-yay ay-teh…
• very good.	• *très bien.*	• treh BYEHN.
• excellent.	• *excellents.*	• ehx-say-LAHN.
• rude.	• *impolis.*	• uhm-poh-lee.
• incompetent.	• *incompétents.*	• ehn-kohn-pay-TAHN.
• unfriendly.	• *désagréables.*	• day-zah-gray-AH-bluh.
I didn't receive my wake-up call.	*On ne m'a pas appelé(e) pour me réveiller.*	Ohn nuh mah PAH ah-puh-LAY poor muh ray-vay-YAY.
I'm very disappointed with the level of service in this hotel.	*Je suis très déçu(e) par la qualité du service dans cet hôtel.*	Zhuh swee treh day-sew pahr lah kah-lee-tay dew sehr-veess dahn seht oh-TEHL.
This is the worst hotel I've ever seen.	*C'est le pire hôtel que j'aie jamais vu.*	Say luh peer oh-tehl kuh zheh zhah-meh VEW.

CONCIERGE

Please let me make the situation right.	*Laissez-moi arranger la situation.*	Leh-say mwah ah-rahn-zhay lah see-tew-ah-SYOHN.
I'm certain we can straighten out the problem.	*Je suis sûr(e) que nous pouvons résoudre ce problème.*	Zhuh swee sewr kuh noo poo-vohn ray-zoodr suh proh-BLEHM.
You won't pay for anything that wasn't completely up to your standards.	*Vous ne serez pas facturé pour tout ce qui n'a pas répondu à votre attente.*	Voo nuh suh-ray pah fahk-tew-RAY poor too suh kee nah pah ray-pohn-DEW ah voh-truh ah-TAHNT.

Please tell me what I can do to correct this terrible situation.	*S'il vous plaît, dites-moi ce que je peux faire pour remédier à cette pénible situation.*	Seel voo PLEH, deet-mwah suh kuh zhuh puh FEHR poor ruh-may-dyay ah seht pay-nee-bluh see-tew-ah-SYOHN.
We'll take _____ percent off your bill.	*Nous allons réduire votre note de _____ pour cent.*	Nooz ah-lohn ray-dweer voh-truh noht duh _____ poor SAHN.
We're going to give you _____ night(s), compliments of the hotel.	*Nous allons vous offrir _____ nuit(s) aux frais de l'hôtel.*	Nooz ah-lohn vooz oh-FREER _____ nwee oh freh duh loh-TEHL.
Your entire bill is compliments of the house.	*Votre note est entièrement aux frais de l'hôtel.*	Voh-truh noht ay ahn-tyehr-mahn oh freh duh loh-TEHL.

GUEST

Yes, that would be satisfactory.	*Oui, cela serait satisfaisant.*	WEE, suh-lah suh-reh sah-teess-fuh-ZAHN.
No, that would not be satisfactory.	*Non, cela ne me satisferait pas.*	NOHN, seh-lah nuh muh sah-teess-fuh-reh PAH.
I appreciate all your efforts.	*J'apprécie vos efforts.*	Zhah-pray-see vohz ay-FOHR.
Thank you, that would be very nice.	*Merci, ça serait très bien.*	Mer-SEE, sah suh-reh treh BYEHN.
I will never come here again.	*Je ne reviendrai jamais ici.*	Zhuh nuh ruh-vyehn-dreh ZHAH-meh ee-SEE.

MANAGEMENT COMPLAINTS

MANAGER

We have had some complaints about the noise coming from your room.	*Nous avons eu des réclamations à cause du bruit venant de votre chambre.*	Nooz ah-vohn ew day ray klah-mah-SYOHN ah kohz duh brwee vuh-nahn duh voh-truh SHAHN-bruh.
You are disturbing…	*Vous dérangez…*	Voo day-rahn-ZHAY…
• the people in the room next door.	• *les gens de la chambre d'à côté.*	• lay ZHAHN duh lah shahn-bruh dah koh-TAY.

• the people at the next table.	***• les gens de la table d'à côté.***	• lay ZHAHN duh lah tah-bluh dah koh-TAY.
• our other guests.	***• les autres clients.***	• layz oh-truh KLYAHN.

GUEST

We're sorry.	***Nous sommes désolé(e)s.***	Noo sohm day-zoh-LAY.
We understand.	***Nous comprenons.***	Noo kohn-pruh-NOHN.
We'll take care of it.	***Nous nous en occupons.***	Noo nooz ahn oh-kew-POHN.
We'll keep it down from now on.	***Nous ferons désormais moins de bruit.***	Noo foh-rohn day-zohr-meh mwehn duh BRWEE.
Who cares!	***On s'en moque!***	Ohn sahn MOHK!
Leave us alone!	***Laissez-nous tranquilles!***	Leh-say noo trahn-KEEL!

MANAGER

If you don't cooperate, I'm afraid I'll have to…	***Si vous refusez de coopérer, je vais être obligé(e)…***	See voo ruh-few-zay duh koh-oh-pay-RAY, zhuh vehz ehtr oh-blee-zhay…
• ask you to leave the hotel (restaurant).	***• de vous demander de quitter l'hôtel*** *(le restaurant).*	• duh voo duh-mahn-day duh kee-tay loh-TEHL (luh rehss-toh-RAHN).
• call security.	***• d'appeler le guardien.***	• dah-puh-lay luh gahrd-YEHN.
• call the police.	***• d'appeler la police.***	• dah-puh-lay lah poh-LEESS.

D. EMERGENCIES AND SAFETY

EMPLOYEE

Please note the emergency exits on this card.	***Je vous prie de prendre note des issues de secours indiquées sur cette carte.***	Zhuh voo pree duh prahn-druh NOHT dayz ee-sew duh suh-KOOR ehn-dee-kay sewr seht KAHRT.

FRENCH

Please note the emergency escape route on the door.	***Je vous prie de prendre note de la voie d'évacuation d'urgence indiquée sur la porte.***	Zhuh voo pree duh prahn-druh NOHT duh lah vwah day-vah-kew-ah-syohn dewr-ZHAHNSS ehn-dee-kay sewr lah POHRT.
Your room is equipped with smoke alarms.	***Votre chambre est dotée de détecteurs de fumée.***	Voh-truh shahn-bruh ay doh-TAY duh day-tehk-tuhr duh few-MAY.
Here is the fire alarm.	***Voici l'alarme d'incendie.***	Vwah-SEE lah-LAHRM dehn-sahn-DEE.
In an emergency, dial _____.	***En cas d'urgence, composez le _____.***	Ahn kah dewr-ZHAHNSS, kohn-poh-zay luh _____.

GUEST

Help!	***Au secours!***	Oh suh-KOOR!
Fire!	***Au feu!***	Oh FUH!
I need a doctor.	***J'ai besoin d'un médecin.***	Zheh buh-zwehn dayn mayd-SEHN.
I'm…	*Je suis…*	Zhuh swee…
My husband (wife) is…	*Mon mari (Ma femme) est…*	Mohn mah-ree (mah fahm) ay…
Someone is…	*Quelqu'un est…*	Kehl-kehn ay…
• very sick.	• *très malade.*	• treh mah-LAHD.
• having a heart attack.	• *victime d'une crise cardiaque.*	• veek-teem dewn kreez kahr-DYAHK.
• nauseated.	• *en proie à des nausées.*	• ahn PRWAH ah day noh-ZAY.
• choking.	• *en train d'étouffer.*	• ahn trehn day-too-FAY.
• losing consciousness.	• *en train de perdre connaissance.*	• ahn trehn duh PEHR-druh koh-neh-SAHNSS.
• about to vomit.	• *sur le point de vomir.*	• sewr luh PWEHN duh voh-MEER.
• having a seizure.	• *en train d'avoir une attaque.*	• ahn trehn dah-vwahr ewn ah-TAHK.
• stuck.	• *coincé(e).*	• kwehn-SAY.

I can't breathe.	*J'ai du mal à respirer.*	Zheh dew mahl ah rehss-pee-RAY.
MANAGER		
I'll call an ambulance.	*Je vais appeler une ambulance.*	Zhuh veh ah-puh-lay ewn ahn-bew-LAHNSS.
Don't move.	*Ne bougez pas.*	Nuh BOO-zhay PAH.
The doctor will be here very soon.	*Le médecin va bientôt arriver.*	Luh mayd-sehn vah byehn-toh ah-ree-VAY.
Are you hurt?	*Êtes-vous blessé(e)?*	Eht-voo bleh-SAY?
What happened?	*Qu'est-ce qui s'est passé?*	Kehss kee say pah-SAY?
GUEST		
I tripped and fell.	*J'ai trébuché et je suis tombé(e).*	Zheh tray-bew-shay ay zhuh swee tohn-BAY.
I cut myself.	*Je me suis coupé(e).*	Zhuh muh swee koo-PAY.
I drank too much.	*J'ai trop bu.*	Zheh troh BEW.
I don't know.	*Je ne sais pas.*	Zhuh nuh seh PAH.
I've injured…	*Je me suis fait mal…*	Zhuh muh swee feh mahl…
• my head.	• *à la tête.*	• ah lah TEHT.
• my neck.	• *au cou.*	• oh KOO.
• my back.	• *au dos.*	• oh DOH.
• my arm.	• *au bras.*	• oh BRAH.
• my leg.	• *à la jambe.*	• ah lah ZHAHNB.
• my foot.	• *au pied.*	• oh PYAY.
• my eye(s).	• *à l'oeil (aux yeux).*	• ah LUH-YUH (oh ZYUH).
DOCTOR (MEDICAL TECHNICIAN)		
You'll be fine; try to relax.	*Cela va aller; essayez de vous calmer.*	Suh-lah vah ah-LAY; ay-say yay duh voo kahl-MAY.
We're taking you to the hospital.	*Nous allons vous emmener à l'hôpital.*	Nooz ah-lohn vooz ahn-muh-nay ah loh-pee-TAHL.

Whom should we notify?	*Qui devons-nous prévenir?*	Kee duh-vohn noo prehv-NEER?
GUEST		
I've been robbed.	***J'ai été victime d'un vol.***	Zhay eh-tay veek-TEEM duhn VOHL.
MANAGER		
What did they take?	***Qu'est-ce qu'on vous a pris?***	Kehss-kohn vooz ah PREE?
Let me call the police.	***J'appelle la police.***	Zhah-pehl lah poh-LEESS.
Attention, ladies and gentlemen.	***Attention, mesdames et messieurs.***	Ah-tahn-SYOHN, may-dahm-zay may-SYUH.
May I have your attention, please?	***Puis-je avoir votre attention, s'il vous plaît?***	Pweej ah-vwahr vohtr ah-tahn-SYOHN, seel voo PLEH?
Please…	***Je vous prie…***	Zhuh voo pree…
• remain calm.	***• de rester calme.***	• duh rehss-tay KAHLM.
• follow the instructions of the staff.	***• de suivre les instructions du personnel.***	• duh swee-vruh layz ehns-trewk-syohn dew payr-soh-NEHL.
• wait in your rooms.	***• d'attendre dans vos chambres.***	• dah-tahn-druh dahn voh SHAHN-bruh.
• get under a table or doorway.	***• de vous mettre sous une table ou dans un chambranle de porte.***	• duh voo mehtr sooz ewn TAH-bluh oo dahnz ehn shahn-brahnl duh POHRT.
• follow the evacuation plan (route) **printed on your door** (in the hallways).	***• de suivre le plan*** *(la voie)* ***d'évacuation sur votre porte (dans le couloir).***	• duh swee-vroh luh plahn (lah vwah) day-vah-kew-ah-syohn sewr voh-truh POHRT (dahn luh koo-LWAHR).
We'll have the situation under control as soon as possible.	***Tout rentrera dans l'ordre au plus vite.***	Too ruhn-truh-rah dahn LOHR-druh oh ploo VEET.
Thank you for your patience.	***Je vous remercie de votre patience.***	Zhuh voo ruh-mehr-see duh voh-truh pah-SYAHNSS.

4. Checking In

A. AT THE FRONT DESK

FRONT DESK CLERK

Good morning (afternoon, evening).	*Bonjour (Bonjour, Bonsoir).*	Bohn-ZHOOR (Bohn-ZHOOR, Bohn-SWAHR).
How may I help you?	*En quoi puis-je vous aider?*	Ahn kwah pweej-voo zeh-DAY?

GUEST

I have a reservation under the name _____.	*J'ai une réservation au nom de _____.*	Zheh ewn ray-zayr-vah-syohn oh nohn duh _____.
Do you have a room for one (two)?	*Avez-vous une chambre pour une (deux) personne(s)?*	Ah-vay-voo ewn SHAHN-bruin poor ewn (duh) pehr-SOHNN?

CLERK

Yes, we have your reservation.	*Oui, nous avons votre réservation.*	WEE, nooz ah-vohn voh-truh ray-zayr-vah-SYOHN.
Yes, for how many nights?	*Oui, pour combien de nuits?*	WEE, poor kohn-byehn duh NWEE?
No, I'm sorry, we're full.	*Non, je suis désolé(e), nous sommes complet.*	NOHN, zhuh swee day-zoh-LAY, noo sohm kohn-PLEH.

GUEST

For _____ night(s), please.	*Pour _____ nuit(s), s'il vous plaît.*	Poor _____ NWEE, seel voo PLEH.
What are your rates?	*Quels sont vos tarifs?*	Kehl sohn voh tah-REEF?

CLERK

• For a single,	• *Pour une chambre simple,*	• Poor ewn shahn-bruh SEHN-pluh,
• For a double,	• *Pour une chambre double,*	• Poor ewn shahn-bruh DOO-bluh,
• For adjoining rooms,	• *Pour des chambres contiguës,*	• Poor day shan-bruh kohn-tee-GEW,

FRENCH

• For a suite,	• *Pour une suite,*	• Poor ewn SWEET,
…the rate is ____ per night.	*…le prix est de ____ la nuit.*	…luh pree ay duh ____ lah nwee.
GUEST		
Are any meals included?	*Est-ce que cela comprend les repas?*	Ehss-kuh suh-lah kohn-prahn lay ruh-PAH?
Is breakfast included?	*Est-ce que le petit déjeuner est compris?*	Ehss-kuh luh puh-tee day zhuh-nay ay kohn-PREE?
CLERK		
No, meals are extra.	*Non, les repas sont en supplément.*	NOHN, lay ruh-pah sohn ahn sew-play-MAHN.
Yes, breakfast is included.	*Oui, le petit déjeuner est compris.*	WEE, luh puh-tee day zhuh-nay ay kohn-PREE.
You can choose…	*Vous avez le choix entre…*	Vooz ah-vay luh shwah ahn-truh…
• the American plan (all meals included).	• *la pension complète (tous les repas sont compris).*	• lah pahn-syohn kohn-PLEHT (too lay ruh-pah sohn kohn-PREE).
• the modified American plan (breakfast and dinner).	• *la demi-pension (petit déjeuner et dîner compris).*	• lah duh-mee pahn-SYOHN (puh-tee day zhuh-nay ay dee-nay kohn-PREE).
• the European plan (no meals included).	• *la chambre seule (repas non compris).*	• lah shahn-bruh SUHL (ruh-pah NOHN kohn PREE).
GUEST		
I'd like a room…	*J'aimerais une chambre…*	Zheh-muh-reh ewn SHAHN-bruh…
• that faces the back (front).	• *qui donne sur l'arrière (devant).*	• kee dohnn sewr lah-RYEHR (duh-VAHN).
• that faces the water (pool).	• *qui donne sur l'eau (la piscine).*	• kee dohnn sewr LOH (lah pee-SEEN).
• with a private bath/toilet/shower.	• *avec salle de bains privée/toilettes/douche.*	• ah-vehk sahl duh behn pree-VAY/twah-LEHT/DOOSH.

• with a handicapped-accessible bathroom.	• *avec une salle de bains accessible aux personnes à mobilité réduite.*	• ah-vehk ewn sahl duh behn ahk-seh-see-bluh oh pehr-sohnn ah moh-bee-lee-tay ray-DWEET.
• with air-conditioning.	• *climatisée.*	• klee-mah-tee-ZAY.
• with a TV.	• *avec la télévision.*	• ah-vehk lah tay-lay-vee-ZYOHN.
• with cable.	• *avec la télévision par cable.*	• ah-vehk lah tay-lay-vee-zyohn pahr KAH-bluh.
• with a fax machine.	• *avec un fax.*	• ah-vehk ehn fahx.
• with a phone.	• *avec un téléphone.*	• ah-vehk ehn tay-lay-FOHNN.
• with a network hookup for my computer.	• *équipée d'une connection sur réseau pour mon ordinateur.*	• ay-kee-pay dewn koh-nehk-syohn sewr ray-ZOH poor mohn ohr-dee-nah TUHR.
• with a view.	• *avec une vue.*	• ah-vehk ewn VEW.
• with a whirlpool bath/Jacuzzi.	• *avec un bain à remous/ bouillonnant.*	• ah-vehk ehn behn ah ruh-MOO/boo-yohn-NAHN.
• with two double beds.	• *avec deux lits doubles.*	• ah-vehk duh lee DOO-bluh.
• with a king-size bed.	• *avec un grand lit.*	• ah-vehk ehn grahn LEE.
• with an extra bed.	• *avec un lit supplémentaire.*	• ah-vehk ehn lee sew-play-mahn-TEHR.
• with a baby crib.	• *avec un berceau.*	• ah-vehk ehn behr-SOH.
• with a balcony.	• *avec un balcon.*	• ah-vehk ehn bahl-KOHN.
• with a sitting area.	• *avec un coin pour s'asseoir.*	• ah-vehk ehn kwehn poor sah-SWAHR.
• with a bar.	• *avec un bar.*	• ah-vehk ehn BAHR.
• with a kitchenette.	• *avec une kitchenette.*	• ah-vehk ewn kee-tchuh-NEHT.

• away from the elevator.	• *éloignée de l'ascenseur.*	• ay-lwah-nyay duh lah-sahn-SUHR.
• with no meals.	• *sans repas compris.*	• sahn ruh-pah kohn-PREE.

CLERK

No problem.	*Il n'y a pas de problème.*	Eel nee ah pah duh proh-BLEHM.
I'm sorry.	*Je suis désolé(e).*	Zhuh swee day-zoh-LAY.
There is none available.	*Il n'y en a pas de libre.*	Eel nee ahn nah pah duh LEE-bruh.
We don't provide/ offer that.	*Nous ne fournissons/ n'offrons pas cela.*	Noo nuh foor-nee-sohn/noh-frohn pah suh-LAH.

GUEST

Does the hotel have…	*Est-ce que l'hôtel a…*	Ehss-kuh loh-tehl ah…
• a restaurant?	• *un restaurant?*	• ehn rehss-toh-RAHN?
• a bar?	• *un bar?*	• ehn BAHR?
• room service?	• *le service à l'étage?*	• luh sehr-veess ah lay-TAHJ?
• a gym/health club?	• *un gymnase/une salle de remise en forme?*	• ehn geem-NAHZ/ewn sahl duh ruh-meez ahn FOHRM?
• a spa hot tub?	• *un bain de relaxation?*	• ehn behn duh ruh-lah-xah-SYOHN?
• a swimming pool?	• *une piscine?*	• ewn pee-SEEN?
• baby-sitting?	• *un service de baby-sitting?*	• ehn sehr-veess duh bay-bee-see-TEENG?
• tennis courts?	• *des courts de tennis?*	• day koor duh tay-NEESS?
• laundry (dry-cleaning) service?	• *un service de pressing (de nettoyage à sec)?*	• ehn sehr-veess duh preh-SEENG (duh neh-twah-yahj ah SEHK)?
• a garage?	• *un parking couvert?*	• ehn pahr-keeng koo-VEHR?

May I see the room?	*Puis je voir la chambre?*	Pweej vwahr lah SHAHN-bruh?
CLERK		
Yes, certainly. Here's the key.	*Oui, bien sûr. Voici la clé.*	WEE, byehn SEWR. Vwah-see lah KLAY.
Would you like another room?	*Est-ce que vous désirez une autre chambre?*	Ehss-kuh voo day-zee-ray ewn oh-truh SHAHN-bruh?
GUEST		
I'd like something...	*J'aimerais quelque chose de...*	Zheh-muh-reh kehl-kuh shohz duh...
• smaller.	• *plus petit.*	• plew puh-TEE.
• larger.	• *plus grand.*	• plew GRAHN.
• quieter.	• *plus calme.*	• plew KAHLM.
• better.	• *mieux.*	• MYUH.
• cheaper.	• *moins cher.*	• mwehn SHEHR.
• on another floor.	• *situé à un autre étage.*	• see-tew-ay ah ehn nohtr ay-TAHJ.
I'll take the room, please.	*Je vais prendre la chambre, s'il vous plaît.*	Zhuh veh prahn-druh lah SHAHN-bruh, seel voo PLEH.
CLERK		
Very well, how will you be paying?	*Très bien. Comment comptez-vous payer?*	Treh BYEHN. Koh-mahn kohn-tay-voo pay-YAY?
GUEST		
I'll pay with...	*Je vais payer...*	Zhuh veh pay-yay...
• cash.	• *en liquide.*	• ahn lee-KEED.
• a credit card.	• *avec ma carte de crédit.*	• ah-vehk mah kahrt duh kray-DEE.
• traveler's checks.	• *par chèques de voyage.*	• pahr shehk duh vwah-YAHJ.
CLERK		
Thank you.	*Merci.*	Mehr-SEE.

FRENCH

To charge meals and services to your room, I'll need a credit card.	*Pour mettre vos repas et autres services sur le compte de votre chambre, je vais avoir besoin de votre carte de crédit.*	Poor mehtr voh ruh-pah ay oh-truh sehr-VEESS sewr luh kohnt duh voh-truh SHAHN-bruh, zhuh vehzah-vwahr buh-ZWEHN duh voh-truh kahrt duh kray-DEE.
You may settle the bill with traveler's checks (cash).	*Vous pouvez régler votre note avec des chèques de voyage (en liquide).*	Voo poo-vay ray-gray voh-truh NOHT ah-vehk day shehk duh vwah-YAHJ (ahn lee-KEED).
If you would like to store valuables, we have a safe.	*Si vous désirez entreposer vos objets de valeur, nous avons un coffre à votre disposition.*	See voo day-zee-ray ahn-truh-poh-zay voh zohb-zheh duh vah-LUHR, nooz ah-vohn ehn kohfr ah voh-truh deess-poh-zee-SYOHN.
Please note that…	*Je vous prie de prendre note que…*	Zhuh voo pree duh prahn-druh NOHT kuh…
• quiet hours are between _____ and _____.	• *les heures de calme sont entre _____ et _____.*	• layz uhr duh kahlm sohn ahn-truh _____ ay _____.
• there are no pets allowed.	• *les animaux de compagnie sont interdits.*	• layz ah-nee-moh duh kohn-pah-NEE sohn ehn tehr-DEE.
• children under _____ stay free.	• *c'est gratuit pour les enfants âgés de moins de _____.*	• say grah-TWEE poor lay zahn-fahn ah-zhay duh mwehn duh _____.
• smoking is allowed only in the bar.	• *il est permis de fumer seulement au bar.*	• eel ay pehr-mee duh few-may suhl-mahn oh BAHR.
• we do not allow cooking in the rooms.	• *nous ne permettons pas aux clients de cuisiner dans la chambre.*	• noo nuh pehr-meh-tohn pah oh klee-YAHN duh kwee-zee-nay dahn lah SHAHN-bruh.

GUEST

Do I (we) have any messages?	*Est-ce qu'il y a des messages pour moi (nous)?*	Ehss-keel ee ah day may-SAHJ poor MWAH (NOO)?
I would like a wake-up call, please.	*J'aimerais qu'on m'appelle pour me réveiller, s'il vous plaît.*	Zheh-muh-reh kohn mah-pehl poor muh ray-vay-YAY, seel voo PLEH.
May we have…, please?	*Est-ce qu'on pourrait avoir…, s'il vous plaît?*	Ehss-kohn poo-reh ah-vwahr…, seel voo PLEH?
• extra blankets	• *des couvertures supplémentaires*	• day koo-vehr-tewr sew-play-mahn-TEHR
• extra towels	• *des serviettes supplémentaires*	• day sehr-vyeht sew-play-mahn-TEHR
• a hair dryer	• *un séchoir à cheveux*	• ehn say-shwahr ah shuh-VUH
• an iron	• *un fer à repasser*	• ehn fehr ah ruh-pah-SAY
• ice	• *de la glace*	• duh lah glahss

CLERK

I'll have that brought to your room right away.	*Je vais le faire monter dans votre chambre tout de suite.*	Zhuh veh luh fehr mohn-tay dahn voh-truh SHAHN-bruin too duh SWEET.

GUEST

Where is…	*Où est…*	Oo ay…
• the room attendant?	• *l'employé(e) chargé(e) de ma chambre?*	• lahn-plwah-yay shahr-zhay duh mah SHAHN-bruh?
• the bellman (bell attendant)?	• *le chasseur?*	• luh shah-SUHR?
• the manager?	• *le gérant (la gérante)?*	• luh zhay-RAHN (lah zhay-RAHNT)?
• the dining room?	• *la salle à manger?*	• lah sahl ah mahn-ZHAY?
• the gift shop?	• *la boutique de souvenirs?*	• lah boo-teek duh soov-NEER?

• the newsstand?	• *le kiosque à journaux?*	• luh kyohsk ah zhoor-NOH?
CLERK		
Just over there.	*Là-bas.*	Lah-BAH.
GUEST		
How do I use the telephone?	*Comment marche le téléphone?*	Koh-mahn mahrsh luh tay-lay-FOHNN?
CLERK		
The instructions are next to the phone.	*Le mode d'emploi est près du téléphone.*	Luh mohd dahn-PLWAH ay preh dew tay-lay-FOHNN.
Dial ____ for a local (long-distance) call, wait for the tone, then dial the number.	*Composez le ____ pour un appel local (de longue distance), attendez la tonalité, puis composez le numéro.*	Kohn-poh-zay luh ____ poor ehn ah-pohl loh-KAHL (de lohng dees-TAHNSS), ah-tahn-day lah toh-nah-lee-TAY, pwee kohn-poh-zay luh new-may-ROH.
Dial ____ for an operator.	*Composez le ____ pour avoir la standardiste.*	Kohn-poh-zay luh ____ poor ah-vwahr lah stahn-dahr-DEEST.
To use a credit card, dial ____.	*Pour payer par carte de crédit, composez le ____.*	Poor pay-yay pahr kahrt duh kray-DEE, kohn say luh ____.
GUEST		
Please have our luggage brought to our room.	*Faites monter nos bagages dans la chambre, s'il vous plaît.*	Feht mohn-tay noh bah-gahj dahn lah SHAHN-bruh, seel voo PLEH.
We'll need a wheelchair.	*Nous allons avoir besoin d'un fauteuil roulant.*	Nooz ah-lohn ah-vwahr buh-zwehn dehn foh-tuh-yuh roo-LAHN.
CLERK		
Yes, right away.	*Oui, tout de suite.*	WEE, too duh SWEET.
GUEST		
We'd like to order a pizza, please.	*Nous aimerions commander une pizza, s'il vous plaît.*	Nooz eh-muh-ryohn koh-mahn-day ewn pee-ZAH, seel voo PLEH.

MANAGER

I'll be happy to call someone for you.	*J'appellerai quelqu'un pour vous avec plaisir.*	Zha-peh-luh-reh kehl-kehn poor VOO ah-vehk pleh-ZEER.
We have room service, but we don't allow outside vendors into the hotel.	*Nous avons le service à l'étage, mais nous n'autorisons pas les commerçants de l'extérieur à l'hôtel.*	Nooz ah-vohn luh sehr-veess ah lay-TAHJ, meh noo noh-toh-ree-zhohn pah lay koh-mehr-sahn duh lehx-tay RYUHR ah loh-TEHL.

GUEST

We'd like to entertain a few friends in our room.	*Nous aimerions recevoir des amis dans notre chambre.*	Nooz eh-muh-ryohn ruh-suh-vwahr dayz ah-MEE dahn noh-truh SHAHN-bruh.

MANAGER

We allow guests in the rooms until _____.	*On peut recevoir des invités jusqu'à _____.*	Ohn puh ruh-suh-VWAHR-dayz ehn-vee-tay zhews-kah _____.

B. SHOWING GUESTS TO THEIR ROOMS

BELLMAN (BELL ATTENDANT)

My name is _____, and I'm your bell attendant.	*Je m'appelle _____, et je suis votre chasseure.*	Zhuh mah-pehl _____, ay zhuh swee voh-truh shah-SUHR.
May I show you to your room?	*Puis-je vous conduire à votre chambre?*	Pweej voo kohn-dweer ah voh-troh SHAHN-bruh?

GUEST

No, thanks. We'll find it ourselves. it ourselves.	*Non, merci. Nous la trouverons nous-mêmes.*	NOHN, mehr-SEE. Noo lah troo-vuh-rohn noo-MEHM.
Yes, please.	*Oui, s'il vous plaît.*	WEE, seel voo PLEH.

BELLMAN

This way, please.	*Suivez-moi, je vous prie.*	Swee-vay-MWAH, zhuh voo PREE.
The elevator is over here.	*L'ascenseur est là-bas.*	Lah-sahn-suhr ay lah-BAH.

TIP! ••••

International guests in particular may have questions about using the telephone and will appreciate seeing how the television and pay movies work.

May I show you the features of your room?	*Puis-je vous montrer comment votre chambre est équipée?*	Pweej voo mohn-TRAY koh-mahn voh-truh SHAHN-bruh ay tay-kee-PAY?
This is the key to the minibar.	*Voici la clé du mini-bar.*	Vwah-see lah klay dew mee-nee BAHR.
• Any movie you select	• *Chaque film que vous choisissez*	• Shahk FEELM kuh voo shwah-zee-SAY
• Any long-distance calls you make	• *Chaque appel de longue distance que vous faites*	• Shahk ah-petal duh lohng deess-TAHNSS kuh voo feht
• Any snack or beverage you take from the refrigerator	• *Chaque casse-croûte ou boisson que vous prenez dans le réfrigérateur*	• Shahk kahss-kroot oo bwah-SOHN kuh voo pruh-nay dahn luh ray-free-zhay-rah-TUHR
...will be charged to your room.	*...sera facturé sur la note de votre chambre.*	...suh-rah fahk-tew-RAY sewr lah noht duh voh-truh SHAHN-bruh.
Here is the control for the heating (air-conditioning).	*Voici le bouton de réglage du chauffage (de la climatisation).*	Vwah-see luh boo-tohn duh ray-glahj dew shoh-FAHJ (duh lah klee-mah-tee-zah-SYOHN).

GUEST

How do I call Room Service?	*Comment est-ce que j'appelle le service à l'étage?*	Koh-mahn ehss-kuh zhah-pehl luh sehr-veess ah lay-TAHJ?

BELLMAN		
Dial _____.	*Composez le _____.*	Kohn-poh-zay luh _____.
GUEST		
This room…	*Cette chambre…*	Seht shahn-bruh…
• is too close to the elevator(s).	• *est trop près de l'ascenseur (des ascenseurs).*	• ay troh preh duh lah-sahn-SUHR (dayz ah-sahn-SUHR).
• hasn't been made up.	• *n'a pas été faite.*	• nah pah ay-tay FEHT.
• smells (like cigarettes).	• *sent (la cigarette).*	• sahn (lain see-gah-REHT).
The toilet (bathtub, sink) is clogged.	*Les toilettes sont bouchées. (La baignoire, le lavabo est bouché(e).)*	Lay twah-leht sohn boo-SHAY. (Lah beh-nwahr, luh lah-vah-boh ay boo-SHAY.)
May I (we) change rooms, please?	*Est-ce je peux (nous pouvons) changer de chambre, s'il vous plaît?*	Ehss-kuh zhuh puh (noo poo-vohn) shahn-zhay duh SHAHN-bruh, seel voo PLEH?
BELLMAN		
Please let me check our availability with the front desk.	*Je vais demander ce qu'il y a de libre à la réception.*	Zhuh veh duh-mahn-DAY suh keel ee ah duh LEE-bruh ah lah ray-sehp-SYOHN.
Sure, I'll be happy to assist you.	*Oui, bien sûr. Je serais heureux (heureuse) de vous aider.*	WEE, byehn SEWR. zhuh suh-reh uh-ruh (uh-ruhz) duh vooz eh-DAY.
Here is my card. Please call if I can help you with anything else.	*Voici ma carte. N'hésitez pas à m'appeler si vous avez besoin de quelque chose.*	Vwah-see mah KAHRT. Nay-zee-tay pah ah mah-puh-LAY see vooz ah-vaybuh-zwehn duh kehl-kuh SHOHZ.

VOCABULARY ••••

THE GUEST ROOM

air-conditioning	*la climatisation*	lah klee-mah-tee-zah-SYOHN
balcony	*le balcon*	luh bahl-kohn
bath mat	*le tapis de bain*	luh tah-pee duh BEHN
bathtub	*la baignoire*	lah beh-NWAHR
bed	*le lit*	luh lee
bedspread	*le couvre-lit*	luh koovr-LEE
blanket	*la couverture*	lah koo-vehr-TEWR
blinds	*les volets*	lay voh-LEH
carpet	*la moquette*	lah moh-KEHT
ceiling	*le plafond*	luh plah-FOHN
chair	*la chaise*	lah shehz
closet	*le placard*	luh plah-KAHR
conditioner	*le climatiseur*	luh klee-mah-tee-ZUHR
couch	*le divan*	luh dee-VAHN
crib	*le berceau*	luh behr-SOH
desk	*le bureau*	luh bew-ROH
Do Not Disturb sign	*la pancarte "ne pas déranger"*	lah pahn-kahrt "nuh pah day-rahn-ZHAY"
door	*la porte*	lah pohrt
drapes	*les rideaux*	lay ree-DOH
dresser	*la commode*	lah koh-MOHD
fan	*le ventilateur*	luh vahn-tee-lah-TUHR
floor	*le sol*	luh sohl
glass(es)	*le(s) verre(s)*	luh (lay) vehr
hair dryer	*le séchoir à cheveux*	luh say-shwahr ah shuh-VUH
(coat) hanger	*le portemanteau*	luh pohrt-mahn-TOH
heat	*le chauffage*	luh shoh-FAHJ
ice bucket	*le seau à glace*	luh soh ah GLAHSS

(cont'd.)

The Guest Room *(cont'd.)*

iron	*le fer à repasser*	luh fehr ah ruh-pah-SAY
lamp	*la lampe*	lah lahnp
light	*la lumière*	lah lew-MYEHR
lock	*la serrure*	lah seh-REWR
minibar	*le mini-bar*	luh mee-nee-BAHR
mirror	*le miroir*	luh mee-RWAHR
nightstand	*la table de nuit*	lah tah-bluh duh NWEE
pillow	*l'oreiller*	loh-ray-YAY
radio	*la radio*	lah rah-dyoh
razor	*le rasoir*	luh rah-ZWAHR
sewing kit	*la trousse à couture*	lah trooss ah koo-TEWR
shampoo	*le shampooing*	luh shahn-PWEHN
sheets	*les draps*	lay drah
shower	*la douche*	lah doosh
shower cap	*le bonnet de douche*	luh boh-nay duh DOOSH
sink	*le lavabo*	luh lah-vah-BOH
soap	*le savon*	luh sah-VOHN
telephone	*le téléphone*	luh tay-lay-FOHNN
television	*la télévision*	lah tay-lay-vee-ZYOHN
thermostat	*le thermostat*	luh tayr-mohss-TAH
toilet	*les toilettes*	lay twah-LEHT
toilet paper	*le papier hygiénique*	luh pah-pyay ee-zhyay-NEEK
toothbrush	*la brosse à dents*	lah brohss ah DAHN
toothpaste	*le dentifrice*	luh dahn-tee-FREESS
towel	*la serviette de toilette*	lah sehr-vyeht duh twah-LEHT
VCR	*le magnétoscope*	luh mah-nyay-tohss-KOHP
wall	*le mur*	luh mewr
window	*la fenêtre*	lah fuh-NEHTR

5. Providing Assistance

A. GIVING DIRECTIONS

CONCIERGE		
Good morning. May I help you?	*Bonjour. En quoi puis-je vous être utile?*	Bohn-ZHOOR. Ahn kwah pweej vooz EHT-ruh oo-TEEL?
GUEST		
Yes, where is (are) the...	*Où est (sont)...*	Oo ay (sohn)...
• bathrooms?	• *les toilettes?*	• lay twah-LEHT?
• lounge/bar?	• *le salon/le bar?*	• luh sah-LOHN/luh BAHR?
• coffee shop/ restaurant?	• *le café-restaurant/le restaurant?*	• luh kah-fay rehss-toh-RAHN/luh rehss-toh-RAHN?
• barbershop/ hairdresser's?	• *le coiffeur pour hommes/le salon de coiffure?*	• luh kwah-fuhr poor OHM/luh sah-lohn duh kwah-FEWR?
• gift shop?	• *la boutique de souvenirs?*	• lah boo-teek duh soov-NEER?
• health club/gym?	• *le club de santé/la salle de gymnastique?*	• luh kluhb duh sahn-TAY/lah sahl duh geem nahss-TEEK?
• ballroom?	• *la salle de bal?*	• lah sahl duh BAHL?
• elevator?	• *l'ascenseur?*	• lah-sahn-SUHR?
• pay phones?	• *les cabines téléphoniques?*	• lay kah-been tay-lay-foh-NEEK?
ice machine?	• *la machine à glaçons?*	• lah main-sheen ah glah-SOHN?
CONCIERGE		
Take...	*Prenez...*	pruh-NAY...
• the escalator.	• *l'escalier roulant.*	• layss-kah-lyay roo-LAHN.
• the elevator.	• *l'ascenseur.*	• lah-sahn-SUHR.
• the stairs.	• *les escaliers.*	• layz ayss-kah-LYAY.

TIP! ••••

You can simply explain many directions, but when they're more complex, you should use either a map or written instructions (or both). Hotels should keep preprinted directions to major sites on hand. Also, many cultures don't speak of distance in terms of city blocks but will understand if you use the word "streets" instead. And remember that most international guests use the metric system and may have difficulties figuring a distance given in miles, yards, or feet.

Go…	*Allez…*	Ah-LAY…
• up.	• *en haut.*	• ahn OH.
• down.	• *en bas.*	• ahn BAH.
• left.	• *à gauche.*	• ah GOHSH.
• right.	• *à droite.*	• ah DRWAHT.
• straight ahead.	• *tout droit.*	• too DRWAH.
• around the corner.	• *juste après le coin.*	• zhewst ah-preh luh KWEHN.
• left, then right.	• *à gauche, puis à droite.*	• ah GOHSH, pweez ah DRWAHT.
• past the elevators.	• *après les ascenseurs.*	• ah-preh layz ah-sahn-SUHR.
• to the first (second, third, fourth) floor.	• *jusqu'au premier (deuxième, troisième, quatrième) étage.*	• jews-koh pruh-myay (duh-zyehm, trwah-zyehm, kah-tryehm) ay-TAHJ.
• left (right) when you exit the elevator.	• *à gauche (à droite) quand vous sortez de l'ascenseur.*	• ah GOHSH (ahDRWAHT) kahn voo sohr-tay duh lah-sahn-SUHR.
• in through the second set of doors.	• *passez les deuxièmes portes.*	• pah-say lay duh-zyehm POHRT.

It will be…	*Ça sera…*	Sah suh-rah…
• on your right.	• *sur votre droite.*	• sewr voh-truh DRWAHT.
• on your left.	• *sur votre gauche.*	• sewr voh-truh GOHSH.
• right in front of you.	• *juste en face de vous.*	• zhewst ahn fahss duh VOO.

GUEST

How do I get…	*Comment est-ce que je vais…*	Koh-mahn ehss-kuh zhuh veh…
• to the hospital?	• *à l'hôpital?*	• ah loh-pee-TAHL?
• to city hall?	• *à la mairie?*	• ah lah meh-REE?
• to the _____ restaurant/hotel?	• *au restaurant/à l'hôtel _____?*	• oh rehss-toh-rahn/ah loh-tehl _____?
• to the train station?	• *à la gare?*	• ah lah GAHR?
• to the bus station?	• *à la gare routière?*	• ah lah gahr roo-TYEHR?
• to the nearest bus stop?	• *à l'arrêt de bus le plus proche?*	• ah lah-reh duh bewss luh plew PROHSH?
• to the mall?	• *à la galerie marchande?*	• ah lah gahl-ree mahr-SHAHND?
• to the post office?	• *à la poste?*	• ah lah POHST?
• to the airport?	• *à l'aéroport?*	• ah lah-ay-roh-POHR?
• downtown?	• *en ville?*	• ahn VEEL?
• to the car rental agency?	• *à l'agence de location de voitures?*	• ah lah-zhahnss duh loh-kah-syohn duh wah-TEWR?
• to _____ Street/Avenue?	• *rue/avenue _____?*	• rew/ahv-new _____?

CONCIERGE

When you exit the hotel, go…	*Quand vous sortez de l'hôtel, allez…*	Kahn voo sohr-tay duh loh-tehl, ah-lay…
• left.	• *à gauche.*	• ah GOHSH.
• right.	• *à droite.*	• ah DRWAHT.
• straight ahead.	• *tout droit.*	• too DRWAH.
• north.	• *vers le nord.*	• vehr luh NOHR.

• south.	• *vers le sud.*	• vehr luh SEWD.
• east.	• *vers l'est.*	• vehr LEHST.
• west.	• *vers l'ouest.*	• vehr LWEHST.

GUEST

How far is it?	*Est-ce que c'est loin?*	Ehss-kuh say LWEHN?

CONCIERGE

It's about _____…	*C'est à environ _____…*	Say tah ahn-vee-rohn _____…
• blocks (streets).	• *pâtés de maisons (rues).*	• pah-tay duh meh-SOHN (REW).
• miles.	• *miles.*	• MEEL.
• kilometers.	• *kilomètres.*	• kee-loh-MEHTR.
• minutes…	• *minutes…*	• mee-newt…
• on foot.	• *à pied.*	• ah PYAY.
• by car.	• *en voiture.*	• ahn vwah-TEWR.
• by bus.	• *en bus.*	• ahn BEWSS.
• by metro (subway).	• *en métro.*	• ahn may-TROH.

GUEST

Can you show me on the map?	*Est-ce que vous pouvez me montrer sur le plan?*	Ehss-kuh voo poo-veh muh mohn-tray sewr luh PLAHN?

CONCIERGE

Sure, it's right here.	*Oui, bien sûr. C'est ici.*	WEE, byehn SEWR. Say tee-SEE.
Let me draw you a little map.	*Je vais vous faire le plan.*	Zhuh veh voo fehr luh PLAHN.

GUEST

Can you tell me where I can…around here?	*Pouvez-vous me dire où je peux…par ici?*	Poo-vay-voo muh DEERoo zhuh puh… pahr ee-SEE?
• take a walk	• *me promener*	• muh proh-muh-nay
• ride a bike	• *faire du vélo*	• fehr dew vay-loh
• jog	• *faire du jogging*	• fehr dew joh-geeng

CONCIERGE

Yes, we have maps of...trails right here.	*Oui, nous avons des cartes ici qui montrent les...*	WEE, nooz ah-vohn day kahrt ee-SEE kee mohn-truh lay...
• jogging	• *sentiers de jogging.*	• sahn-tyay duh joh-GEENG.
• walking	• *sentiers de randonnée.*	• sahn-tyehr duh rahn-doh-NAY.
• bike	• *pistes cyclables.*	• peess-tuh see-klah-bluh.

B. RECOMMENDING PLACES OF INTEREST

GUEST

Can you recommend any places to visit?	*Pouvez-vous me recommander quelques endroits intéressants a voir?*	Poo-vay-voo muh ruh-koh-mahn-DAY kehl-kuh zahn drwah ehn-tay-ray-sahn ah VWAHR?

CONCIERGE

There are lots. Are you interested in...	*Il y en a beaucoup. Est-ce vous vous intéressez...*	Eel ee ahn ah boh-KOO. Ehss-kuh voo vooz ehn-tay-ray-say...
• art?	• *à l'art?*	• ah LAHR?
• theater?	• *au théâtre?*	• oh tay-AH-truh?
• shopping?	• *aux magasins?*	• oh mah-gah-ZEHN?
• museums?	• *aux musées?*	• oh mew-ZAY?
• sports?	• *aux sports?*	• oh SPOHR?
• sight-seeing?	• *au tourisme?*	• oh too-REEZ-muh?
• music?	• *à la musique?*	• ah lah mew-ZEEK?
• outdoor activities?	• *aux activités en plein air?*	• oh zahk-tee-vee-tay ahn plehn EHR?
• children's activities?	• *aux activités pour enfants?*	• oh zahk-tee-vee-tay poor ahn-FAHN?

GUEST

What do you recommend?	*Qu'est-ce que vous recommandez?*	Kehss kuh voo ruh-koh-mahn-DAY?

CONCIERGE

If you're interested in art, I'd suggest…	*Si vous vous intéressez à l'art, je vous suggère…*	See voo vooz ehn-tay-ray-say ah LAHR, zhuh voo sewg-zhehr…
• the _____ gallery.	• *la galerie _____.*	• lah gahl-ree _____.
• the _____ art museum.	• *le musée des beaux-arts _____.*	• luh mew-zay day bohz-ahr _____.
If you're interested in theater, I can get you tickets to…	*Si le théâtre vous intéresse, je peux vous obtenir des billets pour…*	See luh tay-ah-truh vooz ehn-tay-REHSS, zhuh poh vooz ohb-tuh-neer day bee-yay poor…
• a show.	• *un spectacle.*	• ehn spehk-TAH-kluh.
• an opera.	• *l'opéra.*	• loh-pay-RAH.
• a movie.	• *le cinéma.*	• luh see-nay-MAH.
For shopping, I'd recommend…	*Pour ce qui est du shopping, je vous recommande…*	Poor suh kee ay dew shoh-PEENG, zhuh voo ruh-koh-mahnd…
• downtown.	• *d'aller en ville.*	• dah-lay ahn VEEL.
• the mall.	• *la galerie marchande.*	• lah gahl-ree mahr-SHAHND.
• the discount outlets.	• *les magasins de vente au rabais.*	• lay mah-gah-zehn duh vahnt oh rah-BEH.

GUEST

Do they have…there?	*Est-ce qu'on y trouve…*	Ehss kohn nee troov…
• clothes	• *des vêtements?*	• day veht-MAHN?
• furniture	• *des meubles?*	• day MUHBL?
• rugs (carpets)	• *des tapis?*	• day tah-PEE?
• souvenirs	• *des souvenirs?*	• day soov-NEER?
• books	• *des livres?*	• day LEEVR?
• sporting goods	• *des articles de sport?*	• dayz ahr-tee-kluh duh SPOHR?
• candy	• *des bonbons?*	• day bohn-bohn?
• antiques	• *des antiquités?*	• dayz ahn-tee-kee-TAY?

• electronics	• *des gadgets électroniques?*	• day gahd-zheht ay-lehk-troh-NEEK?
• computers	• *des ordinateurs?*	• dayz ohr-dee-nah-TUHR?
• a farmers' market	*un marché fermier?*	• ehn mahr-shay fehr-MYAY?
• a supermarket	• *un supermarché?*	• ehn sew-pehr-mahr-SHAY?
• a flea market	• *un marché aux puces?*	• ehn mahr-shay oh PEWSS?

CONCIERGE

Perhaps you'd like a museum.	*Vous aimeriez peut-être visiter un musée.*	Vooz eh-muh-ryay puh-TEHTR vee-zee-tay ehn mew-ZAY.
A local favorite is the… museum.	*L'un de nos préférés est le musée…*	Lehn duh noh pray-fay-RAY ay luh mew-zay…
• natural history	• *d'histoire naturelle.*	• dees-twahr nah-tew-REHL.
• modern art	• *d'art moderne.*	• dahr moh-DEHRN.
• science	• *des sciences.*	• day SYAHNSS.
• local history	• *d'histoire locale.*	• deess-twahr loh-KAHL.

GUEST

We were thinking of sight-seeing.	*Nous pensions faire du tourisme.*	Noo pahn-syohn fehr dew too-REEZ-muh.

CONCIERGE

I'd be happy to arrange a city tour.	*Je vous arrangerai une visite guidée de la ville avec plaisir.*	Zhuh vooz ah-rahn-zhuh-reh ewn vee-zeet gee-DAY duh lah veel ah-vehk pleh-ZEER.

GUEST

How about…	*Est-ce qu'il y a…*	Ehss keel ee ah…
• interesting architecture?	• *des exemples d'architecture intéressants?*	• dayz ehx-zahm-pluh dahr-shee-tehk-tewr ehn-tay-ray SAHN?
• churches?	• *des églises?*	• dayz ay-GLEEZ?
• a vineyard?	• *des vignobles?*	• day vee-NYOHBL?

• the business district?	• *un quartier d'affaires?*	• ehn kahr-tyay dah-FEHR?
• the government buildings?	• *des bâtiments officials?*	• day bah-tee-mahn oh-fee-SYEHL?
• the university?	• *une université?*	• ewn ew-nee-vehr-see-TAY?
• monuments?	• *des monuments?*	• day moh-new-MAHN?
• the countryside?	• *la campagne?*	• lah kahn-PAH-nyuh?

CONCIERGE

There are many sports events.	*Il y a beaucoup d'événements sportifs.*	Eel ee ah boh-koo day-vaynn-mahn spohr-TEEF.
Would you like tickets to...	*Aimeriez-vous des billets pour...*	Eh-muh-ryay-voo day bee-yay poor...
• a baseball game?	• *un match de base-ball?*	• ehn mahtch duh behz-BOHL?
• a basketball game?	• *un match de basket?*	• ehn mahtch duh bahss-KEHT?
• a football game?	• *un match de football?*	• ehn mahtch duh foot-BOHL?
• a hockey game?	• *un match de hockey?*	• ehn mahtch duh oh-KAY?
• a tennis match?	• *un match de tennis?*	• ehn mahtch duh teh-NEESS?

GUEST

Are there any musical events?	*Y a-t-il des manifestations musicales?*	Ee ah-feel day mah-nee-fehss-tah-syohn mew-zee KAHL?

CONCIERGE

There is a...concert tonight.	*Il y a un concert de...ce soir.*	Eel ee ah ehn kohn-sehr duh...suh SWAHR.
• rock-and-roll	• *rock*	• rohk
• blues	• *blues*	• blooz
• classical music	• *musique classique*	• mew-zeek klah-seek
• jazz	• *jazz*	• jahz

There's musical entertainment at ____.	*Il y a une manifestation musicale à ____.*	Eel ee ah ewn mah-nee fehss-tah-syohn mew-zee-kahl ah ____.
GUEST		
Is there anything else going on tonight?	*Est-ce qu'il y a quelque chose d'autre à faire ce soir?*	Ehss keel ee ah kehl-kuhshohz DOHTR ah fehr suh SWAHR?
CONCIERGE		
Other than the movies, I'd suggest…	*À part le cinéma, je vous suggère…*	Ah pahr luh see-nay-MAH, zhuh voo sewg-zhehr…
• bowling.	• *le bowling.*	• luh boh-LEENG.
• a nightclub.	• *une boîte de nuit.*	• ewn bwaht duh NWEE.
• a video rental.	• *de louer une cassette.*	• duh loo-ay ewn kah-SEHT.
GUEST		
What do you suggest for outdoor activities?	*Quelles activités de plein air suggérez-vous?*	Kehl zahk-tee-vee-tay duh plehnn ehr sewg-zhay-ray VOO?
CONCIERGE		
How about…	*Aimeriez-vous…*	Eh-muh-ryay-voo…
• hiking?	• *faire une randonnée?*	• fehr ewn rahn-doh-NAY?
• fishing?	• *aller à la pêche?*	• ah-lay ah lah PEHSH?
• skiing?	• *faire du ski?*	• fehr dew SKEE?
• skating?	• *patiner?*	• pah-tee-NAY?
• Rollerblading?	• *faire du roller?*	• fehr dew roh-LUHR?
• swimming?	• *nager?*	• nah-ZHAY?
• surfing?	• *faire du surf?*	• fehr dew SUHRF?
Or you might like to go…	*Ou peut-être aimeriez-vous…*	Oo puh-tehtr eh-muh-ryay voo…
• to the river.	• *aller au bord du fleuve.*	• ah-lay oh bohr dew FLUHV.
• to the lake.	• *au lac.*	• oh LAHK.
• to the mountains.	• *à la montagne.*	• ah lah mohn-TAH-nyuh.

• for a drive.	• *faire un tour en voiture.*	• fehr ehn toor ahn vwah-TEWR.
• to the beach.	• *aller à la plage.*	• ah-lay ah lah PLAHJ.
• to the forest.	• *aller en forêt.*	• ah-lay ahn foh-REH.
GUEST		
Is there anything for children?	*Est-ce qu'il y a des choses intéressantes à faire pour les enfants?*	Ehss-keel ee ah day shohz ehn-tay-ray-sahnt ah FEHR poor layz ahn-FAHN?
CONCIERGE		
Yes, there's…	*Oui, il y a…*	WEE, eel ee ah…
• a zoo.	• *un zoo.*	• ehn ZOO.
• a children's museum.	• *un musée pour les enfants.*	• ehn mew-zay poor layz ahn-FAHN.
• an amusement park.	• *un parc d'attraction.*	• ehn pahrk dah-trahk-SYOHN.
• a water park.	• *un parc d'attraction nautique.*	• ehn pahrk dah-trahk-syohn noh-TEEK.
Would you like to rent…	*Aimeriez-vous louer…*	Eh-muh-ryay-voo loo-ay…
• a bicycle?	• *un vélo?*	• ehn vay-LOH?
• a car?	• *une voiture?*	• ewn vwah-TEWR?
• a boat?	• *un bateau?*	• ehn bah-TOH?
• some skis?	• *des skis?*	• day SKEE?
• some Rollerblades?	• *des rollers?*	• day roh-LUHR?
Would you like a tour guide who speaks French?	*Aimeriez-vous avoir un guide qui parle français?*	Eh-muh-ryay-voo ah-vwahr ehn GEED kee pahrl frahnSEH?
May I make a reservation for you?	*Puis-je faire la réservation pour vous?*	Pweej fehr lah ray-zayr-vah-syohn poor VOO?
GUEST		
Can you recommend a good restaurant?	*Pouvez-vous recommander un bon restaurant?*	Poo-vay-voo ruh-koh-mahn-day ehn bohn rehss-toh-RAHN?
CONCIERGE		
What type of cuisine would you like?	*Quel genre de cuisine aimeriez-vous?*	Kehl zhahnr duh kwee-zeen eh-muh-ryay-VOO?

GUEST

We'd like a(n)... restaurant.	*Nous aimerions aller dans un restaurant...*	Nooz eh-muh-ryohn ah-lay dahnz ehn rehss-toh-rahn...
• cajun	• *cajun.*	• kah-ZHEHN.
• California	• *californien.*	• kah-lee-fohr-NYEHN.
• casual	• *assez simple.*	• ah-say SEHN-pluh.
• creole	• *créole.*	• kray-OHL.
• elegant	• *élégant.*	• ay-lay-GAHN.
• fast-food	• *de restauration rapide.*	• duh rehss-toh-rah-syohnrah-PEED.
• inexpensive	• *pas cher.*	• pah SHEHR.
• kosher	• *kasher.*	• kah-SHEHR.
• seafood	• *spécialisé dans les fruits de mer.*	• spay-syah-lee-zay dahn lay frwee duh MEHR.
• vegetarian	• *végétarien.*	• vay-zhay-tah-RYEHN.
We'd like an authentic American steakhouse.	*Nous aimerions aller dans un authentique restaurant américain spécialisé dans les steaks.*	Nooz eh-muh-ryohn ah-lay dahnz ehn oh-tahn-teek rehss-toh-rahn ah-may-ree KEHN spay-syah-lee-zay dahn lay STEHK.

CONCIERGE

You can get there by...	*Vous pouvez y aller en...*	Voo poo-vay ee ah-lay ahn...
• bus.	• *bus.*	• BEWSS.
• train.	• *train.*	• TREHN.
• subway.	• *métro.*	• may-TROH.
Take the...bound for _____.	*Prenez le...direction _____.*	Pruh-nay luh...dee-rehk-syohn _____.
• number _____ bus	• *bus numéro _____*	• bewss new-may-roh _____
• train	• *train*	• trehn
• subway	• *métro*	• may-troh

You'll need to transfer to...at ____.	*Vous devrez changer pour...à ____.*	Voo duh-vray shahn-zhay poor... ah ____.
• the ____ line	• *la ligne ____*	• lah lee-nyuh ____
• the number ____ bus	• *le bus numéro ____*	• luh bewss new-may-roh ____
Get off at ____.	*Descendez à ____.*	Day-sahn-day ah ____.
May I call you a taxi?	*Puis-je vous appeler un taxi?*	Pweej vooz ah-puh-lay ehn tahk-XEE?
We have a free shuttle bus service available to ____.	*Nous avons une navette gratuite qui va à ____.*	Nooz ah-vohn ewn nah-veht grah-TWEET kee vah ah ____.
It leaves every ____ minutes.	*Elle part toutes les ____ minutes.*	Ehl pahr toot lay ____ mee-NEWT.
It leaves every hour.	*Elle part toutes les heures.*	Ehl pahr toot layz UHR.
GUEST		
What's the price range?	*Pouvez-vous me donner une idée des prix?*	Poo-vay-voo muh doh-nay ewn ee-day day PREE?

6. Business Services and Clientele

A. BOOKING A BUSINESS MEETING

TIP! ••••

Clients who do business from the hotel need a great deal of service from you. They tend to be seasoned travelers who don't want a lot of explanation from hotel employees, just competent action. Attending to their every need often yields substantial financial rewards!

EMPLOYEE		
Good morning.	*Bonjour.*	Bohn-ZHOOR.
How may I help you today?	*En quoi puis je vous être utile aujourd'hui?*	Ahn kwah pweej vooz EHT-ruh oo-TEEL oh-zhoor-DWEE?
GUEST		
I'd like to make arrangements for a business meeting.	*J'aimerais prendre des dispositions pour une réunion d'affaires.*	Zheh-muh-reh prahn-druh day deess-poh-zee-SYOHN poor ewn ray-ew-nyohn dah-FEHR.
EMPLOYEE		
For how many people?	*Pour combien de personnes?*	Poor kohn-byehn duh pehr-SOHNN?
GUEST		
For _____ people on _____.	*Pour _____ le _____.*	Poor _____ luh _____.
EMPLOYEE		
Fine.	*Très bien.*	Treh BYEHN.
We have space available.	*Nous avons de la place.*	Nooz ah-vohn duh lah PLAHSS.
We can provide all your meals, as well as your meeting needs.	*Nous pouvons vous fournir tous vos repas et tout ce dont vous avez besoin pour la réunion.*	Noo poo-vohn voo foor-neer too voh ruh-PAH ay too suh dohn vooz ah-vay buh-ZWEHN poor lah ray-ew-NYOHN.
GUEST		
That's good. We'd like… for each day.	*Très bien. J'aimerais… chaque jour.*	Treh BYEHN. Zheh-muh-reh…shahk ZHOOR.
• a continental breakfast	• *un petit déjeuner continental*	• ehn puh-tee day-zhuh-nay kohn-tee-nahn-tahl
• coffee breaks	• *des pauses-café*	• day pohz-kah-FAY
• a working lunch	• *un déjeuner de travail*	• eehn day-zhuh-nay duh trah-vai
• snacks	• *des collations*	• day koh-lah-syohn

• a cocktail reception	• *un cocktail*	• ehn kohk-tehl
• dinner	• *un dîner*	• ehn dee-nay
Also, we'll require… for the meeting room.	*Nous aurons aussi besoin…dans la salle de conférence.*	Nooz oh-rohn oh-see buh-zwehn…dahn lah sahl duh kohn-fay-RAHNSS.
• a VCR with a large-screen monitor	• *d'un magnétoscope et d'un moniteur à grand écran*	• dehn mah-nyay-tohss-KOHP ay dehn moh-nee-tuhr ah grahn tay-KRAHN
• an overhead projector with transparencies and markers	• *d'un rétroprojecteur avec un film transparent et des feutres*	• dehn ray-troh-proh-zhek-tuhr ah-vehk ehn feelm trahnss-pah-RAHN ay day FUHTR
• a chalkboard	• *d'un tableau*	• dehn tah-BLOH
• a flip chart	• *d'un tableau de conférence*	• dehn tah-bloh duh kohn-fay-RAHNSS
• a slide projector	• *d'un projecteur de diapositives*	• dehn proh-zhehk-tuhr duh dyah-poh-see-TEEV
• a computer with a large-screen monitor	• *d'un ordinateur avec un moniteur à grand écran*	• dehn ohr-dee-nah-tuhr ah-vehk ehn moh-nee-tuhr ah grahn tay-KRAHN
And please be sure to provide…	*Et n'oubliez pas de nous donner…*	Ay noo-blyay pah duh noo doh-nay…
• water.	• *de l'eau.*	• duh LOH.
• pads with pencils.	• *des bloc-notes et des crayons.*	• day blohk-noht ay day kray-YOHN.
• ashtrays.	• *des cendriers.*	• day sahn-DRYAY.
EMPLOYEE		
Let's decide on what time you'd like everything, and we'll be all set.	*Décidons pour quelle heure vous voulez tout cela et tout sera réglé.*	Day-see-dohn poor kehl uhr voo voo-lay too suh-LAH ay TOO suh-rah ray-glay.
GUEST		
Okay. How will the room be set up?	*D'accord. Comment allez-vous placer les sièges?*	Dah-KOHR. Koh-mahn ah-lay-voo plain-say lay SYEHJ?

EMPLOYEE

We can set up the room…	*Nous pouvons placer les sièges…*	Noo poo-vohn plain-say lay syehj…
• theater style.	• *comme dans un théâtre.*	• kohm dahnz ehn tay-AH-truh.
• in a square.	• *en carré.*	• ahn kah-RAY.
• horseshoe ("U") style.	• *en fer à cheval (en "U").*	• ahn fehr ah shuh-VAHL (ahn "EW").
• classroom style.	• *comme dans une salle de classe.*	• kohm dahnz ewn sahl duh KLAHSS.
• boardroom style.	• *comme pour un conseil d'adminis-tration.*	• kohm poor ehn kohn-sail dahd-mee-neess-trah SYOHN.
We're looking forward to having your group here.	*Nous attendons votre groupe avec impatience.*	Nooz ah-tahn-dohn voh-truh GROOP ah-vehk ehn-pah-SYAHNSS.

B. AT THE MEETING

ATTENDANT

I'm _____, the meeting-room attendant.	*Mon nom est _____, et je suis le (la) préposé(e) à la salle de conférence.*	Mohn nohn ay _____, ay zhuh swee luh (lah) pray-poh-zay ah lah sahl duh kohn-fay-RAHNSS.
How is everything?	*Êtes-vous satisfait(e)?*	Eht-voo sah-teess-FEH(T)?

GUEST

Everything is fine, thank you.	*Oui, tout est très bien, merci.*	WEE, toot ay treh BYEHN, mehr-SEE.
We need…	*Nous avons besoin…*	Nooz ah-vohn buh-zwehn…
• more chairs.	• *de chaises supplémentaires.*	• duh shehz sew-play-mahn-TEHR.
• more coffee.	• *de plus de café.*	• duh plewss duh kah-FAY.
• the ashtrays emptied.	• *qu'on vide les cendriers.*	• kohn veed lay sahn-DRYAY.

• more water.	• *de plus d'eau.*	• duh plewss DOH.
ATTENDANT		
I'll take care of it right away.	*Je m'en occupe tout de suite.*	Zhuh mahn oh-kewp too duh SWEET.
Is everything else satisfactory?	*Est-ce que le reste vous convient?*	Ehss-kuh luh rehsst voo kohn-VYEHN?
GUEST		
It's quite nice, but the room…	*Oui, ce n'est pas mal, mais la salle…*	WEE, suh nay pah MAHL, meh lah sahl…
• needs more light.	• *a besoin de plus de lumière.*	• ah buh-zwehn duh plewss duh lew-MYEHR.
• is too bright.	• *est trop éclairée.*	• ay troh ay-kleh-RAY.
• needs more ventilation.	• *a besoin d'être mieux aérée.*	• ah buh-zwehn dehtr myuh ah-ay-RAY.
• is too hot (cold).	• *est trop chaude (froide).*	• ay troh SHOHD (FRWAHD).
• is a little noisy.	• *est un peu trop bruyante.*	• ay ehn puh troh brwee-YAHNT.
• is crowded.	• *est bondée.*	• ay bohn-DAY.
Can you take care of it?	*Est-ce que vous pouvez vous en occuper?*	Ehss-kuh voo poo-vay vooz ahn oh-kew-PAY?
Can we get another room?	*Est-ce que nous pouvons changer de salle?*	Ehss-kuh noo poo-vohn shahn-zhay duh SAHL?
ATTENDANT		
Let me see what we can do.	*Je vais voir ce que je peux faire.*	Zhuh veh vwahr suh kuh zhuh puh FEHR.

C. CATERING TO BUSINESS GUESTS

CONCIERGE		
How may I help you?	*En quoi puis-je vous être utile?*	Ahn kwah pweej vooz EHT-ruh oo-TEEL?
GUEST		
Where is breakfast for the _____ group?	*Où est le petit déjeuner du groupe _____?*	Oo ay luh puh-tee day-zhuh-nay dew groop _____?

Where is the exhibits hall?	*Où est la salle d'exposition?*	Oo ay lah sahl dehx-poh-zee-SYOHN?
CONCIERGE		
There's a buffet set up outside your meeting room.	*Il y a un buffet à côté de votre salle de conférence.*	Eel ee ah ehn bew-feh ah koh-tay duh voh-truh sahl duh kohn-fay-RAHNSS.
Just down the hall.	*Au bout du couloir.*	Oh boo dew koo-LWAHR.
In the dining room.	*Dans la salle à manger.*	Dahn lah sahl ah mahn-ZHAY.
GUEST		
Thank you.	*Merci.*	Mehr-SEE.
I need…	*J'ai besoin…*	Zheh buh-zwhen…
• a fax sent.	• *d'envoyer un fax.*	• dahn-vwah-yay ehn FAHX.
• some typing done.	• *de faire taper quelque chose.*	• duh fehr tah-pay kehl-kuh SHOHZ.
• a hookup to the Internet.	• *de me connecter à internet.*	• duh muh kohn-nehk-tay ah uhn-tehr-NEHT.
• a computer.	• *d'un ordinateur.*	• dehn ohr-dee-nah-TUHR.
• a package sent overnight.	• *d'envoyer un paquet en express.*	• dahn-vwah-yay ehn pah-keh ahn ehx-PREHSS.
• courier service.	• *d'un coursier.*	• dehn koor-SYAY.
• some letters mailed.	• *de poster des lettres.*	• duh pohss-tay day LEHTR.
• some copies made.	• *de faire faire des photocopies.*	• duh fehr fehr day foh-toh-koh-PEE.
CONCIERGE		
I'll take care of that right away.	*Je m'en occupe tout de suite.*	Zhuh mahn oh-kewp too duh SWEET.
GUEST		
Later, I'd like to host a small reception.	*J'aimerais donner une petite réception plus tard.*	Zheh-muh-reh doh-nay ewn puh-teet ray-sehp-syohn plew TAHR.

Can you arrange that?	*Est-ce que vous pouvez l'organiser?*	Ehss-kuh voo poo-vay lohr-gah-nee-ZAY?
CONCIERGE		
Certainly. What would you like?	*Bien sûr. Qu'est-ce que vous aimeriez?*	Byehn SEWR. Kehss-kuh vooz eh-muh-RYAY?
GUEST		
We need a full bar and some hors d'oeuvres.	*J'aurais besoin d'un bar complet et de hors-d'oeuvre.*	Zhoh-reh buh-zwehn dehn bahr kohn-pleh ay duh ohr-DUHVR.
Make sure there are plenty of chilled shrimp.	*Assurez vous qu'il y a assez de crevettes.*	Ah-soo-ray voo keel ee ah ah-say duh kruh-veht.
Lots of champagne, please.	*Beaucoup de champagne, s'il vous plaît.*	Boh-koo duh shahn-PAH-nyuh, seel voo PLEH.
CONCIERGE		
I'll have Room Service put together a proposal right away, and get back to you.	*Je vais demander au service à l'étage de dresser une liste de suggestions et de vous rappeller.*	Zhuh veh duh-mahn-day oh sehr-veess ah lay-tahj duh dreh-say ewn leesst duh sewg-zheh-SYOHN ay duh voo rah-puh-LAY.

7. Checking Out

GUEST		
At what time is checkout?	*À quelle heure est-ce que je dois quitter la chambre?*	Ah kehl uhr ehss-kuh zhuh dwah kee-tay lah SHAHN-bruh?
FRONT DESK CLERK		
Checkout is at…	*Vous devez quitter la chambre à…*	Voo duh-vay kee-tay lah shahn-bruh ah…
• 10 A.M.	• *dix heures du matin.*	• deez uhr dew mah-TEHN.
• noon.	• *midi.*	• mee-DEE.
• 3 P.M.	• *trois heures de l'après-midi.*	• trwahz uhr duh lah-preh mee-DEE.

You may audit your bill on channel _____ on your television.	*Vous pouvez évaluer votre note sur la chaîne _____ de votre télévision.*	Voo poo-vay ay-vah-lew-ay voh-truh NOHT sewr lah shehn _____ duh voh-truh tay-lay-vee-ZYOHN.
We provide an express checkout service.	*Nous avons un service de règlement express.*	Nooz ah-vohn ehn sehr-veess duh reh-gluh-mahn ehx-PREHSS.
Your bill will be left under your door the night before you check out.	*Vous trouverez la note sous votre porte la nuit qui précède votre départ.*	Voo troo-vuh-ray lah noht soo voh-truh POHRT lah NWEE kee pray-sehd voh-truh day-PAHR.
If you're satisfied with your bill, simply sign it,	*Si tout est en ordre, signez simplement votre note,*	See toot ay ahn OHRDR, see-nyay sehn-pluh-mahn voh-truh NOHT,
and leave your key in your room.	*et laissez la clé dans votre chambre.*	ay leh-say lah klay dahn voh-truh SHAHN-bruh.
Any late charges such as breakfast or minibar will be added automatically.	*Tous frais de dernière minute, comme le petit déjeuner et le mini-bar, seront automatiquement ajoutés.*	Too freh duh dehr-nyehr mee-NEWT, kohm luh puh-tee day-zhuh-nay ay luh mee-nee BAHR, suh ohn oh-toh-mah-tee-kuh mahn ah-zhoo-TAY.

GUEST

I'd like to check out, please.	*J'aimerais régler ma note, s'il vous plaît.*	Zheh-muh-reh ray-gray mah NOHT, seel voo PLEH.

CLERK

May I have your luggage brought down?	*Est-ce que je peux faire descendre vos bagages?*	Ehss-kuh zhuh puh fehr day-sahn-druh voh bah GAHJ?

GUEST

Yes, please.	*Oui, s'il vous plaît.*	WEE, seel voo PLEH.
No, I brought (will bring) it myself.	*Non, je les ai descendus (vais les descendre) moi-même.*	NOHN, zhuh layz eh day-sahn-dew (veh lay day-sahn-druh) mwah-MEHM.

CLERK

How was everything?	*Êtes-vous satisfait(e) de votre séjour?*	Eht-voo sah-teess-feh(t) duh voh-truh say-ZHOOR?

GUEST

It was very nice, thank you.	*C'était très bien, merci.*	Say-teh treh BYEHN, mehr-SEE.
I want to speak with the manager.	*Je veux parler au gérant (à la gérante).*	Zhuh vuh pahr-lay oh zhay-RAHN (ah lah zhay-RAHNT).

CLERK

Certainly. The manager on duty is _____. One moment, please.	*Bien sûr. Le gérant (La gérante) de service est _____. Un moment, s'il vous plaît.*	Byehn SEWR. Luh zhay-rahn (lain zhay-rahnt) duh sehr-veess ay _____. Ehn moh-MAHN, seel voo PLEH.

GUEST

Our experience was…	*Nous avons passé un…séjour.*	Nooz ah-vohn pain-say ehn…say-ZHOOR.
• good.	• *bon*	• bohn
• excellent.	• *excellent*	• ehx-seh-lahn
• poor.	• *mauvais*	• moh-veh
• very bad.	• *très mauvais*	• treh moh-veh

MANAGER ON DUTY

That's nice to hear.	*C'est gentil de votre part.*	Say zhahn-tee duh voh-truh PAHR.
I'm sorry to hear that.*	*Je suis désolé(e) d'apprendre cela.*	Zhuh swee day-zoh-lay duh-PRAHN-druh suh-lah.
Thank you. Please come again.	*Merci. Au plaisir de vous revoir.*	Mehr-SEE. Oh pleh-zeer duh voo ruh-VWAHR.

*Please refer to "Guest Complaints in the Hotel" on page 74 for more on handling dissatisfied clients.

GERMAN

1. The Bare Essentials

A. THE GERMAN ALPHABET

a	ah	*ö*	uh
ä	eh	*p*	peh
b	beh	*q*	koo
c	tseh	*r*	ehr
d	deh	*s*	ehs
e	eh	*ß*	ehs (TSEHT/ SHAHR-fehs EHS)
f	ehf		
g	geh	*t*	teh
h	hah	*u*	oo
i	ee	*ü*	ew
j	yoht	*v*	fow
k	kah	*w*	veh
l	ehl	*x*	eeks
m	ehm	*y*	EWP-see-lohn
n	ehn	*z*	tseht
o	oh		

B. PRONUNCIATION CHART

VOWELS

GERMAN SOUND	APPROXIMATE SOUND IN ENGLISH	EXAMPLE
a	(bottle)	*hat* (has)
ä/e	(ace, but cut off sharply)	*Hälfte* (half)

i	(sit)	*in* (in)
o	(more)	*Hotel* (hotel)
ö	(hurt)	*Öl* (oil)
u	(moo)	*und* (and)
ü/y	Closest equivalent in English is *ew* (few). To pronounce *ü*, purse lips as if to whistle, and say, "ee."	*über* (over)

Note: Vowel sounds are generally short when followed by two or more consonants, and long if followed by one consonant, another vowel, or an *h*.

DIPHTHONGS

GERMAN SOUND	APPROXIMATE SOUND IN ENGLISH	EXAMPLE
ai/ay/ei/ey	(my)	*Wein* (wine)
au	(cow)	*Haus* (house)
äu/eu	(boy)	*Fräulein* (Miss)
ie	(fee)	*Wien* (Vienna)

CONSONANTS

GERMAN SOUND	APPROXIMATE SOUND IN ENGLISH	EXAMPLE
f/h/k/l/m/n/p/t/x	similar to English	
b	at the end of a syllable or word, as p (up)	*ob* (if)
	elsewhere, similar to English	*Butter* (butter)
c (before ä/e/i/ö)	ts (hats)	*Celsius* (centigrade)
	elsewhere, k (coat)	*Café* (café)
ch (after a/o/u/au)	hard, like Scottish loch or like Spanish Juan; pronounce as if clearing throat	*nach* (after)
ch (after e/i/umlauts/consonants)	soft, as exaggerated h in human	*ich* (I)
chs	usually as ks (packs)	*sechs* (six)

d	at the end of a syllable or word, as t (at)	*Hand* (hand)
	elsewhere similar to English	*Dienst* (service)
g	at the end of a syllable or word, as k (tack), except following i	*weg* (away)
	following i at end of syllable or word as exaggerated h in human	*hungrig* (hungry)
	elsewhere, similar to English	*gehen* (go)
j	y (yet)	*ja* (yes)
qu	k (kite)+v (vase) as in Yiddish kvetch	*Quittung* (receipt)
r	single trill (throw) or gargle (crowd)	*rot* (red), *Krieg* (war)
	when unstressed, as r in (pepper)	*Bauer* (farmer)
s	before or between vowels as z (zebra) or as s (sit)	*sieben* (seven)
	at the beginning of a syllable before *p* or *t*, as sh (shoe)	*spielen* (play), *Stimme* (voice)
	elsewhere, as s (sit)	*Maus* (mouse)
sch	sh (shoe)	*Schwein* (pig)
ß	s (sit)	*ißt* (eats)
th	t (toast)	*Thunfisch* (tuna)
tsch	ch (chalk)	*deutsch* (German)
tz	ts (pits)	*sitzen* (sit)
v	in most words, f (fit)	*vier* (four)
	in borrowed words, v (visit)	*Vase* (vase)
w	v (visit)	*Wien* (Vienna)
z	ts (pits)	*Zeitung* (newspaper)

C. THE GERMAN LANGUAGE

Word Order Word order in a simple German sentence is the same as English, subject-verb-object: *Ich sehe den Mann.* (I see the man.) However, the main verb must remain in the second position. If a word other than the subject precedes the verb, this reverses the order of the subject and the verb: *Jetzt sehe ich den Mann.* (Now I see the man.) Unlike verbs in English, German verbs or verbal elements are often found at the end of the sentence: *Ich sage, daß ich den Mann sehe.* (I'm saying that I see the man.) *Ich habe den Mann gestern gesehen.* (I saw the man yesterday.)

Nouns All German nouns are capitalized and are one of three genders: masculine, feminine, or neuter. The definite articles *der* (m.), *die* (f.), and *das* (n.), and the indefinite articles *ein* (m. and n.) and *eine* (f.) change to indicate the case of the noun or the function the noun serves gramatically. *Der Mann ist in der Küche.* (The man is in the kitchen. *Der Mann* = nominative case, subject.) *Wir sehen den Mann.* (We see the man. *Den Mann* = accusative case, direct object.) *Die Frau spricht mit dem Mann.* (The woman speaks to the man. *Dem Mann* = dative case, indirect object.) *Der Hut des Mannes ist schwarz.* (The Man's hat is black. *Des Mannes* = genetive case, possessive.) Gender and case also play very important roles in pronoun usage and adjective agreement.

Verbs The endings of German verbs change to agree with their subjects in number and person: *Ich komme.* (I come.) *Du kommst.* (You come.) *Wir kommen.* (We come.) German verb tenses are very similar to English verb tenses. Many tenses are formed with auxilliary verbs such as *haben* (to have): *Ich sehe.* (I see.) *Ich habe gesehen.* (I have seen./I saw.) *Ich hatte gesehen.* (I had seen.) *Ich werde sehen.* (I will see.) *Ich werde gesehen haben.* (I will have seen.)

D. THE GERMAN CULTURE

It is customary to greet someone with a handshake in German-speaking countries. Therefore, it is considered impolite to keep your hands in your pockets while speaking to someone.

As the tip is included in the bill in restaurants in German-speaking countries, German-speaking guests sometimes don't concern themselves with the American tipping standard of 15 percent. Like so many international guests, they may not understand the entire economic basis of tipping that much. It is advisable to mention the fact that the waiter's gratuity is not included in the bill. If your restaurant allows it, consider adding the appropriate service charge to the check.

2. Useful Expressions

A. GENERAL

Hello.	*Guten Tag.*	GOO tehn tahk.
Good-bye.	*Auf Wiedersehen.*	Owf VEE-duhr ZEH-uhn.
Yes.	*Ja.*	Ya.
No.	*Nein.*	Nain.
Maybe.	*Vielleicht.*	Fee-LAIKHT.
Please.	*Bitte.*	BEE-teh.
Thank you (very much).	*Danke (vielmals).*	AHN-keh (FEEL-mahls).
You're welcome.	*Bitte.*	BEE-teh.
Excuse me.	*Entschuldigen Sie.*	Ehn-CHOOL-dee-gehn zee.
I beg your pardon.	*Entschuldigung./ Verzeihung.*	Ehnt-CHOOL-dee-goong./Fuhr-TSAI-oong).
I'm sorry.	*Es tut mir leid.*	Ehs TOOT meer lait.
One moment, please.	*Einen Moment bitte./Einen Augenblick bitte.*	AI-nehn moh-MEHNT BEE-teh./AI-nehn OW-gehn-bleek BEE-teh.

Do you speak English?	*Sprechen Sie Englisch?*	SHPREH-khehn zee EHN-gleesh?
• Yes, I do.	• *Ja, ich spreche Englisch.*	• Yah, eekh SHPREH-kheh EHN-gleesh.
• No, I don't.	• *Nein, ich spreche kein Englisch.*	• Nain, eekh SHPREH kheh kain EHN-gleesh.
• A little.	• *Nur wenig.*	• Noor VEH-neekh.
• No, not at all.	• *Nein, überhaupt nicht.*	• Nain, ew-buhr-HOWPT neekht.
That's okay.	*Das ist okay.*	Dahs eest oh-KEH.
It doesn't matter.	*Das macht nichts.*	Dahs MAKHT neekhts.
I don't speak German.	*Ich spreche kein Deutsch.*	Eekh SHPREH-kheh kain doych.
I can speak a little.	*Ich spreche ein wenig.*	Eekh SHPREH-khe ain VEH-neekh.
I understand a little.	*Ich verstehe ein wenig.*	Eekh fuhr-SHTEH ain VEH-neekh.
I don't understand.	*Ich verstehe nicht.*	Eekh fuhr-SHTEH neekht.
Please speak more slowly.	*Bitte sprechen Sie etwas langsamer.*	BEE-teh SHPREH-khehn zee EHT-vahs LAHNG-sah-muhr.
Would you repeat that, please?	*Würden Sie das bitte wiederholen?*	VEWR-dehn zee dahs BEE-teh vee-duhr-HOH-lehn?
No problem.	*Kein Problem.*	Kain proh-BLEHM.
It's my pleasure.	*MitVergnügen.*	Meet fuhr-GNEW-gehn.

B. NEEDS

I'd like _____.	*Ich hätte gern _____.*	Eekh HEH-teh gehrn _____.
I need _____.	*Ich brauche _____.*	Eekh BROW-kheh _____.
What would you like?	*Was möchten Sie?*	Vahs MUHKH-tehn zee?

Please bring me ____.	*Bitte bringen Sie mir ____.*	BEE-teh BREEN-gehn zee meer ____.
I'm looking for ____.	*Ich suche ____.*	Eekh ZOO-kheh ____.
I'm hungry.	*Ich habe Hunger.*	Eekh HAH-beh HOON-guhr.
I'm thirsty.	*Ich habe Durst.*	Eekh HAH-beh doorst.
It's important.	*Es ist wichtig.*	Ehs eest VEEKH-tikh.
It's urgent.	*Es ist dringend.*	Ehs eest DREEN-gehnt.

C. QUESTION WORDS

How?	*Wie?*	Vee?
How much?	*Wieviel?*	Vee-FEEL?
How many?	*Wie viele?*	Vee FEE-leh?
Which?	*Welche(r)(s)?*	VEHL-kheh(r)?
What?	*Was?*	Vahs?
What kind of?	*Was für?*	VAHS fewr?
Who?	*Wer?*	Vehr?
Where?	*Wo?*	Voh?
When?	*Wann?*	Vahn?
What does this mean?	*Was bedeutet?*	Vahs beh-DOY-teht?
What does that mean?	*Was bedeutet das?*	Vahs beh-DOY-teht dahs?
How do you say ____ in German?	*Wie sagt man ____ auf Deutsch?*	Vee sahgt mahn ____ owf doych?

D. COLORS

black	*schwarz*	shvahrts
blue	*blau*	blow
brown	*braun*	brown
gold	*gold*	gohlt
gray	*grau*	grow
green	*grün*	grewn

orange	*orange*	oh-RAHNSH
pink	*rosa*	ROH-zuh
purple	*violett/lila*	LEE-lah
red	*rot*	roht
silver	*silbern*	ZEEL-buhrn
violet	*violett*	vee-oh-LETT
white	*weiß*	vais
yellow	*gelb*	gehlp

E. CARDINAL NUMBERS

1	*eins*	ains
2	*zwei*	tsvai
3	*drei*	drai
4	*vier*	feer
5	*fünf*	fewnf
6	*sechs*	zehks
7	*sieben*	ZEE-behn
8	*acht*	akht
9	*neun*	noyn
10	*zehn*	tsehn
11	*elf*	ehlf
12	*zwölf*	tsvuhlf
13	*dreizehn*	DRAI-tsehn
14	*vierzehn*	FEER-tsehn
15	*fünfzehn*	FEWNF-tsehn
16	*sechzehn*	ZEHK-tsehn
17	*siebzehn*	ZEEP-tsehn
18	*achtzehn*	AHKH-tsehn
19	*neunzehn*	NOYN-tsehn
20	*zwanzig*	TSVAHN-tseekh
21	*einundzwanzig*	AIN-oon-TSVAHN-tseekh

22	*zweiundzwanzig*	TSVAI-oon-TSVAHN-tseekh
23	*dreiundzwanzig*	DRAI-oon-TSVAHN-tseekh
24	*vierundzwanzig*	FEER-oon-TSVAHN-tseekh
25	*fünfundzwanzig*	FEWNF-oon-TSVAHN-tseekh
26	*sechsundzwanzig*	SEHKS-oon-TSVAHN-tseekh
27	*siebenundzwanzig*	ZEE-bekn-oon-TSVAHN-tseekh
28	*achtundzwanzig*	AHKHT-oon-TSVAHN-tseekh
29	*neunundzwanzig*	NOYN-oon-TSVAHN-tseekh
30	*dreißig*	DRAI-seekh
31	*einunddreißig*	AIN-oon-DRAI-seekh
32	*zweiunddreißig*	TSVAI-oon-DRAI-seekh
40	*vierzig*	FEER-tseekh
50	*fünfzig*	FEWNF-tseekh
60	*sechzig*	ZEHKH-tseekh
70	*siebzig*	ZEEP-tseekh
80	*achtzig*	AHCH-tseekh
90	*neunzig*	NOYN-tseekh
100	*hundert (einhundert)*	HOON-duhrt (ein-hoon-duhrt)
101	*hunderteins*	hoon-duhrt-AINS
102	*hundertzwei*	hoon-duhrt-TSVAI
110	*hundertzehn*	hoon-duhrt-TSEHN
120	*hundertzwanzig*	hoon-duhrt-TSVAHN-tseekh
200	*zweihundert*	TSVAI-hoon-duhrt
210	*zweihundertzehn*	tsvai-hoon-duhrt-TSEHN

300	*dreihundert*	DRAI-hoon-duhrt
400	*vierhundert*	FEER-hoon-duhrt
500	*fünfhundert*	FEWNF-hoon-duhrt
600	*sechshundert*	ZEHKS-hoon-duhrt
700	*siebenhundert*	ZEE-behn-hoon-duhrt
800	*achthundert*	AHKHT-hoon-duhrt
900	*neunhundert*	NOYN-hoon-duhrt
1,000	*tausend (ein tausend)*	TOW-zehnt (ain tow-zehnt)
1,100	*tausendeinhundert*	TOW-zehnt-AIN-hoon-duhrt
1,200	*tausendzweihundert*	TOW-zehnt-TSVAI-hoon-duhrt
2,000	*zweitausend*	TSVAI-tow-zehnt
10,000	*zehntausend*	TSEHN-tow-zehnt
50,000	*fünfzigtausend*	FEWNF-tsikh-TOW-zehnt
100,000	*hunderttausend*	HOON-duhrt-TOW-zehnt
1,000,000	*eine Million*	AI-neh meel-YON
1,000,000,000	*eine Milliarde*	AI-neh meel-YAHR-deh

F. ORDINAL NUMBERS

first	*erste*	EHRS-teh
second	*zweite*	TSVAI-teh
third	*dritte*	DREE-teh
fourth	*vierte*	FEER-teh
fifth	*fünfte*	FEWNF-teh
sixth	*sechste*	ZEHKS-teh
seventh	*siebte*	ZEEP-teh
eighth	*achte*	AHKH-teh
ninth	*neunte*	NOYN-teh
tenth	*zehnte*	TSEHN-teh
eleventh	*elfte*	EHLF-teh

twelfth	*zwölfte*	TSVULF-teh
thirteenth	*dreizehnte*	DRAI-tsehn-teh
fourteenth	*vierzehnte*	FEER-tsehn-teh
fifteenth	*fünfzehnte*	FEWNF-tsehn-teh
sixteenth	*sechzeknte*	SEHKH-tsehn-teh
seventeenth	*siebzehnte*	ZEEP-tsehn-teh
eighteenth	*achtzehnte*	AHKH-tsehn-teh
nineteenth	*neunzehnte*	NOYN-tsehn-teh
twentieth	*zwanzigste*	TSVAHN-tseekh-steh
twenty-first	*einundzwanzigste*	AIN-oon-TSVAHN-tseekh-steh
twenty-second	*zweiundzwanzigste*	TSVAI-oon-TSVAHN-tseekh-steh
thirtieth	*dreißigste*	DRAI-seekh-steh
fortieth	*vierzigste*	FEER-tseekh-steh
fiftieth	*fünfzigste*	FEWNF-tseekh-steh
sixtieth	*sechzigste*	ZEHKH-tseekh-steh
seventieth	*siebzigste*	ZEEP-tseekh-steh
eightieth	*achtzigste*	AHKH-tseekh-steh
ninetieth	*neunzigste*	NOYN-tseekh-steh
hundredth	*hundertste*	HOON-duhrt-steh
thousandth	*tausendste*	TOW-zehnt-steh

G. TIME OF DAY

1:00	*ein Uhr*	ain oor
2:00	*zwei Uhr*	tsvai oor
3:00	*drei Uhr*	drai oor
4:00	*vier Uhr*	feer oor
5:00	*fünf Uhr*	fewnf oor
6:00	*sechs Uhr*	zehks oor
7:00	*sieben Uhr*	ZEE-behn oor
8:00	*acht Uhr*	ahkht oor
9:00	*neun Uhr*	noyn oor

10:00	*zehn Uhr*	tsehn oor
11:00	*elf Uhr*	ehlf oor
12:00	*zwölf Uhr*	tsvuhlf oor
1:00 A.M.	*ein Uhr morgens*	ain oor MOR-gehns
3:00 P.M.	*drei Uhr nachmittags/fünfzehn Uhr*	drai oor NACH-meet-taks/FEWNF-tsehn oor
noon	*zwölf Uhr mittags*	tsvuhlf oor MEET-taks
midnight	*Mitternacht*	MEE-tuhr-nahkht
1:15	*ein Uhr fünfzehn/Viertel nach eins/Viertel zwei*	ain oor FEWNF-tsehn/FEER-tuhl nahkh ains/FEER-tuhl tsvai
12:45	*zwölf Uhr fünfundvierzig/Viertel vor eins/Dreiviertel eins*	tsvuhlf oor fewnf-oont-FEER-tseekh/FEER-tuhl fohr ains/drai-FEER-tuhl ans
1:30	*ein Uhr dreißig/halb zwei*	ain oor DRAI-seekh/hahlp tsvai
7:05	*sieben Uhr fünf*	ZEE-behn oor fewnf
4:55	*vier Uhr fünfundfünfzig/fünf Minuten vor fünf*	feer oor fewnf-oont-FEWNF-tseekh/fewnf mee-NOO-tehn fohr fewnf

H. DAYS OF THE WEEK

Monday	*Montag*	MOHN-tahk
Tuesday	*Dienstag*	DEENS-tahk
Wednesday	*Mittwoch*	MEET-vohkh
Thursday	*Donnerstag*	DOH-nuhrs-tahk
Friday	*Freitag*	FRAI-tahk
Saturday	*Samstag/Sonnabend*	ZAHMS-tahk/SOHN-ah-behnt
Sunday	*Sonntag*	ZOHN-tahk

I. MONTHS

January	*Januar*	YAH-noo-ahr
February	*Februar*	FEH-broo-ahr
March	*März*	Mehrts
April	*April*	Ah-PREEL
May	*Mai*	Mai
June	*Juni*	YOO-nee
July	*Juli*	YOO-lee
August	*August*	Ow-GOOST
September	*September*	Zehp-TEHM-buhr
October	*Oktober*	Ohk-TOH-buhr
November	*November*	Noh-VEHM-buhr
December	*Dezember*	Deh-TSEHM-buhr

J. DATES

1998	*Neunzehnhundert-achtundneunzig*	NOYN-tsehn-HOON-duhrt-AHKHT-oont-NOYN-tseekh
1999	*Neunzehnhundert-neunundneunzig*	NOYN-tsehn-HOON-duhrt-NOYN-oont-NOYN-tseekh
2000	*Zweitausend*	Tsvai-tow-sehnt
2001	*Zweitausendeins*	Tsvai-tow-sehnt-AINS
2002	*Zweitausendzwei*	Tsvai-tow-sehnt-TSVAI
2003	*Zweitausenddrei*	Tsvai-tow-sehnt-DRAI
2004	*Zweitausendvier*	Tsvai-tow-sehnt-FEER
2005	*Zweitausendfünf*	Tsvai-tow-sehnt-FEWNF
Today is Thursday, September 22.	*Heute ist Donnerstag, der zweiundzwanzigste September.*	HOY-teh eest DOH-nuhrs-tahk, dehr TSVAI-oont-tsvahn-tseekh-steh sehpt-TEHM-buhr.

Yesterday was Wednesday, September 21.	*Gestern war Mittwoch, der einundzwanzigste September.*	GEH-stuhrn vahr MEET-wohkh, dehr AIN-oont-tsvahn-tseekh-steh sehp-TEHM-buhr.
The day before yesterday was Tuesday, September 20.	*Vorgestern war Dienstag, der zwanzigste September.*	FOHR-geh-stuhrn vahr DEENS-tahk, dehr TSVAHN-tseekh-steh sehp-TEHM-buhr.
Tomorrow is Friday, September 23.	*Morgen ist Freitag, der dreiundzwanzigste September.*	MOHR-gehn eest FRAI-tahk, dehr DRAI-oont-tsvahn-tseekh-steh sehp-TEHM-buhr.
The day after tomorrow is Saturday, September 24.	*Übermorgen ist Samstag (Sonnabend), der vierundzwanzigste September.*	EW-buhr-mohr-gehn eest SAHMS-tahk (SOHN-ah-behnt), dehr FEER-oont-tsvahn-tseekh-steh sehp-TEHM-buhr.
Next Friday is September 30.	*Nächsten Freitag ist der dreißigste September.*	NEHK-stehn FRAI-tahk eest dehr DRAI-seekh-steh sehp-TEHM-buhr.
Last Friday was September 16.	*Vorigen Freitag war der sechzehnte September.*	FOH-ree-gehn FRAI-tahk wahr dehr zekh-tsehn-teh sehp-TEHM-huhr.

TIP! ••••

As do most European countries, German-speaking countries use the decimal system for measurements. Thus, they use milligrams, grams, kilograms, and liters to measure weight and volume; centimeters, meters, and kilometers to measure distances.

K. MEASUREMENTS: DISTANCE

inch	*Inch*	eench
foot	*Fuß*	foos
yard	*Yard*	yahrd
mile	*Meile*	MAI-leh
millimeter	*Millimeter*	mee-lee-MEH-tuhr
meter	*Meter*	MEH-tuhr
kilometer	*Kilometer*	kee-loh-MEH-tuhr

3. Common Hospitality Scenarios

A. GREETINGS AND INTRODUCTIONS

GREETING THE GUEST

EMPLOYEE

Good morning,…	***Guten Morgen,…***	GOO-tehn MOHR-gehn,…
• Mr. _____.	***• Herr _____.***	• hehr _____.
• Mrs. _____.	***• Frau _____.***	• frow _____.
• Miss _____.	***• Fräulein _____.***	• fROY-lain _____.
• sir.	***• mein Herr.***	• main hehr.
• ma'am.	***• meine Dame.***	• MAI-neh DAH-meh.
• ladies and gentlemen.	***• meine Damen und Herren.***	• mai-neh DAH-mehn oont HEH-rehn.
• everyone.	***• alle.***	• AH-leh.
Good afternoon, Mr. _____.	***Guten Tag, Herr _____.***	GOO-tehn tahk, hehr _____.
Good evening, Mr. _____.	***Guten Abend, Herr _____.***	GOO-tehn AH-behnt, hehr _____.
Hello, Mr. _____.	***Grüß Gott, Herr _____.***	Grews GOHT, hehr _____.
Welcome…	***Willkommen…***	Veel-KOH-mehn…
• to the hotel.	***• im Hotel.***	• eem hoh-TEHL.

• to the restaurant.	• *im Restaurant.*	• eem rehs-tow-RAHNT.
• to our city.	• *in unserer Stadt.*	• een OON-zuh-ruhr shtaht.
• to the United States.	• *in den Vereinigten Staaten.*	• een dehn fuhr-AI-neekh-tehn SHTAH-tehn.
If there is anything I can do to make your stay more pleasant, please let me know.	*Wenn Sie noch einen Wunsch haben, bitte sagen Sie es mir.*	Vehn zee nohkh AI-nehn voonsh HAH-behn, BEE-teh SAH-gehn zee ehs meer.
May I…	*Darf ich…*	Dahrf eekh…
• take your coat(s)?	• *Ihren Mantel (ihre Mäntel) nehmen?*	• EE-rehn MAHN-tuhl (EEH-reh MEHN-tuhl) NEH-mehn?
• carry your…for you?	• *Ihre/n…für Sie tragen?*	• EE-reh/n…fewr zee TRAH-gehn?
• bags	• *Taschen*	• TAH-shehn
• suitcase	• *Koffer*	• KOH-fuhr
How are you today?	*Wie geht es Ihnen heute?*	Vee geht ehs EE-nehn HOY-teh?

TIP! ••••

Most American employees are used to greeting guests jovially and asking them how they are. However, in any but the most informal settings, this behavior may actually be considered impolite. Asking guests how they are is stepping outside the bounds of your position and throws the burden onto the guest to answer you. Other cultures usually observe this principle to a much greater extent than we do.

GUEST

I am…	*Mir geht es…*	Meer geht ehs…
• fine, thank you.	• *gut, danke.*	• goot, DAHN-keh.
• okay.	• *okay.*	• oh-KEH.
I am very tired.	*Ich bin sehr müde.*	Eekh been sehr MEW-deh.
I am not feeling well.	*Ich fühle mich nicht wohl.*	Eekh FEW-leh meekh neekht vohl.
And you?	*Und Ihnen?*	Oont EE-nehn?

INTRODUCTIONS

EMPLOYEE

My name is ____.	*Ich heiße ____.*	Eekh HAI-seh ____.
I am…	*Ich bin…*	Eekh been…
• the door attendant (doorman).	• *der Portier.*	• dehr por-TYEH.
• the bell attendant (bellman).	• *der Page.*	• dehr pehch.
• the valet-parking attendant.	• *der Parkplatzwächter.*	• dehr PAHRK-plahts VEKH-tuhr.
• the driver.	• *der Fahrer.*	• dehr FAH-ruhr.
• the captain.	• *der Kapitän.*	• dehr kah-pee-TEHN.
• the concierge.	• *der Concierge.*	• dehr kohn-SYEHRSH.
• the room attendant.	• *das Dienstmädchen.*	• dahs DEENST-meht-khehn.
• the host.	• *der Oberkellner/der Gastgeber.*	• dehr OH-buhr-kehl-nuhr/dehr GAHST-geh-buhr.
• the hostess.	• *die Oberkellnerin/die Gastgeberin.*	• dee OH-buhr-kehl-nuh-een/dee GAHST-geh-buh-reen.
• the manager.	• *der Direktor/die Direktorin.*	• dehr dee-REHK-tohr/dee dee-rehk-TOH-reen.
• the server (waiter/waitress).	• *der Kellner/die Kellnerin.*	• dehr KEHL-nuhr/dee KEHL-nuh-reen.

TIP! ••••

It is typical of American employees to introduce themselves to the guest. This practice allows the guest to call an employee by name when s/he needs something. This is not a common practice in other countries, however, so the international guest may simply ignore your introduction.

• **the chef.**	• ***der Küchenchef/****die Küchenchefin.*	• dehr KEW-khehn-shehf/dee KEW-khehn-SHEH-feen.
• **the activities director.**	• ***der Aktivitäts-direktor/****die Aktivitatsdirektorin.*	• dehr ahk-tee-vee-TEHTS-dee-REK-tohr/dee ahk-tee-vee-TEHTS dee-rek-TOH-reen.
Mr. (Mrs., Miss) **____, this is Mr.** (Mrs., Miss) **____, the manager.**	***Herr*** *(Frau, Fräulein)* ***____, das ist Herr*** *(Frau, Fräulein)* ***____, der Direktor*** *(die Direktorin).*	Hehr (frow, FROY-lain) ____, dahs eest hehr (frow, FROY-lain) ____, dehr dee-REHK-tohr (dee dee-rehk-TOH-reen).
Mr. (Mrs., Miss) **____, may I introduce our manager, Mr.** (Mrs., Miss) **____?**	***Herr*** *(Frau, Fräulein)* ***____, darf ich unseren Direktor*** *(unsere Direktorin)* ***vorstellen, Herr*** *(Frau, Fräulein)* ***____?***	Hehr (frow, FROY-lain) ____, dahrf eekh OON-suh-rehn dee-REHK-tohr (oon-zuh-reh dee-rehk-TOH-reen) FOHR-shteh-ehn, hehr (frow, FROY-lain) ____?

B. RESERVATIONS

HOTEL RESERVATIONS

OPERATOR

Good morning (afternoon, evening), **____ Hotel.**	***Guten Morgen*** *(Tag, Abend),* ***Hotel ____.***	GOO-tehn MOHR-gehn (tahk, AH-behnt), hoh-TEHL ____.

How may I direct your call?	*Mit wem kann ich Sie verbinden?*	Meet vehm kahn eekh zee fuhr-BEEN-dehn?
GUEST		
Hello. Do you speak German?	*Hallo. Sprechen Sie Deutsch?*	HAH-loh. SHPREH-khehn zee doych?
OPERATOR		
One moment, please.	*Einen Moment, bitte.*	AI-nehn moh-MEHNT, BEE-teh.
I'll connect you with a bilingual operator.	*Ich verbinde Sie mit einem/einer zweisprachigen Telefonist/in.*	Eekh fuhr-BEEN-deh zee meet AI-nehm/AI-nuhr TSVAI-shprah-khee-gehn teh-leh-foh-NEEST/een.
I have a book here to help me.	*Ich habe ein Buch dabei, das mir hilft.*	Eekh HAA-beh ain bookh dah-BAI, dahs meer heelft.
Please speak slowly.	*Bitte sprechen sie langsam.*	BEE-teh SHPREH-khehn zee LAHNG-zahm.
GUEST		
I would like to make a reservation, please.	*Ich möchte etwas reservieren, bitte.*	Eekh MUHKH-teh EHT-vahs reh-zehr-VEE rehn, BEE-teh.
OPERATOR		
For a room or for one of the restaurants?	*Ein Zimmer oder einen Tisch in einem Restaurant?*	Ain TSEE-muhr OH-duhr AI-nehn teesh een AI-nehm rehs-tow-RAHNT?
GUEST		
For a room, please.	*Ein Zimmer, bitte.*	Ain TSEE-muhr, BEE-teh.
For the _____ Restaurant, please.	*Im Restaurant _____, bitte.*	Eem rehs-tow-RAHNT _____, BEE-teh.
OPERATOR		
One moment, please. I will direct your call to Reservations.	*Einen Moment, bitte. Ich verbinde Sie mit dem Reservierungsschalter.*	AI-nehn moh-MEHNT, BEE-teh. Eekh fuhr-BEEN-deh zee meet dehm reh-zehr-VEE-roongs-shahl-tuhr.

One moment, please. I will direct your call to the restaurant.	*Einen Moment, bitte. Ich verbinde Sie mit dem Restaurant.*	AI-nehn moh-MEHNT, BEE-teh. Eekh fuhr-BEEN-deh zee meet dehm reh-stow-RAHNT.
CLERK		
Hello. This is Reservations. What date would you like?	*Guten Tag. Hier ist der Reservierungs-schalter. Wann möchten Sie kommen?*	GOO-tehn tahk. Heer eest dehr reh-zehr-VEE-roongs-shahl-tuhr. Vahn MUHKH-tehn zee KOH-mehn?
GUEST		
May 27th.	*Am siebenundzwanzigsten Mai.*	Ahm ZEE-behn-oont-TSVAHN-tseekh-stehn mai.
CLERK		
For how many nights?	*Für wie viele Nächte?*	Fewr VEE fee-leh NEHKH-teh?
GUEST		
For three nights, please.	*Für drei Nächte, bitte.*	Fewr drai NEHKH-teh, BEE-teh.
For a week.	*Für eine Woche.*	Fewr AI-neh VOH-kheh.
Just one night.	*Nur für eine Nacht.*	Noor fewr AI-neh nahkht.
CLERK		
For how many people?	*Für wie viele Personen?*	Fewr wie FEE-leh pehr-ZOH-nehn?
GUEST		
For two people.	*Für zwei Personen.*	Fewr tsvai pehr-ZOH-nehn.
For one person.	*Für eine Person.*	Fewr AI-neh pehr-ZOHN.
For two adults and a child.	*Für zwei Erwachsene und ein Kind.*	Fewr tsvai ehr-VAHK-seh-neh oont ain keent.
CLERK		
Do you have any special requests (needs)?	*Hätten Sie besondere Wünsche?*	HEH-tehn zee beh-ZOHN-deh-reh VEWN-sheh?

GUEST

No, thank you.	***Nein, danke.***	Nain, DAHN-keh.
Yes, I (we, my spouse) would like…	***Ja, ich möchte (wir möchten, meine Frau/mein Mann möchte)…***	Yah, eekh MUHKH-teh (veer MUHKH-tehn, MAI-neh frow MUHKH-tehf/main mahn MUHKH-teh)…
• to be near the stairs.	***• den Stufen nahe sein.***	• dekn SHTOO-fehn NAH-eh zain.
• to be near an exit.	***• einem Ausgang nahe sein.***	• AI-nehm OWS-gahng NAH-eh zain.
• a cot for our child.	***• ein Kinderbett für unser Kind.***	• ain KEEN-dehr-beht fewr OON-zuhr keent.
• a handicapped-accessible room.	***• ein Zimmer mit Einrichtungen für Behinderte.***	• ain TSEE-muhr meet AIN-reekh-toon-gehn fewr beh-HEEN-duhr-teh.

CLERK

The rate is _____ per night.	***Es kostet _____ pro Nacht.***	Ehs KOH-steht _____ proh nahkht.
Would you like to guarantee the reservation with a credit card?	***Möchten Sie die Reservierung mit einer Kreditkarte garantieren?***	MUHKH-tehn zee dee reh-zehr-VEE-roong meet AI-nehr kreh-DEET-kahr-teh gah-rahn-TEE-rehn?

GUEST

Yes, here is my _____ card.	***Ja, hier ist meine _____ Karte.***	Yah, heer eest MAI-neh _____ KAHR-teh.
My credit card number is _____.	***Meine Kreditkarte-nummer ist _____.***	MAI-neh kreh-DEET-kahr-teh-NOO-muhr eest _____.

CLERK

What is the expiration date?	***Bis wann ist die Karte gültig?***	Bees vahn eest dee KAHR-teh GUHL-teeg?
Thank you.	***Danke.***	DAHN-keh.

RESTAURANT RESERVATIONS

RESTAURANT HOST

Good morning (afternoon, evening), _____ Restaurant.	*Guten Morgen (Tag, Abend), Restaurant _____.*	GOO-tehn MOHR-gehn (tahk, AH-behnt), reh-stow-RAHNT _____.

GUEST

I'd like to reserve a table for...	*Ich möchte einen Tisch zum... reservieren lassen.*	Eekh MUHKH-teh AI-nehn teesh tsoom... reh-sehr-VEE-rehn LAH-suhn.
• breakfast.	• *Frühstück*	• FREW-shtewk
• lunch.	• *Mittagessen*	• MIT-tahk-eh-suhn
• dinner.	• *Abendessen*	• AH-behnt-eh-suhn

HOST

For what time?	*Um wieviel Uhr?*	Oom VEE-feel oor?

GUEST

For...o'clock.	*Um... Uhr.*	Oom...oor.
• seven	• *sieben*	• ZEE-behn
• eight	• *acht*	• akht
• nine	• *neun*	• noyn
For eight-thirty.	*Um acht Uhr dreißig (halb neun).*	Oom akht oor DRAI-seekh (hahlp-noyn).

HOST

For how many people?	*Für wieviele Personen?*	Fewr VEE-fee-leh pehr-SOH-nekn?

GUEST

For one person.	*Für eine Person.*	Fewr AI-neh pehr-ZOHN.
For...people.	*Für...Personen.*	Fewr...pehr-ZOH-nehn.
• two	• *zwei*	• tsvai
• four	• *vier*	• drai
• six	• *sechs*	• sehks

GERMAN

HOST		
And your name, please?	*Und Ihr Name, bitte?*	Oont eehr NAH-meh, BEE-teh?
GUEST		
My name is ____.	*Mein Name ist ____.*	Main NAH-meh eest ____.
HOST		
And is there a phone number where we can reach you?	*Und gibt es eine Telefonnummer, wo wir Sie erreichen können?*	Oont geebt ehs AI-neh teh-leh-FON-noo-muhr, voh veer zee ehr-RAI-khehn KUH-nehn?
GUEST		
Yes, the number is ____.	*Ja, die Nummer ist ____.*	Yah, dee NOO-muhr eest ____.
By the way, do you have any…items on the menu?	*Übrigens, hätten Sie… Gerichte auf der Speisekarte?*	EW-bree-gehns, HEH-tehn zee…geh-REEKH-teh owf dehr SHPAI-zeh-kahr-teh?
• vegetarian	• *vegetarische*	• veh-geh-TAH-ree-sheh
• macrobiotic	• *makrobiotische*	• mahk-roh-bee-OH-tee-scheh
• low-fat	• *fettarme*	• FEHT-ahr-meh
• low-sodium	• *natriumarme*	• NAH-tree-oom-ahr-meh
HOST		
Would you like smoking or nonsmoking?	*Möchten Sie einen Tisch in der Raucherecke oder in der Nichtraucherecke?*	MUHKH-tehn zee AI-nehn teesh een dehr ROW-khur-eh-keh OH-duh een dehr NEEKHT-row-khur-eh-keh?
GUEST		
We would like…	*Wir hätten gern…*	Veer HEH-tehn gehrn…
• smoking.	• *die Raucherecke.*	• dee ROW-khur-eh-keh.

• nonsmoking.	• *die Nichtraucherecke.*	• dee NEEKHT-row-khur-eh-keh.

HOST

Thank you.	*Danke.*	DAHN-keh.
That will be two people at eight o'clock.	*Also zwei Personen um acht Uhr.*	AHL-zoh tsvai pehr-ZOH-nehn oom akht oor.
That's a party of six at seven-thirty.	*Eine Gruppe von sechs um sieben Uhr dreißig.*	AI-neh GROO-peh fohn sehks oom ZEE-behn oor DRAI-zikh.

C. COURTESY AND COMPLAINTS

GENERAL EXPRESSIONS OF COURTESY

Please.	***Bitte.***	BEEH-teh.
Thank you.	***Danke (schön).***	DAHN-keh (shuhn).
You're welcome.	***Bitte (schön).***	BEE-teh (shuhn).
Excuse me.	***Entschuldigen Sie (mich).***	Ehn-CHOOL-dee-gehn zee (meekh).
I beg your pardon.	***Entschuldingung./ Verzeihung.***	Ehn-CHOOL-dee-goong./Fuhr-TSAI-oong.
I'm (terribly) sorry.	***Es tut mir (schrecklich) leid.***	Ehs toot meer (SHREHK-leekh) lait.
That's okay.	***Das ist okay.***	Dahs eest oh-KEH.
No problem.	***Kein Problem.***	Kain proh-BLEHM.
It doesn't matter.	***Es macht nichts.***	Ehs MAHKHT neekhts.

COURTESY IN THE HOTEL

CONCIERGE

Good morning, sir, ma'am.	***Guten Morgen, mein Herr, meine Dame.***	GOO-tehn MOHR-gehn, main hehr, MAI-neh DAH-meh.
May I help you with something?	***Darf ich Ihnen mit etwas behilflich sein?***	Dahrf eekh EEH-nehn meet EHT-vahs be-HEELF-leekh zain?

GUEST

Yes, I need…	*Ja, ich möchte…*	Yah, eekh MUHKH-teh…
• more towels, please.	• *mehr Handtücher, bitte.*	• mehr HAHNT-tew-khuhr, BEE-teh.
• a rental car.	• *ein Mietauto.*	• ain MEE-TOW-toh.
• a taxi.	• *ein Taxi.*	• ain TAHK-see.
• a fax sent.	• *ein Fax schicken.*	• ain fahks SHEE-kehn.
• some letters mailed.	• *Briefe schicken.*	• BREE-feh SHEE-kehn.
• to make arrangements for a business meeting.	• *eine Besprechung organisieren.*	• AI-neh beh-SHPREH-khoong ohr-gah-nee-ZEE-rehn.
• tickets to a show.	• *Theaterkarten.*	• teh-AH-tuhr-KAHR-tehn.
• tickets to a concert.	• *Konzertkarten.*	• kohn-TSEHRT-KAHR-tehn.
• tickets to a football game.	• *Fußballkarten.*	• FOOS-bahl-KAHR-tehn.

GUEST COMPLAINTS IN THE HOTEL

CONCIERGE

Is everything satisfactory?	*Ist alles in Ordnung?*	Eest AH-lehs een OHRD-noong?

GUEST

No, there is a problem.	*Nein, es gibt ein Problem.*	Nain, ehs geept ain proh-BLEHM.
• The light	• *Das Licht*	• Dahs leekht
• The toilet	• *Die Toilette*	• Dee toy-LEH-teh
• The television	• *Der Fernseher*	• Dehr FEHRN-zeh-uhr
• The radio	• *Das Radio*	• Dahs RAHD-yo
• The air-conditioning	• *Die Klimaanlage*	• Dee KLEE-mah-ahn-lah-geh
• The alarm clock	• *Der Wecker*	• Dehr VEH-kuhr
• The heat	• *Die Heizung*	• Dee HAIT-soong
• The key	• *Der Schlüssel*	• Dehr SHLEW-suhl

• The lock	• *Das Schloß*	• Dahs shlohs
• The fan	• *Der Ventilator*	• Dehr vehn-tee-LAH-tohr
...doesn't work.	...*funktioniert nicht.*	...foonk-tsyoh-NEERT neekht.

CLERK

I'll have Maintenance fix that right away.	*Ich kümmere mich darum, daß das sofort repariert wird.*	Eekh KUH-meh-reh meekh data-room, dahs dahs soh-FOHRT reh-pah-REERTveers.
I apologize.	*Entschuldigung.*	Ehn-CHOOL-dee-goong.

GUEST

My room...	***Mein Zimmer...***	Main TSEE-muhr...
• wasn't clean.	***• war nicht sauber.***	• vahr neekht SOW-buhr.
• was noisy.	***• war laut.***	• vahr lowt.
The bed was uncomfortable.	***Das Bett war unbequem.***	Dahs beht vahr OON-beh-kvehm.
The water wasn't hot.	***Das Wasser war nicht warm.***	Dahs VAH-suhr vahr neekht vahrm.
Room service was late.	***Der Zimmerservice kam spät.***	Dee TSEE-muhr-seuhr-vees kahm shpeht.
The servicc was very poor.	***Die Bedienung war sehr schlecht.***	Dee beh-DEE-noong vahr sehr shlehkht.
The employees were...	***Die Angestellten waren...***	Dee AHN-geh-shtehl VAH-rehn...
• very good.	***• sehr gut.***	• sehr goot.
• excellent.	***• hervorragend.***	• hehr-FOHR-rah-gehnt.
• rude.	***• unhöflich.***	• OON-huhf-leekh.
• incompetent.	***• unfähig.***	• OON-feh-eekh.
• unfriendly.	***• unfreundlich.***	• OON-froynt-leekh.
The room attendant is rude (incompetent).	***Das Zimmermädchen ist unhöflich*** *(unfähig).*	Dahs TSEE-muhr-meht-khehn eest OON-huhf-leekh (OON-feh-eekh).

I didn't receive my wake-up call.	*Man hat mich heute nicht geweckt.*	Mahn haht meekh HOY-teh neekht geh-VEHKT.
I'm very disappointed with the level of service in this hotel.	*Ich bin von der Bedienung in diesem Hotel enttäuscht.*	Eekh been vohn dehr beh-DEE-noong een DEE-zehm hoh-TEHL ehnt-TOYSHT.
This is the worst hotel I've ever seen.	*Das ist das schlechteste Hotel, das ich je gesehen habe.*	Dahs eest dahs SHLEHKH-teh-steh hoh-TEHL, dahs eekh yeh geh-ZEH-ehn HAH-beh.

CONCIERGE

Please let me make the situation right.	*Bitte lassen Sie mich die Situation wiedergutmachen.*	BEE-teh LAH-sehn zee meekh dee see-too-ah-TSYOHN VEE-duhr-goot-MAH-khehn.
I'm certain we can straighten out the problem.	*Ich bin sicher, daß wir das Problem lösen können.*	Eekh been SEE-khuhr, dahs weer dahs proh-BLEHM LUH-zehn KUH-nehn.
You won't pay for anything that wasn't completely up to your standards.	*Sie werden für nichts zahlen, womit Sie nicht ganz zufrieden waren.*	Zee VEHR-dehn fewr neekhts TSAH-lehn, voh MEET zee neekht gahnts tsoo-FREE-dehn WAH-rehn.
Please tell me what I can do to correct this terrible situation.	*Bitte sagen Sie mir, was ich machen kann, um diese schreckliche Situation wieder-gutzumachen.*	BEE-teh ZAH-gehn zee meer, vahs eekh MAH-khehn kahn, oom DEE-zeh SHREHK-lee-khch see-too-ah-TSYOHN vee-duhr-GOOT-tsoo-MAH-khehn.
We'll take ____ percent off your bill.	*Wir ziehen ____ Prozent von Ihrer Rechnung ab.*	Veer TSEE-ehn ____ proh-TSEHNT fohn EE-ruhr REHKH-noong ahp.

We're going to give you _____ night(s), compliments of the hotel.	*Wir geben Ihnen _____ Nacht (Nächte) gratis, mit den besten Empfehlungen von der Geschäftsleitung.*	Veer GEH-behn EEH-nehn _____ nakht (NEHKH-teh) GRAH-tees, meet dehn BEHS-tehn ehmp-FEH-loon-gehn fohn dehr geh-SHEHFTS-lai-toong.
Your entire bill is compliments of the house.	*Ihre ganze Rechnung wird von der Geschäftsleitung bezahlt.*	EE-reh GAHN-tseh REHKH-noong veert fohn dehr geh-SHEHFTS-lai-toong beh-TSAHLT.

GUEST

Yes, that would be satisfactory.	*Ja, ich war (wir waren) damit zufrieden.*	Yah, eekh VEH-reh (veer VEH-rehn) dah-MEET tsoo-FREE-dehn.
No, that would not be satisfactory.	*Nein, ich war (wir waren) nicht damit zufrieden.*	Nain, eekh **be**VEH-reh (veer VEH-rehn) neekht dah-MEET tsoo-FREE-dehn.
I appreciate all your efforts.	*Danke für Ihre Mühe.*	DAHN-keh fewr EE-reh MEW-eh.
Thank you, that would be very nice.	*Danke, das wäre sehr nett.*	DAHN-keh, dahs VEH-reh sehr neht.
I will never come here again.	*Ich komme nie zurück.*	Eekh KOH-meh nee tsoo-REWK.

MANAGEMENT COMPLAINTS

MANAGER

We have had some complaints about the noise coming from your room.	*Es beschweren sich Gäste bei uns über den Lärm, der von Ihrem Zimmer kommt.*	Ehs beh-SCHWEH-rehn zeekh GEHS-teh bai oons EW-behr dehn lehrm, dehr fohn EE-rehm TSEE-muhr kohmt.
You are disturbing...	*Sie stören...*	Zee SHTUH-rehn...
• the people in the room next door.	• *die Gäste nebenan.*	• dee GEHS-teh neh-behn-AHN.
• the people at the next table.	• *die Gäste am nächsten Tisch.*	• dee GEHS-teh ahm NEKHS-tehn teesh.

• our other guests.	• *die anderen Gäste.*	• dee AHN-duh-rehn GEH-steh.

GUEST

We're sorry.	*Es tut uns leid.*	Ehs toot oons LAIT.
We understand.	*Wir verstehen.*	Veer fuhr-SHTEH-ehn.
We'll take care of it.	*Wir werden uns darum kümmern.*	Veer VEHR-dehn oons dah-ROOM KEW-muhrn.
We'll keep it down from now on.	*Ab jetzt werden wir leise sein.*	Ahp yehtst VEHR-dehn veer LAI-zeh zain.
Who cares!	*Ist doch egal!*	Eest dohkh eh-GAHL!
Leave us alone!	*Lassen Sie uns alleine!*	LAH-sehn zee oons ah-LAI-neh!

MANAGER

If you don't cooperate, I'm afraid I'll have to…	*Wenn Sie nicht kooperativ sind, muß ich…*	Vehn zee neekht koh-oh-peh-rah-TEEF scent, moos eekh…
• ask you to leave the hotel (restaurant).	• *Sie leider bitten das Hotel (das Restaurant) zu verlassen.*	• zee LAI-duhr BEE-tehn dahs hoh-TEHL (dahs reh-stow-RAHNT) tsoo fuhr-LAH-sehn.
• call security.	• *leider den Sicherheitsdienst rufen.*	• LAI-dahr dehn ZEE-khuhr-haits-deenst ROO-fehn.
• call the police.	• *leider die Polizei rufen.*	• LAI-duhr dee poh-lee-TSAI ROO-fehn.

D. EMERGENCIES AND SAFETY

EMPLOYEE

Please note the emergency exits on this card.	*Bitte merken Sie sich die Nottausgänge auf dieser Karte.*	BEE-teh MEHR-kehn zee zeekh dee NOHT-ows-GEHN-geh owf DEE-zuhr KAHR-teh.
Please note the emergency escape route on the door.	*Bitte merken Sie sich den Notfluchtweg, der an der Tür notiert ist.*	BEE-teh MEHR-kehn zee zeekh dehn NOHT-flookht-wehk, dehr ahn dehr tewr noh-TEERT eest.

Your room is equipped with smoke alarms.	***Ihr Zimmer ist mit einem Rauchmelder ausgerüstet.***	Eehr TSEE-muhr eest meet AI-nehm ROWKH-mehl-duhr OWS-geh-rew-steht.
Here is the fire alarm.	***Dies ist der Feuermelder.***	Dees eest dehr FOH-yuhr-mehl-duhr.
In an emergency, dial ____.	***Im Notfall wählen Sie ____.***	Eem NOHT-fahl VEH-lehn zee ____.
GUEST		
Help!	***Hilfe!***	HEEL-feh!
Fire!	***Es brennt!/Feuer!***	Ehs brehnt!/FEW-ehr!
I need a doctor.	***Ich brauche einen Arzt.***	Eekh BROW-kheh AI-nehn ahrtst.
I/My wife/My Husband/ Someone…	*Ich/Mein Mann/ Meine Frau/ Jemand…*	Eekh/main mahn/MAI-neh frow/YEH-mahnt…
• am/is very sick.	• *bin/ist sehr krank.*	• been/eest zehr krahnk.
• am/is having a heart attack.	• *haben/hat einen Herzinfarkt.*	• HAH-behn/haht AI-nehn HEHRTS-een-fahrkt.
• am/is choking.	• *ersticke/erstickt.*	• ehr-SHTEE-keh/ehr-SHTEEKT.
• am/is losing consciousness.	• *werde/wird ohnmächtig.*	• VEHR-deh/veert OH-mehkh-teekh.
• am/is about to vomit.	• *werde mich/wird sich gleich übergeben.*	• VEHR-deh meekh/veert seekh glaikh ew-buhr-GEH-behn.
• am/is having a seizure.	• *haben/hat einen Anfall.*	• HAH-behn/haht AI-nehn AHN-fahl.
• am/is stuck.	• *bin/ist steckengeblieben.*	• been/eest SHTEH-kehn geh-BLEE-behn.
I can't breathe.	Ich kann nicht atmen.	Eekh kahn neekht AHT-mehn.
MANAGER		
I'll call an ambulance.	*Ich werde einen Krankenwagen rufen.*	Eekh VEHR-deh AI-nehn KRAHN-kehn VAH-gehn ROO-fehn.

Don't move.	*Bewegen Sie sich nicht.*	Beh-VEH-gehn zee zeekh neekht.
The doctor will be here very soon.	*Der Arzt kommt in einem Augenblick.*	Dehr rtst kohmt een AI-nehm OW-gehn-bleek.
Are you hurt?	*Sind Sie verletzt?*	Zeent zee fuhr-LEHTST?
What happened?	*Was ist passiert?*	Vahs eest pah-SEERT?
GUEST		
I tripped and fell.	*Ich bin gestürzt.*	Eekh been geh-SHTEWRTST.
I cut myself.	*Ich habe mich geschnitten.*	Eekh HAH-beh meekh geh-SHNEE-tehn.
I drank too much.	*Ich habe zuviel getrunken.*	Eekh HAH-beh tsoo-FEEL geh-TROON-kehn.
I don't know.	*Ich weiß nicht.*	Eekh vaiss neekht.
I've injured my…	*Ich habe…verletzt.*	Eekh HAH-beh…fuhr-LEHTST.
• head.	• *den Kopf*	• dehn kohpf
• neck.	• *das Genick*	• dahs geh-NEEK
• back.	• *den Rücken*	• dehn REW-kehn
• arm.	• *den Arm*	• dehn ahrm
• leg.	• *das Bein*	• dahs bain
• foot.	• *den Fuß*	• dehn foos
• eye(s).	• *das Auge (die Augen)*	• dahs OW-geh (dee OW-gehn)
DOCTOR (MEDICAL TECHNICIAN)		
You'll be fine; try to relax.	*Es wird schon gut werden; beruhigen Sie sich nur.*	Ehs veers shohn GOOT VEHR-dehn; beh-ROO-ee gehn zee zeekh noor.
We're taking you to the hospital.	*Wir bringen Sie ins Krankenhaus.*	Veer BREEN-gehn zee eens KRAHN-kehn-hows.
Whom should we notify?	*Wen sollen wir benachrichtigen?*	Vehn zoh-lekn veer beh-NAHKH-reekh-tee-gehn?

GUEST

I've been robbed.	*Ich bin bestohlen worden.*	Eekh been beh-SHTOH-lehn vohr-dehn.

MANAGER

What did they take?	*Was hat man gestohlen?*	Vahs haht mahn geh-SHTOH-lehn?
Let me call the police.	*Ich rufe die Polizei.*	Eekh ROO-feh dee poh-lee-TSSAI.
Attention, ladies and gentlemen.	*Achtung, meine Damen und Herren.*	AHKH-toong, MAI-neh DAH-mehn oont HEH-rehn.
May I have your attention, please?	*Ich bitte um Ihre Aufmerksamkeit?*	Eekh BEE-theh oom EE-reh OWF-mehrk-sahm-kait?
Please…	*Bitte…*	BEE-teh…
• remain calm.	• *bleiben Sie ruhig.*	• BLAI-behn zee ROO-eekh.
• follow the instructions of the staff.	• *befolgen Sie die Anweisungen des Personals.*	• beh-FOHL-gehn zee dee AHN-vai-zoon-gehn dehs PEHR-zoh-nahls.
• wait in your rooms.	• *warten Sie in Ihren Zimmern.*	• VAHR-tehn zee een EE-rehn TSEE-muhrn.
• get under a table or doorway.	• *stellen Sie sich unter einen Tisch oder eine Tür.*	• SHTEH-lehn zee zeekh OON-tehr AI-nehn teesh OH-dehr AI-neh tewr.
• follow the evacuation plan (route) printed on your door (in the hallways).	• *folgen Sie dem Notplan (Fluchtweg), der an Ihrer Tür (in den Gängen) notiert ist.*	• FOHL-gehn zee dehm NOHT-plahn (FLOOKHT-vehk), dehr ahn EE-ruhr tewr (een dehn GEHN-gehn) noh-TEERT eest.
We'll have the situation under control as soon as possible.	*Wir werden die Situation so bald wie möglich unter Kontrolle haben.*	Veer VEHR-dehn dee see-too-ah-TSYON zoh BAHLT vee MUHK-leekh OON-tuhr kohn-TROH-leh HAH-behn.

Thank you for your patience.	*Danke für Ihre Geduld.*	DAHN-keh fewr EE-reh geh-DOOLT.

4. Checking In

A. AT THE THE FRONT DESK

FRONT DESK CLERK

Good morning (afternoon, evening).	*Guten Morgen (Tag, Abend).*	Goo-tehnMOHR-gehn (TAHK, AH-behnt).
How may I help you?	*Was kann ich für Sie tun?*	Vahs kahn eekh fewr zee soon?

GUEST

I have a reservation under the name ____.	*Ich habe ein Zimmer auf den Namen ____ reservieren lassen.*	Eekh HAH-beh ain TSEE-muhr owf dehn NAH-mehn ____ reh-zehr-VEE-rehn lah-suhn.
Do you have a room for one (two)?	*Haben Sie ein Einzelzimmer (Doppelzimmer)?*	HAH-behn zee ain AIN-tsehl-tsee-muhr (DOH-puhl-tsee-muhr)?

CLERK

Yes, we have your reservation.	*Ja, wir haben Ihre Reservierung hier.*	Yah, veer HAH-behn EE-reh reh-zehr-VEE-roong heer.
Yes, for how many nights?	*Ja, für wieviele Nächte?*	Yah, fewr VEE-fee-leh NEHKH-teh?
No, I'm sorry, we're full.	*Nein, leider sind wir ausgebucht.*	Nain, LAI-duhr zeent weer OWS-geh-bookht.

GUEST

For ____ night(s), please.	*Für ____ Nacht (Nächte), bitte.*	Fewr ____ nahkht (NEHKH-teh) BEE-teh.
What are your rates?	*Wieviel kostet es?*	VEE-feel KOHS-teht ehs?

CLERK

• For a single,	• *Ein Einzelzimmer*	• Ain AIN-tsuhl-tsee-muhr
• For a double,	• *Ein Doppelzimmer*	• Ain DOH-puhl-tsee-muhr

• For adjoining rooms,	• *Nebenzimmer*	• NEH-behn-tsee-muhr
• For a suite,	• *Eine Suite*	• AI-neh sveet
...the rate is ____ per night.	*...kostet/kosten ____ pro Nacht.*	...KOHS-teht/KOHS-tehn ____ proh nahkht.

GUEST

Are any meals included?	*Sind Mahlzeiten im Preis inbegriffen?*	Seent MAHL-tsai-tehn eem prais EEN-beh-gree-fehn?
Is breakfast included?	*Ist Frühstück im Preis inbegriffen?*	Eest FREW-shtewk eem prais EEN-beh-gree-fehn?

CLERK

No, meals are extra.	*Nein, Mahlzeiten sind extra.*	Nain, MAHL-tsai-tehn zeent EHKS-trah.
Yes, breakfast is included.	*Ja, Frühstück ist inbegriffen.*	Yah, FREW-shtewk eest EEN-beh-gree-fehn.
You can choose...	*Sie können...wählen.*	Zee KUH-nehn...VEH-lehn.
• the American plan (all meals included).	• *den amerikanischen Plan (Vollpension)*	• dehn ah-meh-ree-KAH-nee-shehn plahn (FOHL-pohns-yohn)
• the modified American plan (breakfast and dinner).	• *den modifizierten amerikanischen Plan (Frühstück und Abendessen)*	• dehn moh-dee-fee-TSEER-tehn ah-meh-ree-KAH-nee-shehn plahn (FREW-shtewk oont AH-behnt-eh-sehn)
• the European plan (no meals included).	• *den europäischen Plan (keine Mahlzeiten inbegriffen)*	• dehn oy-roh-PEH-ee-shehn plahn (KAI-neh MAHL-tsai-tehn EEN-beh-gree-fehn)

GUEST

I'd like a room...	*Ich hätte gern ein Zimmer...*	Eekh HEH-teh gehrn ain TSEE-muhr...
• that faces the back (front).	• *nach hinten (vorne) hinaus.*	• nahkh HEEN-tehn (FOR-neh) hee-NOWS.
• that faces the water (pool).	• *zum Wasser (Schwimmbad).*	• tsoom VAH-suhr (SHVEEM-baht).

• with a private bath/ toilet/shower.	• *mit Privatbad/ Privattoilette/ Privatdusche.*	• meet pree-VAHT-baht/pree-VAHT-toy-LEH-teh/pree-VAHT-DOO-sheh.
• with a handicapped-accessible bathroom.	• *mit einem Badezimmer mit Einrichtungen für Behinderte.*	• meet AI-nehm BAH-deh-zee-muhr meet AIN-reekh-toon-gehn fewr beh-HEEN-duhr-teh.
• with air-conditioning.	• *mit Klimaanlage.*	• meet KLEE-mah-ahn-lah-geh.
• with a TV.	• *mit Fernseher.*	• meet FEHRN-zehr.
• with cable.	• *mit Kabelfernseher.*	• meet KAH-buhl-fehrn-zehr.
• with a fax machine.	• *mit Telefaxmaschine.*	• meet teh-leh-fahks-mah-SHEE-neh.
• with a phone.	• *mit Telefon.*	• meet teh-leh-FOHN.
• with a network hookup for my computer.	• *mit Netzwerk-einrich-tungen für meinen Computer.*	• meet NEHTS-vehr-keh-ain-reekh-toon-gehn fewr MAI-nen kohmp-YEW-tuhr.
• with a view.	• *mit Aussicht.*	• meet OWS-zeekht.
• with a whirlpool bath/Jacuzzi.	• *mit Whirlpool/ Strudel.*	• meet VUHRL-pool/SHTROO-duhl.
• with two double beds.	• *mit zwei Doppelbetten.*	• meet tsvai DOH-puhl-beh-tehn.
• with a king-size bed.	• *mit einem extra großem Bett.*	• meet AI-nehm EHKS-trah GROH-sehn beht.
• with an extra bed.	• *mit einem zusätzlichen Bett.*	• meet AI-nehm TSOO-zehts-lee-khchn beht.
• with a baby crib.	• *mit Kinderbett.*	• meet KEEN-duhr-beht.
• with a balcony.	• *mit Balkon.*	• meet bahl-KOHN.
• with a sitting area.	• *mit Salon.*	• meet sah-LOHN.
• with a bar.	• *mit einer Bar.*	• meet AI-nuhr bahr.
• with a kitchenette.	• *mit einer kleinen Küche.*	• meet AI-nuhr klai-nehn KEW-kheh.

• away from the elevator.	• *weit vom Fahrstuhl.*	• vait fohm FAHR-shtool.
• with no meals.	• *ohne Mahlzeiten.*	• OH-neh MAHL-tsai-tehn.

CLERK

No problem.	*Kein Problem.*	Kain proh-BLEHM.
I'm sorry.	*Es tut mir leid.*	Ehs toot meer LAIT.
There is none available.	*Das haben wir im Moment nicht.*	Dahs HAH-behn veer eem moh-MEHNT neekht.
We don't offer that.	*Das bieten wir nicht an.*	Dahs BEE-tehn veer neekht ahn.

GUEST

Does the hotel have…	*Gibt es im Hotel…*	Geept ehs eem hoh-TEHL…
• a restaurant?	• *ein Restaurant?*	• ain rehs-tow-RAHNT?
• a bar?	• *eine Bar?*	• AI-neh bahr?
• room service?	• *Zimmerservice?*	• TSEE-muhrsuhr-vees?
• a gym/health club?	• *ein Fitnesscenter?*	• ain FEET-nehs-tsehn-tuhr?
• a spa hot tub?	• *eine Mineralquelle/einen Strudel?*	• AI-neh mee-neh-RAHL-kveh-leh/AI-nehn SHTROO-duhl?
• a swimming pool?	• *ein Schwimmbad?*	• ain SHVEEM-baht?
• baby-sitting?	• *einen Babysitter?*	• AI-nehn BEH-bee-see-tuhr?
• tennis courts?	• *einen Tennisplatz?*	• AI-nehn TEH-nees-plahts?
• laundry (dry-cleaning service?	• *einen Wäschedienst/chemischen Reinigungsdienst?*	• AI-nehn VEH-sheh-deenst/KHE-mee-shch RAI-nee-goongs-deenst?
• a garage?	• *eine Garage?*	• AI-neh gah-RAHSH?
May I see the room?	• *Kann ich das Zimmer sehen?*	• Kahn eekh dahs TSEE-muhr ZEH-uhn?

GERMAN

CLERK		
Yes, certainly. Here's the key.	*Ja, selbstverständlich. Hier ist der Schlüssel.*	Yah, sehlpst-fuhr-SHTEHNT-leekh. Heer eest dehr SHLEW-suhl.
Would you like another room?	*Möchten Sie ein anderes Zimmer haben?*	MUHKH-tehn zee ain AHN-deh-rehs TSEE-muhr HAH-behn?
GUEST		
I'd like something…	*Ich hätte gern etwas…*	Eekh HEH-teh gehrn EHT-vahs…
• smaller.	• *kleineres.*	• KLAI-nuh-rehs.
• larger.	• *größeres.*	• GROH-suh-rehs.
• quieter.	• *ruhigeres.*	• ROO-ee-guh-rehs.
• better.	• *besseres.*	• BEH-suh-rehs.
• cheaper.	• *billigeres.*	• BEE-lee-guh-rehs.
• on another floor.	• *auf einem anderen Stock.*	• owf AI-nehm AHN-duh-rehn shtohk.
I'll take the room, please.	*Ich nehme das Zimmer, bitte.*	Eekh NEH-meh dahs TSEE-muhr BEE-teh.
CLERK		
Very well, how will you be paying?	*Gut, und wie möchten Sie zahlen?*	Goot, oont vee MUHKH-tehn zee TSAH-lehn?
GUEST		
I'll pay with…	*Ich bezahle…*	Eekh beh-TSAH-leh…
• cash.	• *bar.*	• bahr.
• a credit card.	• *mit Kreditkarte.*	• meet kreh-DEET-kahr-teh.
• traveler's checks.	• *mit Reiseschecks.*	• meet RAI-zeh-shehks.
CLERK		
Thank you.	*Dankeschön.*	DAHN-keh-shuhn.

To charge meals and services to your room, I'll need a credit card.	*Wenn Sie wollen, daß Mahlzeiten auf die Zimmerrechnung geschrieben werden, brauche ich eine Kreditkarte.*	Vehn zee VOH-lehn, dahs MAHL-tsai-tehn owf dee TSEE-muhr-rehkh-noong geh-SHREE-behn VEHR-dehn, BROW-kheh eekh AI-neh kreh-DEET-kahr-teh.
You may settle the bill with traveler's checks (cash).	*Sie können die Rechnung mit Reiseschecks (Bar) bezahlen.*	Zee KUH-nehn dee REHKH-noong meet RAI-seh-shehks (bahr) beh TSAH-lehn.
If you would like to store valuables, we have a safe.	*Wir haben einen Tresor, falls Sie Ihre Wertsachen aufbewahren möchten.*	Veer hah-behn AI-nehn treh-SOHR, fahls zee EE-reh VEHRT-zah-khehn OWF-beh-vah-rehn MUHKH-tehn.
Please note that…	*Wir möchten auf folgendes hinweisen…*	Veer MUHKH-tehn owf VOHL-gehn-dehs HEEN-wai-sehn…
• quiet hours are between _____ and _____.	• *ruhestunden sind zwischen _____ und _____.*	• ROO-eh-shtoon-dehn zeent TSVEE-shehn _____ oont _____.
• there are no pets allowed.	• *haustiere sind nicht erlaubt.*	• HOWS-tee-reh zeent neekht ehr-LOWPT.
• children under _____ stay free.	• *kinder unter _____ wohnen bei uns gratis.*	• KEEN-duhr OON-tuhr _____ voh-nehn bai oons GRAH-tees.
• smoking is allowed only in the bar.	• *das Rauchen ist nur an der Bar erlaubt.*	• dahs ROW-KHEHN eest noor ahn dehr bahr ehr-LOWPT.
• we do not allow cooking in the rooms.	• *des Kochen ist in den Zimmern verboten.*	• dahs KOH-khehn eest een dehn TSEE-muhrn fuhr-BOH-tehn.

GUEST

Do I (we) have any messages?	*Hat jemand eine Nachricht für mich (uns) hinterlassen?*	Haht YEH-mahnt AI-neh NAHKH-reekht fewr meekh (oons) heen-tuhr-LAH-sehn?
I would like a wake-up call, please.	*Bitte wecken Sie mich um _____.*	BEE-teh VEH-kehn zee meekh oom _____.

May we have…, please?	*Könnten wir bitte… haben?*	KUHN-tehn weer BEE-teh…HAH-behn?
• extra blankets	• *zuszätzliche Decken*	• TSOO-zehts-lee-kheh DEH-kehn
• extra towels	• *zusätzliche Badetücher*	• TSOO-zehts-lee-khe BAH-deh-tew-khuhr
• a hair dryer	• *einen Haartrockner*	• AI-nehn HAHR-trohk-nuhr
• an iron	• *ein Bügeleisen*	• ain BEW-gubl-ai-zehn
• ice	• *Eiswürfel*	• AIS-vewr-fuhl
CLERK		
I'll have that brought to your room right away.	*Das wird sofort auf Ihr Zimmer gebracht.*	Dahs veers soh-FOHRT ouf eer TSEE-muhr geh-brahkht.
GUEST		
Where is…	*Wo ist…*	Voh Best…
• the room attendant?	• *das Zimmermädchen?*	• dahs TSEE-muhr-meht-khehn?
• the bellman (bell attendant)?	• *der Hotelpage?*	• dehr hoh-TEHL-pehch?
• the manager?	• *der Direktor/die Direktorin?*	• dehr dee-REHK-tohr/dee dee-rehk-TOH-reen?
• the dining room?	• *der Speisesaal?*	• dehr SHPAI-zeh-zaal?
• the gift shop?	• *das Souvenirgeschäft?*	• dahs soo-veh-NEER geh-SHEHFT?
• the newsstand?	• *der Zeitungsstand?*	• dehr TSAI-toongs-shtahnt?
CLERK		
Just over there.	*Nur dort drüben.*	Noor dohrt DREW-behn.
GUEST		
How do I use the telephone?	*Wie funktioniert das Telefon?*	Vee foonk-tsyoh-NEERT dahs teh-leh-FOHN?

CLERK

The instructions are next to the phone.	*Die Gebrauchsanweisungen sind neben dem Telefon.*	Dee geh-BROWKHS-ahn-VAI-zoon-gehn zeent NEH-ben dehm teh-leh-FOHN.
Dial ____ for a local (long-distance) call,	*Wählen Sie ____ für ein Lokalgespräch (Ferngespräch),*	VEH-lehn zee ____ fewr ain loh-KAHL-geh-shprehkh (FEHRN-geh-shprehkh),
wait for the tone,	*Warten Sie auf den Ton,*	VAHR-tehn zee owf dehn TOHN,
then dial the number.	*dann wählen Sie die Nummer.*	dahn VEH-lehn zee dee NOO-muhr.
Dial ____ for an operator.	*Wählen Sie ____ für die Vermittlung.*	VEH-lehn zee ____ fewr dee fuhr-MEET-loong.
To use a credit card, dial ____.	*Wenn Sie eine Kreditkarte benützen wollen, wählen Sie ____.*	Vehn zee AI-neh kreh-DEET-kahr-teh beh-NEW-tsehn voh-lehn, VEH-lehn zee ____.

GUEST

Please have our luggage brought to our room.	*Bitte schicken Sie unser Gepäck zu unserem Zimmer hinauf.*	BEE-teh SHEE-kehn zee OON-zuhr geh-PEHK tsoo OON-zuh-rehm TSEE-muhr hee-NOWF.
We'll need a wheelchair.	*Wir brauchen einen Rollstuhl.*	Veer BROW-khehn AI-nehn ROHL-shtool.

CLERK

Yes, right away.	*Ja, sofort.*	Yah, soh-FOHRT.

GUEST

We'd like to order a pizza, please.	*Wir möchten eine Pizza bestellen, bitte.*	Veer MUHKH-tehn Ai-neh PEE-tsah beh-SHTEH-lehn, BEE-teh.

MANAGER

I'll be happy to call someone for you.	*Ich rufe gern jemanden für Sie an.*	Eekh ROO-feh gehrn YEH-mahn-dehn fewr zee ahn.

We have room service, but we don't allow outside vendors into the hotel.	*Wir haben Zimmer-service, aber wenn Sie von Restaurants außerhalb des Hotels bestellen, darf das Essen nicht ins Hotel geliefert werden.*	Veer HAH-behn TZEE-muhrsuhr-vees, AH-buhr wehn zee vohn rehs-tow-RAHNZ OW-suhr-hahlp dehs hoh-TEHLS beh-STEH-lehn, dahrf dahs EH sehn neekht eens hoh-TEHL geh-LEE-fuhrt VEHR-dehn.

GUEST

We'd like to entertain a few friends in our room.	*Wir möchten ein paar Freunde auf unser Zimmer einladen.*	Veer MUHKH-tehn ain pahr FROYN-dehn ouf OON-suhr TSEE-muhr AIN-lah-dehn.

MANAGER

We allow guests in the rooms until _____.	*Gäste sind bis _____ in den Zimmern erlaubt.*	GEHS-teh zeent bees _____ een dehn TSEE-muhrn ehr-LOWPT.

B. SHOWING GUESTS TO THEIR ROOMS

BELLMAN (BELL ATTENDANT)

My name is _____, and I'm your bell attendant.	*Ich heiße _____, und ich bin Ihr Page.*	Eekh HAI-seh _____, oont eekh been eer pehch.
May I show you to your room?	*Darf ich Ihnen das Zimmer zeigen?*	Dahrf eekh EEH-nehn dahs TSEE-muhr TSAI-gehn?

GUEST

No, thanks. We'll find it ourselves.	*Nein, danke. Wir können es selbst finden.*	Nain, DAHN-keh. Veer KUH-nehn ehs sehlbst FEEN-dehn.
Yes, please.	*Ja, bitte.*	Yah, BEE-teh.

BELLMAN

This way, please.	*Hier entlang, bitte.*	Heer ehnt-LAHNG, BEE-teh.
The elevator is over here.	*Der Fahrstuhl ist drüben.*	Dehr FAHR-shtoohl eest DREW-behn.

May I show you the features of your room?	*Darf ich Ihnen zeigen, was Sie im Zimmer haben?*	Dahrf eekh EEH-nehn TSAI-gehn, vahs zee eem TSEE-muhr HAH-behn?
This is the key to the minibar.	*Dieser Schlüssel ist für die Minibar.*	DEE-zuhr SHLEW-suhl eest fewr dee MEE-nee-bahr.
• Any movie you select…	• *Wenn Sie einen Film wählen…*	• Vehn zee AI-nehn feelm VEH-lehn…
• Any long-distance calls you make…	• *Wenn Sie ein Ferngespräch führen…*	• Vehn zee ain FEHRN-geh-shprehkh FEW-rehn…
• Any snack or beverage you take from the refrigerator…	• *Wenn Sie etwas aus dem Kühlschrank nehmen…*	• Vehn zee EHT-vahs ous dehm KEWL-shrahnk NEH-mehn…
…will be charged to your room.	*…wird das auf Ihre Zimmerrechnung geschrieben.*	…weert dahs owf EE-reh TSEE-muhr-rehkh-noong geh-SHREE-behn.
Here is the control for the heating (air-conditioning).	*Hier regulieren Sie die Heizung (Klimaanlage).*	Heer reh-goo-LEE-rehn zee dee HAI-tsoong (KLEE-mah-ahn-lah-geh).
GUEST		
How do I call Room Service?	*Wie rufe ich den Zimmerservice?*	Vee ROO-feh eekh dee TSEE-muhr-suhr-vees?
BELLMAN		
Dial ____.	*Wählen Sie ____.*	VEH-lehn zee ____.

GERMAN

TIP! ••••

International guests in particular may have questions about using the telephone and will appreciate seeing how the television and pay movies work.

GUEST

This room…	*Dieses Zimmer…*	DEE-zehs TZEE-muhr…
• is too close to the elevator.	• *ist zu nah am Fahrstuhl.*	• eest tsoo nah ahm FAHR-shtool.
• hasn't been made up.	• *ist nicht gemacht.*	• eest neekht geh-MAHKHT.
• smells (like cigarettes).	• *riecht (nach Zigaretten).*	• reekht (nahkh tsee-gah-REH-tehn).
The toilet (bathtub, sink) is clogged.	*Die Toilette (die Badewanne, das Spülbecken) ist verstopft.*	Dee toy-LEH-teh (dee BAH-deh-vah-neh, dahs SHPEWL-beh-kehn) eest fuhr-SHTOHPFT.
May I (we) change rooms, please?	*Könnte ich (könnten wir) das Zimmer wechseln?*	KUHN-teh eekh (KUHN-tehn veer) dahs TSEE-muhr VEHK-suhln?

BELLMAN

Please let me check our availability with the front desk.	*Ich werde die Rezeption fragen, welche Zimmer noch frei sind.*	Ekh VEHR-deh dee reh-tsehp-TSYOHN FRAH-gehn, VEHL-kheh TSEE-muhr nohkh frai zeent.
Sure, I'll be happy to assist you.	*Selbstverständlich, ich helfe Ihnen gern.*	ZEHLBST-fuhr-SHTEHNT-leekh, eekh HEHL-feh EE-nehn gehrn.
Please call if I can help you with anything else.	*Bitte rufen Sie mich, wenn Sie sonst noch etwas brauchen.*	BEE-teh ROO-fehn zee meekh, vehn zie nohkh EHT-vahs BROW-khehn.

VOCABULARY ••••

THE GUEST ROOM

air-conditioning	*Klimaanlage*	KLEE-mah-ahn-lah-geh
balcony	*Balkon*	bahl-KOHN
bath mat	*Badematte*	BAH-deh-mah-teh
bathtub	*Badewanne*	BAH-deh-vah-neh
bed	*Bett*	beht
bedspread	*Tagesdecke*	TAH-gehs-deh-keh
blanket	*Decke*	DEH-keh
blinds	*Rolladen*	ROH-lah-dehn
carpet	*Teppich*	TEH-peekh
ceiling	*Zimmerdecke*	TSEE-muhr-deh-keh
chair	*Stuhl*	shtool
closet	*Schrank*	shrahnk
conditioner	*Pflegespülung*	PFLEH-geh-shpew-loong
couch	*Couch*	kowch
crib	*Kinderbett*	KEEN-duhr-beht
desk	*Schreibtisch*	SHRAIP-teesh
Do Not Disturb sign	*Schild auf dem "Bitte nicht stören" steht*	sheelt ouf dehm "BEE-teh neekht SHTUH-rehn" shteht
door	*Tür*	tewr
drapes	*Vorhänge*	FOHR-hehn-geh
dresser	*Frisierkommode*	free-ZEER-koh-moh-deh
fan	*Ventilator*	vehn-tee-LAH-tohr
floor	*Boden*	BOH-dehn
glass(es)	*Glas (Gläser)*	glahs (GLEH-zuhr)
hair dryer	*Haartrockner*	HAHR-trohk-nuhr
(coat) hanger	*Kleiderbügel*	KLAI-duhr-bew-guhl

(cont'd.)

The Guest Room *(cont'd.)*

heat	*Heizung*	HAI-tsoong
ice bucket	*Eiskühler*	AIS-kew-luhr
iron	*Bügeleisen*	BEW-guhl-ai-zehn
lamp	*Lampe*	LAHM-peh
light	*Licht*	leekht
lock	*Schloß*	shlohs
minibar	*Mini-Bar*	MEE-nee-bahr
mirror	*Spiegel*	SHPEE-guhl
nightstand	*Nachttisch*	NAHKHT-teesh
pillow	*Kopfkissen*	KOHPF-kee-sehn
radio	*Radio*	RAHD-yo
razor	*Rasierapparat*	rah-zeer-ah-pah-RAHT
sewing kit	*Nähkorb*	NEH-kohrp
shampoo	*Schampoo*	SHAHM-poo
sheets	*Bettücher*	BEHT-tew-khuhr
shower	*Dusche*	DOO-sheh
shower cap	*Duschhaube*	DOOSH-how-beh
sink	*Spülbecken*	SHPEWL-beh-kehn
soap	*Seife*	ZAI-feh
telephone	*Telefon*	teh-leh-FOHN
television	*Fernseher*	FEHRN-seh-uhr
thermostat	*Thermostat*	tehr-mohs-TAHT
toilet	*Toilette*	toy-LEH-teh
toilet paper	*Toilettenpapier*	toy-LEH-tehn-pah-PEER
toothbrush	*Zahnbürste*	TSAHN-bewrs-teh
toothpaste	*Zahnpasta*	TSAHN-pahs-tah
towel	*Handtuch*	HAHNT-tookh
VCR	*Videorekorder*	VEED-yo-reh-kohr-duhr
wall	*Wand*	vahnt
window	*Fenster*	FEHNS-tuhr

5. Providing Assistance

A. GIVING DIRECTIONS

CONCIERGE

Good morning. May I help you?	*Guten Morgen! Kann ich Ihnen behilflich sein?*	GOO-tehn MOHR-gehn! Kahn eekh EE-nehn beh-HEELF-leekh zain?

GUEST

Yes, where is (are) the…	*Ja, wo ist (sind)…*	Yah, voh eest (zeent)…
• bathrooms?	• *die Toiletten?*	•dee toy-LEH-tehn?
• lounge/bar?	• *die Bar?*	• dee bahr?
• coffee shop/ restaurant?	• *das Kaffeehaus/ Restaurant?*	• dahs kah-FEH-hows/ rehs-tow-RAHNT?
• barbershop/ hairdresser's?	• *der Friseur?*	• dehr free-ZUHR?
• gift shop?	• *die Geschenke-boutique?*	• dee geh-SHEHN-keh-boo-teek?
• health club/gym?	• *das Fitnesscenter?*	• dahs FEET-nehs-TSEHN-tuhr?
• ballroom?	• *der Ballsaal?*	• dehr BAHL-sahl?

TIP! ••••

You can simply explain many directions, but when they're more complex, you should use either a map or written instructions (or both). Hotels should keep preprinted directions to major sites on hand. Also, German-speaking countries do not measure distances in terms of city blocks, but rather in an approximation of minutes it takes on foot, by car, or by public transportation to get to the desired destination.

• elevator?	• *der Fahrstuhl?*	• dehr FAHR-shtool?
• pay phones?	• *ein öffentliches Telefon?*	• ain UHF-ehnt-LEE-khehs teh-leh-FOHN?
• ice machine?	• *die Eiswürfel-maschine?*	• dee AIS-vewr-fuhl-mah-shee-neh?

CONCIERGE

Take…	*Nehmen Sie…*	NEH-mehn zee…
• the escalator.	• *die Rolltreppe.*	• deeROHL-treh-peh.
• the elevator.	• *den Fahrstuhl.*	• dehn FAHR-shtool.
• the stairs.	• *die Treppe.*	• dee TREH-peh.
Go…	*Gehen Sie…*	GEH-ehn zee…
• up.	• *hinauf.*	• hee-NOWF.
• down.	• *hinunter.*	• hee-NOON-tuhr.
• left.	• *links.*	• leenks.
• right.	• *rechts.*	• rehkhts.
• straight ahead.	• *geradeaus.*	• geh-RAH-deh-ows.
• around the corner.	• *um die Ecke.*	• oom dee EH-keh.
• left, then right.	• *links, dann rechts.*	• leenks, dahn rehkhts.
• past the elevators.	• *an den Fahrstühlen vorbei.*	• ahn dehn FAHR-shtew-lehn VOHR-bai.
• to the first (second, third, fourth) floor.	• *zum ersten (zweiten, dritten, vierten) Stock.*	• tsoom EHRS-tehn (TSVAI-tehn, DREE-tehn, FEER-tehn) shtohk.
• left (right) when you exit the elevator.	• *links (rechts), wenn Sie den Fahrstuhl verlassen.*	• leenks (rehkhts), vehnn zee dehn FAHR-shtool fuhr-LAH-sehn.
It will be…	*Es ist…*	Ehs eest…
• on your right.	• *auf Ihrer rechten Seite.*	• sowf EE-ruhr REHKH-tehn ZAI-teh.
• on your left.	• *auf Ihrer linken Seite.*	• owf EE-ruhr LEEN-kehn ZAI-teh.
• right in front of you.	• *direkt vor Ihnen.*	• dee-REHKT FOHR EE-nehn.

GUEST

How do I get…	*Wie komme ich…*	Vee KOH-meh eekh…
• to the hospital?	• *zum Spital/ Krankenhaus?*	• tsoom shpee-TAHL/KRAHN-kehn-hous?
• to city hall?	• *zum Rathaus?*	• tsoom RAHT-hows?
• to the _____ restaurant/hotel?	• *zum Restaurant/ Hotel _____?*	• tsoom rehs-tow-RAHNT/boh-TEHL _____?
• to the train station?	• *zum Bahnhof?*	• tsoom BAHN-hohf?
• to the bus station?	• *zum Busbahnhof?*	• tsoom BOOS-bahn-hohf?
• to the nearest bus stop?	• *zur nächsten Bushaltestelle?*	• tsoor NEHKS-tehn BOOS-hahl-teh-shteh-leh?
• to the mall?	• *zum Einkauf-szentrum?*	• tsoom AIN-kowfs-tsehn-troom?
• to the post office?	• *zum Postamt?*	• tsoom POHST-ahmt?
• to the airport?	• *zum Flughafen?*	• tsoom FLOOK-hah-fuhn?
• downtown?	• *zur Innenstadt?*	• tsoor EE-nuhn-shtaht?
• to the car rental agency?	• *zum Autoverleih?*	• tsoom OW-to-fuhr-LAI?
• to _____ Street/Avenue?	• *zur _____ Straße/Avenue?*	• tsoor _____ SHTRAH-seh/ah-veh-NEW?

CONCIERGE

When you exit the hotel, go…	*Wenn Sie das Hotel verlassen, gehen Sie…*	Vehn zee dahs hoh-TEHL fuhr-LAH-sehn, GEH-ehn zee…
• left.	• *links.*	• leenks.
• right.	• *rechts.*	• rehkhts.
• straight ahead.	• *geradeaus.*	• geh-rah-deh-OWS.
• north.	• *nach Norden.*	• nahkh NOHR-dehn.
• south.	• *nach Süden.*	• nahkh SEW-dehn.
• east.	• *nach Osten.*	• nahkh OHS-tehn.

• west.	• *nach Westen.*	• nahkh VEHS-tehn.
GUEST		
How far is it?	*Wie weit ist es?*	Vee vait eest ehs?
CONCIERGE		
It's about _____...	*Es ist ungefähr _____...*	Ehs eest OON-geh-fehr _____...
• blocks (streets).	• *Straßen.*	• SHTRAH-sehn.
• miles.	• *Meilen.*	• MAI-lehn.
• kilometers.	• *Kilometer.*	• kee-loh-MEH-tuhr.
• minutes...	• *Minuten...*	• mee-NOO-tehn...
• on foot.	• *zu Fuß.*	• tsoo FOOS.
• by car.	• *mit dem Auto.*	• meet dehm OW-toh.
• by bus.	• *mit dem Bus.*	• meet dehm boos.
• by metro (subway).	• *mit der U-Bahn.*	• meet dehr OO-Bahn.
GUEST		
Can you show me on the map?	*Können Sie mir das auf dem Stadtplan zeigen?*	KUH-nekn zee meer dahs owf dehm SHTAHT-plahn TSAI-gehn?
CONCIERGE		
Sure, it's right here.	*Selbstverständlich, hier ist es.*	Zehlbst-fuhr-SHTEHNT-leekh, heer est es.
Let me draw you a little map.	*Ich zeichnen Ihnen einen kleinen Plan.*	Eekh TSAIKH-neh EE-nehn AI-nehn KLAI-nehn plahn.
GUEST		
Can you tell me where I can... around here?	*Können Sie mir sagen, wo ich in der Nähe...kann?*	KUH-nehn zee meer ZAH-gehn, voh eekh een dehr NEH-eh... kahn?
• take a walk	• *spazierengehen*	• shpah-TSEEH-rehn-geh-ehn
• ride a bike	• *radfahren*	• RAHT-fah-rehn
• jog	• *joggen*	• CHOH-gehn

CONCIERGE

Yes, we have maps of…trails right here.	*Ja, hier haben wir Karten mit…*	Yah, heer HAH-behn veer KAHR-tehn meet…
• jogging	• *Joggingpfaden.*	• CHO-geeng PFAH-dehn.
• walking	• *Spazierwegen.*	• shpah-TSEER-veh-gehn.
• bike	• *Radfahrwegen.*	• RAHT-fahr-veh-gehn.

B. RECOMMENDING PLACES OF INTEREST

GUEST

Can you recommend any places to visit?	*Könnten Sie einige Sehenswürdigkeiten empfehlen?*	KUHN-tehn zee AI-nee-geh ZEH-ehns-vewr-deekh-kai-tehn ehm-PFEH-lehn?

CONCIERGE

There are lots. Are you interested in…	*Es gibt eine Menge. Interessieren Sie sich für…*	Ehs geept AI-neh MEHN-geh. EEN-teh-reh-SEE-rehn zee zeekh fewr…
• art?	• *Kunst?*	• koonst?
• theater?	• *Theater?*	• teh-AH-tuhr?
• shopping?	• *Einkaufen?*	• AIN-kow-fohn?
• museums?	• *Museen?*	• moo-ZEH-ehn?
• sports?	• *Sport?*	• shpohrt?
• sight-seeing?	• *Besichtigung?*	• beh-ZEEKH-tee-goong-ekn?
• music?	• *Musik?*	• moo-ZEEK?
• outdoor activities?	• *Aktivitäten im Freien?*	• ahk-tee-vee-TEH-tehn-eem-FRAI-ehn?
• children's activities?	• *Kinderaktivitäten?*	• KEEN-duhr-ahk-tee-vee-TEH-tehn?

GUEST

What do you recommend?	*Was würden Sie empfehlen?*	Vahs VEWR-dehn zee ehmp-FEH-lehn?

CONCIERGE

If you're interested in art, I'd suggest...	*Wenn Sie sich für Kunst interessieren, würde ich... empfehlen.*	Vehn zee zeekh fewr koonst een-teh-reh-SEE-rehn, VEWR-deh eekh...FEH-lehn.
• the _____ gallery.	• *die _____ Gallerie*	• dee _____ gah-leh-REE
• the _____ art museum.	• *das _____ Kunstmuseum*	• dahs _____ KOONST-moo-zeh-oom
If you're interested in theater, I can get you tickets to...	*Wenn Sie sich für Theater interessieren, könnte ich Ihnen Karten für... besorgen.*	Vehn zee zeekh fewr teh-AH-tuhr een-teh-reh-SEE-rehn, KUHN-teh eekh EE-nuhn KAHR-tehn fewr...beh-ZOHR-gehn.
• a show.	• *eine Vorstellung*	• AI-neh FOHR-shteh-loong
• an opera.	• *eine Oper*	• AI-neh OH-puhr
• a movie.	• *einen Film*	• AI-nehn feelm
For shopping, I'd recommend...	*Wenn Sie einkaufen gehen möchten, würde ich... empfehlen.*	Vehn zee AIN-kow-fehn GEH-ehn MUHKH-tehn, VEWR-deh eekh... FEH-lehn.
• downtown.	• *die Innenstadt*	• dee EE-nuhn-shtaht
• the mall.	• *das Einkaufs-zentrums*	• dahs AIN-kowfs-tehn-troom
• the discount outlets.	• *die Discount-geschäfte*	• dee DEES-kownt-geh-shehf-teh

GUEST

Do they have... there?	*Gibt es dort...*	Geept ehs dohrt...
• clothes	• *Kleider?*	• KLAI-duhr?
• furniture	• *Möbel?*	• MUH-buhl?
• rugs (carpets)	• *Teppiche?*	• TEH-pee-kheh?
• souvenirs	• *Souvenirs?*	• soo-veh-NEER?
• books	• *Bücher?*	• BEW-khuhr?

• sporting goods	• *Sportartikel?*	• SHPOHRT-ahr-tee-kuhl?
• candy	• *Bonbons?*	• bohn-BOHN?
• antiques	• *Antiquitäten?*	• ahn-tee-kvee-TEHT-ehn?
• electronics	• *Elektronik?*	• eh-lehk-TROH-neek?
• computers	• *Computer?*	• kohmp-YEW-tuhr?
• a farmers' market	• *einen Bauernmarkt?*	• AI-nehn BOW-uhrn-mahrkt?
• a supermarket	• *einen Supermarkt?*	• AI-nehn ZOO-puhr-mahrkt?
• a flea market	• *einen Flohmarkt?*	• AI-nehn FLOH-mahrkt?

CONCIERGE

Perhaps you'd like a museum.	*Vielleicht mögen Sie ein Museum?*	Fee-LAIKHT MUH-ken zee ain moo-ZEH-oom?
A local favorite is the...museum.	*Ein sehr beliebtes Museum hier ist das...*	Ain zehr beh LEEP-tehs moo-ZEH-oom heer eest dahs...
• natural history	• *Naturhistorische Museum.*	• Nah-TOOR-hees-toh-ree-sheh moo-ZEH-oom.
• modern art	• *Museum für moderne Kunst.*	• moo-ZEH-oom fewr moh-DEHR-neh koonst.
• science	• *Wissenschafts-museum.*	• VEE-sehn-shahfts-moo-ZEH-oom.
• local history	• *Lokalhistorische Museum.*	• Loh-KAHL-hees-TOH-ree-shch moo-ZEH-oom.

GUEST

We were thinking of sight-seeing.	*Wir dachten daran, die Stadt zu besichtigen.*	Veer DAHKH-tehn DAH-ahn, dee shtaht tsoo beh-ZEEKH-tee-gehn.

English	German	Pronunciation
CONCIERGE		
I'd be happy to arrange a city tour.	*Ich arrangiere Ihnen gern eine Stadtrundfahrt.*	Eekh ah-rahn-SHEE-reh EE-nehn gehrn AI-neh SHTAHT-roont-fahrt.
GUEST		
How about…	*Wie wär es mit…*	Vee vehr ehs meet…
• interesting architecture?	• *interessanter Architektur?*	• een-teh-reh-SAHN-tuhr ahr-khee-tehk-TOOR?
• churches?	• *Kirchen?*	• KEER-khehn?
• a vineyard?	• *einem Weingarten?*	• AI-nehm VAIN-gahr-tehn?
• the business district?	• *dem Geschäftsviertel?*	• dehm geh-SHEHFTS-feer-tuhl?
• the government buildings?	• *den staatlichen Gebäuden?*	• dehn SHTAHT-lee-khehn geh-BOY-dehn?
• the university?	• *der Universität?*	• dehr oo-nee-vehr-see-TEHT?
• monuments?	• *Monumenten?*	• moh-noo-MEHN-tehn?
• the countryside?	• *der Landschaft?*	• dehr LAHNT-shahft?
CONCIERGE		
There are many sports events.	*Es gibt viele Wettkämpfe.*	Es geept FEE-leh VEHT-kehmp-feh.
Would you like tickets to…	*Möchten Sie Karten für…*	MUKH-tehn zee KAHR-tehn fewr…
• a baseball game?	• *ein Baseballspiel?*	• ain BEHS-bahl-shpeel?
• a basketball game?	• *ein Basketballspiel?*	• ain BAHS-keht-bahl-shpeel?
• a football game?	• *ein amerikanisches Fußballspiel?*	• ain ah-meh-ree-KAH-nee-shehs FOOS-bahl-shpeel?
• a hockey game?	• *ein Hockeyspiel?*	• ain HOH-kee-shpeel?
• a tennis match?	• *ein Tennisspiel?*	• ain TEH-nees-shpeel?

GUEST

Are there any musical events?	*Gibt es musikalische Ereignisse?*	Geept ehs moo-zee-KAH-lee-sheh eh-RAIK-nee-seh?

CONCIERGE

There is a…concert tonight.	*Es gibt ein…heute Abend.*	Ehs geept ain…HOY-teh AH-behnt.
• rock-and-roll	• *Rock and Roll Konzert*	• rohk ehnt rohl kohn-TSEHRT
• blues	• *Blues Konzert*	• bloos kohn-TSEHRT
• classical music	• *Konzert für klassische Musik*	• kohn-TSEHRT fewr KLAH-see-shch moo-ZEEK
• jazz	• *Jazz Konzert*	• chehz kohn-TSEHRT
There's musical entertainment at _____.	*Es gibt musikalische Unterhaltung in _____.*	Ehs geept moo-zee-KAH-lee-sheh oon-tuhr-HAHL-toong een _____.

GUEST

Is there anything else going on tonight?	*Ist heute Abend noch etwas los?*	Eest HOY-teh AH-behnt nohkh EHT-vahs lohs?

CONCIERGE

Other than the movies, I'd suggest…	*Außer Filmen, würde ich empfehlen, daß Sie vielleicht…*	OW-zuhr FEEL-mehn, VEWR-deh eekh ehmp-FEH-lehn, dahs zee fee-LAIKHT…
• bowling.	• *kegeln gehen.*	• KEH-guhln GEH-ehn.
• a nightclub.	• *in einen Nachtklub gehen.*	• een AI-nehn NAHKHT-kloop GEH-ehn.
• a video rental.	• *ein Video leihen.*	• ain VEED-yoh LAI-ehn.

GUEST

What do you suggest for outdoor activities?	*Was gibt es im Freien zu tun, das Sie empfehlen?*	Vahs geept ehs eem FRAI-ehn tsoo soon, dahs zee ehmp-FEH-lehn?

CONCIERGE

How about…	*Wie wäre es mit…*	Vee VEH-reh ehs meet…
• hiking?	• *wandern?*	• VAHN-duhrn?
• fishing?	• *fischen?*	• FEE- shehn?
• skiing?	• *skifahren?*	• SHEE-fah-rehn?
• skating?	• *Schlittschuh laufen?*	• SHLEET-shoo LOW-fehn?
• Rollerblading?	• *Rollerbladen?*	• ROH-luhr-bleh-dehn?
• swimming?	• *schwimmen?*	• SHVEE-mehn?
• surfing?	• *surfen?*	• ZUHR-fehn?
Or you might like to go…	*Oder hätten Sie vielleicht Lust…zu gehen.*	OH-duhr HEH-tehn zee fee-LAIKHT roost…tsoo GEH-ehn.
• to the river.	• *an den Fluß*	• ahn dehn FLOOS
• to the lake.	• *an den See*	• ahn dehn ZEH
• to the mountains.	• *in die Berge*	• een dee BEHR-geh
• to the beach.	• *an den Strand*	• ahn dehn SHTRAHNT
• to the forest.	• *in den Wald*	• een dehn VAHLT

GUEST

Is there anything for children?	*Gibt es etwas für Kinder?*	Geept ehs EHT-vahs fewr KEEN-duhr?

CONCIERGE

Yes, there's…	*Ja, es gibt…*	Ya, ehs geept…
• a zoo.	• *einen Zoo.*	• AI-nehn TSOH.
• a children's museum.	• *ein Kindermuseum.*	• ain KEEN-duhr-moo-zeh-oom.
• an amusement park.	• *einen Vergnügungs-park.*	• AI-nehn fuhr-GNEW-goongs-pahrk.
• a water park.	• *einen Wasserpark.*	• AI-nehn VAH-suhr-pahrk.
Would you like to rent…	*Möchten Sie… mieten?*	MUHKH-tehn zee… MEE-tehn?
• a bicycle?	• *ein Fahrrad*	• ain FAHR-raht

• a car?	• *ein Auto*	• ain OW-toh
• a boat?	• *ein Boot*	• ain BOHT
• some skis?	• *Skier*	• SHEE-uhr
• some Rollerblades?	• *Rollerblades*	• ROH-luhr-blehts
Would you like a tour guide who speaks German?	*Möchten Sie einen/eine Fremdenführer/in, der/die Deutsch spricht?*	MUHKH-tehn zee AI-nehn/AI-neh FREHM-dehn-few-ruhr/een, dehr/dee doych shpreekht?
May I make a reservation for you?	*Darf ich das für Sie reserverien lassen?*	Dahrf eekh dahs fewr zee reh-zehr-VEE-rehn lah-sehn?
GUEST		
Can you recommend a good restaurant?	*Können Sie ein gutes Restaurant empfehlen?*	KUH-nehn zee ain goo-tehs rehs-tow-RAHNT ehmp-FEH-lehn?
CONCIERGE		
What type of cuisine would you like?	*Was für eine Küche hätten Sie gern?*	Vahs fewr aineh KEW-kheh HEH-tehn zee gehrn?
GUEST		
We'd like a(n)... restaurant.	*Wir hätten gern ein... Restaurant.*	Veer HEH-tehn gehrn ain...rehs-tow-RAHNT.
• casual	• *bequemes*	• beh-KVEH-mehs
• elegant	• *elegantes*	• eh-leh-GAHN-tehs
• fast-food	• *Schnell-*	• shnehl-
• inexpensive	• *preiswertes*	• PRAIS-vehr-tehs
• seafood	• *Fisch*	• feesh
• vegetarian	• *vegetarisches*	• veh-geh-TAH-ree-shehs
We'd like an authentic American steakhouse.	*Wir hätten gern ein echtes amerikanisches Steakhaus.*	Veer HEH-tehn gehrn ain EHKH-tehs ah-meh-ree-KAH-nee-shehs STEHK-house.
CONCIERGE		
You can get there by...	*Sie kommen... dorthin.*	Zee KOH-mehn... HEEN.

• bus.	• *mit dem Bus*	• meet dehm BOOS
• train.	• *mit dem Zug*	• meet dehm TSOOK
• subway.	• *mit der U-Bahn*	• meet dehr OO-bahn
Take the...bound for ____.	*Nehmen Sie... Richtung____.*	NEH-mehn zee... toong ____.
• number ____ bus	• *den Bus Nummer ____*	• dehn boos NOO-muhr ____
• train	• *den Zug*	• dehn tsook
• subway	• *die U-Bahn*	• dee OO-bahn
You'll need to transfer to...at ____.	*Sie werden bei ____ zu...umsteigen müssen.*	Zee VEHR-dehn bai ____ tsoo...OOM-shtai-gehn MEW-sehn.
• the ____ line	• *der Linie ____*	• dehr LEEN-yeh ____
• the number ____ bus	• *dem Bus Nummer ____*	• dehm boos NOO-muhr ____
Get off at ____.	*Steigen Sie bei ____ aus.*	SHTAI-gehn zee bai ____ ows.
May I call you a taxi?	*Darf ich Ihnen ein Taxi rufen?*	Darf eekh EE-nehn ain TAH-ksee ROO-fehn?
We have a free shuttle bus service available to ____.	*Es gibt einen gratis Pendelverkehr zu ____.*	Ehs geept AI-nehn grain-tees PEHN-duhl-fur-kehr tsoo ____.
It leaves every ____ minutes.	*Er fährt alle ____ Minuten ab.*	Ehr fehrt AH-leh ____ mee-NOO-tehn ahp.
It leaves every hour.	*Er fährt jede Stunde ab.*	Ehr fehrt YEH-deh SHTOON-deh ahp.

GUEST

What's the price range?	*Wieviel kostet das?*	VEE-feel KOHS-teht dahs?

6. Business Services and Clientele

A. BOOKING A BUSINESS MEETING

EMPLOYEE

Good morning.	*Guten Morgen.*	GOO-tehn MOHR-gehn.

How may I help you today?	*Wie kann ich Ihnen heute behilflich sein?*	Vee kahn eekh EE-nehn HOY-teh beh-HEELF-leekh zain?
GUEST		
I'd like to make arrangements for a business meeting.	*Ich möchte für eine Geschäftsbesprechung Vorbereitungen treffen.*	Eekh MUHKH-teh fewr AI-neh geh-SHEHFTS-beh-shpreh-khoong vohr-beh-RAI-toon-gehn TREH-fehn.
EMPLOYEE		
For how many people?	*Für wieviele Personen?*	Fewr vee-FEE-leh pehr-ZOH-nehn?
GUEST		
For ____ people on ____.	*Für ____ Personen am ____.*	Fewr ____ pehr-ZOH-nehn ahm ____.
EMPLOYEE		
Fine.	*Gut.*	Goot.
We have space available.	*Wir haben dafür noch Platz.*	Veer HAH-behn dah-FEWR nohkh plaints.
We can provide all your meals.	*Wir können Ihnen alle Mahlzeiten servieren.*	Veer KUH-nehn EE-nehn Ah-leh MAHL-tsai-tehn sehr-VEE-rehn.

TIP! ••••

Clients who do business from the hotel need a great deal of service from you. They tend to be seasoned travelers who don't want a lot of explanation from hotel employees, just competent action. Attending to their every need often yields substantial financial rewards!

GUEST

That's good. We'd like… for each day.	*Das ist gut. Für jeden Tag hätten wir gern…*	Dahs eest goot. Fewr YEH-dehn tahk HEH-tehn veer gehrn…
• a continental breakfast	• *ein kleines Frühstück (Kaffee und Brötchen).*	• ain KLAI-nehs FREW-shtewk (KAH-feh oont BRUHT-khehn).
• coffee breaks	• *Kaffeepausen.*	• KAH-feh-pow-zehn.
• a working lunch	• *Mittagsessen während der Besprechung.*	• MEET-tahks-eh-sehn WEH-rehnd dehr beh-SHPREH-khoong.
• snacks	• *Kleinigkeiten zu essen.*	• KLAI-neekh-kai-tehn tsoo EH-sehn.
• a cocktail reception	• *einen Cocktailempfang.*	• AI-neRn KOHK-tehl-ehmp-fahng.
• dinner	• *Abendessen.*	• AH-behnt-eh-sehn.
Also, we'll require… for the meeting room.	*Wir werden auch…für das Besprechungszimmer brauchen.*	Veer VEHR-dehn owkh…fewr dahs beh-SHPREH-khoons-ZEE-muhr BROW-khehn.
• a VCR with a large-screen monitor	• *einen Videorekorder mit einem großen Monitor*	• AI-nehn VEED-yo-reh-kohr-duhr meet AI-nehm GROH-sen MOH-nee-tohr
• an overhead projector with transparencies and markers	• *einen Overhead-projektor mit Transparenten und Markierstiften*	• AI-nehn OH-vuhr-heht-proh-yehk-tohr meet TRAHNS-pah-rehn-tehn oont mahr-KEER-shteef-tehn
• a chalkboard	• *eine Wandtafel*	• AI-neh VAHNT-tah-fuhl
• a flip chart	• *ein Flip-Chart*	• AIN FLEEP-chahrt
• a slide projector	• *einen Diaprojektor*	• AI-nehn DEE-ah-proh yehk-tohr
• a computer with a large-screen monitor	• *einen Computer mit einem großen Monitor*	• AI-nehn kohmp-YEW-tuhr meet AI-nehm GROH-sehm MOH-nee-tohr

And please be sure to provide…	*Und bitte bringen Sie ganz bestimmt…*	Oont BEE-teh BREEN-gehn zee gahnts beh-SHTEEMT…
• water.	• *Wasser.*	• VAH-suhr.
• pads with pencils.	• *Schreibblöcke mit Bleistiften.*	• SHRAIB-bluh-keh meet BLAI-shteef-tehn.
• ashtrays.	• *Aschenbecher.*	• AH-shehn-beh-khuhr.

EMPLOYEE

Let's decide on what time you'd like everything, and we'll be all set.	*Entscheiden wir uns doch, um wieviel Uhr Sie alles gern hätten, und dann wird alles in Ordnung gehen.*	Ehnt-SHAI-dehn veer oons dokh, oom VEE-feel oor zee AH-lehs gehrn HEH-tehn, oont dahn veers AH-lehs een OHRD-noong GEH-ehn.

GUEST

Okay. How will the room be set up?	*Okay. Wie wird das Zimmer eingerichtet sein?*	Oh-KEH. Vee veert dahs TSEE-muhr AIN-geh-reekh-teht zain?

EMPLOYEE

We can set up the room…	*Es kann…eingerichtet sein.*	Ehs kahn…AIN-geh-reekh-teht zain.
• theater style.	• *im Theaterstil*	• eem teh-AH-tuhr-steel
• in a square.	• *in einem Quadrat*	• een AI-nehm kvah-DRAHT
• horseshoe ("U") style.	• *im Hufeisen-("U"-) stil*	• eem HOOF-ai-sehn-("oo") steel
• classroom style.	• *im Klassenzimmerstil*	• eem KLAH-sehn-tsee-muhr-steel
• boardroom style.	• *im Konferenzstil*	• eem kohn-fuh-REHNTS-steel
We're looking forward to having your group here.	*Wir freuen uns auf den Besuch Ihrer Gruppe.*	Veer FRO-yehn oons owf dehn beh-ZOOKH EE-ruhr GROO-poh.

GERMAN

B. AT THE MEETING

ATTENDANT

I'm ____, the meeting-room attendant.	*Ich heiße ____, und ich bin der Aufseher/die Aufseherin für die Besprechung.*	Eekh HAI-seh ____, oont eekh been dehr OWF-seh-uhr/dee OWF-seh-uh-reen fewr dee beh-SHPREH-khoong.
How is everything?	*Ist alles in Ordnung?*	Eest AH-lehs een OHRD-noong?

GUEST

Everything is fine, thank you.	*Ja, alles ist in Ordnung, danke.*	Yah, AH-lehs eest een OHRD-noong, DAHN-keh.
We need…	*Wir brauchen…*	Veer BROW-khehn…
• more chairs.	• *mehr Stühle.*	• mehr SHTEW-leh.
• more coffee.	• *mehr Kaffee.*	• mehr KAH-feh.
• the ashtrays emptied.	• *saubere Aschenbecher.*	• SOW-buh-reh AH-shehn-beh-khuhr.
• more water.	• *mehr Wasser.*	• mehr VAH-suhr.

ATTENDANT

I'll take care of it right away.	*Das wird sofort erledigt.*	Dahs veers soh-FOHRT ehr-LEH-deekht.
Is everything else satisfactory?	*Sind Sie mit dem Dienst zufrieden?*	Zeent zee meet dehm deenst tsoo-FREE-dehn?

GUEST

It's quite nice, but the room…	*Es ist ganz gut, aber das Zimmer…*	Ehs eest gahnts goot, AH-buhr dahs TSEE-muhr…
• needs more light.	• *braucht mehr Licht.*	• browkht mehr LEEKHT.
• is too bright.	• *ist zu hell.*	• eest tsoo hehl.
• needs more ventilation.	• *braucht mehr frische Luft.*	• browkht mehr FREE-sheh looft.
• is too hot (cold).	• *ist zu heiß (kalt).*	• eest tsoo hais (kahlt).

• is a little noisy.	• *ist ein bißchen laut.*	• Best ain BEES-khehn lowt.
• is crowded.	• *ist überfüllt.*	• eest ew-buhr-FEWLT.
Can you take care of it?	*Können Sie sich darum kümmern?*	KUH-nehn zee zeekh dah-ROOM KEW-muhrn?
Can we get another room?	*Könnten wir ein anderes Zimmer haben?*	KUHN-tehn veer ain AHN-duh-rehs TSEE-muhr hah-behn?

ATTENDANT

Let me see what we can do.	*Ich werde nachschauen, was wir machen können.*	Eekh VEHR-deh NAHKH-show-ehn, vahs veer MAH-khehn KUH-nehn.

C. CATERING TO BUSINESS GUESTS

CONCIERGE

Good morning. How may I help you?	*Guten Morgen. Wie kann ich Ihnen behilflich sein?*	GOO-tehn MOHR-gehn. Vee kahn eekh EE-nehn beh-HEELF-leekh zain?

GUEST

Good morning. Where is breakfast for the _____ group?	*Guten Morgen. Wo ist das Frühstück für die _____ Gruppe?*	GOO-tehn MOHR-gehn. VOH eest dahs FREW-shtewk fewr dee _____ GROO-peh?
Where is the exhibits hall?	*Wo ist die Ausstellungshalle?*	Voh eest dee OWS-shteh-loongs-hah-leh?

CONCIERGE

There's a buffet set up outside your meeting room.	*Es gibt ein Büffet vor dem Besprechungs-zimmer.*	Ehs geept ain bew-FEH fohr dehm beh-SHPREH-khoongs-tsee-muhr.
Just down the hall.	*Nur den Gang entlang.*	Noor dehn gahng ehnt-LAHNG.
In the dining room.	*Im Speisesaal.*	Eem SHPAI-zeh-zahl.

GUEST

Thank you.	*Danke.*	DAHN-keh.

I need…	*Ich möchte…*	Eekh MUHKH-teh…
• a fax sent.	• *ein Fax aufgeben.*	• ain fahks OWF-geh-behn.
• some typing done.	• *, daß jemand einen Brief für mich mit der Maschine schreibt.*	• , dahs yeh-MAHNT AI-nehn breef fewr meekh meet dehr mah-SHEE-neh shraipt.
• a hookup to the Internet.	• *eine Internet-verbindung.*	• AI-neh EEN-tuhr-neht-fuhr-been-doong.
• a computer.	• *einen Computer.*	• AI-nehn kohmp-YOO-tuhr.
• a package sent overnight.	• *ein Paket übernacht liefern lassen.*	• ain pah-KEHT ew-buhr-NAHKHT LEE-fuhrn LAH-sehn.
• courier service.	• *dies mit dem Kurier schicken.*	• dees meet dehm KOOR-yuhr SHEE-kehn.
• some letters mailed.	• *einige Briefe aufgeben.*	• AI-nee-geh BREE-feh OWF-geh-behn.
• some copies made.	• *einige Fotokopien machen lassen.*	• AI-nee-geh foh-toh-koh-PEE-ehn MAH-khehn lah-sehn.
CONCIERGE		
I'll take care of that right away.	*Das wird sofort erledigt.*	Dahs veers soh-FOHRT ehr-LEH-deekht.
GUEST		
Later, I'd like to host a small reception.	*Ich möchte für später einen Empfang organisieren.*	Eekh MUHKH-teh fewr SHPEH-tuhr AI-nehn EHMP-fahng OHR-gah-nee-zee-rehn.
Can you arrange that?	*Können Sie das arrangieren?*	KUH-nehn zee dahs ah-rahn-SHEE-rehn?
CONCIERGE		
Certainly. What would you like?	*Sicher. Was hätten Sie gern?*	ZEE-khuhr. Vahs HEH-tehn zee gehrn?

GUEST

We need a full bar and some hors d'oeuvres.	*Wir brauchen eine volle Bar und einige Vorspeisen.*	Veer BROW-khehn AI-neh FOH-leh bahr oont AI-nee-geh FOHR-shpai-zehn.
Make sure there are plenty of chilled shrimp.	*Kümmern Sie sich bitte darum, daß es genug kaltgestelle Shrimp gibt.*	KUH-mehr zee zeekh BEE-teh DAH-room, dahs ehs geh-NOOK KAHLT-geh-shtehl-teh shreemp geept.
Lots of champagne, please.	*Viel Sekt, bitte.*	Feel sehkt, BEE-teh.

CONCIERGE

I'll have Room Service put together a proposal right away, and get back to you.	*Der Zimmerservice wird sofort einen Vorschlag organisieren, und dann werde ich mit Ihnen darüber diskutieren.*	Dehr TSEE-muhr-suhr-vees veers soh-FOHRT AI-nehn FOHR-shlahk ohr-gah-nee-SEE-rehn, oont dahn VEHR-deh eekh meet EE-nehn dah-REW-buhr dees-koo-TEE-rehn.

7. Checking Out

GUEST

At what time is checkout?	*Wann muß ich das Zimmer verlassen?*	Vahn moos eekh dahs TSEE-muhr fuhr-LAH-sehn?

FRONT DESK CLERK

Checkout is at…	*Sie müssen das Zimmer um… verlassen.*	Zee MEW-sehn dahs TSEE-muhr oom… fuhr-LAH-sehn.
• 10 A.M.	• *zehn Uhr vormittags*	• tsekn oor FOHR-meet-tahks
• noon.	• *zwölf Uhr Mittag*	• tsvuhlf oor meet-tahk
• 3 P.M.	• *drei Uhr nachmittags*	• drai oor NAHKH-meet-tags

You may audit your bill on channel _____ on your television.	*Sie können Ihre Rechnung auf Kanal _____ ihres Fernsehers anschauen.*	Zee KUH-nehn EE-reh REHKH-noong owf kah-NAHL _____ EE-rehs FEHRN-seh-ehrs AHN-show-ehn.
We provide an express checkout service.	*Wir haben auch einen Expreß-Checkout Dienst.*	Veer HAH-behn owkh AI-nehn ehks-PREHS-chehk-owt deenst.
Your bill will be left outside your door the night before you check out.	*Am Abend vor Ihrer Abreise werden Sie die Rechnung vor Ihrer Tür finden.*	Ahm AH-behnt fohr EE-ruhr AHP-rai-seh VEHR-dehn zee dee REHKH-noong fohr EE-ruhr tewr FEEN-dehn.
If you're satisfied with your bill, simply sign it,	*Wenn alles in Ordnung ist, unterschreiben Sie die Rechnung einfach,*	Vehn AH-lehs een OHRD-noong eest, oon-tuhr-SHRAI-behn zee dee REHKH-noong AIN-fahkh,
and leave your key in your room.	*und lassen Sie den Schlüssel im Zimmer.*	oont LAH-sehn zee dehn SHLEW-suhl eem TSEE-muhr.
Any late charges such as breakfast or minibar will be added automatically.	*Die Frühstucks- oder Mini-bar-Rechnung wird automatisch dazugerechnet.*	Dee FREW-shtewks-OH-duhr MEE-nee-OH-REHKH-noong veerd ow-toh-MAH-teesh dah-TSOO-geh-rehkh-neht.
GUEST		
I'd like to check out, please.	*Ich möchte bitte ausziehen.*	Eekh MUHKH-teh BEE-teh OUS-tsee-ehn.
CLERK		
May I have your luggage brought down?	*Kann ich ihr Gepäck herunterbringen lassen?*	Kahn eekh eer geh-PEHK heh-ROON-tuhr-breen-gehn LAH-sehn?
GUEST		
Yes, please.	*Ja, bitte.*	Yah, BEE-teh.
No, I brought (will bring) it myself.	*Nein, ich habe es (werde es) schon heruntergebracht (herunterbringen).*	Nain, eekh HAH-beh ehs (VEHR-deh ehs) shohn heh-ROON-tuhr-geh-brahkht (heh-ROON-tuhr-breen-gehn).

CLERK		
How was everything?	*Wie war der Aufenthalt?*	Vee vahr dehr OWF-ehnt-hahlt?
GUEST		
It was very nice, thank you.	*Der Aufenthalt war sehr angenehm, danke.*	Dehr OWF-ehnt-hahlt vahr sehr AHN-geh-nehm, DAHN-keh.
I want to speak with the manager.	*Ich möchte den Direktor/der Direktorin sprechen.*	Eekh MUHKH-teh dehn dee-REHK-tohr/dehr dee-rehk-DOH-reen SHPREH-khehn.
CLERK		
Certainly. The manager on duty is _____. One moment, please.	*Selbstverstandlich. Der Direktor/Die Direktorin im Dienst ist _____. Einen Moment, bitte.*	Sehlpst-fuhr-SHTEHNT-leekh. Dehr dee-REHK-tohr/dee dee-rehk-DOH-reen eem deenst eest _____. AI-nehn moh-MEHNT, BEE-teh.
GUEST		
Our experience was…	*Der Aufenthalt war…*	Dehr OWF-ehnt-hahlt vahr…
• good.	• *gut.*	• goot.
• excellent.	• *ausgezeichnet.*	• ows-geh-TSAIKH-neht.
• poor.	• *schlecht.*	• shlehkht.
• very bad.	• *sehr schlecht.*	• sehr shlehkht.
MANAGER ON DUTY		
That's nice to hear.	*Das freut mich.*	Dahs FROYT meekh.
I'm sorry to hear that.*	*Das tut mir leid.*	Dahs toot meer LAIT.
Thank you. Please come again.	*Danke. Bitte kommen Sie wieder.*	DAHN-keh. BEE-teh KOH-mehn zee VEE-duhr.

*Please refer to "Guest Complaints in the Hotel" on page 138 for more on handling dissatisfied clients.

ITALIAN

1. The Bare Essentials

A. THE ITALIAN ALPHABET

a	ah	*q*	ku
b	bee	*r*	EHR-reh
c	chee	*s*	EHS-seh
d	dee	*t*	tee
e	eh	*u*	oo
f	EHF-feh	*v*	voo
g	jee	*z*	ZEH-tah
h	AHK-kah		
i	ee	*j*	ee-LOON-gah
l	EHL-leh	*k*	KAHP-pah
m	EHM-meh	*w*	DOHP-pia-VOO
n	EHN-neh		
o	oh	*x*	eeks
p	pee	*y*	EEPS-ee-lohn

Note: The letters *j, k, w, x,* and *y* occur only in words of foreign origin.

B. PRONUNCIATION CHART

VOWELS

ITALIAN SOUND	APPROXIMATE SOUND IN ENGLISH	EXAMPLE
a	(f<u>a</u>ther)	*casa* (house)
e (closed)	(l<u>a</u>te)	*sete* (thirst)

e (open)	(quest)	*bello* (beautiful)
i	(marine)	*pizza* (pizza)
o	(cozy)	*nome* (name)
u	(rude)	*luna* (moon)

DIPHTHONGS

ITALIAN SOUND	APPROXIMATE SOUND IN ENGLISH	EXAMPLE
ai	(aisle)	*mai* (never)
au	(now)	*auto* (car)
ei	(may)	*sei* (six)
ia	(yarn)	*foglia* (leaf)
ie	(yet)	*piegare* (to bend)
io	(yodel)	*foglio* (sheet)
iu	(you)	*chiuso* (closed)
oi	(ahoy)	*noi* (we)
ua	(wand)	*quando* (when)
ue	(wet)	*questo* (this)
ui	(sweet)	*qui* (here)

CONSONANTS

Most Italian consonants do not differ greatly from English. The following are some important exceptions and special combinations.

c (before *a, o, u*)	hard c (cat)	*cane* (dog) *cosa* (thing) *curioso* (curious)
ch	hard c (cat)	*Michele* (Michael) *Chianti* (Chianti)
c (before *e, i*)	soft c (church)	*cena* (dinner) *cinema* (cinema)
g (before *a, o, u*)	hard g (go)	*gatto* (cat) *gonna* (skirt) *gusto* (taste)
g (before *e, i*)	soft g (joy)	*gelato* (ice cream) *giorno* (day)
gl (before final *i* and before *i* + vowel)	ll (million)	*figlio* (son) *gli* (the/to him)
gl (in all other contexts)	gl (glad)	*glicerina* (glycerine) *globo* (globe)

gn	ny (canyon)	*signore* (sir, Mr.) *ignorante* (ignorant) *gnocchi* (gnocchi)
h	always silent	*ho* (I have)
ps (word initial)	ps (jeeps)	*psicologo* (psychologist)
r	like r in "throw" but lightly rolled	*Roma* (Rome) *però* (but) *radio* (radio)
s (word initial)	s (sad)	*sera* (evening)
s (between vowels)	s (rose)	*rosa* (rose)
s (before *ce, ci*)	sh (should)	*scegliere* (to choose) *scena* (scene)
z	ts (quits)	*negozio* (store)
z (word initial)	dz (seeds)	*zero* (zero) *zeffiro* (zephyr)

The letters *j, k, w, x,* and *y* are pronounced the same as they are in the foreign words in which they appear.

DOUBLE CONSONANTS

All Italian consonants except *q* have a corresponding double form, whose pronunciation is similar to, yet distinct from, that of the single consonant. The difference between the two corresponds to a difference in meaning. Hence, correct pronunciation is very important. Compare, for example:

sete (thirst)	*sette* (seven)
papa (pope)	*pappa* (baby food)
dona (he/she gives)	*donna* (woman)
casa (house)	*cassa* (cash register)

The sounds of the consonants *f, l, m, n, r, s,* and *v* are simply lengthened when they appear in doubled form. Some consonants' sounds cannot be lengthened (*b, c, g, p, t,* and *z*), in which case, the vowel sound that precedes them is shortened and accented.

C. THE ITALIAN LANGUAGE

Word Order The basic word order of Italian is the same as in English—subject-verb-object:

Il camariere	*porta*	*la pizza.*	The waiter	brings	the pizza.
S	V	O	S	V	O

Nouns and Adjectives All nouns in Italian have gender. *Il* (the) and *un* (a/an) are used with masculine nouns, and *la* and *una* are used with feminine nouns. To form the plural, a final *-o* or a final *-e* changes to *-i,* a final *-a* changes to *-e. I* is the article used with plural masculine nouns, and *le* is used with plural feminine nouns. Adjectives in Italian change to agree with the nouns they modify. Adjective endings follow the same pattern as nouns: *un ragazzo curioso* (a curious boy), *la ragazza curiosa* (the curious girl), *i ragazzi curiosi* (the curious boys), and *le ragazze curiose* (the curious girls). Notice that most adjectives in Italian come after the nouns they modify.

Verbs Italian verbs undergo various changes to indicate subject, tense, or mood. *Il cameriere porta la pizza.* (The waiter brings the pizza.) *Portiamo una bottiglia.* (We bring a bottle.) *Portavano dei fiori.* (They were bringing some flowers.) *Porterei del formaggio.* (I would bring some cheese.) *Mi porti una birra!* (Bring me a beer!) *Signor Martini porterà il denaro.* (Mr. Martini will bring the money.)

These simple rules will help you communicate on a basic level in Italian. The phrases and sentences in the Italian sections are written so that you can use them as printed. All you have to do is familiarize yourself with them, and you'll be ready to go. *Buona fortuna!*

D. THE ITALIAN CULTURE

Italians place a great deal of importance on dressing well, although not necessarily formally, and will always look fashionable in your establishment. The common greeting is a handshake. While northern Italians will tend to be punctual, southern

Italians may not be as concerned with time and should be told if punctuality is important.

Like so many international guests, Italians may not understand the financial realities of the American tipping system, so it may be wise to include a service charge in the bill.

2. Useful Expressions

A. GENERAL

Hello.	*Buon giorno.*	Bwohn JOR-noh.
Good-bye.	*Arrivederci.*	Ah-ree-veh-DEHR-chee.
Yes.	*Sì.*	See.
No.	*No.*	Noh.
Maybe.	*Forse.*	FOHR-seh.
Please.	*Per favore.*	Pehr fah-VOR-eh.
Thank you (very much).	*Grazie (mille).*	GRAH-tsee-eh (MEEL-leh).
You're welcome.	*Prego.*	PREH-go.
Excuse me.	*Mi scusi.*	Mee SKOO-zee.
I beg your pardon.	*Chiedo scusa.*	KYEH-doh SKOO-zah.
I'm sorry.	*Mi dispiace.*	Mee dee-SPYAH-cheh.
One moment, please.	*Un momento, per favore.*	Oon moh-mehn-toh, pehr fah-VOHR-eh.
Do you speak English?	*Parla inglese?*	Pahr-lah een-GLEH-zeh?
• Yes, I do.	• *Sì, parlo inglese.*	• SEE, PAHR-loh een-GLEH-zeh.
• No, I don't.	• *No, non parlo inglese.*	• NOH, nohn PAHR-loh een-GLEH-zeh.
• A little.	• *Un poco.*	• Oon POH-koh.
• No, not at all.	• *No, per niente.*	• NOH, pehr NYEHN-teh.
That's okay.	*Va bene.*	VAH BEH-neh.
It doesn't matter.	*Non importa.*	Nohn eem-POHR-tah.

I don't speak Italian.	*Non parlo italiano.*	Nohn PAHR-loh ee-tahl-YAH-noh.
I can speak a little.	*Lo parlo un poco.*	Loh PAHR-loh oon POH-koh.
I understand a little.	*Lo capisco un poco.*	Loh kah-PEES-koh oon POH-koh.
I don't understand.	*Non capisco.*	Nohn cah-PEES-koh.
Please speak more slowly.	*Parli più lentamente per favore.*	PAHR-lee PYOO lehn-tah-MEHN-teh, pehr fah-VOH-reh.
Would you repeat that, please?	*Può ripetere, per favore?*	Pwoh ree-PEH-teh-reh, pehr fah-VOR-eh?
Yes, sir/ma'am.	*Sì, signore/a.*	SEE see-NYO-reh/ah.
No problem.	*Volentieri.*	Vo-lehn-TYEH-ree.
It's my pleasure.	*Con piacere.*	Cohn pee-ah-CHEH-reh.

B. NEEDS

I'd like ____.	*Vorrei ____.*	Vohr-RAY ____.
I need ____.	*Ho bisogno di ____.*	Oh bee-ZO-nyo dee ____.
What would you like?	*Desidera?*	Deh-ZEE-deh-rah?
Please bring me ____.	*Per favore, mi porti ____.*	Pehr fah-VOR-eh, mee POHR-tee ____.
I'm looking for ____.	*Cerco ____.*	CHEHR-koh ____.
I'm hungry.	*Ho fame.*	Oh FAH-meh.
I'm thirsty.	*Ho sete.*	Oh SE-teh.
It's important.	*È importante.*	Eh eem-pohr-TAHN-teh.
It's urgent.	*È urgente.*	Eh oor-JEHN-teh.

C. QUESTION WORDS

How?	*Come?*	KOH-meh?
How much?	*Quanto?*	KWAHN-toh?
How many?	*Quanti/e?*	KWAHN-tee/teh?
Which?	*Quale?*	KWAH-leh?

What?	*Cosa?*	KOH-zah?
What kind of?	*Che tipo di?*	Keh TEE-poh dee?
Who?	*Chi?*	Kee?
Where?	*Dove?*	DOH-veh?
When?	*Quando?*	KWAHN-doh?
What does this mean?	*Cosa vuol dire?*	KOH-zah vwohl DEE-reh?
What does that mean?	*Cosa vuol dire quello?*	KOH-zah vwohl DEE-reh KWEHL-loh?
How do you say ____ in Italian?	*Come si dice ____ in italiano?*	KOH-meh see DEE-cheh ____ een ee-tahl-YAH-noh?

D. COLORS

black	*nero*	NEH-roh
blue	*azzurro*	ah-DSOOR-roh
brown	*marrone*	mahr-ROH-neh
gold	*oro*	OH-roh
gray	*grigio*	GREEjoh
green	*verde*	VEHR-deh
orange	*arancione*	ah-rahn-CHOH-neh
pink	*rosa*	ROH-zah
purple	*porpora*	POHR-poh-rah
red	*rosso*	ROHS-soh
silver	*argento*	ahr-JEHN-toh
violet	*viola*	vee-OH-lah
white	*bianco*	bee-YAHN-koh
yellow	*giallo*	JAHL-loh

E. CARDINAL NUMBERS

1	*uno*	OO-noh
2	*due*	DOO-eh
3	*tre*	treh
4	*quattro*	KWAHT-troh

5	*cinque*	CHEEN-kweh
6	*sei*	say
7	*sette*	SEHT-teh
8	*otto*	OHT-toh
9	*nove*	NOH-veh
10	*dieci*	DYEH-chee
11	*undici*	OON-dee-chee
12	*dodici*	DOH-dee-chee
13	*tredici*	TREH-dee-chee
14	*quattordici*	kwaht-TOHR-dee-chee
15	*quindici*	KWEEN-dee-chee
16	*sedici*	SEH-dee-chee
17	*diciassette*	dee-chahs-SEHT-teh
18	*diciotto*	dee-CHO-toh
19	*diciannove*	dee-chahn-NOH-veh
20	*venti*	VEHN-tee
21	*ventuno*	vehn-TOO-noh
22	*ventidue*	vehn-tee-DOO-eh
23	*ventitré*	vehn-tee-TREH
24	*ventiquattro*	vehn-tee-KWAH-troh
25	*venticinque*	vehn-tee-CHEEN-kweh
26	*ventisei*	vehn-tee-SAY
27	*ventisette*	vehn-tee-SEHT-teh
28	*ventotto*	vehn-TOHT-toh
29	*ventinove*	vehn-tee-NOH-veh
30	*trenta*	TREHN-tah
31	*trentuno*	trehn-TOO-noh
32	*trentadue*	trehn-tah-DOO-eh
40	*quaranta*	kwah-RAHN-tah
50	*cinquanta*	cheen-KWAHN-tah
60	*sessanta*	sehs-SAHN-tah
70	*settanta*	seht-TAHN-tah

80	*ottanta*	oht-TAHN-tah
90	*novanta*	noh-VAHN-tah
100	*cento*	CHEHN-toh
101	*centouno*	chehn-toh-OO-noh
102	*centodue*	chehn-toh-DOO-eh
110	*centodieci*	chehn-toh-DYEH-chee
120	*centoventi*	chehn-toh-VEHN-tee
200	*duecento*	doo-eh-CHEHN-toh
210	*duccentodieci*	doo-eh-chehn-toh-DYEH-chee
300	*trecento*	treh-CHEHN-toh
400	*quattrocento*	kwaht-troh-CHEHN-toh
500	*cinquecento*	cheen-kweh-CHEN-toh
600	*seicento*	say-CHEHN-toh
700	*settecento*	seht-teh-CHEHN-toh
800	*ottocento*	oht-toh-CHEHN-toh
900	*novecento*	noh-veh-CHEHN-toh
1,000	*mille*	MEEL-leh
1,100	*millecento*	meel-leh-CHEHN-toh
1,200	*milleduecento*	meel-leh-doo-eh-CHEHN-toh
2,000	*duemila*	doo-eh-MEE-lah
10,000	*diecimila*	dyeh-chee-MEE-lah
50,000	*cinquantamila*	cheen-kwahn-tah-MEE-lah
100,000	*centomila*	chehn-toh-MEE-lah
1,000,000	*un milione*	oon mee-LYOH-neh
1,000,000,000	*un miliardo*	oon mee-LYAHR-doh

F. ORDINAL NUMBERS

first	*primo*	PREE-moh
second	*secondo*	seh-KOHN-doh
third	*terzo*	TEHR-tsoh

fourth	*quarto*	KWAHR-toh
fifth	*quinto*	KWEEN-toh
sixth	*sesto*	SEHS-toh
seventh	*settimo*	SEHT-tee-moh
eighth	*ottavo*	oht-TAH-voh
ninth	*nono*	NOH-noh
tenth	*decimo*	DEH-chee-moh
eleventh	*undicesimo*	oon-dee-CHEH-zee-moh
twelfth	*dodicesimo*	doh-dee-CHEH-zee-moh
thirteenth	*tredicesimo*	treh-dee-CHEH-zee-moh
fourteenth	*quattordicesimo*	kwah-tohr-dee-CHEH-zee-moh
fifteenth	*quindicesimo*	kween-dee-CHEH-zee-moh
sixteenth	*sedicesimo*	say-dee-CHEH-zee-moh
seventeenth	*diciasettesimo*	dee-chah-seh-TEH-zee-moh
eighteenth	*diciottesimo*	dee-choh-TEH-zee-moh
nineteenth	*diciannovesimo*	dee-chahn-noh-VAY-zee-moh
twentieth	*ventesimo*	vehn-TEH-zee-moh
twenty-first	*ventunesimo*	vehn-too-NEH-zee-moh
twenty-second	*ventiduesimo*	vehn-tee-doo-EH-zee-moh
thirtieth	*trentesimo*	trehn-TEH-zee-moh
fortieth	*quarantesimo*	kwah-rahn-TEH-zee-moh
fiftieth	*cinquantesimo*	cheen-kwahn-TEH-zee-moh
sixtieth	*sessantesimo*	sehs-sahn-TEH-zee-moh
seventieth	*settantesimo*	seh-tahn-TEH-zee-moh
eightieth	*ottantesimo*	oh-tahn-TEH-zee-moh

ninetieth	*novantesimo*	noh-vahn-TEH-zee-moh
hundredth	*centesimo*	chehn-TEH-zee-moh
thousandth	*millesimo*	meel-LEH-zee-moh

G. TIME OF DAY

1:00	*l'una*	LOO-nah
2:00	*le due*	leh DOO-eh
3:00	*le tre*	leh TREH
4:00	*le quattro*	leh KWAHT-troh
5:00	*le cinque*	leh CHEEN-kweh
6:00	*le sei*	leh SAY
7:00	*le sette*	leh SEHT-teh
8:00	*le otto*	leh OHT-toh
9:00	*le nove*	leh NOH-veh
10:00	*le dieci*	leh DYE-chee
11:00	*le undici*	leh OON-dee-chee
12:00	*le dodici*	leh DOH-dee-chee
1:00 A.M.	*l'una di notte*	LOO-nah dee NOHT-teh
3:00 P.M.	*le tre del pomeriggio*	leh TREH dehl poh-meh-REE-joh
noon	*mezzogiorno*	meh-dsoh-JOHR-noh
midnight	*mezzanotte*	meh-dsah-NOH-teh
1:15	*l'una e un quarto*	LOO-nah eh oon KWAHR-toh
12:45	*l'una meno quindici/ un quarto*	LOO-nah MEH-noh KWEEN-dee-chee/oon KWAHR-to
1:30	*l'una e mezzo*	LOO-nah eh MEH-dsoh
7:05	*le sette e cinque*	leh SEH-teh eh CHEEN-kweh
4:55	*le cinque meno cinque*	leh CHEEN-kweh MAY-noh CHEEN-kweh

H. DAYS OF THE WEEK

Monday	*lunedì*	loo-neh-DEE
Tuesday	*martedì*	mahr-teh-DEE
Wednesday	*mercoledì*	mehr-koh-leh-DEE
Thursday	*giovedì*	joh-veh-DEE
Friday	*venerdì*	veh-nehr-DEE
Saturday	*sabato*	SAH-bah-toh
Sunday	*domenica*	doh-MEH-nee-kah

I. MONTHS

January	*gennaio*	jehn-NAH-yoh
February	*febbraio*	feh-BRAH-yoh
March	*marzo*	MAHR-tsoh
April	*aprile*	ah-PREE-leh
May	*maggio*	MAH-joh
June	*giugno*	JOO-nyoh
July	*luglio*	LOO-lyoh
August	*agosto*	ah-GOH-stoh
September	*settembre*	seh-TEHM-breh
October	*ottobre*	oh-TOH-breh
November	*novembre*	noh-VEHM-breh
December	*dicembre*	dee-CHEHM-breh

J. DATES

1998	*il millenovecento-novantotto*	eel meel-leh-noh-veh-chehn-toh-noh-vahn-TOH-toh
1999	*il millenovecento-novantanove*	eel meel-leh-noh-veh-chehn-toh-noh-vahn-tah-NOH-veh
2000	*il duemila*	eel doo-eh-MEE-lah
2001	*il duemilauno*	eel doo-eh-mee-lah-OO-noh
2002	*il duemiladue*	eel doo-eh-mee-lah-DOO-eh

ITALIAN

2003	*il duemilatre*	eel doo-eh-mee-lah-TREH
2004	*il duemilaquattro*	eel doo-eh-mee-lah-KWAH-troh
2005	*il duemilacinque*	eel doo-eh-mee-lah-CHEEN-kweh
Today is Thursday, September 22.	*Oggi è giovedì, il ventidue settembre.*	OH-jee EH joh-veh-DEE, eel vehn-tee-DOO-eh seh-TEHM-breh.
Yesterday was Wednesday, September 21.	*Ieri era mercoledì, il ventuno settembre.*	YEH-ree EH-rah mehr-koh-leh-DEE, eel vehn-TOO-noh seh-TEHM-breh.
The day before yesterday was Tuesday, September 20.	*L'altro ieri era martedì, il venti settembre.*	LAHL-troh YEH-ree EH-rah mahr-teh-DEE, eel VEHN-tee seh-TEHM-breh.
Tomorrow is Friday, September 23.	*Domani è venerdì, il ventitré settembre.*	Doh-MAH-nee eh veh-nehr-DEE, eel vehn-tee-TREH seh-TEHM-breh.
The day after tomorrow is Saturday, September 24.	*Dopo domani è sabato, il ventiquattro settembre.*	DOH-poh doh-MAH-nee Eh SAH-ba-toh, eel vehn-tee-KWAH-troh seh-TEHM-breh.
Next Friday is September 30.	*Venerdì prossimo è il trenta settembre.*	Veh-nehr-DEE PROH-see-moh Eh eel TREHN-tah seh-TEHM-breh.
Last Friday was September 16.	*Venerdì scorso era il sedici settembre.*	Veh-nehr-DEE SCOHR-soh EH-rah eel SAY-dee-chee seh-TEHM-breh.

K. MEASUREMENTS: DISTANCE

inch	*pollice*	POHL-lee-cheh
foot	*piede*	PYEH-deh
yard	*iarda*	YAHR-dah
mile	*miglio*	MEE-lyoh

millimeter	*millimetro*	meel-LEE-meh-troh
meter	*metro*	MEH-troh
kilometer	*chilometro*	kee-LOH-meh-troh

3. Common Hospitality Scenarios

A. GREETINGS AND INTRODUCTIONS

GREETING THE GUEST

EMPLOYEE

Good morning,...	***Buon giorno,...***	Bwohn JOHR-noh,...
• Mr. ____.	***• Signor ____.***	• see-NYOR ____.
• Mrs. ____.	***• Signora ____.***	• see-NYOR-ah ____.
• Miss ____.	***• Signorina ____.***	• see-NYOR-ee-nah ____.
• sir.	***• signore.***	• see-NYOR-eh.
• ma'am.	***• signora.***	• see-NYOR-ah.
• ladies and gentlemen.	***• signori e signore.***	• see-NYOR-ee eh see-NYOR-eh.
• everyone.	***• a tutti.***	• ah TOO-tee.

TIP! ••••

Most American employees are used to greeting guests jovially and asking them how they are. However, in any but the most informal settings, this behavior may actually be considered impolite. Asking guests how they are is stepping outside the bounds of your position and throws the burden onto the guest to answer you. Other cultures usually observe this principle to a much greater extent than we do.

Good afternoon, Mr. _____.	*Buon giorno, Signor _____.*	Bwohn JOHR-noh, see NYOR _____.
Good evening, Mr. _____.	*Buona sera, Signor _____.*	BWOH-nah SEH-rah, see-NYOR _____.
Hello, Mr. _____.	*Salve, Signor _____.*	SAHL-veh, see-NYOR _____.
Welcome to…	*Benvenuto/a…*	Behn-veh-NOO-toh/tah…
• the hotel.	• *all'albergo.*	• ahll ahl-BEHR-goh.
• the restaurant.	• *al ristorante.*	• ahl ree-stohr-AHN-teh.
• our city.	• *nella nostra città.*	• NEHL-lah NOH-strah chee-TAH.
• the United States.	• *negli Stati Uniti.*	• NEH-lyee STAH-tee oo-NEE-tee.
If there is anything I can do to make your stay more pleasant, please let me know.	*Se posso fare qualcosa per rendere la Sua permanenza più piacevole, me lo faccia sapere.*	Seh POHS-soh FAH-reh kwahl-KOH-zah pehr REHN-deh-reh lah SOO-ah pehr-mah-NEHN-tsah pyoo pee-ah-CHEH-voh-leh, meh loh FAH-chah sah-PEH-reh.
May I take your coat?	*Mi vuole dare il cappotto?*	Mee VWOH-leh DAH-reh eel kah-POH-toh?
Can I carry your…for you?	*Le posso portare…*	Leh POHS-soh pohr-TAH-reh…
• bags	• *le borse?*	• leh BOHR-seh?
• suitcase	• *la valigia?*	• lah vah-LEE-jah?
How are you today?	*Come sta?*	KOH-meh STAH?
GUEST		
I am…	*Sto…*	Stoh…
• fine, thank you.	• *bene, grazie.*	• BEH-neh, GRAH-tsee-eh.
• so-so.	• *così, così.*	• koh-ZEE, koh-ZEE.
• very tired.	• *molto stanco/a.*	• MOHL-toh STAHN-koh/kah.
I'm not feeling well.	*Non sto bene.*	Nohn STOH BEH-neh.
And you?	*E Lei?*	Eh LAY?

TIP! ••••

It is typical of American employees to introduce themselves to the guest. This practice allows the guest to call an employee by name when s/he needs something. This is not a common practice in other countries, however, so the international guest may simply ignore your introduction.

INTRODUCTIONS

EMPLOYEE

My name is _____.	***Mi chiamo _____.***	mee kee-YAH-moh _____.
I am your…	***Sono…***	SOH-noh…
• door attendant (doorman).	***• il portiere.***	• eel pohr-TYEH-reh.
• bell attendant (bellman).	***• il facchino.***	• eel fahk-KEE-noh.
• parking attendant.	***• il posteggiatore.***	• eel poh-stehjah-TOH-reh.
• driver.	***• l'autista.***	• lau-TEE-stah.
• captain.	***• il caposquadra dei facchini.***	• eel KAH-poh SKWAH-drah day fah-KEE-nee.
• concierge.	***• il portinaio.***	• eel pohr-tee-NAH-yoh.
• room attendant.	***• il/la cameriere/a.***	• eel/lah kah-mehr-YEHR-eh/ah.
• host.	***• l'albergatore** (hotel)/ **direttore di sala** (restaurant).*	• lahl-behr-gah-TO-reh/dee-reh-TOH-reh dee SAH-lah.
• hostess.	***• l'albergatrice** (hotel)/ **direttrice di sala** (restaurant).*	• lahl-behr-gah-TREE-cheh/dee-reh-TREE-cheh dee SAH-lah.

ITALIAN

• **manager.**	• ***il gestore/direttore d'albergo.***	• eel jeh-STOH-reh/ dee-reh-TOH-reh dahl-BEHR-goh.
• **server** (**waiter/ waitress**).	• ***il/la cameriere/a.***	• eel/lah kah-mehr-YEHR-eh/ah.
• **chef.**	• ***il capocuoco/chef.***	• eel kah-poh-KWOH-koh/chef.
• **activities director.**	• ***il capo animatore.***	• eel KAH-poh ah-nee-mah-TO-reh.
Mr. (Mrs., Miss) **____, this is Mr.** (Mrs., Miss) **____, the manager.**	***Signor*** *(Signora, Signorina)* ____, ***Le presento il Signor*** *(la Signora, la Signorina)*____, ***il/la direttore/direttrice.***	See-NYOHR (see-NYO-rah, see-nyo-REE-nah) ____, leh preh-SEHN-toh eel see-NYOHR (lah see-NYO-rah, lah see-nyo-REE-nah), ____, eel/lah dee reh-TOH-reh/TREE-cheh.
Mr. (Mrs., Miss) **____, may I introduce our manager, Mr.** (Mrs., Miss) **____?**	***Signor*** *(Signora, Signorina)* ____, ***Le posso presentare il/la nostro/a direttore/trice, Signor*** *(Signora, Signorina)* ____?	See-NYOHR (see-NYO-rah, see-nyo-REE-nah) ____, leh POHS-soh preh-sehn-TAH-reh eel/lah NOH-stroh/ah dee-reh-TOH-reh/TREE-cheh, see-NYOHR (see-NYO-rah, see-nyo-REE-nah) ____?

B. RESERVATIONS

HOTEL RESERVATIONS

OPERATOR

Good morning (afternoon, evening), **____ Hotel.**	***Buon giorno*** *(Buon pomeriggio, Buona sera),* ***Albergo*** ____.	Bwohn JOHR-noh (BWOHN poh-meh-REE-joh, BWOH-nah SEH-rah), ahl-BEHR-goh ____.
How may I direct your call?	***Con chi desidera parlare?***	Kohn KEE deh-ZEE-deh-RAH pahr-LAH-reh?

GUEST

Hello. Do you speak Italian?	*Pronto. Parla Italiano?*	PROHN-toh. PAHR-lah ee-tah-LYAH-noh?

OPERATOR

One moment, please.	*Un momento, per favore.*	Oon moh-MEHN-toh, pehr fah-VOH-reh.
I'll connect you with a bilingual operator.	*La metto in comunicazione con un centralinista bilingue.*	Lah MEH-toh een koh-moo-nee-kah-TSYOH-neh kohn oon chehn-trah-lee-NEE-stah bee-LEENG-weh.
I have a book here to help me.	*Ho qui un libro da consultare.*	Oh kwee oon LEE-broh dah kohn-sool-TAH-reh.
Please speak slowly.	*Parli lentamente per favore.*	PAHR-lee lehn-tah-MEHN-teh pehr fah-VOH-reh.

GUEST

I would like to make a reservation, please.	*Vorrei fare una prenotozione, per favore.*	Vohr-RAY FAH-reh OO-nah preh-noh-tah-TSYOH-neh, pehr fah-VOH-reh.

OPERATOR

For a room or for one of the restaurants?	*Per una camera o per uno dei ristoranti?*	Pehr OO-nah KAH-meh-rah oh pehr OO-noh day ree-stoh-RAHN-tee?

GUEST

For a room, please.	*Per una camera, per favore.*	Pehr OO-nah KAH-meh-rah, pehr fah-VOH-reh.
For the _____ Restaurant, please.	*Per il Ristorante _____, per favore.*	Pehr eel ree-stoh-RAHN-teh _____, pehr fah-VOH-reh.

OPERATOR

One moment, please. I will direct your call to Reservations.	*Un momento, per favore. La metto in contatto con l'Ufficio Prenotozioni.*	Oon moh-MEHN-toh, pehr fah-VOH-reh. Lah MEH-toh een kohn-TAH-toh kohn loo-FEE-chyoh preh-noh-tah-TSYOH-nee.

One moment, please. I will direct your call to the restaurant.	*Un momento, per favore. La metto in contatto con il ristorante.*	Oon moh-MEHN-toh, pehr fah-VOH-reh. Lah MEH-toh een kohn-TAH-toh kohn eel ree-stoh-RAHN-teh.
CLERK		
Hello. This is Reservations.	*Pronto. Ufficio Prenotozioni.*	PROHN-toh. Oo-FEE-chyoh preh-nohtah-TSYOH-nee.
What date would you like?	*Per quale data?*	Pehr KWAH-leh DAH-tah?
GUEST		
May 27th.	*Il ventisette maggio.*	Eel vehn-tee-SEH-teh MAH-joh.
CLERK		
For how many nights?	*Per quante notti?*	Pehr KWAHN-teh NOH-tee?
GUEST		
For three nights, please.	*Per tre notti, per favore.*	Pehr treh NOH-tee, pehr fah-VOH-reh.
For a week.	*Per una settimana.*	Pehr OO-nah seh-tee-MAH-nah.
Just one night.	*Solo per una notte.*	SOH-loh pehr OO-nah NOH-teh.
CLERK		
For how many people?	*Per quante persone?*	Pehr KWAHN-teh pehr-SOH-neh?
GUEST		
For two people.	*Per due persone.*	Pehr DOO-eh pehr-SOH-neh.
For one person.	*Per una persona.*	Pehr OO-nah pehr-SOH-nah.
For two adults and a child.	*Per due adulti e un bambino.*	Pehr DOO-eh ah-DOOL-tee eh oon bahm-BEE-noh.

CLERK

Do you have…	*Ha…*	Ah…
• any special needs?	• *delle esigenze particolari?*	• DEHL-leh eh-zee-JEHN-tseh pahr-tee-koh-LAH-ree?
• any special requests?	• *qualche richiesta particolare?*	• KWAHL-keh ree-KYEHS-tah pahr-tee-koh-LAH-reh?

GUEST

No, thank you.	*No, grazie.*	Noh, GRAH-tsyeh.
Yes, I would like…	*Sì, io vorrei…*	See, EE-yoh vohr-RAY…
• to be near the stairs.	• *una camera vicino alle scale.*	• OO-nah KAH-meh-rah vee-CHEE-noh AHL-leh SCAH-leh.
• to be near an exit.	• *una camera vicino ad una uscita.*	• OO-nah KAH-meh-rah vee-CHEE-noh ahd OO-nah oo-SHEE-tah.
• a cot for our child.	• *una branda per il nostro bambino.*	• oo-nah BRAHN-dah pehr eel NOH-stroh bahm-BEE-noh.
• a handicapped-accessible room.	• *una camera con accesso per handicappati.*	• OO-nah KAH-meh-rah kohn ah-CHEHS-soh pehr ahn-dee-kah-PAH-tee.

CLERK

The rate is ____ per night.	*La tariffa è ____ per notte.*	Lah tah-REEF-fah eh ____ pehr NOH-teh.
Would you like to guarantee the reservation with a credit card?	*Vorrebbe assicurare la prenotozione con una carta di credito?*	Vohr-REH-beh ahs-see-koo-RAH-reh lah preh-noh-tah-TSYOH-neh kohn OO-nah KAHR-tah dee KREH-dee-toh?

GUEST

Yes, here is my ____ card.	*Sì, ho una ____.*	See, oh OO-nah ____.

My credit card number is ____.	***Il numero della mia carta di credito è ____.***	Eel NOO-meh-roh DEHL-lah MEE-yah KAHR-tah dee KREH-dee-toh eh ____.
CLERK		
What is the expiration date?	***Qual è la data di scadenza?***	Kwahl EH lah DAH-tah dee skah-DEHN-tsah?
Thank you.	***Grazie.***	GRAH-tsyeh.

RESTAURANT RESERVATIONS

RESTAURANT HOST		
Good morning (afternoon, evening), ____ Restaurant.	*Buon giorno (buona sera), Ristorante ____.*	Bwohn JOHR-noh (BWOH-nah SEH-rah), ree stohr-AHN-teh ____.
GUEST		
I'd like to reserve a table for…	*Vorrei prenotare un tavolo per…*	Vohr-RAY preh-noh-TAH-reh oon TAH-voh-loh pehr…
• breakfast.	• *la (prima) colazione.*	• lah (PREE-mah) koh-lah-TSYOH-neh.
• lunch.	• *il pranzo.*	• eel PRAHN-tsoh.
• dinner.	• *la cena.*	• lah CHEH-nah.
HOST		
For what time?	*Per che ora?*	Pehr keh OH-rah?
GUEST		
For…o'clock.	*Per…*	Pehr…
• seven	• *le sette.*	• leh SEH-teh.
• eight	• *le otto.*	• leh OH-toh.
• nine	• *le nove.*	• leh NOH-veh.
For eight-thirty.	*Per le otto e mezzo.*	Pehr leh OH-toh eh MEH-dsoh.
HOST		
For how many people?	*Per quante persone?*	Pehr KWAHN-teh pehr-SOH-neh?

GUEST		
For one person.	*Per una persona.*	Pehr OO-nah pehr-SOH-nah.
For…people.	*Per…persone.*	Pehr…pehr-SOH-neh.
• two	• *due*	• DOO-eh
• four	• *quattro*	• KWAH-troh
• six	• *sei*	• say
HOST		
And your name, please?	*E il Suo nome, per favore?*	Eh eel SOO-oh NOH-meh, pehr fah-VOHR-eh?
GUEST		
My name is _____.	*Mi chiamo _____.*	Mee KYAH-moh _____.
HOST		
And is there a phone number where we can reach you?	*A quale numero di telefono La possiamo rintracciare?*	Ah KWAH-leh NOO-meh-roh dee teh-LEH-foh-noh lah pohs-SYAH-moh reen-trah-CHAH-reh?
GUEST		
Yes, the number is _____.	*Sì, al _____.*	See, ahl _____.
By the way, do you have any…items on the menu?	*A proposito, nel menù avete…*	Ah proh-POH-zee-toh, nehl meh-NOO ah-VEH-teh…
• vegetarian	• *piatti vegetariani?*	• PYAH-tee veh-jeh-tah-RYAH-nee?
• low-fat	• *piatti ipocalorici?*	• PYAH-tee ee-poh-kah-LOH-ree-chee?
• low-sodium	• *piatti a bassa quantità di sodio?*	• PYAH-tee ah BAHS-sah kwahn-tee-TAH dee SOH-dyoh?
HOST		
Would you like smoking or nonsmoking?	*Vuole un tavolo fumatori o non fumatori?*	VWOH-leh oon TAH-voh-loh foo-mah-TOH-ree oh nohn foo-mah-TOH-ree?

GUEST

We would like...	*Vorremmo un tavolo per...*	Vohr-REH-moh oon TAH-voh-loh pehr...
• smoking.	• *fumatori.*	• foo-mah-TOH-ree.
• nonsmoking.	• *non fumatori.*	• NOHN foo-mah-TOH-ree.

HOST

Thank you.	*Grazie.*	GRAH-tsyeh.
That will be two people at eight o'clock.	*D'accordo, un tavolo per due alle otto.*	Dah-KOHR-doh, oon TAH-voh-loh pehr DOO-eh AHL-leh OH-toh.
That's a party of six at seven-thirty.	*D'accordo, un tavolo per sei alle sette e mezza.*	Dah-KOHR-doh, oon TAH-voh-loh pehr say AHL-leh SEH-teh eh MEH-dsah.

C. COURTESY AND COMPLAINTS

GENERAL EXPRESSIONS OF COURTESY

Please.	***Per favore.***	Pehr fah-VOH-reh.
Thank you.	***Grazie.***	GRAH-tsyeh.
You're welcome.	***Prego.***	PREH-goh.
Excuse me.	***Mi scusi.***	Mee SKOO-zee.
I beg your pardon.	***Chiedo scusa.***	KYEH-doh SKOO-zah.
I'm (terribly) sorry.	***Mi dispiace (molto).***	Mee dee-SPYAH-cheh (MOHL-toh).
That's okay.	***Va bene.***	Vah BEH-neh.
No problem.	***Volentieri.***	Voh-lehn-TYEH-ree.
It doesn't matter.	***Non importa.***	Nohn eem-POHR-tah.

COURTESY IN THE HOTEL

CONCIERGE

Good morning, sir, ma'am.	***Buon giorno, signore, signora.***	Bwohn JOHR-noh, see-NYOHR-yeh, see-NYOHR-yah.
May I help you with something today?	***Posso esserLe di aiuto?***	POHS-soh EHS-sehr-leh dee ah-YOO-toh?

GUEST

Yes, I need…	*Sì, avrei bisogno di…*	See, ah-VRAY bee-ZOH-nyoh dee…
• my room made up between now and ____.	• *di avere la camera rifatta entro le ____.*	• dee ah-VEH-reh lah CAH-meh-rah ree-FAH-tah EHN-troh leh ____.
• more towels, please.	• *altri asciugamani.*	• AHL-tree ah-shoo-gah-MAH-nee.
• a rental car.	• *una macchina da noleggiare.*	• OO-nah MAH-kee-nah dah noh-leh-JAH-reh.
• a taxi.	• *un taxi.*	• oon TAHK-see.
• a fax sent.	• *mandare un fax.*	• mahn-DAH-reh oon fahks.
• some letters mailed.	• *imbucare delle lettere.*	• eem-boo-KAH-reh DEHL-leh LEH-teh-reh.
• to make arrangements for a business meeting.	• *organizzare una riunione di affari.*	• or-gah-nee-DSAH-reh oo-nah ree-oo-NYOH-neh dee ahf-FAH-ree.
• tickets to a show.	• *biglietti per uno spettacolo.*	• bee-LYEH-tee pehr OO-noh speh-TAH-koh-loh.
• tickets to a concert.	• *biglietti per un concerto.*	• bee-LYEH-tee pehr oon kohn-CHEHR-toh.
• tickets to a game.	• *biglietti per una partita.*	• bee-LYEH-tee pehr OO-nah pahr-TEE-tah.

GUEST COMPLAINTS IN THE HOTEL

CONCIERGE

Is everything satisfactory?	*È tutto a posto?*	Eh TOO-toh ah POH-stoh?

GUEST

No, there is a problem.	*No, c'è un problema.*	Noh, cheh oon proh-BLEH-mah.
• The light	• *La luce*	• Lah LOO-cheh

ITALIAN

• The toilet	• *La toilette*	• Lah twah-LEHT
• The television	• *Il televisore*	• Eeel teh-leh-vee-ZOH-reh
• The radio	• *La radio*	• Lah RAH-dee-oh
• The air-conditioning	• *L'aria condizionata*	• LAH-ryah kohn-dee-tsyoh-NAH-tah
• The alarm clock	• *La sveglia*	• Lah ZVEH-lyah
• The heat	• *Il riscaldamento*	• Eel ree-skahl-dah-MEHN-toh
• The key	• *La chiave*	• Lah KYAH-veh
• The lock	• *La serratura*	• Lah sehr-rah-TOO-rah
• The fan	• *Il ventilatore*	• Eel vehn-tee-lah-TOH-reh
...doesn't work.	*...non funziona.*	...nohn foon-TSYOH-nah.
CLERK		
I'll have Maintenance fix that right away.	*Mando subito qualcuno a ripararlo/la.*	MAHN-doh SOO-bee-toh KWAHL-koo-noh ah ree-pah-RAHR-loh/lah.
I apologize.	*Mi dispiace.*	Mee dee-SPYAH-cheh.
GUEST		
My room...	***La camera...***	Lah KAH-meh-rah...
• wasn't clean.	**• *non era pulita.***	• nohn EH-rah poo-LEE-tah.
• was noisy.	**• *era rumorosa.***	• EH-rah roo-moh-ROH-zah.
• was too small.	**• *era troppo piccola.***	• EH-rah TROH-poh PEE-koh-lah.
My room stinks (smells).	***C'è un cattivo odore in camera.***	Cheh oon kah-TEE-voh oh-DOH-reh een KAH-meh-rah.
The bed was uncomfortable.	***Il letto era scomodo.***	Eel LEH-toh EH-rah SKOH-moh-doh.
The water wasn't hot.	***Non c'era l'acqua calda.***	Nohn CHEH-rah LAH-kwah KAHL-dah.

Room service was slow.	*Il servizio in camera era lento.*	Eel sehr-VEE-tsyoh een KAH-meh-rah EH-rah LEHN-toh.
The service was very poor.	*Il servizio è stato pessimo.*	Eel sehr-VEE-tsyoh EH STAH-toh PEHS-see-moh.
The employees were…	*Il personale è stato…*	Eel pehr-soh-NAH-leh EH STAH-toh…
• very good.	• *ottimo.*	• OH-tee-moh.
• excellent.	• *eccellente.*	• eh-cheh-LEHN-teh.
• rude.	• *scortese.*	• skohr-TEH-zeh.
• incompetent.	• *incompetente.*	• een-kohm-peh-TEHN-teh.
• unfriendly.	• *antipatico.*	• ahn-tee-PAH-tee-koh.
I didn't receive my wake-up call.	*Non mi hanno svegliato.*	Nohn mee AHN-noh zveh-LYAH-toh.
I'm very disappointed with the level of service in this hotel.	*Sono molto scontento/a della scarsa qualità del servizio in questo albergo.*	SOH-noh MOHL-toh skohn-TEHN-toh/tah DEHL-lah SKAHR-sah kwah-lee-TAH dehl sehr-VEE-tsyoh een KWEH-stoh ahl-BEHR-goh.
This is the worst hotel I've ever seen.	*Questo è il peggior albergoin cui io sia mai stato/a.*	KWEH-stoh eh eel peh-JOHR ahl-BEHR-goh een KOO-ee EE-oh SEE-ah mai STAH-toh/tah.

CONCIERGE

Please let me make the situation right.	*Per favore, mi permetta di rimediare.*	Pehr fah-VOH-reh, mee pehr-MEH-tah dee ree-meh-DYAH-reh.
I'm certain we can straighten out the problem.	*Sono sicuro/a che possiamo trovare una soluzione.*	SOH-noh see-KOO-roh/rah keh pohs-SYAH-moh troh-VAH-reh OO-nah soh-loo-TSYOH-neh.
You won't pay for anything that wasn't completely up to your standards.	*Non dovrà pagare per quello che non l'ha soddisfatto.*	Nohn doh-VRAH pah-GAH-reh pehr KWEHL-loh keh nohn lah sohd-dees-FAHT-toh.

ITALIAN

Please tell me what I can do to correct this terrible situation.	*Per favore, mi dica cosa posso fare per rimediare a questo problema.*	Pehr fah-VOH-reh, mee DEE-kah KOH-zah POHS-soh FAH-reh pehr ree-meh-DYAH-reh ah KWEH-stoh proh-BLEH-mah.
We'll take ____ percent off your bill.	*Le faremo uno sconto del ____ percento.*	Leh fah-REH-moh OO-noh SKOHN-toh dehl ____ pehr-CHEHN-toh.
We're going to give you ____ night(s), compliments of the hotel.	*Le offriamo ____ notte/i a nostre spese.*	Leh ohf-free-YAH-moh ____ NOH-teh/tee ah NOH-streh SPEH-zeh.
Your entire bill is compliments of the house.	*Pagheremo per tutto.*	Pah-geh-REH-moh pehr TOO-toh.

GUEST

Yes, that would be satisfactory.	*Sì, cosí andrebbe bene.*	See, koh-ZEE ahn-DREH-beh BEH-neh.
No, that would not be satisfactory.	*No, non va bene.*	Noh, nohn vah BEH-neh.
I appreciate all your efforts.	*La ringrazio per quello che ha fatto.*	Lah reen-GRAH-tsyoh pehr KWEHL-loh keh ah FAH-toh.
Thank you, that would be very nice.	*Grazie, sarebbe molto gentile.*	GRAH-tsyeh, sah-REH-beh MOHL-toh jehn-TEE-leh.
I will never come here again.	*Non ci tornerò mai più.*	Nohn chee tohr-neh-ROH mai PYOO.

MANAGEMENT COMPLAINTS

MANAGER

We have had some complaints about the noise coming from your room.	*Ci hanno informato che provengono rumori dalla Sua camera.*	Chee AHN-noh een-fohr-MAH-toh keh proh-VEHN-goh-noh roo-MOH-ree DAHL-lah SOO-ah KAH-meh-rah.
You are disturbing…	*Disturba…*	Dee-STOOR-bah…

• the people in the room next door.	• *gli ospiti della camera accanto.*	• lyee OH-spee-tee DEHL-lah KAH-meh-rah ah-KAHN-toh.
• the people at the next table.	• *le persone al tavolo accanto.*	• leh pehr-SOH-neh ahl TAH-voh-loh ah-KAHN-toh.
• our other guests.	• *gli altri ospiti.*	• lyee AHL-tree OH-spee-tee.

GUEST

We're sorry.	*Ci dispiace.*	Chee dee-SPYAH-cheh.
We understand.	*Capiamo.*	Kah-PYAH-moh.
We'll take care of it.	*Ce ne occupiamo noi.*	Cheh neh oh-koo-PYAH-moh NOY.
We'll keep it down from now on.	*Non faremo più rumore.*	Nohn fah-REH-moh PYOO roo-MOH-reh.
Who cares!	*Chi se ne importa!*	Kee seh neh eem-POHR-tah!
Leave us alone!	*Ci lasci stare!*	Chee LAH-shee STAH-reh!

MANAGER

If you don't cooperate, I'm afraid I'll have to…	*Se non collaborate, sarò purtroppo costretto a…*	Seh nohn coh-lah-boh-RAH-teh, sah-ROH poor-TROH-poh koh-STREH-toh ah…
• ask you to leave the hotel (restaurant).	• *chiedervi di lasciare l'albergo* (*il ristorante*).	• KYEH-dehr-vee dee lah-SHAH-reh lahl-BEHR-goh (eel ree-stoh-RAHN-teh).
• call security.	• *chiamare la sicurezza.*	• kyah-MAH-reh lah see-koo-REH-tsah.
• call the police.	• *chiamare la polizia.*	• kyah-MAH-reh lah poh-leeTSEE-yah.

D. EMERGENCIES AND SAFETY

EMPLOYEE

Please note the emergency exits on this card.	*Per favore, individui le uscite di emergenza su questo cartello.*	Pehr fah-VOH-reh, een-dee-VEE-dwee leh oo-SHEE-teh dee eh-mehr-JEHN-tsah soo KWEH-stoh cahr-TEHL-loh.

Please note the emergency escape route on the door.	*Per favore, individui il percorso delle uscite di emergenza sulla porta.*	Pehr fah-VOH-reh, een-dee-VEE-dwee eel pehr-KOHR-soh DEHL-leh oo-SHEE-teh dee eh-mehr-JEHN-tsah SOOL-lah POHR-tah.
Your room is equipped with smoke alarms.	*La Sua camera è fornita di segnalatori di incendio.*	Lah SOO-ah KAH-meh-rah eh fohr-NEE-tah dee seh-nyah-lah TOH-ree dee een-CHEHN-dyoh.
Here is the fire alarm.	*Ecco il segnalatore di incendio.*	EH-koh eel seh-nyah-lah-TOH-reh dee een-CHEHN-dyoh.
In an emergency, dial _____.	*In caso di emergenza, faccia il numero _____.*	Een KAH-zoh dee eh-mehr-JEHN-zah, FAH-chah eel NOO-meh-roh _____.

GUEST

Help!	*Aiuto!*	Ah-YOO-toh!
Fire!	*Fuoco!*	FWOH-koh!
I need a doctor.	*Ho bisogno di un dottore.*	Oh bee-ZOH-nyoh dee oon doh-TOH-reh.
I'm…	*Sto…*	Stoh…
My husband (wife) is…	*Mio marito (mia moglie) sta…*	MEE-oh mah-REE-toh (MEE-ah MOH-lyeh) stah…
Someone is…	*Qualcuno sta…*	Kwahl-KOO-noh stah…
• very sick.	• *molto male.*	• MOHL-toh MAH-leh.
• having a heart attack.	• *subendo un attacco al cuore.*	• soo-BEHN-doh oon ah-TAH-koh ahl KWOH-reh.
• choking.	• *soffocando.*	• soh-foh-KAHN-doh.
• losing consciousness.	• *svenendo.*	• zveh-NEHN-doh.
• about to vomit.	• *per vomitare.*	• pehr voh-mee-TAH-reh.

• having a seizure.	• *subendo un attacco epileptico.*	• soo-BEHN-doh oon ah-TAH-koh eh-pee-LEHP-tee-koh.
I'm stuck.	*Sono bloccato/a.*	SOH-noh bloh-KAH-toh/tah.
I can't breathe.	*Non posso respirare.*	Nohn POHS-soh reh-spee-RAH-reh.
MANAGER		
I'll call an ambulance.	*Chiamo l'ambulanza.*	KYAH-moh lahm-boo-LAHN-tsah.
Don't move.	*Non si muova.*	Nohn see MUOH-vah.
The doctor will be here very soon.	*Il dottore arriva subito.*	Eel doh-TOH-reh ahr-REE-vah SOO-bee-toh.
What happened?	*Che è successo?*	Keh eh soo-CHEHS-soh?
GUEST		
I fell.	*Sono caduto/a.*	SOH-nohkah-DOO-toh/tah.
I cut myself.	*Mi sono tagliato/a.*	Mee SOH-noh tah-LYAH-toh/tah.
I drank too much.	*Ho bevuto troppo.*	Oh beh-VOO-toh TROH-poh.
I don't know.	*Non lo so.*	Nohn loh SOH.
I hit my head.	*Ho battuto la testa.*	Oh bah-TOO-toh lah TEH-stah.
I've injured my…	*Mi sono fatto/a male…*	Mee SOH-noh FAH-toh/tah MAH-leh…
• neck.	• *al collo.*	• ahl KOHL-loh.
• back.	• *alla schiena.*	• AHL-lah skee-YEH-nah.
• arm.	• *al braccio.*	• ahl BRAH-choh.
• leg.	• *alla gamba.*	• AHL-lah GAHM-bah.
• foot.	• *al piede.*	• ahl PYEH-deh.
• eye.	• *all'occhio.*	• ahll-OH-kyoh.

DOCTOR (MEDICAL TECHNICIAN)

You'll be fine; try to relax.	*Starà meglio; cerchi di stare tranquillo/a.*	Stah-RAH MEH-lyoh; CHEHR-kee dee STAH-reh trahn-KWEEL-loh/lah.
We're taking you to the hospital.	*La portiamo in ospedale.*	Lah pohr-TYAH-moh een oh-speh-DAH-leh.
Whom should we notify?	*Chi dobbiamo avvisare?*	Kee doh-BYAH-moh ahv-vee-ZAH-reh?

GUEST

I've been robbed.	***Sono stato/a derubato/a.***	SOH-noh STAH-toh/tah deh-roo-BAH-toh/tah.

MANAGER

What did they take?	***Cosa hanno preso?***	KOH-zah AHN-noh PREH-zoh?
Let me call the police.	***Mi faccia chiamare la polizia.***	Mee FAH-chah kyah-MAH-reh lah poh-lee-TSEE-ah.
Attention, ladies and gentlemen.	***Attenzione, signore e signori.***	Ah-tehn-TSYOH-neh, see-NYOH-reh eh see-NYOH-ree.
May I have your attention, please?	***La vostra attenzione, per favore?***	Lah VOH-strah ah-tehn-TSYOH-neh, pehr fah-VOH-reh?
Please...	***Per favore...***	Pehr fah-VOH-reh...
• remain calm.	***• rimanete calmi.***	• ree-mah-NEH-teh KAHL-mee.
• follow the instructions of the staff.	***• seguite le istruzioni del personale.***	• seh-GWEE-teh leh ees-troo-TSYOH-nee dehl pehr-soh-NAH-leh.
• wait in your rooms.	***• rimanete nelle vostre camere.***	• ree-mah-NEH-teh NEHL-leh VOH-streh KAH-meh-reh.
• get under a table or doorway.	***• mettetevi sotto un tavolo o nel vano di una porta.***	• MEHT-teh-teh-vee SOH-toh oon TAH-voh-loh oh nehl VAH-noh dee OO-nah POR-tah.

• follow the evacuation plan printed on your door (in the hallways).	***• seguite il piano di evacuazione che è sulle porte delle vostre camere*** *(nei corridoi).*	• seh-GWEE-teh eel PYAH-noh dee eh-vah-koo-ah-TSYOH-neh keh EH SOOL-leh POHR-teh DEHL-leh VOH-streh KAH-meh-reh (nay koh-ree-DOY-ee).
We'll have the situation under control as soon as possible.	***Avremo la situazione sotto controllo il più presto possibile.***	Ah-VREH-moh lah see-too-ah-TSYOH-neh SOH-toh kohn-TROHL-loh eel PYOO PREH-stoh poh-SEE-bee-leh.
Thank you for your patience.	***Grazie per la vostra pazienza.***	GRAH-tsyeh pehr lah VOH-strah pah-tsee-EHN-tsah.

4. Checking In

A. AT THE FRONT DESK

FRONT DESK CLERK

Hello.	*Buon giorno.*	Bwohn JOHR-noh.
How may I help you?	*Desidera?*	Deh-ZEE-deh-rah?

GUEST

I have a reservation under the name ____.	*Ho una prenotazione a nome ____.*	Oh OO-nah preh-noh-tah-TSYOH-neh ah NOH-meh ____.
Do you have a room for one (two)?	*Avete una camera singola (doppia)?*	Ah-VEH-teh OO-nah KAH-meh-rah SEEN-goh-lah (DOH-pyah?)

CLERK

Yes, we have your reservation.	*Sì, abbiamo la Sua prenotazione.*	SEE, ah-BYAH-moh lah SOO-ah preh-noh-tah-TSYOH-neh.
Yes, for how many nights?	*Sì, per quante notti?*	SEE, pehr KWAHN-teh NOH-tee?

English	Italian	Pronunciation
No, I'm sorry, we're full.	*No, mi dispiace. Siamo completi.*	NOH, mee dee-SPYAH-cheh. SYAH-moh kohm-PLEH-tee.
GUEST		
For ____ night(s), please.	*Per ____ notte(i), per favore.*	Pehr ____ NOH-teh(tee), pehr fah-VOH-reh.
What are your rates?	*Quali sono le tariffe?*	KWAH-lee SOH-noh leh tah-REEF-feh?
CLERK		
• For a single…	• *Per una singola…*	• Pehr OO-nah SEEN-goh-lah…
• For a double…	• *Per una doppia…*	• Pehr OO-nah DOH-pyah…
• For adjoining rooms…	• *Per camere comunicanti…*	• Pehr KAH-meh-reh koh-moo-nee-KAHN-tee…
• For a suite…	• *Per una suite…*	• Pehr OO-nah suite…
…the rate is ____ per night.	*…la tariffa è ____ per notte.*	…lah tah-REEF-fah EH ____ pehr NOH-teh.
GUEST		
Are any meals included?	*Sono inclusi i pasti?*	SOH-noh een-KLOO-zee ee PAH-stee.
Is breakfast included?	*È inclusa la prima colazione?*	EH een-KLOO-zah lah PREE-mah koh-lah-TSYOH-neh?
CLERK		
No, meals are extra.	*No, non sono inclusi i pasti.*	NOH, nohn SOH-noh een-KLOO-zee ee PAH-stee.
Yes, breakfast is included.	*Sì, la prima colazione è inclusa.*	SEE, lah PREE-mah koh-lah-TSYOH-neh EH een-KLOO-zah.

You can choose…	*Può scegliere…*	PWOH SHEH-lyeh-reh…
• the American plan (all meals included).	• *il programma americano (pasti compresi).*	• eel proh-GRAHM-mah ah-meh-ree-KAH-noh (PAH-stee kohm-PREH-zee).
• the modified American plan (breakfast and dinner).	• *il programma americano modificato (prima colazione/ pranzo inclusi).*	• eel proh-GRAHM-mah ah-meh-ree-KAH-noh moh-dee-fee-KAH-toh (PREE-mah koh-lah-TSYOH-neh /PRAHN-tsoh een-KLOO-zee).
• the European plan (no meals included).	• *il programma europeo (senza vitto).*	• eel proh-GRAHM-mah eh-oo-roh-PEH-oh (SEHN-tsah VEE-toh).

GUEST

I'd like a room…	*Vorrei una camera…*	Vohr-RAY OO-nah KAH-meh-rah…
• that faces the back (front).	• *sul retro (sul davanti).*	• sool REH-troh (sool dah-VAHN-tee).
• that faces the pool.	• *di fronte alla piscina.*	• dee FROHN-teh AHL-lah pee-SHEE-nah.
• with a private bath/ shower.	• *con bagno e doccia.*	• kohn BAH-nyoh eh DOH-chah.
• with a handicapped-accessible bathroom.	• *con un bagno accessibile agli handicappati.*	• kohn oon BAH-nyoh ah-chehs-SEE-bee-leh AH-lyee ahn-dee-kah-PAH-tee.
• with air-conditioning.	• *con l'aria condizionata.*	• kohn LAH-ree-ah kohn-dee-tsyoh-NAH-tah.
• with a TV.	• *col televisore.*	• kohl teh-leh-vee-ZOH-reh.
• with cable.	• *col televisore via cavo.*	• kohl teh-leh-vee-ZOH-rehVEE-ah KAH-voh.

• with a fax machine.	• *con fax.*	• kohn FAH-ks.
• with a phone.	• *con telefono.*	• kohn teh-LEH-foh-noh.
• with a network hookup for my computer.	• *con un collegamento per il computer.*	• kohn oon kohl-leh-gah-MEHN-toh pehr eel computer.
• with a view.	• *con una bella vista.*	• kohn OO-nah BEHL-lah VEE-stah.
• with a whirlpool bath/Jacuzzi.	• *con una vasca a idromassaggio/ Jacuzzi.*	• kohn OO-nah VAH-skah ah ee-droh-mahs-SAH-joh/yah-KOO-tsee.
• with two double beds.	• *con due letti doppi.*	• kohn DOO-eh LEH-tee DOH-pyee.
• with a king-size bed.	• *con un letto doppio molto grande.*	• kohn oon LEH-toh DOH-pyoh MOHL-toh GRAHN-deh.
• with an extra bed.	• *con un letto in più.*	• kohn oon LEH-toh een PYOO.
• with a baby crib.	• *con un lettino.*	• kohn oon leh-TEE-noh.
• with a balcony.	• *con un balcone.*	• kohn oon bahl-KOH-neh.
• with a sitting area.	• *con un salotto.*	• kohn oon sah-LOH-toh.
• with a bar.	• *con bar.*	• kohn bar.
• with a kitchenette.	• *con angolo cottura.*	• kohn AHN-goh-loh koh-TOO-rah.
• away from the elevator.	• *lontano dall'ascensore.*	• lohn-TAH-noh dahl-lah-shehn-SOH-reh.
• with no meals.	• *senza pasti.*	• SEHN-tsah PAH-stee.

CLERK

No problem.	*Va bene.*	Vah BEH-neh.
I'm sorry.	*Mi dispiace.*	Mee dee-SPYAH-cheh.
There is none available.	*Non ce n'è.*	Nohn cheh NEH.
We don't offer that.	*Non offriamo questo servizio.*	Nohn ohf-FRYAH-moh KWEH-stoh sehr-VEE-zyoh.

GUEST

Does the hotel have…	*C'è…in albergo?*	Cheh…een ahl-BEHR-goh?
• a restaurant?	• *un ristorante*	• oon ree-stoh-RAHN-teh
• a bar?	• *un bar*	• oon bar
• room service?	• *servizio in camera*	• sehr-VEE-tsyoh een KAH-meh-rah
• a gym/health club?	• *una palestra*	• OO-nah pah-LEH-strah
• a spa hot tub?	• *una vasca a idromassaggio*	• OO-nah VAH-skah ah ee-droh-mahs-SAH-joh
• a swimming pool?	• *una piscina*	• OO-nah pee-SHEE-nah
• baby-sitting?	• *un servizio "baby-sitting"*	• oon sehr-VEE-tsyoh "baby-sitting"
• tennis courts?	• *un campo da tennis*	• oon KAHM-poh dah TEHN-nees
• laundry service (dry-cleaning)?	• *una lavanderia/lavaggio a secco*	• OO-nah lah-vahn-deh-REE-ah/lah-VAH-joh ah SEH-koh
• a garage?	• *un garage*	• oon garage
May I see the room?	• *Potrei vedere la camera?*	• Poh-TRAY veh-DEH-reh lah KAH-meh-rah?

CLERK

Yes, certainly. Here's the key.	*Sì, certo. Ecco la chiave.*	SEE, CHEHR-toh. EH-koh lah KYAH-veh.
Would you like another room?	*Vorrebbe un'altra camera?*	Vohr-REH-beh oon-AHL-trah KAH-meh-rah?

GUEST

I'd like something…	*Vorrei qualcosa di…*	Vohr-RAY kqahl-KOH-zah dee…
• smaller.	• *più piccolo.*	• PYOO PEE-koh-loh.

• larger.	• *più grande.*	• PYOO GRAHN-deh.
• quieter.	• *più silenzioso.*	• PYOO see-lehn-TSYOH-zoh.
• better.	• *più bello.*	• PYOO BEHL-loh.
• cheaper.	• *meno costoso.*	• MEH-noh koh-STOH-zoh.
• on another floor.	• *su un altro piano.*	• soo oon AHL-troh PYAH-noh.
I'll take the room, please.	*Prendo la camera, grazie.*	PREHN-doh lah KAH-meh-rah, GRAH-tsyeh.
CLERK		
Very well, how will you be paying?	*Bene, come vuole pagare?*	BEH-neh, KOH-meh VWOH-leh pah-GAH-reh?
GUEST		
I'll pay with…	*Pago con…*	PAH-goh kohn…
• cash.	• *contati.*	• kohn-TAHN-tee.
• a credit card.	• *carta di credito.*	• KAHR-tah dee KREH-dee-toh.
• traveler's checks.	• *"traveler's checks."*	• "traveler's checks."
CLERK		
Thank you.	*Grazie.*	GRAH-tsyeh.
To charge meals and services to your room, I'll need a credit card.	*Per addebitare i pasti e servizio alla Sua camera, avrei bisogno di una carta di credito.*	Pehr ah-deh-bee-TAH-reh ee PAH-stee eh sehr-VEE-tsyoh AHL-lah SOO-ah KAH-meh-rah, ah-VRAY bee-ZOH-nyoh dee oo-nah KAHR-tah dee KREH-dee-toh.
You may settle the bill with traveler's checks (cash).	*Può pagare il conto con traveler's checks (contanti).*	PWOH pah-GAH-reh eel KOHN-toh kohn traveler's checks (kohn-TAHN-tee).

If you would like to store valuables, we have a safe.	*Se desidera depositare oggetti preziosi, abbiamo una cassaforte.*	Seh deh-ZEE-deh-rah deh-poh-zee-TAH-reh oh-JEH-tee preh-TSYOH-zee, ah-BYAH-moh OO-nah kahs-sah-FOHR-teh.
Please note that…	*Noti per favore che…*	NOH-tee pehr-fah-VOH-reh keh…
• quiet hours are between_____ and _____.	• *è richiesto silenzio tra le _____ e le _____.*	• EH ree-KYEH-stoh eel see-LEHN-tsyoh trah leh _____ eh leh _____.
• there are no pets allowed.	• *non sono ammessi animali domestici.*	• nohn SOH-noh ahm-MEHS-see ah-nee-MAH-leedoh-MEH-stee-chee.
• children under _____ stay free.	• *i bambini di età inferiore a _____ anni non pagano.*	• ee bahm-BEE-nee dee eh-TAH een-feh-ree-OH-reh ah _____ AHN-nee nohn PAH-gah-noh.
• smoking is allowed only in the bar.	• *si può fumare solo al bar.*	• see PWOH foo-MAH-reh SOH-loh ahl bar.
• we do not allow cooking in the rooms.	• *è vietato cucinare in camera.*	• EH vee-eh-TAH-toh koo-chee-NAH-reh een KAH-meh-rah.

GUEST

Do I (we) have any messages?	*Ci sono dei messaggi per me (per noi)?*	Chee SOH-noh day mehs-SAH-jee pehr MEH (pehr NOY)?
I would like a wake-up call, please.	*Vorrei la sveglia, per favore.*	Vohr-RAY lah ZVEH-lyah,pehr-fah-VOH-reh.
May we have…, please?	*Potremmo avere…, per favore?*	Poh-TREH-moh ah-VEH-reh…, pehr fah-VOH-reh?
• extra blankets	• *altre coperte*	• AHL-treh koh-PEHR-teh

• extra towels	• *altri asciugamani*	• AHL-tree ah-shoo-gah-MAH-nee
• a hair dryer	• *un asciugacapelli*	• oon ah-shoo-gah-kah-PEHL-lee
• an iron	• *un ferro*	• oon FEHR-roh
• ice	• *del ghiaccio*	• dehl GYAH-choh
CLERK		
I'll have that brought to your room right away.	*Lo faccio mandare subito alla Sua camera.*	Loh FAH-choh mahn-DAH-reh SOO-bee-toh AHL-lah SOO-ah KAH-meh-rah.
GUEST		
Where is…	*Dov'è…*	Doh-VEH…
• the room attendant?	• *il/la cameriere/a?*	• eel/lah kah-mehr-YEH-reh/rah?
• the bellman (bell attendant)?	• *il facchino?*	• eel fah-KEE-noh?
• the manager?	• *il direttore di albergo?*	• eel dee-reh-TOH-reh dee ahl-BEHR-goh?
• the dining room?	• *la sala da pranzo?*	• lah SAH-lah dah PRAHN-tsoh?
• the gift shop?	• *il negozio di articoli da regalo?*	• eel neh-GOH-tsyoh dee ahr-TEE-koh-lee dah reh-GAH-loh?
• the newsstand?	• *l'edicola?*	• leh-DEE-koh-lah?
CLERK		
Just over there.	*Proprio là.*	PROH-pree-oh LAH.
GUEST		
How do I use the telephone?	*Come si usa il telefono?*	KOH-meh see OO-zah eel teh-LEH-foh-noh?
CLERK		
The instructions are next to the phone.	*Ci sono le istruzioni accanto al telefono.*	Chee SOH-noh leh ee-stroo-TSYOH-nee ah-KAHN-toh ahl teh-LEH-foh-noh.

Dial ____ for a local (long-distance) call,	*Faccia ____ per una telefonata urbana (interurbana),*	FAH-chah ____ pehr OO-nah teh-leh-foh-NAH-tah oor-BAH-nah (een-tehr-oor-BAH-nah),
wait for the tone,	*aspetti il segnale acustico,*	ah-SPEH-tee eel seh-NYAH-leh ah-KOO-stee-koh,
then dial the number.	*poi faccia il numero.*	POY FAH-chah eel NOO-meh-roh.
Dial ____ for an operator.	*Faccia ____ per parlare con un centralinista.*	FAH-chah ____ pehr pahr-LAH-reh kohn oon chehn-trah-lee-NEE-stah.
To use a credit card, dial ____.	*Per usare la carta di credito, faccia ____.*	Pehr oo-ZAH-reh lah KAHR-tah dee KREH-dee-toh, FAH-chah ____.
GUEST		
Please have our luggage brought to our room.	*Vorremmo che i nostri bagagli fossero portati in camera, per favore.*	Vohr-REHM-moh keh ee NOH-stree bah-GAH-lyee FOHS-seh-roh pohr-TAH-tee een KAH-meh-rah, pehr fah-VOH-reh.
We'll need a wheelchair.	*Abbiamo bisogno di una sedia a rotelle.*	Ah-BYAH-moh bee-ZOH-nyoh dee OO-nah SEH-dyah ah roh-TEHL-leh.
CLERK		
Yes, right away.	*Sì, subito.*	SEE, SOO-bee-toh.
GUEST		
We'd like to order a pizza, please.	*Vorremmo ordinare una pizza, per favore.*	Vohr-REHM-moh ohr-dee-NAH-reh OO-nah PEE-tsah, pehr fah-VOH-reh.
MANAGER		
I'll be happy to call someone for you.	*Chiamo volentieri per Lei.*	KYAH-moh voh-lehn-TYEH-ree pehr LAY.

We have room service, but we don't allow outside vendors into the hotel.	*Abbiamo servizio in camera, ma non permettiamo venditori in albergo.*	Ah-BYAH-moh sehr-VEE-tsyoh een KAH-meh-rah, mah nohn pehr-meh-TYAH-moh vehn-dee-TOH-ree een ahl-BEHR-goh.

GUEST

We'd like to entertain a few friends in our room.	*Vorremmo ospitare qualche amico in camera nostra.*	Vohr-REHM-moh ohs-pee-TAH-reh KWAHL-keh ah-MEE-coh een KAH-meh-rah NOH-strah.

MANAGER

We allow guests in the rooms until ____.	*Le ore di visita finiscono alle ____.*	Leh OH-reh dee VEE-zee-tah fee-NEE-skoh-noh AHL-leh ____.

B. SHOWING GUESTS TO THEIR ROOMS

BELLMAN (BELL ATTENDANT)

My name is ____, and I'm your bell attendant.	*Mi chiamo ____, e sono il facchino.*	Mee KYAH-moh ____, eh SOH-noh eel fah-KEE-noh.
May I show you to your room?	*Posso accompagnarvi in camera?*	POHS-soh ah-kohm-pah-NYAR-vee een KAH-meh-rah?

GUEST

No, thanks. We'll find it ourselves.	*No, grazie. La troviamo noi.*	Noh, GRAH-tsyeh. Lah troh-VYAH-moh NOY.
Yes, please.	*Sì, grazie.*	SEE, GRAH-tsyeh.

BELLMAN

This way, please.	*Di qua, prego.*	Dee KWAH, PREH-goh.
The elevator is over here.	*L'ascensore è di qua.*	Lah-shehn-SOH-reh EH dee KWAH.
May I show you the features of your room?	*Posso mostrarvi i vari servizi disponibili nella vostra camera?*	POHS-soh moh-STRAHR-vee ee VAR-ee sehr-VEE-tsee dee-spoh-NEE-bee-lee NEL-lah VOH-strah KAH-meh-rah?

This is the key to the minibar.	*Questa è la chiave del mini-bar.*	KWEH-stah EH lah KYAH-veh dehl MEE-nee-BAR.
• Any movie you select…	• *Se scegliete un film…*	• Seh sheh-LYEH-teh oon FEELM…
• Any long-distance calls you make…	• *Se fate una telefonata interurbana…*	• Seh FAH-teh OO-nah teh-leh-foh-NAH-tah een-tehr-oor-BAH-nah…
• Any snack or beverage you take from the refrigerator…	• *Se prendete uno snack dal frigo…*	• Seh prehn-DEH-teh OO-noh snack dahl FREE-goh…
…will be charged to your room.	*…sarà addebitato alla vostra camera.*	…sah-RAH ah-deh-bee-TAH-toh AHL-lah VOH-strah KAH-meh-rah.
Here is the control for the heating.	*Ecco il pannello per il riscaldamento.*	EH-koh eel pahn-NEHL-loh pehr eel ree-skahl-dah-MEHN-toh.

GUEST

How do I call Room Service?	*Come faccio a chiamare il servizio in camera?*	KOH-meh FAH-choh ah kyah-MAH-reh eel sehr-VEE-tsyoh een KAH-meh-rah?

TIP! ••••

International guests in particular may have questions about using the telephone and will appreciate seeing how the television and pay movies work.

BELLMAN

Dial ____.	*Faccia il ____.*	FAH-chah eel ____.

GUEST

This room…	*Questa camera…*	KWEH-stah KAH-meh-rah…
• is too close to the elevator.	• *è troppo vicino all'ascensore.*	• EH TROH-poh vee-CHEE noh ahll-ah-shehn-SOH-reh.
• hasn't been made up.	• *non è stata preparata.*	• nohn EH STAH-tah preh-pah-RAH-tah.
• smells (like cigarettes).	• *puzza (di fumo).*	• POO-tsah (dee FOO-moh).
The toilet (bathtub, sink) is clogged.	*La toilette (vasca da bagno, lavandino) è intasato/a.*	Lah twah-LEHT (VAH-skah dah BAH-nyoh, lah-vahn-DEE-noh) EH een-tah-ZAH-toh/tah.
May I (we) change rooms, please?	*Posso (possiamo) cambiare camere, per favore?*	POHS-soh (pohs-SYAH-moh) kahm-BYAH-reh KAH-meh-reh, pehr fah-VOH-reh?

BELLMAN

Please let me check our availability with the front desk.	*Chiedo alla reception.*	KYEH-doh AHL-lah reception.
Sure, I'll be happy to assist you.	*Certo. Vi aiuto volentieri.*	CHER-toh. Vee ai-OO-toh voh-lehn-TYEH-ree.
Please call if I can help you with anything else.	*Mi chiamate se posso esservi di aiuto.*	Mee kyah-MAH-teh seh POHS-soh EHS-sehr-vee dee ai-OO-toh.

VOCABULARY ••••

THE GUEST ROOM

air-conditioning	*l'aria condizionata*	LAH-ree-yah kohn-dee-tsyoh-NAH-tah
balcony	*balcone*	bahl-KOH-neh
bath mat	*tappetino da bagno*	tah-peh-TEE-noh dah BAH-nyoh
bathtub	*vasca da bagno*	VAH-skah dah BAH-nyoh
bed	*letto*	LEH-toh
bedspread	*copriletto*	koh-pree-LEH-toh
blanket	*coperta*	koh-PEHR-tah
blinds	*tendine*	tehn-DEE-neh
carpet	*tappeto*	tah-PEH-toh
ceiling	*soffitto*	sohf-FEE-toh
chair	*sedia*	SEH-dyah
closet	*armadio a muro*	ahr-MAH-dyoh ah MOO-roh
couch	*divano*	dee-VAH-noh
crib	*culla*	KOOL-lah
desk	*scrivania*	skree-vah-NEE-yah
Do Not Disturb sign	*cartellino "non disturbare"*	kahr-tehl-LEE-noh "nohn dee-stoor-BAH-reh"
door	*porta*	POHR-tah
drapes	*tende*	TEHN-deh
dresser	*cassettone*	kahs-seh-TOH-neh
fan	*ventilatore*	vehn-tee-lah-TOH-reh
floor	*pavimento*	pah-vee-MEHN-toh
glass(es)	*bicchiere/i*	bee-KYEH-reh/ree
hair dryer	*asciugacapelli*	ah-shoo-gah-kah-PEHL-lee
(coat) hanger	*attaccapanni*	ah-tah-kah-PAHN-nee

(cont'd.)

ITALIAN

The Guest Room *(cont'd.)*

heat	*riscaldamento*	ree-skahl-dah-MEHN-toh
ice bucket	*secchiello per il ghiacco*	seh-KYEHL-loh pehr eel GYAH-choh
iron	*ferro*	FEHR-roh
lamp	*lampada*	LAHM-pah-dah
light	*luce*	LOO-cheh
lock	*serratura*	sehr-rah-TOO-rah
minibar	*mini-bar*	mini-bar
mirror	*specchio*	SPEH-kyoh
nightstand	*comodino*	koh-moh-DEE-noh
pillow	*cuscino*	koo-SHEE-noh
radio	*radio*	RAH-dyoh
razor	*rasoio*	rah-ZOY-oh
sewing kit	*borsa per il cucito*	BOHR-sah pehr eel koo-CHEE-toh
shampoo	*shampoo*	SHAHM-poh
sheets	*lenzuola*	lehn-TSWOH-lah
shower	*doccia*	DOH-chah
shower cap	*cuffia da bagno (doccia)*	KOO-fyah dah BAH-nyoh (DOH-chah)
sink	*lavandino*	lah-vahn-DEE-noh
soap	*sapone*	sah-POH-neh
telephone	*telefono*	teh-LEH-foh-noh
television	*televisore*	teh-leh-vee-ZOH-reh
thermostat	*termosifone*	tehr-moh-see-FOH-neh
toilet	*toilette*	twah-LEHT
toilet paper	*carta igenica*	KAHR-tah ee-JEHN-ee-kah
toothbrush	*spazzolino*	spah-tsoh-LEE-noh
toothpaste	*dentifricio*	dehn-tee-FREE-choh
towel	*asciugamano*	ah-shoo-gah-MAH-noh
VCR	*videoregistratore*	vee-deh-oh-reh-jee-strah-TOH-reh
wall	*muro*	MOO-roh
window	*finestra*	fee-NEH-strah

5. Providing Assistance

A. GIVING DIRECTIONS

CONCIERGE		
Good morning. May I help you?	*Buon giorno. Desidera?*	Bwohn JOHR-noh. Deh-ZEE-deh-rah?
GUEST		
Yes, where is the…	*Sì, dov'è…*	SEE, doh-VEH…
• bathroom?	• *il bagno?*	• eel BAH-nyoh?
• lounge/bar?	• *il bar/la lounge?*	• eel bar/lah lounge?
• coffee shop/ restaurant?	• *il caffè/il ristorante?*	• eel kahf-FEH/eel ree-stoh-RAHN-teh?
• barbershop/ hairdresser's?	• *il barbiere/ il parucchiere?*	• eel bahr-BYEH-reh/ eel pahr-roo-KYEH-reh?
• gift shop?	• *il negozio di articoli da regalo?*	• eel neh-GOH-tsyoh dee ahr-TEE-koh-lee dah reh-GAH-loh?
• health club/gym?	• *la palestra?*	• lah pah-LEH-strah?
• ballroom?	• *la sala da ballo?*	• lah SAH-lah dah BAHL-loh?

TIP! ••••

You can simply explain many directions, but when they're more complex, you should use either a map or written instructions (or both). Hotels should keep preprinted directions to major sites on hand. Also, many cultures don't speak of distance in terms of city blocks but will understand if you use the word "streets" instead. And remember that most international guests use the metric system and may have difficulties figuring a distance given in miles, yards, or feet.

• elevator?	• *l'ascensore?*	• lah-shehn-SOH-reh?
• pay phone?	• *il telefono pubblico?*	• eel teh-LEH-foh-noh POO-blee-koh?
• ice machine?	• *la macchina per il ghiaccio?*	• lah MAH-kee-nah pehr eel GYAH-choh?

CONCIERGE

Take…	*Prenda…*	PREHN-dah…
• the escalator.	• *la scala mobile.*	• lah SKAH-lah MOH-bee-leh.
• the elevator.	• *l'ascensore.*	• lah-shehn-SOH-reh.
• the stairs.	• *le scale.*	• leh SKAH-leh.
Go…	*Vada…*	VAH-dah…
• up.	• *sù.*	• SOO.
• down.	• *giù.*	• JOO.
• left.	• *a sinistra.*	• ah see-NEE-strah.
• right.	• *a destra.*	• ah DEH-strah.
• straight ahead.	• *diritto.*	• dee-REE-toh.
• around the corner.	• *dietro l'angolo.*	• DYEH-troh LAHN-goh-loh.
• left, then right.	• *a sinistra, poi a destra.*	• ah see-NEE-strah, poy ah DEH-strah.
• past the elevator.	• *dopo l'ascensore.*	• DOH-poh lah-shehn-SOH-reh.
• to the first (second, third, fourth) floor.	• *al primo (secondo, terzo, quarto) piano.*	• ahl PREE-moh (seh-KOHN-doh, TEHR-tsoh, KWAHR-toh) PYAH-noh.
• left (right) when you exit the elevator.	• *a sinistra (a destra) appena esce dall'ascensore.*	• ah see-NEE-strah (ah DEH-strah) ah-PEH-nah EH-sheh dahl lah-shen-SOH-reh.
• in through the second set of doors.	• *alla seconda porta.*	• AHL-lah seh-KOHN-dah POHR-tah.
It will be…	*È…*	EH…
• on your right.	• *a destra.*	• ah DEH-strah.
• on your left.	• *a sinistra.*	• ah see-NEES-trah.

• right in front of you.	• *davanti a Lei.*	• dah-VAHN-tee ah LAY.

GUEST

How do I get…	*Come si arriva…*	KOH-meh see ahr-REE-vah…
• to the hospital?	• *all'ospedale?*	• ahl loh-speh-DAH-leh?
• to city hall?	• *al municipio?*	• ahl moo-nee-CHEE-pyoh?
• to the _____ restaurant/hotel?	• *al ristorante/albergo _____?*	• ahl ree-stoh-RAHN-teh/ahl-BEHR-goh _____?
• to the train station?	• *alla stazione ferroviaria?*	• AHL-lah stah-TSYOH-neh fehr-roh-VYAH-ree-ah?
• to the bus station?	• *alla stazione dell'autobus?*	• AHL-lah stah-TSYOH-neh dehl LAU-toh-boos?
• to the nearest bus stop?	• *alla fermata d'autobus più vicina?*	• AHL-lah fehr-MAH-tah DAU-toh-boos PYOO vee-CHEE-nah?
• to the mall?	• *al centro commerciale?*	• ahl CHEHN-troh kohm-mehr-CHAH-leh?
• to the post office?	• *all'ufficio postale?*	• ahl oo-FEE-choh poh-STAH-leh?
• to the airport?	• *all'aeroporto?*	• ah-lah-reh-oh-POHR-toh?
• downtown?	• *in centro?*	• een CHEHN-troh?
• to the car rental agency?	• *all'autonoleggio?*	• ah-lau-toh-noh-LEH-joh?
• to _____ Street/Avenue?	• *in Via _____?*	• een VEE-ah _____?

CONCIERGE

When you exit the hotel, go…	*Appena esce dall'albrgo, vada…*	Ah-PEH-nah EH-sheh dahl lahl-BEHR-goh, VAH-dah…
• left.	• *a sinistra.*	• ah see-NEE-strah.

ITALIAN

• right.	• *a destra.*	• ah DEH-strah.
• straight ahead.	• *diritto.*	• dee-REE-toh.
• north.	• *verso nord.*	• VEHR-soh NOHRD.
• south.	• *verso sud.*	• VEHR-soh SOOD.
• east.	• *verso est.*	• VEHR-soh EHST.
• west.	• *verso ovest.*	• VEHR-soh OH-vehst.
GUEST		
How far is it?	*Quanto è lontano?*	KWAHN-toh EH lohn-TAH-noh?
CONCIERGE		
It's about _____...	*Circa _____...*	CHEER-kah _____...
• blocks (streets).	• *isolati.*	• ee-zoh-LAH-tee.
• miles.	• *miglia.*	• MEE-lyah.
• kilometers.	• *chilometri.*	• kee-LOH-meh-tree.
• minutes...	• *minuti...*	• mee-NOO-tee...
• on foot.	• *a piedi.*	• ah PYEH-dee.
• by car.	• *in macchina.*	• een MAH-kee-nah.
• by bus.	• *in autobus.*	• een AU-toh-boos.
• by metro (subway).	• *in metro.*	• een MEH-troh.
GUEST		
Can you show me on the map?	*Me lo può indicare sulla mappa?*	Meh loh PWOH een-dee-KAH-reh SOOL-lah MAH-pah?
CONCIERGE		
Sure, it's right here.	*Certo, eccolo qui.*	CHEHR-toh, EH-koh-loh KWEE.
Let me draw you a little map.	*Le faccio una piccola mappa.*	Leh FAH-choh OO-nah PEE-koh-lah MAH-pah.
GUEST		
Can you tell me where I can...around here?	*Mi sa dire dove posso...*	Mee SAH DEE-reh DOH-veh POHS-soh...
• take a walk	• *fare una passeggiata?*	• FAH-reh OO-nah pahs-seh-JAH-tah?

• ride a bike	• *andare in bicicletta?*	• ahn-DAH-reh een bee-chee-KLEH-tah?
• jog	• *fare jogging?*	• FAH-reh jogging?

CONCIERGE

Yes, we have maps of…trails right here.	*Sì, abbiamo delle mappe che indicano gli itinerari…*	SEE, ah-BYAH-moh DEHL-leh MAH-peh keh EEN-dee-kah-noh lyee ee-tee-neh-RAH-ree…
• jogging	• *per il "jogging."*	• pehr eel "jogging."
• walking	• *per passeggiare.*	• pehr pahs-seh-JAH-reh.
• bike	• *per andare in bicicletta.*	• pehr ahn-DAH-reh een bee-chee-KLEH-tah.

B. RECOMMENDING PLACES OF INTEREST

GUEST

Can you recommend any places to visit?	*Può raccomandare dei luoghi di interesse?*	PWOH rah-koh-mahn-DAH-reh LWOH-gee dee een-teh-REHS-seh?

CONCIERGE

There are lots. Are you interested in…	*Ce ne sono molti. Le interessa…*	Cheh neh SOH-noh MOHL-tee. Leh een-teh-REHS-sah…
• art?	• *l'arte?*	• LAHR-teh?
• theater?	• *il teatro?*	• eel teh-AH-troh?
• shopping?	• *lo shopping?*	• loh SHOH-peeng?
• museums?	• *i musei?*	• ee moo-ZAY-ee?
• sports?	• *lo sport?*	• loh SPOHRT?
• sight-seeing?	• *i tour?*	• ee TOUR?
• music?	• *la musica?*	• lah MOO-zee-kah?
• outdoor activities?	• *attività all'aperto?*	• ah-tee-vee-TAH ahl ah-PEHR-toh?
• children's activities?	• *attività per bambini?*	• ah-tee-vee-TAH pehr-bahm-BEE-nee?

GUEST

What do you recommend?	*Cosa mi consiglia?*	KOH-zah mee kohn-SEE-lyah?

CONCIERGE

If you're interested in art, I'd suggest…	*Se le interessa l'arte, suggerirei…*	Seh leh een-teh-REHS-sah LAHR-teh, soo-jeh-ree-RAY…
• the _____ gallery.	• *la galleria _____.*	• lah gahl-leh-REE-ah _____.
• the _____ art museum.	• *il museo _____.*	• eel moo-ZEH-oh _____.
If you're interested in theater, I can get you tickets to…	*Se le interessa il teatro, Le posso procurare biglietti per…*	Seh leh een-teh-REHS-sah eel teh-AH-troh, leh POHS-soh proh-koo-RAH-reh bee LYEH-tee-pehr…
• a show.	• *uno spettacolo.*	• OO-noh speh-TAH-koh-loh.
• an opera.	• *l'opera.*	• LOH-peh-rah.
• a movie.	• *un film.*	• oon FEELM.
For shopping, I'd recommend…	*I migliori posti per lo shopping sono…*	Ee mee-LYOH-ree POH-stee pehr lo shopping SOH-noh…
• downtown.	• *il centro.*	• eel CHEHN-troh.
• the mall.	• *il centro commerciale.*	• eel CHEHN-troh kohm-mehr-CHAH-leh.
• the discount outlets.	• *i grandi magazzini.*	• ee GRAHN-dee mah-gah-DSEE-nee.

GUEST

Do they have…there?	*Ci si può comprare…*	Cee see PWOH kohm-PRAH-reh…
• clothes	• *vestiti?*	• veh-STEE-tee?
• furniture	• *mobili?*	• MOH-bee-lee?
• rugs (carpets)	• *tappeti?*	• tah-PEH-tee?
• souvenirs	• *souvenirs?*	• souvenirs?
• books	• *libri?*	• LEE-bree?

• sporting goods	• *articoli sportivi?*	• ahr-TEE-koh-lee spohr-TEE-vee?
• candy	• *caramelle?*	• kah-rah-MEHL-leh?
• antiques	• *oggetti di antiquariato?*	• oh-JEH-tee dee ahn-tee-kwahr-YAH-toh?
• electronics	• *oggetti elettronici?*	• oh-JEH-tee eh-leh-TROH-nee-chee?
• computers	• *computer?*	• computer?
Is there…there?	*C'è un…*	CHEH oon…
• a farmer's market	• *mercato ortofrutticolo?*	• mehr-KAH-toh ohr-toh-froo-TEE-koh-loh?
• a supermarket	• *un supermercato?*	• oon soo-pehr-mehr-KAH-toh?
• a flea market	• *un mercato delle pulci?*	• oon mehr-KAH-toh DEHL-leh POOL-chee?

CONCIERGE

Perhaps you'd like a museum.	*Forse preferisce visitare un museo.*	FOHR-seh preh-feh-REE-sheh vee-zee-TAH-reh oon moo-ZEH-oh.
A local favorite is the…museum.	*Un luogo molto visitato è il museo…*	Oon LWOH-goh MOHL-toh vee-zee-TAH-toh EH eel moo-ZEH-oh…
• natural history	• *di storia naturale.*	• dee STOH-ree-ah nah-too-RAH-leh.
• modern art	• *di arte moderna.*	• dee AHR-teh moh-DEHR-nah.
• science	• *delle scienze.*	• DEHL-leh SHEHN-tseh.
• local history	• *della storia locale.*	• DEHL-lah STOH-ree-ah loh-KAH-leh.

GUEST

We were thinking of sight-seeing.	*Pensavamo di fare un giro turistico.*	Pehn-sah-VAH-moh dee FAH-reh oon JEE-roh too-REE-stee-koh.

CONCIERGE

I'd be happy to arrange a city tour.	*Vi posso organizzare un tour della città.*	Vee POHS-soh ohr-gah-nee-DSAH-reh oon TOOR DEHL-lah chee-TAH.

GUEST

How about…	*Se volessimo vedere…*	Seh voh-LEHS-see-moh veh-DEH-reh…
• interesting architecture?	• *alcune opere architettoniche?*	• ahl-KOO-neh OH-peh-reh ahr-kee-teh-TOH-nee-keh?
• churches?	• *chiese?*	• KYEH-zeh?
• a vineyard?	• *vigne?*	• VEE-nyeh?
• the business district?	• *il centro financiario?*	• eel CHEHN-troh fee-nahn-ZYAH-ree-oh?
• the government buildings?	• *gli edifici governativi?*	• lyee eh-dee-FEE-chee goh-vehr-nah-TEE-vee?
• the university?	• *l'università?*	• loo-nee-vehr-see-TAH?
• monuments?	• *monumenti?*	• moh-noo-MEHN-tee?
• the countryside?	• *la campagna?*	• lah kahm-PAH-nyah?

CONCIERGE

There are many sports events.	*Ci sono anche molti eventi sportivi.*	Chee SOH-noh AHN-keh MOHL-tee eh-VEHN-tee spohr-TEE-vee.
Would you like tickets to a…game (match)?	*Vuole biglietti per una partita di…*	VWOH-leh bee-LYEH-tee pehr OO-nah pahr-TEE-tah dee…
• baseball	• *baseball?*	• BAYZ-bol?
• basketball	• *"basketball"?*	• "basketball"?
• football	• *"football" americano?*	• "football" ah-meh-ree-KAH-noh?
• hockey	• *"hockey"?*	• "hockey"?
• tennis	• *tennis?*	• TEHN-nees?

GUEST		
Are there any musical events?	*Ci sono eventi musicali?*	Chee SOH-noh eh-VEHN-tee moo-zee-KAH-lee?
CONCIERGE		
There is a _____ concert tonight.	*Stasera c'è un concerto di _____.*	Stah-SEH-rah CHEH oon kohn-CHEHR-toh dee _____.
There's live music at _____.	*Suonano dal vivo a _____.*	SWOH-nah-noh dahl VEE-voh ah _____.
GUEST		
Is there anything else going on tonight?	*Cos'altro c'è da fare stasera?*	Koh-ZAHL-troh CHEH dah FAH-reh stah-SEH-rah?
CONCIERGE		
Other than the movies, I'd suggest…	*A parte il cinema, suggerirei…*	Ah PAHR-teh eel CHEE-neh-mah, soo-jeh-ree-RAY…
• bowling.	• *il "bowling."*	• eel "bowling."
• a nightclub.	• *la discoteca.*	• lah dee-skoh-TEH-kah.
• a video rental.	• *di noleggiare un film.*	• dee noh-leh-JAH-reh oon FEELM.
GUEST		
What do you suggest for outdoor activities?	*Cosa può consigliare come attività all'aperto?*	KOH-zah PWOH kohn-see-LYAH-reh KOH-meh ah-tee-vee-TAH ahl lah-PEHR-toh?
CONCIERGE		
How about…	*Le piacerebbe…*	Leh pyah-cheh-REH-beh…
• hiking?	• *fare un'escursione?*	• FAH-reh oon eh-skoor-SYOH-neh?
• fishing?	• *andare a pescare?*	• ahn-DAH-reh ah peh-SKAH-reh?
• skiing?	• *andare a sciare?*	• ahn-DAH-reh ah shee-YAH-reh?

• skating?	• *andare a pattinare?*	• ahn-DAH-reh ah pah-tee-NAH-reh?
• Rollerblading?	• *fare il "rollerblading"?*	• FAH-reh eel "rollerblading"?
• swimming?	• *nuotare?*	• nwoh-TAH-reh?
• surfing?	• *fare "surf"?*	• FAH-reh "surf"?
Or you might like to go…	*O forse potrebbe andare…*	Oh FOHR-seh poh-TREH-beh ahn-DAH-reh…
• to the river.	• *al fiume.*	• ahl FYOO-meh.
• to the lake.	• *al lago.*	• ahl LAH-goh.
• to the mountains.	• *in montagna.*	• een mohn-TAH-nyah.
• for a drive.	• *a fare un giro in macchina.*	• ah FAH-reh oon JEE-roh een MAH-kee-nah.
• to the beach.	• *alla spiaggia.*	• AHL-lah SPYAH-jah.
• to the forest.	• *nei boschi.*	• NAY BOH-skee.
GUEST		
Is there anything for children?	*C'è qualche luogo o attività adatto/a ai bambini?*	CHEH KWAHL-keh LWOH-goh oh ah-tee-vee-TAH ad-DAH-toh/tah ahy bahm-BEE-nee?
CONCIERGE		
Yes, there's…	*Sì, c'è…*	SEE, CHEH…
• a zoo.	• *uno zoo.*	• OO-noh DSOH-oh.
• a children's museum.	• *un museo per bambini.*	• oon moo-SEH-oh pehr bahm-BEE-nee.
• an amusement park.	• *un parco divertimenti.*	• oon PAHR-koh dee-vehr-tee-MEHN-tee.
• a water park.	• *un parco acquatico.*	• oon PAHR-koh ah-KWAH-tee-koh.
Would you like to rent…	*Vuole affittare…*	VWOH-leh ahf-fee-TAH-reh…
• a bicycle?	• *una bicicletta?*	• OO-nah bee-chee-KLEH-tah?
• a car?	• *una macchina?*	• OO-nah MAH-kee-nah?

• a boat?	• *una barca?*	• OO-nah BAHR-kah?
• some skis?	• *un paio di sci?*	• oon PAI-oh dee SHEE?
• some Rollerblades?	• *un paio di "rollerblades"?*	• oon PAI-oh dee "rollerblades"?
Would you like a tour guide who speaks Italian?	*Vorrebbe una guida che parla italiano?*	Vohr-REH-beh OO-nah GWEE-dah keh PAHR-lah ee-tahl-YAH-noh?
May I make a reservation for you?	*Posso fare una prenotazione per Lei?*	POHS-soh FAH-reh OO-nah preh-noh-tah-TSYOH-neh pehr-LAY?
GUEST		
Can you recommend a good restaurant?	*Può raccomandarmi un buon ristorante?*	PWOH rah-koh-mahn-DAHR-mee oon BWOHN ree-stoh-RAHN-teh?
CONCIERGE		
What type of cuisine would you like?	*Quale tipo di cucina vorrebbe provare?*	KWAH-leh TEE-poh dee koo-CHEE-nah vohr-REH-beh proh-VAH-reh?
GUEST		
We'd like a(n)... restaurant.	*Vorremmo provare un ristorante...*	Vohr-REH-moh proh-VAH-reh oon ree-stoh-RAHN-teh...
• California	• *californiano.*	• kah-lee-fohr-NYAH-noh.
• casual	• *informale.*	• een-fohr-MAH-leh.
• creole	• *creolo.*	• creh-OH-loh.
• elegant	• *elegante.*	• eh-leh-GAHN-teh.
• fast-food	• *"fast food."*	• "fast food."
• inexpensive	• *modesto.*	• moh-DEH-stoh.
• kosher	• *kosher.*	• kosher.
• seafood	• *che serve pesce.*	• keh SEHR-veh PEH-sheh.
• vegetarian	• *vegetariano.*	• veh-jeh-tah-RYAH-noh.

We'd like an authentic American steakhouse.	*Vorremmo provare una autentica "steakhouse" americana.*	Vohr-REHM-moh proh-VAH-reh OO-nah au-TEHN-tee-kah "steakhouse" ah-meh-ree-KAH-nah.

CONCIERGE

You can get there by…	*Ci si può arrivare…*	Chee see PWOH ahr-ree-VAH-reh…
• bus.	• *in autobus.*	• een AH-oo-toh-boos.
• train.	• *in treno.*	• een TREH-noh.
• subway.	• *in metro.*	• een MEH-troh.
Take the…bound for _____.	*Prenda il… verso _____.*	PREHN-dah eel… VEHR-soh _____.
• number _____ bus	• *l'autobus numero _____*	• LAH-oo-toh-boos NOO-meh-roh _____
• train	• *il treno*	• eel TREH-noh
• subway	• *la metro*	• lah MEH-troh
You'll need to transfer to…at _____.	*Dovrà cambiare… a _____.*	Doh-VRAH kahm-BYAH-reh… ah _____.
• the _____ line	• *la linea _____*	lah LEE-neh-ah _____
• the number _____ bus	• *l'autobus numero _____*	LAH-oo-toh-boos NOO-meh-roh _____
Get off at _____.	*Scenda a _____.*	SHEHN-dah ah _____.
May I call you a taxi?	*Posso chiamar Le un taxi?*	POHS-soh kyah-MAHR-Leh oon taxi?
We have a free shuttle bus service available to _____.	*L'albergo ha un pendolino gratuito che va a _____.*	Lahl-BEHR-goh ah oon pehn-doh-LEE-noh grah-TOO-ee-toh keh vah ah _____.
It leaves every _____ minutes.	*Parte ogni _____ minuti.*	PAHR-teh OH-nyee _____ mee-NOO-tee.
It leaves every hour.	*Parte ogni ora.*	PAHR-teh OH-nyee OH-rah.

GUEST

What's the price range?	*Quanto costa?*	KWAHN-toh KOH-stah?

6. Business Services and Clientele

A. BOOKING A BUSINESS MEETING

EMPLOYEE		
Good morning.	*Buon giorno.*	Bwohn JOHR-noh.
How may I help you today?	*La posso aiutare?*	Lah POHS-soh ah-yoo-TAH-reh?
GUEST		
I'd like to make arrangements for a business meeting.	*Vorrei organizzare un incontro di affari.*	Vohr-RAY ohr-gah-nee-DSAH-reh oon een-KOHN-troh dee ahf-FAH-ree.
EMPLOYEE		
For how many people?	*Per quante persone?*	Pehr KWAHN-teh pehr-SOH-neh?
GUEST		
For ____ people on ____.	*Per ____ persone.*	Pehr ____ pehr-SOH-neh.
EMPLOYEE		
Fine.	*Bene.*	BEH-neh.
We have space available.	*Abbiamo lo spazio a disposizione.*	Ah-BYAH-moh loh SPAH-tsyoh ah dee-spoh-zee-TSYOH-neh.

TIP! ••••

Clients who do business from the hotel need a great deal of service from you. They tend to be seasoned travelers who don't want a lot of explanation from hotel employees, just competent action. Attending to their every need often yields substantial financial rewards!

We can provide all your meals, as well as your meeting needs.	*Possiamo provvedere ai pasti e a tutto ciò che vi serve per il meeting.*	Pohs-SYAH-moh prohv-VEH-deh-reh ai PAH-stee eh ah TOO-toh CHOH keh vee SEHR-veh pehr eel meeting.
GUEST		
That's good. We'd like…for each day.	*Bene. Vorremmo… tutti i giorni.*	BEH-neh. Vohr-REHM-moh…TOO-tee ee JOHR-nee.
• breakfast	• *la prima colazione*	• lah PREE-mah koh-lah-TSYOH-neh
• coffee breaks	• *pause (caffè)*	• PAU-zeh (kahf-FEH)
• a working lunch	• *il pranzo*	• eel PRAHN-tsoh
• snacks	• *spuntini*	• spoon-TEE-nee
• a cocktail reception	• *un cocktail*	• oon cocktail
• dinner	• *la cena*	• lah CHEH-nah
Also, we'll require… for the meeting room.	*Abbiamo anche bisogno di…nella salsa di conferenza.*	ah-BYAH-moh AHN-kehbee-ZOH-nyoh dee …NEHL-lah SAH-lah dee kohn-feh-REHN-tsah.
• a VCR with a large-screen monitor	• *un videoregistratore con schermo grande*	• oon VEE-deh-oh-reh-jee-strah-TOH-reh kohn SKEHR-moh GRAHN-deh
• an overhead projector with transparencies and markers	• *un proiettore con i lucidi e evidenziatori*	• oon proh-yeh-TOH-reh kohn LOO-chee-dee eh eh-vee-dehn-tsyah-TOH ree
• a chalkboard	• *una lavagna*	• OO-nah lah-VAH-nyah
• a flip chart	• *una lavagna di carta*	• OO-nah lah-VAH-nyah dee KAHR-tah
• a slide projector	• *un proiettore di diapositive*	• oon proh-yeh-TOH-reh dee dee-ah-poh-zee-TEE-veh
• a computer with a large-screen monitor	• *un computer con schermo grande*	• oon computer kohn SKEHR-moh GRAND-deh

And please be sure to provide…	*Abbiamo bisogno in particolare di…*	Ah-BYAH-moh bee-ZOH-nyoh een pahr-tee-koh-LAH-reh dee…
• water.	• *acqua.*	• AH-kwah.
• pads with pencils.	• *matite e carta.*	• mah-TEE-teh eh KAHR-tah.
• ashtrays.	• *portaceneri.*	• pohr-tah-CHEH-neh-ree.

EMPLOYEE

Let's decide on what time you'd like everything, and we'll be all set.	*Fissiamo un orario e del resto ce ne occupiamo noi.*	Fees-SYAH-moh oon oh-RAH-ryoh eh dehl REH-stoh cheh neh oh-koo-PYAH-moh NOY.

GUEST

Okay. How will the room be set up?	*Va bene. Come sarà sistemata la sala di conferenza?*	Vah BEH-neh. KOH-meh sah-RAH see-steh-MAH-tah lah SAH-lah dee kohn-feh-REHN-tsah?

EMPLOYEE

We can set up the room…	*Possiamo arrangiare le sedie…*	Pohs-SYAH-moh ahr-rahn-JAH-reh leh SEH-dyeh…
• theater style.	• *in anfiteatro.*	• een ahn-fee-teh-AH-troh.
• in a square.	• *in forma quadrata.*	• een FOHR-mah kwah-DRAH-tah.
• horseshoe ("U") style.	• *a forma di ferro di cavallo.*	• ah FOHR-mah dee FEHR-roh dee kah-VAHL-loh.
• classroom style.	• *in file.*	• een FEE-leh.
• boardroom style.	• *intorno a un lungo tavolo.*	• een-TOHR-noh ah oon LOON-goh TAH-voh-loh.
We're looking forward to having your group here.	*Saremo lieti di ospitare il Suo gruppo.*	Sah-REH-moh LYEH-tee dee oh-spee-TAH-reh eel SOO-oh GROO-poh.

B. AT THE MEETING

ATTENDANT		
I'm ____, the meeting-room attendant.	*Mi chiamo ____. Sono l'assistente.*	Mee KYAH-moh ____. SOH-noh lahs-see-STEHN-teh.
How is everything?	*Va tutto bene?*	Vah TOO-toh BEH-neh?
GUEST		
Everything is fine, thank you.	*Va tutto bene, grazie.*	Vah TOO-toh BEH-neh, GRAH-tsyeh.
We need…	*Abbiamo bisogno di…*	Ah-BYAH-moh bee-ZOH-nyoh dee…
• more chairs.	• *più sedie.*	• PYOO SEH-dyeh.
• more coffee.	• *più caffè.*	• PYOO kahf-FEH.
• the ashtrays emptied.	• *portaceneri puliti.*	• pohr-tah-CHE-neh-ree poo-LEE-tee.
• more water.	• *più acqua.*	• PYOO AH-kwah.
ATTENDANT		
I'll take care of it right away.	*Me ne occupo subito.*	Meh neh OH-koo-poh SOO-bee-toh.
Is everything else satisfactory?	*E il resto va bene?*	Eh eel REH-stoh vah BEH-neh?
GUEST		
Yes, but…	*Sì, però…*	SEE, peh-ROH…
• the room needs more light.	• *la sala è troppo buia.*	• lah SAH-lah EH TROH-poh BOO-yah.
• the room is too bright.	• *c'è troppa luce nella sala.*	• CHEH TROH-pah LOO-cheh NEHL-lah SAH-lah.
• the room needs more ventilation.	• *manca l'aria in sala.*	• MAHN-kah LAH-ryah een SAH-lah.
• the room is too hot (cold).	• *fa troppo caldo (freddo).*	• fah TROH-poh KAHL-doh (FREH-doh).
• the room is a little noisy.	• *la sala è rumorosa.*	• lah SAH-lah EH roo-moh-ROH-zah.

• the room is crowded.	• *è affollata.*	• EH ahf-fohl-LAH-tah.
Can you take care of it?	*Potrebbe occuparsene?*	Poh-TREH-beh oh-koo-PAHR-seh-neh?
Can we get another room?	*Possiamo cambiare sala?*	Pohs-SYAH-moh kahm-BYAH-reh SAH-lah?
ATTENDANT		
Let me see what we can do.	*Addesso vedo che possiamo fare.*	Ah-DEHS-soh VEH-doh keh pohs-SYAH-moh FAH-reh.

C. CATERING TO BUSINESS GUESTS

CONCIERGE		
How may I help you?	*Posso esserLe di aiuto?*	POHS-soh EHS-sehr-leh dee ah-YOO-toh?
GUEST		
Where is breakfast for the _____ group?	*Dove si riunisce il gruppo _____ per la colazione?*	DOH-veh see ree-oo-NEE-sheh eel GROO-poh _____ pehr lah koh-lah-TSYOH-neh?
Where is the exhibits hall?	*Dov'è il salone di esposizione?*	Doh-VEH eel sah-LOH-neh dee eh-spoh-zee-TSYOH-neh?
CONCIERGE		
There's a buffet set up outside your meeting room.	*C'è un buffet fuori della sala.*	CHEH oon buffet FWOH-ree DEHL-lah SAH-lah.
Just down the hall.	*In fondo al corridoio.*	Een FOHN-doh ahl kohr-ree-DOY-oh.
In the dining room.	*In sala da pranzo.*	Een SAH-lah dah PRAHN-tsoh.
GUEST		
Thank you.	*Grazie.*	GRAH-tsyeh.
I need…	*Ho bisogno di…*	Oh bee-ZOH-nyoh dee…
• a fax sent.	• *spedire un fax.*	• speh-DEE-reh oon FAH-ks.

ITALIAN

• some typing done.	• *qualcosa dattilografato.*	• kwahl-KOH-zah DAH-tee-loh-grah-FAH-toh.
• a hookup to the Internet.	• *un collegamento con l'Internet.*	• oon kohl-leh-gah-MEHN-toh kohn l'internet.
• a computer.	• *un computer.*	• oon computer.
• a package sent overnight.	• *spedire un pacco in posta celere.*	• speh-DEE-reh oon PAH-koh een POH-stah CHEH-leh-reh.
• courier service.	• *un corriere.*	• oon kohr-RYEH-reh.
• some letters mailed.	• *imbucare delle lettere.*	• eem-boo-KAH-reh DEHL-leh LEH-teh-reh.
• some copies made.	• *fare delle fotocopie.*	• FAH-reh DEHL-leh foh-toh-KOH-pyeh.
CONCIERGE		
I'll take care of that right away.	*Lo faccio subito.*	Loh FAH-choh SOO-bee-toh.
GUEST		
Later, I'd like to host a small reception.	*Vorrei preparare un piccolo ricevimento per più tardi.*	Vohr-RAY preh-pah-RAH-reh oon PEE-koh-loh ree-cheh-vee-MEHN-toh pehr PYOO TAHR-dee.
Can you arrange that?	*Lo può organizzare?*	Loh PWOH ohr-gah-nee-DSAH-reh?
CONCIERGE		
Certainly. What would you like?	*Certo. Cosa desidera?*	CHEHR-toh. KOH-zah deh-ZEE-deh-rah?
GUEST		
We need a full bar and some hors d'oeuvres.	*Abbiamo bisogno di un bar e di antipasti.*	Ah-BYAH-moh bee-ZOH-nyoh dee oon bar eh dee ahn-tee-PAH-stee.
Make sure there are plenty of chilled shrimp.	*Vorremmo molti gamberi.*	Vohr-REHM-moh MOHL-tee GAHM-beh-ree.

Lots of champagne, please.	*Molto champagne, per favore.*	MOHL-toh shahm-PAH-ny, pehr fah-VOH-reh.
CONCIERGE		
I'll have Room Service put together a proposal right away, and get back to you.	*Comunico le Sue esigenze al Servizio in Camera, e La richiamo.*	Koh-MOO-nee-koh leh SOO-eh eh-zee-JEHN-tseh ahl sehr-VEE-tsyoh een KAH-meh-rah, eh lah ree-KYAH-moh.

7. Checking Out

GUEST		
At what time is checkout?	*A che ora bisogna lasciare l'albergo?*	Ah keh OH-rah bee-ZOH-nyah lah-SHAH-reh lahl-BEHR-goh?
FRONT DESK CLERK		
At 10 A.M.	*Alle dieci di mattina.*	AHL-leh DYEH-chee dee mah-TEE-nah.
At noon.	*A mezzogiorno.*	Ah meh-dsoh-JOHR-noh.
At 3 P.M.	*Alle tre del pomeriggio.*	AHL-leh TREH dehl poh-meh-REE-joh.
You may audit your bill on channel _____ on your television.	*Può controllare il conto sul canale _____ del televisore.*	PWOH kon-trohl-LAH-reh eel KOHN-toh sool kah-NAH-leh _____ dehl teh-leh-vee-ZOH-reh.
We provide an express checkout service.	*Offriamo un servizio espresso per saldare il conto.*	Ohf-free-YAH-moh oon serh-VEE-tsyoh eh-SPREHS-soh pehr sahl-DAH-reh eel KOHN-toh.
Your bill will be left outside your door the night before you check out.	*Troverà il conto sulla porta la sera prima.*	Troh-veh-RAH eel KOHN-toh SOOL-lah POHR-tah lah SEH-rah PREE-mah.

ITALIAN

If you're satisfied with your bill, simply sign it,	*Se è soddisfatto, lo può firmare,*	Seh EH soh-dees-FAH-toh, loh PWOH feer-MAH-reh,
and leave your key in your room.	*e lasciare la chiave in camera.*	eh lah-SHAH-reh lah KYAH-veh een KAH-meh-rah.
Any late charges will be added automatically.	*Ulteriori addebiti saranno aggiunti automaticamente al conto.*	Ool-teh-ree-YOH-ree ah-DEH-bee-tee sah-RAHN-noh ah-JOON-tee au-toh-mah-tee-kah-MEHN-teh ahl KOHN-toh.
GUEST		
I'd like to check out, please.	*Vorrei saldare il conto, per favore.*	Vohr-RAY sahl-DAH-reh eel KOHN-toh, pehr fah-VOH-reh.
CLERK		
May I have your luggage brought down?	*Le faccio portare giù i bagagli?*	Leh FAH-choh pohr-TAH-reh JOO ee bah-GAH-lyee?
GUEST		
Yes, please.	*Sì, grazie.*	SEE, GRAH-tsyeh.
No, I brought (will bring) it myself.	*No, li ho portati (porto), giù io.*	Noh, lee oh pohr-TAH-tee (POHR-toh) JOO EE-oh.
CLERK		
How was everything?	*Com'è stata la permanenza?*	KOH-meh STAH-tah lah pehr-mah-NEHN-tsah?
GUEST		
It was very nice, thank you.	*Molto bene, grazie.*	MOHL-toh BEH-neh, GRAH-tsyeh.
I want to speak with the manager.	*Vorrei parlare col direttore.*	Vohr-RAY pahr-LAH-reh kohl dee-reh-TOH-reh.
CLERK		
Certainly. The manager on duty is _____. One moment, please.	*Certo. Il direttore di turno è _____. Un momento, per favore.*	CHEHR-toh. Eel dee-reh-TOH-reh dee TOOR-noh EH _____. Oon moh-MEHN-toh, pehr fah-VOH-reh.

GUEST

Our experience was…	*La nostra permanenza è stata…*	Lah NOH-strah pehr-mah-NEHN-tsah EH STAH-tah…
• good.	• *piacevole.*	• pee-ah-CHEH-voh-leh.
• excellent.	• *eccellente.*	• eh-chehl-LEHN-teh.
• poor.	• *scarsa.*	• SKAHR-sah.
• very bad.	• *molto brutta.*	• MOHL-toh BROO-tah.

MANAGER ON DUTY

That's nice to hear.	*Ci fa piacere.*	Chee FAH pyah-CHEH-reh.
I'm sorry to hear that.*	*Mi dispiace.*	Mee dee-SPYAH-cheh.
Thank you. We hope to see you again.	*Grazie. Speriamo di rivederLa.*	GRAH-tsyeh. Spehr-YAH-moh dee ree-veh-DEHR-lah.

*Please refer to "Guest Complaints in the Hotel" on page 203 for more on handling dissatisfied clients.

SECTION E

JAPANESE

1. The Bare Essentials

A. PRONUNCIATION CHART

VOWELS

ah	father	*oh*	spoke
eh	bet	*oo*	moose
ee	bee		

CONSONANTS

b	bat	*s*	song, cease
d	dock	*t*	tongue
f	flag	*y*	yes
g	get	*z*	zest
h	house		
k	cat	*j*	judge
m	mouse	*ts*	dots
n	nest	*ds*	seeds
p	pass	*sh*	short
r	rolling r	*ch*	chicken

DIPHTHONGS

ai	aye	*oy*	boy
ay	day		

B. THE JAPANESE LANGUAGE

Nouns Japanese does not distinguish between masculine and feminine or singular and plural, and there are no equivalents for the articles *a* or *the*. Thus, the word *hon* can be translated as "book," "a book," "the book," "books," or "the books." The exact meaning is always apparent from context.

Particles Particles are suffixes that are attached to the ends of nouns or pronouns to indicate a specific grammatical function in a sentence or to slightly alter the meaning of that noun or pronoun. The meaning of the noun *gakkoh* (school) can be changed by the following particles: *gakkoh wa* (the school, as a subject of a sentence), *gakkoh e* (to the school), *gakkoh o* (the school, as direct object of a sentence), *gakkoh no* (of the school, the school's), and *gakkoh mo* (the school as well; the school, too.)

Verbs Unlike English verbs, Japanese verbs are positioned at the end of the clause or sentence. There are only two tenses, the present and the past, and two forms, called normal and plain. Number and gender distinctions do not affect verb conjugation, but the distinction between positive and negative does. *Watashi wa Ohsaka e ikimasu.* (I am going to Osaka.) *Watashi wa Ohsaka e ikimasen.* (I am not going to Osaka.) *Watashi wa Ohsaka e ikimashita.* (I went to Osaka.) *Watashi wa Ohsaka o ikimasen deshita.* (I did not go to Osaka.)

Although this discussion of Japanese grammar is meant only as a very simplified presentation, it will help you as you try to communicate in Japanese.

C. THE JAPANESE CULTURE

The Japanese are generally very familiar with American customs. They have an elaborate system of bowing but prefer Westerners to shake hands. Japanese guests will tend to dress in a fashionable American style. Reserve and good manners are highly valued, and where you may find Japanese guests a bit vague in expressing their preferences or displeasure, it's really their way of being polite; straightforward complaints are rare.

In Japan, businessmen often get together after work and drink a great deal of alcohol. This is a custom that allows the dismantling of some of the strict facade of stoicism otherwise expected in the culture. The men act silly and speak more freely than they dare during business hours. Don't be surprised if such occasions arise; seldom is anyone truly out of control. Above all, never mention the antics of the night before when you encounter your guests in the light of a new business day.

Customers from Japan will generally tip, but they will not be offended by an added service charge.

2. Useful Expressions

A. GENERAL

Hello.	*KohNNEECHEEWAH.*
Good-bye.	*SahYOHNAHRAH.*
Yes.	*HAye.*
No.	*EEeh.*
Maybe.	*OhSOHrahkoo.*
Please.	*OhNEHGAYESHEEMAHsoo.*
Thank you (very much).	*AhRE gahtoh(gohZAYEMAHsoo).*
You're welcome.	*DOHeeTAHSHEEMAHSHEEteh.*
Excuse me.	*SooMEEMAHSEHn.*
I beg your pardon.	*SooMEEMAHSEHn.*
I'm sorry.	*MOHSHEEWAHKEH gohZAYEMAHSEHn.*
One moment, please.	*SHOHshoh ohMAHCHEE, kooDAHSAYE.*
Do you speak English?	*EHGOHWA ohHAHNAHSHEENEE nahREEMAHsooKAH?*
• Yes, I do.	• *HAye, hahNAHSHEEMAHsoo.*
• No, I don't.	• *EEeH, hahNAHSHEEMAHSEHn.*
• A little.	• *SooKOHshee, hahNAHSHEEMAHsoo.*

• No, not at all.	• *EEeh, mahTAHKOO hahNAHSHEEMAHSEHn.*
That's okay.	*DAYEJOHboo dehsoo.*
It doesn't matter.	*KAHNKEH ahREEMAHSEHn.*
I don't speak Japanese.	*Nee-HOHN goh wah hahNAH-SHEEMAHSEHn.*
I can speak a little.	*SooKOHshee, hahNAHSEH-MAHsoo.*
I understand a little.	*SooKOHshee, wahKAHREE-MAHsoo.*
I don't understand.	*WahKAHREEMAHSEHn.*
Please speak more slowly.	*MOHtoh yooKOOree hahNAH-sheeteh, kooDAHSAYE.*
Would you repeat that, please?	*MOHEECHEEDOH ohSHAHteh, kooDAHSAYE.*
Yes, sir/ma'am.	*HAye.*
No problem.	*MOHNDAYE ahREEMAHSEHn.*
It's my pleasure.	*YohROHKOHndeh.*

B. NEEDS

I'd like _____.	_____ *gah hohSHEE dehsoo.*
I need _____.	_____ *gah heeTSOOYOH DEHsoo.*
What would you like?	*NAHneenee eeTAHSHEEMAH-SHOH?*
Please bring me _____.	_____ *oh mohTEHKEEteh, koo-DAHSAYE.*
I'm looking for _____.	_____ *oh sahGAHSHEETEH EEMAHsoo.*
I'm hungry.	*OhNAHKAHGAH sooEETEH EEMAHsoo.*
I'm thirsty.	*NOHdohgah kahWAHeeteh ee-MAHsoo.*
It's important.	*KohREHWAH JOOYOH DEHsoo.*
It's urgent.	*KohREHWAH KEENKYOO DEHsoo.*

C. QUESTION WORDS

How?	*DOHnoh yohnee dehsooKAH?*
How much?	*DohNOHKOORAYE DEH-sooKAH?*
How many?	*EEkootsoo dehsooKAH?*
Which?	*DOHreh dehsooKAH?*
What?	*NAHn dehsooKAH?*
What kind of?	*DOHnnah SHOOrooee dehsoo-KAH?*
Who?	*DOHnahtah dehsooKAH?*
Where?	*DOHkoh dehsooKAH?*
When?	*EEtsoo dehsooKAH?*
What does this mean?	*kohREHWAH DOHyoo EEmee dehsooKAH?*
What does that mean?	*ahREHWAH DOHyoo EEmee dehsooKAH?*
How do you say _____ in Japanese?	_____ *oh nee-HOHN-goh deh wah NAH-ntoh EEMAHsooKAH?*

D. COLORS

black	*KOOroh*
blue	*AHoh*
brown	*CHAHeeroh*
gold	*KEEnEEroh*
gray	*gooRE*
green	*meeDOHREE eeroh*
orange	*ohREHNJEE eeroh*
pink	*PEEnkoo eeroh*
purple	*mooRAHSAHKEE eeroh*
red	*AHkah*
silver	*GEEn eeroh*
violet	*sooMEEREH eeroh*
white	*SHEEroh*
yellow	*KEEroh*

E. CARDINAL NUMBERS

1	*EEchee*	32	*SAHNjoo nee*
2	*nee*	40	*YOHNjoo*
3	*sahn*	50	*gohJOO*
4	*shee/yohn*	60	*rohKOOJOO*
5	*goh*	70	*nahNAJjoo*
6	*rohKOO*	80	*hahCHEEJOO*
7	*sheeCHEE/NAHnah*	90	*KYOOjoo*
8	*hahCHEE*	100	*hyahKOO*
9	*koo/kyoo*	101	*hyahKOO eechee*
10	*joo*	102	*hyahKOO NEE*
11	*JOO eechee*	110	*hyah KOO JOO*
12	*JOO nee*	120	*hyahKOO NEEjoo*
13	*JOO sahn*	200	*neeHYAHKOO*
14	*JOO shee/JOO yohn*	210	*neeHYAHKOO JOO*
15	*JOO goh*	300	*SAHMbyahkoo*
16	*JOO rohkoo*	400	*YOHNhyahkoo*
17	*JOO sheeCHEE/ JOO NAHnah*	500	*gohHYAHKOO*
18	*JOO hahCHEE*	600	*rohPYAHKOO*
19	*JOO koo/JOO kyoo*	700	*nahNAHhyakoo*
20	*NEEjoo*	800	*hahPYAHKOO*
21	*NEEjoo eechee*	900	*KYOOhyahkoo*
22	*NEEjoo nee*	1,000	*SEHn*
23	*NEEjoo sahn*	1,100	*SEHn hyahKOO*
24	*NEEjoo shee/ NEEjoo yohn*	1,200	*sehn neeHYAHKOO*
25	*NEEjoo goh*	2,000	*neeSEHn*
26	*NEEjoo rohKOO*	10,000	*eeCHEEMAHn*
27	*NEEjoo sheeCHEE/ NEEjoo NAHnah*	50,000	*gohMAHn*
28	*NEEjoo hahCHEE*	100,000	*JOOMAHn*
29	*NEEjoo koo/ NEEjoo kyoo*	1,000,000	*hyahKOOMAHn*
30	*SAHNjoo*	1,000,000,000	*JOO-ohkoo*
31	*SAHNjoo eechee*		

F. ORDINAL NUMBERS

first	*eeCHEE BAHNmeh*
second	*nee BAHNmeh*
third	*sahn bahnmeh*
fourth	*yohn bahnmeh*
fifth	*goh BAHNmeh*
sixth	*rohKOO BAHNmeh*
seventh	*nahNAH BAHNmeh*
eighth	*hahCHEE BAHNmeh*
ninth	*kyoo bahnmeh*
tenth	*joo bahnmeh*
eleventh	*jooeechee bahnmeh*
twelfth	*joonee bahnmeh*
thirteenth	*joosahn bahnmeh*
fourteenth	*jooyohn bahnmeh*
fifteenth	*joogoh bahnmeh*
sixteenth	*joorohkoo bahumeh*
seventeenth	*joonahnah bahnmeh*
eighteenth	*joohahchee bahnmeh*
nineteenth	*jookyoo bahnmeh*
twentieth	*neeJOO BAHNMEH*
twenty-first	*NEEjooeeCHEE BAHNMEH*
twenty-second	*NEEjoonee BAHNMEH*
thirtieth	*sahnjoo bahnmeh*
fortieth	*yohnJOO BAHNMEH*
fiftieth	*gohJOO BAHNMEH*
sixtieth	*rohKOOJOO BAHNMEH*
seventieth	*nahNAHJOO BAHNMEH*
eightieth	*hahCHEEJOO BAHNMEH*
ninetieth	*kyoojoo bahnmeh*
hundredth	*hyaKOO BAHNMEH*
thousandth	*SEHN bahnmeh*

G. TIME OF DAY

1:00	*eeCHEEjee*
2:00	*NEE jee*
3:00	*SAHN jee*
4:00	*YOH jee*
5:00	*GOH jee*
6:00	*rohKOO jee*
7:00	*sheeCHEE jee*
8:00	*hahCHEE jee*
9:00	*KOO jee*
10:00	*JOO jee*
11:00	*JOOEECHEE jee*
12:00	*JOONEE jee*
1:00 A.M.	*GOHzehn eeCHEE jee*
3:00 P.M.	*GOHgoh SAHN jee*
noon	*SHOHgoh*
midnight	*mahYOHnahkah*
1:15	*eeCHEE jee JOOGOH hoon*
12:45	*JOONEE jee YOHNjooGOH hoon*
1:30	*eeCHEE JEE HAHn*
7:05	*sheeCHEE jee GOH hoon*
4:55	*YOH jee gohJOOGOH hoon*

H. DAYS OF THE WEEK

Monday	*gehTSOOYOHhbee*
Tuesday	*kahYOHbee*
Wednesday	*SOOEEYOHbee*
Thursday	*mohKOOYOHbee*
Friday	*KEENYOHbee*
Saturday	*dohYOHbee*
Sunday	*neeCHEEYOHbee*

I. MONTHS

January	*eeCHEE GAHTSOO*
February	*nee GAHTSOO*
March	*SAHN gahtsoo*
April	*shee GAHTSOO*
May	*GOH gahtsoo*
June	*rohKOO GAHTSOO*
July	*sheeCHEE GAHTSOO*
August	*hahCHEE GAHTSOO*
September	*KOO gahtsoo*
October	*joo gahtsoo*
November	*jooeechee gahtsoo*
December	*joonee gahtsoo*

J. DATES

1998	*SEHn KYOOhyahkoo KYOOjoo hahCHEE nehn*
1999	*SEHn KYOOhyahkoo KYOOjoo KYOOnehn*
2000	*nee SEHN NEHN*
2001	*nee SEHN eeCHEE nehn*
2002	*nee SEHN NEE nehn*
2003	*nee SEHN SAHN NEHN*
2004	*nee SEHN yoh NEHN*
2005	*nee SEHN goh NEHN*
Today is Thursday, September 22.	*KYOH wah KOOgahtsoo NEE-jooneeNEECHEE, mohKOOYO-Hbee dehsoo.*
Yesterday was Wednesday, September 21.	*KeeNOHwah KOOgahtsoo NEEjooeeCHEE NEECHEE, sooEEYOHbee dehsheetah.*
The day before yesterday was Tuesday, September 20.	*OhTOHTOHY wah KOOgaht-soohaTSOOKAH, kahYOHbee dehsheetah.*

Tomorrow is Friday, September 23.	*AhSHEETAH wah KOOgahtsoo NEEjooSAHN neechee, KEENYO-Hbeedehsoo.*
The day after tomorrow is Saturday, September 24.	*AhSAHteh wah KOOgahtsoo NEEjooyohKAH, dohYOHbee dehsoo.*
Next Friday is September 30.	*RaYESHOO NOH KEENYOH-bee wahKOOgahtsoo SAHNJOO neechee dehsoo.*
Last Friday was September 16.	*SEHNSHOO NOH KEENYO-Hbee wahKOOgahtsoo JOO-ROHKOO NEECHEE dehsheetah.*

K. MEASUREMENTS: DISTANCE

inch	*EEnchee*
foot	*HOOtoh*
yard	*YAHdoh*
mile	*MAYEroo*
millimeter	*meeREE MEHtohroo*
meter	*mehtohroo*
kilometer	*keeROH MEHtohroo*

JAPANESE

3. Common Hospitality Scenarios

A. GREETINGS AND INTRODUCTIONS

GREETING THE GUEST

EMPLOYEE

Good morning,...	***OhHAHYOH gohZAYEMAH-soo,...***
• Mr./Mrs./Miss ____.	**• ____ *sahmah.***
• ladies and gentlemen.	***• meeNAHsahmah.***
• everyone.	***• meeNAHsahmah.***
Good afternoon, Mr. ____.	***KONneecheewah, ____ sahmah.***
Good evening, Mr. ____.	***KOHNbahnwah, ____ sahmah.***

TIP! ••••

Most American employees are used to greeting guests jovially and asking them how they are. However, in any but the most informal settings, this behavior may actually be considered impolite. Asking guests how they are is stepping outside the bounds of your position and throws the burden onto the guest to answer you. Other cultures usually observe this principle to a much greater extent than we do.

Hello, Mr. _____.	*KOHNneecheewah, _____ sahmah.*
Welcome to…	*…ni YOHkohsoh.*
• the hotel.	• *TOH HOHtehroo*
• the restaurant.	• *TOH REHsootohrahn*
• our city.	• *WahTAHsheetahchee noh mahCHEE*
• the United States.	• *AhMEHREEKAH*
If there is anything I can do to make your stay more pleasant, please let me know.	*YohREE kaYETEHKEENAH gohTAYEZAYENOH tahMEHnee, wahTAHKOOSHEENEE dehKEErookohTOHgah gohZAYEMAHsheetahrah, NAHndehmoh ohSHAHteh, kooDAHSAYE.*
May I…	*…yohROHSHEEdeh shohkah?*
• take your coat(s)?	• *KOHtoh oh ohAHZOO-KAHREEsheeTEHmoh*
• carry your…for you?	• *…oh ohHAHKOHBEE shee-TEHmoh.*
• bags	• *BAHgoo*
• suitcase	• *SOOTSOOKEHsoo*
How are you today?	*GohKEEGEHN eeKAHgah dehsooKAH?*

GUEST

I am…	…*dehsoo.*
• fine, thank you.	• *OhKAHGEHSAHMAHDEH GEHnkee*
• okay.	• *MAHMAH*
• very tired.	• *TohTEHMOH tsooKAHreeteh eeMAHsoo*
• not feeling well.	• *KEEboongah wahROOee*
And you?	*GohKEEGEHN eeKAHgah dehsooKAH?*

INTRODUCTIONS

EMPLOYEE

My name is _____.	*WahTAHSHEENOH nah-MAHEH WAH _____ dehsoo.*
I am the…	*OhKYAHKOOSAHMAH noh tahNTOHnoh…dehsoo.*
• door attendant (doorman).	• *dohAHmahn*
• bell attendant (bellman).	• *behroomahn*
• valet-parking attendant.	• *PAHKEENGOO GAHkahree*
• driver.	• *OONTEHnshoo*
• captain.	• *KYAHpootehn*
• concierge.	• *kohnsheeEHj oo*

TIP! ••••

It is typical of American employees to introduce themselves to the guest. This practice allows the guest to call an employee by name when s/he needs something. This is not a common practice in other countries, however, so the international guest may simply ignore your introduction.

• room attendant.	• *hehYAH GAHkahree*
• host.	• *HOHsootoh*
• hostess.	• *HOHsootehsoo*
• manager.	• *mahNEHJAH*
• server (waiter/waitress).	• *wayTAH/WAYtohrehsoo*
• chef.	• *SHEHhoo*
• activities director.	• *ahKOOTEEBEETEE deeREHKOOtah*
Mr. (Mrs., Miss) ____, this is Mr. (Mrs., Miss) ____, the manager.	(guest) *sahmah, koh-CHEERAHWAHmahNEH-JAH NOH ____ dehsoo.*
Mr. (Mrs., Miss) ____, may I introduce our manager, Mr. (Mrs., Miss) ____?	(guest) *sahmah, wahTAH-KOOSHEE DOHmohno mahNEHJAH NOH ____ oh gohSHOHKAYE sheeMAHsoo.*

B. RESERVATIONS

HOTEL RESERVATIONS

OPERATOR

Good morning (afternoon, evening), ____ Hotel.	*OhHAHYOH gohZAYE-MAHsoo (KOHNneecheewah/KOHNbahnwah), ____ HOHteh-roo de gohZAYEMAHsoo.*
How may I direct your call?	*DOHnohyohnee ohTSOONAHGEE eeTAHSHEEMAH SHOH?*

GUEST

Hello. Do you speak Japanese?	*MOHsheemohshee. NeeHOHN GOH wah hahNAHSHEEMAH sooKAH?*

OPERATOR

One moment, please.	*SHOHshoh ohMAHCHEE, kooDAHSAYE.*
I'll connect you with a bilingual operator.	*BAYEREENgahroo noh ohPEH-REHTAH NEE ohTSOON-AHGEE sheeMAHsoo.*
I have a book here to help me.	*KohKOHNEE SAHNKOHNEE NAHroo HOHN oh MOHteheemahsoo.*

Please speak slowly.	*YooKOOree hahNAHsheeteh, kooDAHSAYE.*

GUEST

I would like to make a reservation, please.	*YohYAHKOO OH, ohNEHGAYE sheeMAHsoo.*

OPERATOR

For a room or for one of the restaurants?	*OhHEHYAH DEHsooKAH, sohREETOHmoh REHsootohrahn dehsooKAH?*

GUEST

For a room, please.	*HehYAHoh, ohNEHGAYE sheeMahsoo.*
For the _____ Restaurant, please.	*_____ REHsootohrahn oh, ohNEHGAYE sheeMAHsoo.*

OPERATOR

One moment, please. I will direct your call to Reservations.	*SHOHshoh ohMAHCHEE, kooDAHSAYE. YohYAHKOO-KAHNREE ohTSOONAHGEE sheeMAHsoo.*
One moment, please. I will direct your call to the restaurant.	*SHOHshoh ohMAHCHEE, kooDAHSAYE. REHsootohrahn nee ohTSOONAHGEE sheeMAHsoo.*

CLERK

Hello. This is Reservations.	*YohYAHKOOKAHDEH. GohZAYEMAHsoo.*
What date would you like?	*EEtsoo oh gohKEEBOH dehsooKAH?*

GUEST

May 27th.	*GOHgahtsu NEEjoo-sheeCHEE NEECHEE dehsoo.*

CLERK

For how many nights?	*NAHmpahkoo dehsooKAH?*

GUEST

For three nights, please.	*SAHmpahkoo, ohNEGAYE sheeMAHsoo.*
For a week.	*EeSHOOkan, ohNEHGAYE sheeMAHsoo.*

Just one night.	*EePAHKKOO dehsoo.*
CLERK	
For how many people?	*NAHnmeh sahmah dehsooKAH?*
GUEST	
For two people.	*HooTAHREE dehsoo.*
For one person.	*HeeTOHree dehsoo.*
For two adults and a child.	*OhTOHNAH hooTAHREE toh kohDOHMOH heeTOHree dehsoo.*
CLERK	
Do you have…	*…wah ahREEMAHsooKAH?*
• any special needs?	• *TohKOOBEHTSOONEE heeTSOOYOHNAH kohTOH*
• any special requests?	• *TohKOOBEHTSOONAH reeKOOEHsootoh*
GUEST	
No, thank you.	*EEeh, ahREEMAHSEHn.*
I would like…	*WahTAHSHEE wah…gah EEno dehsoogah.*
• to be near the stairs.	• *KAYEDAHN noh cheeKAHkoo*
• to be near an exit.	• *DEHgoochee noh cheeKAHkoo*
• a cot for our child.	• *kohDOHMOHNOH BEHdoh*
• a handicapped-accessible room.	• *HAHNDEEKYAHpoo AHkoo-sehsoogah AHroo hehYAH*
CLERK	
The rate is _____ per night.	*HeeTOHbahn _____ deh gohZAYEMAHsoo.*
Would you like to guarantee the reservation with a credit card?	*KooREHJEETOHKAHdohdeh yohYAHKOONOO kahKOOTE-HEEOH nahSAYEMAHsooKAH?*
GUEST	
Yes, here is my _____ card.	*HAye, _____ KAHdoh dehsoo.*
My credit card number is _____.	*KooREHJEETOH KAHdoh noh bahNGOH wah _____ dehsoo.*

CLERK	
What is the expiration date?	*YOOKOHKEEgehn wah EEtsoo dehsooKAH?*
Thank you.	***AhREEgahtoh gohZAHyemah-sheetah.***

RESTAURANT RESERVATIONS

RESTAURANT HOST	
Good morning (afternoon, evening), ____ Restaurant.	*OhHAHYOH gohZAYE-MAHsoo (KOHNneecheewah, KOHbahnwah) ____, REHsoo-tohrahn de gohZAYEMAHsoo.*
GUEST	
I'd like to reserve a table for…	*…noh yohYAHKOO OH sheeTAYE noh dehsoogah.*
• breakfast.	• *Chohshohkoo*
• lunch.	• *Chooshohkoo*
• dinner.	• *Yooshohkoo*
HOST	
For what time?	*NAHnjee dehsooKAH?*
GUEST	
For…o'clock.	*…deh, ohNEHGAYE shee-MAHsoo.*
• seven.	• *SheeCHEE jee*
• eight	• *HahCHEE jee*
• nine	• *KOO jee*
For eight-thirty.	*HahCHEE JEE HAHn.*
HOST	
For how many people?	*NAHnmeh sahmah dehsooKAH?*
GUEST	
For one person.	*HeeTOHree dehsoo.*
For…people.	*…dehsoo.*
• two	• *HooTAHREE*
• four	• *YohNEEn*

• six	• *RohKOOneen*
HOST	
And your name, please?	*OhNAHMAHEH OH, ohNEH-GAYE sheeMAHsoo.*
GUEST	
My name is ____.	*____ dehsoo.*
HOST	
And is there a phone number where we can reach you?	*GohREHNRAHKOO dehKEEroo ohDEHNWAH BAHngoh wah gohZAYEMAHsooKAH?*
GUEST	
Yes, the number is ____.	*HAye, ____ dehsoo.*
By the way, do you have any…items on the menu?	*TohKOHROHdeh,…MEHnyoo wah ahREEMAHsooKAH?*
• vegetarian	• *behJEETAHreeahn noh*
• macrobiotic	• *zehnsheekee noh*
• low-fat	• *TAYSHEEboh noh*
• low-sodium	• *EHnboon noh sooKOOnaye/ taYEN noh*
HOST	
Would you like smoking or nonsmoking?	*KeeTSOOEHN SEHKEE toh KEENEHNsehkee noh DOH-cheerahneenahSAYEMAH-sooKAH?*
GUEST	
We would like…	*…nee sheeTEH kooDAHSAYE.*
• smoking.	• *KeeTSOOEHN sehkee*
• nonsmoking.	• *KEENEHN sehkee*
HOST	
Thank you.	*AhREEgahtoh gohZAYEMAHsoo.*
That will be two people at eight o'clock.	*HahCHEEjee nee ohHOOT-AHREE SAHMAH dehsoo.*
That's a party of six at seven-thirty.	*SheeCHEE JEE HAhn goh-YOHYAHKOONOH, rohKOOmeh sahmah noh gooROOpoo dehsoo.*

C. COURTESY AND COMPLAINTS

GENERAL EXPRESSIONS OF COURTESY

Please.	*OhNEHGAYE sheeMAHsoo.*
Thank you.	*AhREEgahto gohZAYEMAHsoo.*
You're welcome.	*DOHeeTAHSHEEMAHsheeteh.*
Excuse me.	*SooMEEMAHSEHn.*
I beg your pardon.	*SooMEEMAHSEHn.*
I'm (terribly) sorry.	*MOHSHEEWAHKEH gohZAYEMAHSEHn.*
That's okay.	*DaYEJOHboo dehsoo.*
No problem.	*MOHNDAYE goh-ZAYEMAHSEHn.*
It doesn't matter.	*KAHNKEH ahREEMAHSEHn.*

COURTESY IN THE HOTEL

CONCIERGE

Good morning, sir, ma'am.	*OhHAHYOH gohZAYEMAHsoo.*
May I help you with something today?	*NAHneekah gohZAYEMAHsoo dehshohKAH?*

GUEST

Yes, I need...	*...gah heeTSOOYOH DEHsoo.*
• my room made up between now and _____.	• *_____ jeemahdeenee hehYAHoh SOHJEEohSHEETEH eetahdah-noh koonoh.*
• more towels, please.	• *TAHohroo oh kooDAHSAYE*
• a rental car.	• *RehNTAH kah*
• a taxi.	• *TAHkooshee*
• a fax sent.	• *FAHkoosoo oh ohKOOROOnoh.*
• some letters mailed.	• *TehGAHMEE oh ohKOOROOnoh.*
• to make arrangements for a business meeting.	• *SHOHDAHN NOH YOY oh sheeTEHKOODAHSAroonah.*
• tickets to a show.	• *SHOH noh cheeKEHtoh*

• tickets to a concert.	***• KOHnsahtoh noh cheeKEHhtoh***
• tickets to a game.	***• SheeAYE NOH cheeKEHtoh***

GUEST COMPLAINTS IN THE HOTEL

CONCIERGE

Is everything satisfactory?	***SOObehteh yohROHSHEEde shohkah?***

GUEST

No, there is a problem.	***MOHNDAYE GAH ahREE-MAHsoo.***
• The light	*• DEHnkee*
• The toilet	*• TOYreh*
• The television	*• TEHrehbee*
• The radio	*• RAHjeeoh*
• The air-conditioning	*• KOOchoh, ehAHKOHn*
• The alarm clock	*• MehZAHMAHSHEE DOHkeh*
• The heat	*• AHtsoosah*
• The key	*• KahGEE*
• The lock	*• KahGEE*
• The fan	*• SehmPOOkee*
…doesn't work.	*…gah kohwahrehteeMAHSOO.*

CLERK

I'll have Maintenance fix that right away.	*SOOgoonee mehNTEHNAHNSOO GAHkahreenee nahOHSAHSEHMAHsoo.*
I apologize.	*MOHsheewahkeh gohZAYEMAHSEHn.*

GUEST

My room wasn't clean.	***HehYAHgah KEEraynee NAHteh eeMAHSEHndehsheetah.***
My room was noisy.	***OhTOHgah ooROOSAHkahtah dehsoo.***
My room stinks (smells).	***HehYAHgah eeYAHnah neeOYgah sheeMAHsoo.***

The bed was uncomfortable.	*BEHdohnoh nehGOHKOH-CHEEGAH wahROOkahtah.*
The water wasn't hot.	*OhYOOGAH nooROOkahtah.*
Room service was late.	*ROOMOOSAHbeesoogah ohSOHkahtah.*
The service was very poor.	*SAHbeesoogah wahROOkahrah.*
The employees were…	*JOOGYOHeen wah…*
• very good.	• *tohTEHMOH YOHkahtah.*
• excellent.	• *sooBAHRAHSHEEkahtah.*
• rude.	• *TAYEdohgah wahROOkahtah.*
• incompetent.	• *yahKOOnee tahTAHnahkahtah.*
• unfriendly.	• *ahEESOHgah wahROOkahtah.*
I didn't receive my wake-up call.	*MOHNEENGOO KOHroo gah ahREEMAHSEHNn dehsheetah.*
I'm very disappointed with the level of service in this hotel.	*KohNOH HOHtehroo noh SAHbeesoo NEEwah toh TEHmoh gahKAHree sheemahsheetah.*
This is the worst hotel I've ever seen.	*KOHNNAHNEE heeDOYnohwah MEEtahkohtohgah naye.*

CONCIERGE

Please let me make the situation right.	*NAHntohkah eeTAH-SHEEMAHsoo.*
I'm certain we can straighten out the problem.	*KahNAHRAHZOO mohNDAYE oh KAYEKEHTSOO dehKEE-rootoh ohMOYMAHsoo.*
You won't pay for anything that wasn't completely up to your standards.	*GohMAHNZOHkoo sahREHNAHkahtah BOONnoh ohDAYEwah eeTAHDAHKEE-MAHSEHn.*
Please tell me what I can do to correct this terrible situation.	*KohNOH JOHKYOH OH kahEHROO tahMEHnee wahTAHKOOSHEENEE deh-KEErookohtoh oh ohSHAHteh, kooDAHSAYE.*
We'll take ____ percent off your bill.	*DAYEkeen noh ____ PAHSE-Hntoh oh ohHEEKEE eeTAHSHEEMAHsoo.*

We're going to give you ____ night(s), compliments of the hotel.	*____ HAHKOOkahn moo-RYODEH ohTOHMAHREE eeTAHDAHKEHROO YOHnee eeTAHSHEEMAHsoo.*
Your entire bill is compliments of the house.	*DAYEkeenwah SOObehteh moo-RYOtoh sahSEHTEH eeTAHDAHKEEMAHsoo.*

GUEST

Yes, that would be satisfactory.	*SohREEDEH KEHkoh dehsoo.*
No, that would not be satisfactory.	*SohREEDEHwah hooJOOboon dehsoo.*
I appreciate all your efforts.	*GohKYOHRYOHKOO ahREE-gahtoh gohZAYEMAHsheetah.*
Thank you, that would be very nice.	*DOHmoh, ahREEgahtoh gohZAYEMAHsoo.*
I will never come here again.	*MOH neeDOHTOH kohKOH-NEEwah keeMAHSEHn.*

MANAGEMENT COMPLAINTS

MANAGER

We have had some complaints about the noise coming from your room.	*OhKYAHKOOSAHMAHnoh ohHEHYAHKAHRAH OHkeenah ohTOHgah keeKOHEHROOtoh kooJOHGAH DEHtehohreem-ahsoo.*
You are disturbing…	*…nee gohMEHwahkoo toh nahreemahsoo.*
• the people in the room next door.	• *TohNAHREENOH hehYAHNOH ohKYAHKOO-SAHMAH*
• the people at the next table.	• *TohNAHREENOH TEH-BOOROOnoh ohKYAHKOO-SAHMAH*
• our other guests.	• *HohKAHNOH ohKYAHKOO-SAHMAH*

GUEST

We're sorry.	*Dohmoh sooMEEMAHSEHn.*
We understand.	*WahKAHREEMAHsheetah.*
We'll take care of it.	*KeeOHTSOOKEHMAHsoo.*

We'll keep it down from now on.	*KohREHKAHRAH SHEEzook-ahnee sheemahsoo.*
Who cares!	*KAHNKEH NAYE dehshoh!*
Leave us alone!	*HohTOYteh kooDAHSAYE!*

MANAGER

If you don't cooperate, I'm afraid I'll have to…	*GohKYOHRYOHKOO eeTAHDAHKAHNAYTOH…*
• ask you to leave the hotel (restaurant).	• *HOHtehroo (REHsootohrahn) kahrah DEHteh eetahdah-keemahsoo.*
• call security.	• *KEHBEEeen oh yohBEE-MAHsoo.*
• call the police.	• *KEHSAHTSOO OH yoh-BEEMAHsoo.*

D. EMERGENCIES AND SAFETY

EMPLOYEE

Please note the emergency exits on this card.	*KohNOH KAHdohdeh heeJOH-goochee oh ohTAHSHEE-KAHMEH, kooDAHSAYE.*
Please note the emergency escape route on the door.	*DOHahnee KAYEte AHroo heeJOHKAYEdahn oh ohTAHSHEEKAHMEH, kooDAHSAYE.*
Your room is equipped with smoke alarms.	*OhKYAHKOOSAHMAH NOH ohHEYYAHNEEwah keh-MOOREE TAHNCHEEKEE-gah TSOOeeteh eeMAHsoo.*
Here is the fire alarm.	*KohREHWAH kahSAYE HOH-CHEEkee dehsoo.*
In an emergency, dial ____.	*KEENKYOOJEEtaye noh tohKEEwah ____ BAHN-woh dayeyahroo sheeTEH kooDAHSAYE.*

GUEST

Help!	*TahSOOKEHTEH!*
Fire!	*KAHJEE dehsoo!*
I need a doctor.	*EeSHAH oh YOHndeh, koo-DAHSAYE.*

JAPANESE

I'm…	*WahTAHSHEEWAH…*
My husband (wife) is…	*WahTAHSHEENOH ohTOH (TSOOmah) wah…*
Someone is…	*DAHREHKAHgah…*
• very sick.	• *heeDOHKOO BYOHKEE dehsoo.*
• having a heart attack.	• *SHEENZOH HOHsah oh ohKOHsheeteh eemahsoo.*
• nauseated.	• *hahKEEKEHgah sheemahsoo.*
• choking.	• *EEkeegah kooROOSHEEn-deemahsoo.*
• losing consciousness.	• *kee OH ooSHEENAHTEH eemahsoo.*
• about to vomit.	• *hahKEESOH dehsoo.*
• having a seizure.	• *hohSAH oh ohKOHSHEETEH eemahsoo.*
I can't breathe.	*EEkeegah dehKEEMAHSEHn.*
MANAGER	
I'll call an ambulance.	*KYOOKYOOshah oh yohBEEMAHsoo.*
Don't move.	*OoGOHKAHnayedeh kooDAHSAYE.*
The doctor will be here very soon.	*SOOgoonee eeSHAHGAH keeMAHsoo.*
Are you hurt?	*EeTAYE dehsooKAH?*
What happened?	*DOHsheetahnoh dehsooKAH?*
GUEST	
I tripped and fell.	*TsooMAHZOOEETEH kohROHBEEMAHsheetah.*
I cut myself.	*KEEteh sheeMAYEMAHsheetah.*
I drank too much.	*NohMEESOOGEE MAHsheetah.*
I don't know.	*WahKAHREEMAHSEHn.*
I hit my head.	*AhTAHMAH oh ooCHEE-MAHsheetah.*
I've injured my…	*…oh kehGAH sheemahsheetah.*
• neck.	• *KooBEE*

• back.	• *SehNAHKAH*
• arm.	• *OoDEH*
• hand.	• *Teh*
• leg.	• *AhSHEE*
• foot.	• *AhSHEE*
• eye(s).	• *Meh*

DOCTOR (MEDICAL TECHNICIAN)

You'll be fine; try to relax.	*DAYJOHboo dehsookahrah; ohCHEETSOOEETEH, kooDAHSAYE.*
We're taking you to the hospital.	*BYOEEN NEE ohTSOOREH sheeMAHsoo.*
Whom should we notify?	*DOHnahtahnee sheeRAHSEH MAHsooKAH?*

GUEST

I've been robbed.	*TOHNAHNNEE AYEMAHsheetah.*

MANAGER

What did they take?	*NAHNEE OH tohRAHreh-tahndehsooKAH?*
Let me call the police.	*KEHSAHTSOO NEE dehnWAH sheeMAHSHOH.*
Attention, ladies and gentlemen.	*MeeNAHsahmah ohKEEKEE, kooDAHSAYE.*
May I have your attention, please?	*OSHEEZOOKAHNEE nehGAYEMAHhsoo?*
Please…	*DOHkah…*
• remain calm.	• *ohCHEETSOOEETEH, kooDAHSAYE.*
• follow the instructions of the staff.	• *KAHkahree noh SHEEjeenee sheeTAHGAHTEH koo-DAHSAYE.*
• wait in your rooms.	• *gohJEEBOON NOH hehYAHdeh ohMAHCHEE kooDAHSAYE.*
• get under a table or doorway.	• *TEHBOOROO NOH sheeTAHKAH DOHhah noh tohKOHROH nee eeTEH kooDAHSAYE.*

JAPANESE

• follow the evacuation plan (route) printed on your door (in the hallways).	• *DOHah (ROHKAH) nee hahTEH AHrooheeNAHN TEHjoon (TOHtoh) nee sheeTAHGAHTEH koo-DAHSAYE.*
We'll have the situation under control as soon as possible.	*EeKOHKOOmoh HAHyahkoo JEEtaye oh KAYEKEHTSOO eeTAHSHEE-MAHsoo.*
Thank you for your patience.	*GohSHEEmboh eeTAHDAH-KEEMAHsheeteh, ahREEgahto gohZAYEMAHsoo.*

4. Checking In

A. AT THE FRONT DESK

FRONT DESK CLERK

Good morning (afternoon, evening).	*OhHAHYOH gohZAHYEMAHsoo (KOHNneecheewah, KOHNbahnwah).*
How may I help you?	*EeRAHSHAYEMAHseh.*

GUEST

I have a reservation under the name ____.	____ *noh nahMAHEH DEHyoh-YAHKOO sheeTAHndeh-soogah.*
Do you have a room for one (two)?	*HeeTOHREEBOON (HOO-TAHreeboon)NOH heYAHwah ahREEMAHsoo-KAH?*

CLERK

Yes, we have your reservation.	*HAye, gohYOHYAHKOO TAHsheekahnee nee ooKEHTAH-MAHWAHTEH ohREEMAHsoo.*
Yes, for how many nights?	*NAHnpahkoo dehsooKAH?*
No, I'm sorry, we're full.	*MOHsheewahkeh gohZAYE-MAHSEHn, mahNSHEETSOO deh gohZAYEMAHsoo.*

GUEST

For ____ night(s), please.	____ *HAHkoo, ohNEHGAYE sheeMAHsoo.*
What are your rates?	*OhEEKOORAH DEHsooKAH?*

CLERK

• For a single,	• *SheeNGOOROO wah,*
• For a double,	• *DAHbooroo wah,*
• For adjoining rooms,	• *TohNAHREEAHoo heeYAHwah,*
• For a suite,	• *SooEETOH ROOmoo wah,*
...the rate is _____ per night.	*...eePAHKOO _____ deh gohZAYEMAHsoo.*

GUEST

Are any meals included?	*ShohKOOJEEWAH KOHmeedehsooKAH?*
Is breakfast included?	*CHOHSHOKOO wah KOKHmeedehsooKAH?*

CLERK

No, meals are extra.	*Ee-eh, behTSOODEH gohZAYEMAHsoo.*
Yes, breakfast is included.	*HAye, CHOHSHOkoowah hooKOOMAHrehteh ohreemahsoo.*
You can choose...	*...oh ohEERAHBEE eeTAHDAHKEHMAHsoo.*
• the American plan (all meals included).	• *AhMEHREEKAHn POOrahn (ZEHnshohKOOJEE KOHmee)*
• the modified American plan (breakfast and dinner).	• *GEHnTEH ahMEHREEKAHn POOrahn (CHOHshohkoo toh YOOshohkoo)*
• the European plan (no meals included).	• *YOHROHPEEahn POOrahn (ohSHOHKOOJEE NAHshee)*

GUEST

I'd like a room...	*...hehYAHoh, ohNEEGAYE sheeMAHsoo.*
• that faces the back (front).	• *OoRAHGAHWAH (ohMOHTEHGAHWAH) NOH*
• that faces the water (pool).	• *MeeZOOGAHWAH (POOrooGAHWAH) NOH*
• with a private bath/toilet/ shower.	• *BAHsoo/toyehREH/shaWAH tsooKEE NOH*

• with a handicapped-accessible bathroom.	• *HaNDEHKYAHpooYOH NOH bahSOOROOMOO tsooKEE NOH*
• with air-conditioning.	• *EhAHKOHn tsooKEE NOH*
• with a TV.	• *TehREHBEE tsooKEE NOH*
• with cable.	• *KEHbooroo tehREHBEE tsooKEE NOH*
• with a fax machine.	• *FAkoosoo tsooKEE NOH*
• with a phone.	• *DehNWAH gah AHroo*
• with a network hookup for my computer.	• *KohmPYOOtah oh tsooNAHGEHRAHREHROO*
• with a view.	• *KEHsheekee noh EE*
• with a whirlpool bath/Jacuzzi.	• *JahKOOJEE tsooKEE NOH*
• with two double beds.	• *DahBOOROO BEHdoh hooTAHTSOOnoh*
• with a king-size bed.	• *KeeNGOO SAyezoonoh BEHdoh noh*
• with an extra bed.	• *BEHdohgah yohBOONnee AHroo*
• with a baby crib.	• *BehBEE BEhdoh tsooKEENOH*
• with a balcony.	• *BahROOKOHNEE tsooKEE NOH*
• with a sitting area.	• *SheeTEHNGOO EEreeah noh ahroo*
• with a bar.	• *BAH tsooKEE NOH*
• with a kitchenette.	• *KeeCHEEN tsooKEE NOH*
• away from the elevator.	• *EhREHBEHtah kahrah TOY*
• with no meals.	• *ShohKOOJEE gah NAYE*

CLERK

No problem.	*KahsheeKOHMAHREE MAHsheetah.*
I'm sorry.	*MOHsheewahkeh gohZAYmahSEHn.*
There is none available.	*TahDAYEmah ahKEEGAH gohZAYEmahSEHn.*

We don't provide/offer that.	*SohREHWAH gohZAYE-mahSEHn.*
GUEST	
Does the hotel have…	*KohNOHHOHtehrooneewah… gah ahREEMAHsooKAH?*
• a restaurant?	• *REHsootohrahn*
• a bar?	• *bah*
• room service?	• *ROOmoo SAHbeesoo*
• a gym/health club?	• *JEEmoo/feeTOHNEHSOO SEHntah*
• a spa hot tub?	• *sooPAH*
• a swimming pool?	• *sooEEMEENGOO POOroo*
• baby-sitting?	• *tahKOOJEESHOH*
• tennis courts?	• *tehNEESOOKOHtoh*
• laundry (dry-cleaning) service?	• *sehNTAHKOO (dohRAYE-kooREEneengoo) SAHbeesoo*
• a garage?	• *gaREHjee*
May I see the room?	*HehYAHoh MEEsehteh mohRAHEHMAHsooKAH?*
CLERK	
Yes, certainly.	*MohCHEErohndehsoo.*
Here's the key.	*KahGEEdeh gohZAYEMAHsoo.*
Would you like another room?	*BehTSOONOH ohHEHYAHNEE eeTAHSHEEMAHsooKAH?*
GUEST	
I'd like something…	*…gah EEdehsoo.*
• smaller.	• *MOHtoh CHEESAYE tohkohroh*
• larger.	• *MOHtoh OHKEE tohkohroh*
• quieter.	• *SHEEzookahnah tohkohroh*
• better.	• *MOHtoh EEtohkohroh*
• cheaper.	• *MOHtoh yahSOOee tohkohroh*
• on another floor.	• *CheeGAHOO KAYE*
I'll take the room, please.	*KohKOHNEE sheeMAHsoo.*

CLERK	
Very well, how will you be paying?	*OhSHEEHAHRAYE wah DOHsahrehmahsooKAH?*
GUEST	
I'll pay with…	*…deh hahRAHeeMAHsoo.*
• cash.	• *GEHnKEEn*
• a credit card.	• *KooREHJEETOH KAHdoh*
• traveler's checks.	• *TohRAHBEHRAHzoo CHEHkoo*
CLERK	
Thank you.	*AhREEgahtoh gohZAYEMAH-sheetah.*
To charge meals and services to your room, I'll need a credit card.	*OhHEHYAHEHnoh ohSHOHKOOJEE toh SAHbeesooneewah kooREHJEETOH KAH, dohgah heeTSOOYOHdehsoo.*
You may settle the bill with traveler's checks (cash).	*TohRAHBEHRAHzoo CHEHkoo (GEHnKEEn) dehohSHEEHAH-RAYE eeTAHDAHKEHMAHsoo.*
If you would like to store valuables, we have a safe.	*KeeCHOHHEEn oh ohMOHCHEEDEHsheetahrah ohAHZOOKAHREE sheeMAHsoo.*
Quiet hours are between ____ and ____.	*____ jeekarhar ____ jeenoh ahEEDAHwah ohSHEEZOOK-AH NEE ohNEGAYE-sheeMAHsoo.*
There are no pets allowed.	*PEHtoh wah haYEREH-MAHSEHn.*
Children under ____ stay free.	*____ saye EEKAHnoh ohKOHSAHMAHWAH mooRYOdehsoo.*
Smoking is allowed only in the bar.	*OhTAHbahkohwah BAHdeh nohmee ohSOOEE eeTAHDAH-KEHMAHsoo.*
We do not allow cooking in the rooms.	*OhHEHYAHDEHnoh CHOHreewah dehKEEMAHSEHn.*

GUEST

Do I (we) have any messages?	*MEHsehjee wah ahREE-MAHsooKAH?*
I would like a wake-up call, please.	*MOHneengoo KOHroowoh, ohNEGAYEsheeMAHsoo.*
May we have..., please?	*...oh eeTAHDAHKEHMAHsoo-KAH, ohNEHGAYEsheeMAHsoo?*
• extra blankets	• *MOHhoo oh NAHnmayeKAH*
• extra towels	• *TAHohroo oh NAHnmayeKAH*
• a hair dryer	• *HeYAH dohRAYEyah*
• an iron	• *AYEROHn*
• ice	• *KOHree*

CLERK

I'll have that brought to your room right away.	*SOOgoonee ohTOHDOHKEH sheeMAHsoo.*

GUEST

Where is...	*...wah DOHkoh dehsooKAH?*
• the bellman (bell attendant)?	• *BehROOBOY*
• the manager?	• *MahNEHJAH*
• the dining room?	• *ShohKOODOH*
• the gift shop?	• *GeeHOOTOH SHOHpoo*
• the newsstand?	• *SHEEMBOON OOreebah*

CLERK

Just over there.	*KohCHEERAHDEH gohZAYEMAHsoo.*

GUEST

How do I use the telephone?	*DEHnwah wah DOHyahteh tsooKAHOOnoh dehsooKAH?*

CLERK

The instructions are next to the phone.	*DEHnwah noh tohNAHREENEE sehTSOOMEHGAH gozayemahsoo.*
Dial _____ for a local (long-distance) call,	*SheNAYEDEHnwah (CHOHkyo-hreeDEHnwah) wah hahJEEMEH-NEE _____ BAHn oh mahWAH-SHEETEH kooDAHSAHee,*

wait for the tone, then dial the number.	*TOHn gah keeKOHEHTAHrah bahnGOH oh DAYEyahroo sheeTEH, kooDAHSAYE.*
Dial ____ for an operator.	*OhPEREHTAH wah ____ BAHn DEHsoo.*

GUEST

Please have our luggage brought to our room.	*NEEmohtsoo oh hehYAHnee hahKOHndeh, kooDAHSAYE.*
We'll need a wheelchair.	*KooROOMAH eesoogah heeTSOOYOH dehsoo.*

CLERK

Yes, right away.	*HAye, tahDAYEmah.*

GUEST

We'd like to order a pizza, please.	*PEEzah oh CHOOmohn sheeTAYEno dehsoogah.*

MANAGER

I'll be happy to call someone for you.	*TahnTOHshah oh ohYOHBEE sheeMAHsoo.*
We have room service, but we don't allow outside vendors into the hotel.	*ROOmooSAHbeesoowah gozayemahsoo gah, SOHtohKAHrahnoh haYEtahtsoowah HOHtehroonee haYEREHMAHSEHn.*

GUEST

We'd like to entertain a few friends in our room.	*TohMOHDAHCHEE oh hehYAHnee yohBEETAyenoh dehsoogah.*

MANAGER

We allow guests in the rooms until ____.	*GEHsootohnoh kahTAHwah ____ mahdehTAYEZAYE dehKEEMAHsoo.*

B. SHOWING GUESTS TO THEIR ROOMS

BELLMAN (BELL ATTENDANT)

My name is ____, and I'm your bell attendant.	*BehROOBOY noh ____, deh gohZAYEMAHsoo.*
May I show you to your room?	*OhHEHYAHEH gohAHNNAYE eeTAHSHEEMAHSHOHKAH?*

GUEST	
No, thanks. We'll find it ourselves.	*KEHkohdehsoo. JeeBOONtah-cheedeh eeKEEMAHsookahrah.*
Yes, please.	*OhNEHGAYE sheeMAHsoo.*
BELLMAN	
This way, please.	*KohCHEERAHdeh gohZAYEMAHsoo.*
The elevator(s) is (are) over here.	*EhREHBEHtahwah kohCHEERAHdeh gohZAYEMAHsoo.*
May I show you the features of your room?	*OhHEHYAHnoh gohAHNNAYEoh eeTAHSHEEMAHSHOHKAH?*
This is the key to the minibar.	*MeeNEEBAH noh kahGEEdeh gohZAYEMAHsoo.*
• Any movie you select	• *EHEEGAH oh gohRAHnnee NAHtah BAHeewah*
• Any long-distance calls you make	• *CHOHkyohree DEHnwah oh nahSAHtah BAHeewah*
• Any snack or beverage you take from the refrigerator	• *REHZOHkohnoh sooNAH-kooyah nohMEEMOHnoh oh mehSHEEAHGAHTAH BAHeewah*
...will be charged to your room.	*...ohHEHYAHnee CHAHjee sahREHMAHsoo.*
Here is the control for the heating (air-conditioning).	*DAHnboh (REHboh) noh CHOHsehtsoowah kohCHEERAHDEHsoo.*

JAPANESE

TIP! ••••

International guests in particular may have questions about using the telephone and will appreciate seeing how the television and pay movies work.

GUEST

How do I call Room Service?	*ROOmooSAHbeesoo wah DOHsoorehbah EEdehsooKAH?*

BELLMAN

Dial ____.	*____ BAHnnee ohkahKEH, kooDAHSAYE.*

GUEST

This room…	*KohNOH HEHYAHwah…*
• is too close to the elevator(s).	• *ehREHBEHtahnee cheeKAHSOOGEEmahsoo.*
• hasn't been made up.	• *kahTAHDSOOeeteh eeMAHSEHn.*
• smells (like cigarettes).	• *eeYAHnah (tahBAHKOHNOH) neeOYgah sheeMAHsoo.*
The toilet (bathtub, sink) is clogged.	*TOYreh (bahsooTAHboo, sehnMEHNDAYE) gah tsooMAHteh eeMAHsoo.*
May I (we) change rooms, please?	*HeyYAH oh kahEHTEH mohRAHEHMAHsooKAH?*

BELLMAN

Please let me check our availability with the front desk.	*FooROHNTOHnee tahSHEEKAHMEHMAHsoo.*
Sure, I'll be happy to assist you.	*MohCHEEROHn, ohTEHtsoodaye eeTAHSHEEMAHsoo.*
Please call if I can help you with anything else.	*NAHneekah gohZAYE-MAHsheetahrah ohYOHBEE kooDAHSAYE.*

VOCABULARY ••••

THE GUEST ROOM

air-conditioning	*rehEEBOH*
balcony	*bahROOkohnee*
bath mat	*bahSOOMAHtoh*
bathtub	*bahSOOTAHBOO*
bed	*BEHdoh*
bedspread	*behDOHSOOPOOREHdoh*
blanket	*MOHhoo*
blinds	*booRAYENDOH*
carpet	*KAHpohtoh*
ceiling	*TEHnJOH*
chair	*eeSOO*
closet	*kooROHzehtoh, ohSHEEEEREH*
conditioner	*kohnDEEshohnah*
couch	*KAHoochee*
crib	*behBEEBEHdoh*
desk	*tsooKOOEH*
Do Not Disturb sign	*ohKOHSAHnayedeh kooDAHSAYE noh TAHboo*
door	*DOHah*
drapes	*dohREHpoo*
dresser	*dohREHsah*
fan	*FAHn*
floor	*yooKAH*
glass(es)	*kohPOO, gooRAHSOO*
hair dryer	*hehAH dohRAYEyah*
(coat) hanger	*(KOHTOH) HAHngah*

(cont'd.)

The Guest Room *(cont'd.)*

heat	*nehTSOO*
ice bucket	*AHEESOO BAHkehtoh*
iron	*AYEROHn*
lamp	*RAHnpoo*
light	*RYEtoh*
lock	*kahGEE, ROHkoo*
minibar	*meeNEEBAH*
mirror	*kahGAHMEE*
nightstand	*mohNOHOHKEEDAYE*
pillow	*mahKOORAH*
radio	*RAHjeeoh*
razor	*kahMEESOHree*
sewing kit	*SAYEHOH SEHtoh*
shampoo	*SHAHmpoo*
sheets	*SHEEtsoo*
shower	*SHAHwah*
shower cap	*shahWAHKYAHpoo*
sink	*nahGAHSHEE*
soap	*sehKEHN*
telephone	*dehNWAH*
television	*TEHrehbee*
thermostat	*ohNDOHKEH*
toilet	*TOYreh*
toilet paper	*TOYREHTOH PEHpah*
toothbrush	*hahBOOrahshee*
toothpaste	*hahMEEGAHkeekoh*
towel	*TAHohroo*
VCR	*beeDEHOHPOOREHyah*
wall	*kahBEH*
window	*MAHdoh*

5. Providing Assistance

A. GIVING DIRECTIONS

CONCIERGE

Good morning. May I help you?	*OhHAHYOH gohZAYEMAHsoo. EeKAHGAH eeTAHSHEE-MAHSHOH?*

GUEST

Yes, where is (are) the…	*…wah DOHkohdehsooKAH?*
• bathrooms?	• *OhTEHAHraye, TOYreh*
• lounge/bar?	• *RahOONJEE/bah*
• coffee shop/restaurant?	• *KOHHEE SHOHpoo/REH-sootohrahn*
• barbershop/hairdresser's?	• *TohKOHYAH/beeYOHeen*
• gift shop?	• *GeeHOOTOH SHOHpoo*
• health club/gym?	• *FeeTOHNEHSOO KOOrahboo/JEEmoo*
• elevator?	• *EhREHBEHtah*
• pay phones?	• *KOHSHOODEHnwah*
• ice machine?	• *KOHreenoh mahSHEEn*

TIP! ••••

You can simply explain many directions, but when they're more complex, you should use either a map or written instructions (or both). Hotels should keep preprinted directions to major sites on hand. Also, many cultures don't speak of distance in terms of city blocks but will understand if you use the word "streets" instead. And remember that most international guests use the metric system and may have difficulties figuring a distance given in miles, yards, or feet.

CONCIERGE

Take...	*...oh ohTSOOKAYE, kooDAHSAYE.*
• the escalator.	• *EhsooKAHREHtah*
• the elevator.	• *EhREHBEHTAH*
• the stairs.	• *KAYEdahn*
Go...	*...kooDAHSAYE.*
• up.	• *OoEH nee eeTEH*
• down.	• *SheeTAH nee eeTEH*
• left.	• *HeeDAHREE nee eeTEH*
• right.	• *MeeGEE nee eeTEH*
• straight ahead.	• *MAHsoogoo eeTEH*
• around the corner.	• *KAHdoh oh mahGAHTEH*
• left, then right.	• *HahJEEMEHNEE heeDAHree, sohREHKAHRAH meeGEE nee*
• past the elevators.	• *EhREHBEHtah oh SOOgeeteh*
• to the first (second, third, fourth) floor.	• *EeKAYE (neeKAYE, sahnKAYE, yohnKAYE) nee*
• left (right) when you exit the elevator.	• *EhREHBEHtah oh OHreeteh heeDAHREE (meeGEE) nee*
• in through the second set of doors.	• *NeeBAHnmehnoh DOHah oh HAYEteh*
It will be...	*...nee ahREEMAHsoo.*
• on your right.	• *MeeGEETEHnee*
• on your left.	• *HeeDAHREETEHnee*
• right in front of you.	• *MehNOHMAHEHnee*

GUEST

How do I get...	*...hehwah DOHyahteh eeKEEMAHsooKAH?*
• to the hospital?	• *BYOHeen*
• to city hall?	• *SheeYAHkooshoh*
• to the _____ restaurant/hotel?	• _____ *HOHtehroo/REH-sootohrahn*
• to the train station?	• *EHkee*
• to the bus station?	• *BahsooTEH*

• to the nearest bus stop?	• *MohYOHREENOH bahsooTEH*
• to the mall?	• *ShohPEENGOO SEHntah*
• to the post office?	• *YOOBEEnkyohkoo*
• to the airport?	• *KOOkoh*
• downtown?	• *DahOONTAHoon*
• to the car rental agency?	• *REHntahKAHyah*
• to _____ Street/Avenue?	• _____ *DOHree/GAYE*
CONCIERGE	
When you exit the hotel, go…	*HOHtehroo oh dehRAHreh-tahrah,…nee mooKAHTEH, kooDAHSAYE.*
• left.	• *heeDAHree*
• right.	• *meeGEE*
• straight ahead.	• *mahSOOGOO*
• north.	• *keeTAH*
• south.	• *meeNAHMEE*
• east.	• *heeGAHSHEE*
• west.	• *neeSHEE*
GUEST	
How far is it?	*DohNOHKOORAYE dehsooKAH?*
CONCIERGE	
It's about _____…	*YAHkoo _____…dehsoo.*
• blocks (streets).	• *booROHkoo (TOHreemeh)*
• miles.	• *MAYEroo*
• kilometers.	• *KEEroh*
• minutes…	•*…hoon.*
• on foot.	• *ahROOEEteh*
• by car.	• *kooROOMAHdeh*
• by bus.	• *BAHsoodeh*
• by metro (subway).	• *cheeKAHTEHTSOOdeh*
GUEST	
Can you show me on the map?	*CHEEzoode ohSHEEEHTEH mohRAHEEMAHsooKAH?*

CONCIERGE

Sure, it's right here. — *HAye, kohKOHdehsoo.*

Let me draw you a little map. — *CHEEzoo oh ohKAHKEE sheeMAHSHOH.*

GUEST

Can you tell me where I can…around here? — *KohKOHDEHwah…wah dehKEEMAHsooKAH?*

- take a walk — *SAHmpoh*
- ride a bike — *jeeTEHNSHAnee nohROOKOHtohwah*
- jog — *johGEENGOO*

CONCIERGE

Yes, we have maps of…trails right here. — *HAye,…KOHsoonoh CHEEzoo-gah gohZAYEMAHsoo.*

- jogging — *johGEENGOO*
- walking — *SAHmpoh*
- bike — *SAYEkooreengoo*

B. RECOMMENDING PLACES OF INTEREST

GUEST

Can you recommend any places to visit? — *DOHkohkah ohMOHSHEEROY tohKOHROHwah ahREEMAH-sooKAH?*

CONCIERGE

There are lots. Are you interested in… — *EeROHEEROH gohZAYEMAHsoo.…wah ohSOOKEEDEHsooKAH?*

- art? — *BEEjootsoo*
- theater? — *EhngehKEE*
- shopping? — *OhKAYEMOHNOH*
- museums? — *HahKOOBOOTSOOkahn*
- sports? — *SooPOHtsoo*
- sightseeing? — *KahnKOH*
- music? — *OHngahkoo*

- outdoor activities? — *AhOOTOHDOHah ahKOOTEEbeetee*
- children's activities? — *KohDOHMOHNOH ahKOOTEEbeetee*

GUEST

What do you recommend? — *NAHneegah ohSOOSOOMEH dehsooKAH?*

CONCIERGE

If you're interested in art, I'd suggest… — *BEEjootsoogah ohSOOKEEDEH-sheetahrah,…gah Eetoh ohMOY-MAHsoo.*

- the _____ gallery. — *_____ GYArahree*
- the _____ art museum. — *_____ beeJOOTSOOkahn*

If you're interested in theater, I can get you tickets to… — *EhngehKEEGAH ohSOOKEE-DEEsheetahrah,…noh TEHhaye oh eeTAHSHEEMAHSOOgah.*

- a show. — *SHOH*
- an opera. — *OHperah*
- a movie. — *EHgah*

For shopping, I'd recommend… — *SHOHpeengoo neewah…gah EEtoh ohMOYMAHsoo.*

- downtown. — *dahOONTAHoon*
- the mall. — *shohPEENGOO SEHntah*
- the discount outlets. — *deesooKAHoontoh ahOOTOHREHtoh*

GUEST

Do they have…there? — *SohKOHNEEwah…gah ahREEMAHsooKAH?*

- clothes — *YOHhookoo*
- furniture — *KAHgoo*
- rugs (carpets) — *JOOtahn (KAHpehtoh)*
- souvenirs — *ohMEEYAHGEH*
- books — *HOHn*
- sporting goods — *sooPOHTSOOYOHheen*
- candy — *ohKAHshee*

• antiques	• *kohTOHHEEN, ahnTEEkoo*
• electronics	• *ehREHKOOTOHROH-NEEKOOSOO SEHYEheen*
• computers	• *kohmPYOOtah*
• a farmers' market	• *NOHGYOH EEcheebah*
• a supermarket	• *SOOPAHMAHkehtoh*
• a flea market	• *nohMEENOHeechee*
CONCIERGE	
Perhaps you'd like a museum.	*BeeJOOTSOOkahngah ohKEENEEMEHsootoh ohMOYMAHsoo.*
A local favorite is the... museum.	*KohkohDEHwah...gah NEEN-keegah ahREEMAHsoo.*
• natural history	• *sheeZEHN hahKOO-BOOTSOOkahn*
• modern art	• *KEENDAYE beeJOOTSOO-kahn*
• science	• *kahGAHKOO hahKOO-BOOTSOOkahn*
• local history	• *CHEEeekeenoh rehKEESHEE hahKOOBOOTSOOkahn*
GUEST	
We were thinking of sight-seeing.	*KAHNKOH OH KAHNGAH-ehteh eeTAHndehsoogah.*
CONCIERGE	
I'd be happy to arrange a city tour.	*SHEEnaye KAHNKOH TSOOah oh TEHhaye eeTAHSHEEMAHSHOH.*
GUEST	
How about...	*...wah eeKAHgahdehsooKAH?*
• interesting architecture?	• *OhMOHSHEEROY KEHncheekoo*
• churches?	• *KYOkaye*
• a vineyard?	• *WAYEn sehEEJOHSHOH, WAYEnahree*
• the business district?	• *BeeJEENEHSOO gaye*
• the government buildings?	• *SEHhooKAHNCHOH BEEroo*
• the university?	• *DAYEGAHkoo*

• monuments?	• *KeeNEHnkahn*
• the countryside?	• *CHEEhoh*

CONCIERGE

There are many sports events.	*TahKOOSAHnnoh sooPOHT-SOO EEbehntoh gah gohZAYE-MAHsoo.*
Would you like tickets to...	*...noh cheeKEHtoh oh gohKEEBOHDEHsooKAH?*
• a baseball game?	• *YahKYOOnoh sheeAYE*
• a basketball game?	• *BahsooKEHTOHBOHroonoh sheeAYE*
• a football game?	• *HooTOHBOHroonoh sheeAYE*
• a hockey game?	• *HOHkehnoh sheeAYE*
• a tennis match?	• *TEHneesoonoh sheeAYE*

GUEST

Are there any musical events?	*OHngahkoonoh eeBEHNTOHWAH ahREEMAHsooKAH?*

CONCIERGE

There is a...concert tonight.	*KOHnbahn...noh KOHnsahtoh gah ahREEMAHsoo.*
• rock-and-roll	• *rohKOONROHroo*
• blues	• *booROOsoo*
• classical music	• *kooRAHSHEEkoonoh*
• jazz	• *JAHzoo*
There's musical entertainment at _____.	*_____ deh OHngahkoo mohYOHOHSHEE GAH ahREEMAHsoo.*

GUEST

Is there anything else going on tonight?	*KOHnbahn hohKAHNEE NAHneekah ahREEMAH-sooKAH?*

CONCIERGE

Other than the movies, I'd suggest...	*EHgahnoh hohKAHNEE-wah...gah ohSOOSOOMEH DEHsoo.*
• bowling.	• *BOHreengoo*

• a nightclub.	• *NAYETOH KOOrahboo*
• a video rental.	• *beeDEHOH REHntahroo*

GUEST

What do you suggest for outdoor activities?	*AhOOTOHDOHahwahdehwah NAHneegah ohSOOSOO-MEHDEHsooKAH?*

CONCIERGE

How about...	*...wah eeKAHgahdehsooKAH?*
• hiking?	• *HAYEkeengoo*
• fishing?	• *TsooREE*
• skiing?	• *SooKEE*
• Rollerblading?	• *ROHRAHbooREHdoh*
• swimming?	• *SOOeeEH*
• surfing?	• *SAHfeen*
Or you might like to go...	*...nee eeKAHREHROOnohmoh EEkahmoh sheeREHMAHSEHn.*
• to the river.	• *KahWAH*
• to the lake.	• *MeeZOOmee*
• to the mountains.	• *YahMAH*
• for a drive.	• *DohRAYEboo*
• to the beach.	• *KAYEgahn, BEchee*
• to the forest.	• *MohREE*

GUEST

Is there anything for children?	*KohDOHMOHNEEwah NAHnee-KAH ahREEMAHsooKAH?*

CONCIERGE

Yes, there's...	*HAye,...gah ahREEMAHsoo.*
• a zoo.	• *DOHBOOTSOOehn*
• a children's museum.	• *jeeDOH hahKOOBOO-TSOOkahn*
• an amusement park.	• *YOOEHnchee*
• a water park.	• *WOHTAHPAHkoo*
Would you like to rent...	*...noh REHntahroooh gohKEEB, OHDEHsooKAH?*
• a bicycle?	• *JeeTEHNSHAH*

• a car?	• *KooROOMAH*
• a boat?	• *BOHtoh*
• some skis?	• *SooKEEYOHheen*
• some Rollerblades?	• *ROHRAHbooREHdoh*
Would you like a tour guide who speaks Japanese?	*Neehongoh oh hahNAHsoo GAYE-dohoh goh KEEBOHDEHsooKAH?*
May I make a reservation for you?	*YohYAHKOOOH ohTOHREE sheMASHOHKAH?*

GUEST

Can you recommend a good restaurant?	*EEREHsootohrahn oh ohSHEEHTEH, kooDAHSAYE?*

CONCIERGE

What type of cuisine would you like?	*DOHnnah RYOHreegah gohKEEBOHDEHsooKAH?*

GUEST

We'd like a(n)...restaurant.	*...REHsootohrahn gah EEndehsoogah.*
• casual	• *KAHjooahroonah*
• elegant	• *EHrehgahntohnah*
• fast-food	• *FAHsootoh HOOdoh noh*
• inexpensive	• *YahSOOee*
• seafood	• *SHEEHOOdoh noh*
• vegetarian	• *BehJEETAHreeahn noh*
We'd like an authentic American steakhouse.	*HohNBAHNOH ahMEHREE-KAHN sooTEHKEE-HAHoosoo gah EEndehsoogah.*

CONCIERGE

You can get there by...	*SohKOHEHwah...deh eeKEHMAHsoo.*
• bus.	• *BAHsoo*
• train.	• *DEHnshah*
• subway.	• *cheeKAHTEHTSOO*
Take the...bound for _____.	*_____ eeKEENOO...nee nohREEMAHsoo.*
• number _____ bus	• *_____ BAHnBAHsoo*

JAPANESE

You'll need to transfer to…at ____.	____ *deh…nee nohREE-KAHehteh, kooDAHSAYE.*
• the ____ line	• ____ *SEHn*
• the number ____ bus	• ____ *BAHn noh BAHsoo*
Get off at ____.	____ *deh ohREEMAHsoo.*
May I call you a taxi?	*TAHkoosheeoh ohYOHBEE sheeMAHSHOHKAH?*
We have a free shuttle bus service available to ____.	____ *eeKEENOH mooRYOH SHAHtohroogah DEHtehohREEMAHsoo.*
It leaves every ____ minutes.	____ *HOONGOHtohnee DEHtehohREEMAHsoo.*
It leaves every hour.	*EeCHEEJEEKAHNGOHtohnee DEHtehohREEMAHsoo.*

GUEST

What's the price range?	*EeKOORAHGOOraye dehsooKAH?*

6. Business Services and Clientele

A. BOOKING A BUSINESS MEETING

EMPLOYEE

Good morning.	*OhHAHYOH gohZAYEMAHsoo.*
How may I help you today?	*KYOHwah eeKAHGAH eeTAHSHEEMAHSHO?*

TIP! ••••

Clients who do business from the hotel need a great deal of service from you. They tend to be seasoned travelers who don't want a lot of explanation from hotel employees, just competent action. Attending to their every need often yields substantial financial rewards!

GUEST	
I'd like to make arrangements for a business meeting.	*SHODAHnnoh DAHNDOHreeoh sheeTAYEnoh deesoogah.*
EMPLOYEE	
For how many people?	*NAHnmeh sahmah dehsooKAH?*
GUEST	
For _____ people on _____.	(date) *nee* (number) *maydehsoo.*
EMPLOYEE	
Fine.	*KahSHEEKOHMAH-REEMAHsheetah.*
We have space available.	*OhHEHYAHWAH ayeTEHohREEMAHsoo.*
We can provide all your meals, as well as your meeting needs.	*KAYEGOH nee heeTSOO-YOHnah mohNOHNOH hoh-KAHNEE, ohSHOHKOOJEE-MOH gohYOY dehKEEMAHsoo.*
GUEST	
That's good. We'd like…for each day.	*EEdehsooneh. MAYEneechee…oh, ohNEHGAYEsheeMAHsoo.*
• a continental breakfast	• *kohncheeNEHntahroo booREHkooFAHsootoh*
• coffee breaks	• *KOHHEEBOOREHkoo*
• a working lunch	• *CHOOshohkoo*
• snacks	• *sooNAHkoo*
• a cocktail reception	• *KAHkootehroo rehSEH-pooshohn*
• dinner	• *YOOshohkoo*
Also, we'll require…for the meeting room.	*SohREHKAHRAH, KAYEGEE-sheetsooneewah…gah heeTSOY-OHDEHsoo.*
• a VCR with a large-screen monitor	• *DAYEGAHmehn noh BEEdehoh*
• an overhead projector with transparencies and markers	• *OHBAHHEHtoh pooROHJEHkootah toh rohRAHNSOOPEHrehnnshee toh MAHKAH.*
• a chalkboard	• *kohKOOBAHn*
• a flip chart	• *hooREEPOOCHAHtoh*

• a slide projector	• *sooRAYEDOH pooROHJEHkootah*
• a computer with a large-screen monitor	• *DAYEGAHmehnnoh KOHNPYOOtah*
And please be sure to provide...	*KAHNAHRAHZOO...oh YOYsheeTEH, kooDAHSAYE.*
• water.	• *meeZOO*
• pads with pencils.	• *kahMEE toh EHNpeetsoo*
• ashtrays.	• *HAYEzahrah*

EMPLOYEE

Let's decide on what time you'd like everything, and we'll be all set.	*NAHnjeemahdehnee JOOnbeeohsooROOkaoh keeMEHMAHSHOH, soh-REHDEH ohWAHREEDEHsoo.*

GUEST

Okay. How will the room be set up?	*WahKAHREEMAHsheetah. OhHEHYAHNOH sehTOHAH DOHnohyohnee sheeMAH-SHOHKAH?*

EMPLOYEE

We can set up the room...	*...ohHEHYAHwah.*
• theater style.	• *SheeAHTAH sooTAYEroo*
• in a square.	• *SheeKAHKOOdeh*
• horseshoe ("U") style.	• *YOOjeegahTAH*
• classroom style.	• *KYOHsheetsoo sooTAYEroo*
• boardroom style.	• *KAYEGEESHEETSOO sooTSYEroo*
We're looking forward to having your group here.	*MeeNAHSAHmahnoh ohKOHSHEEoh ohMAHCHEESHEETEH ohREEMAHsoo.*

B. AT THE MEETING

ATTENDANT

I'm _____, the meeting-room attendant.	*KAYEGEEsheetsoo AHNNAYEGAHkahreenoh _____, toh mohsheemahsoo.*

How is everything?	*MeeNAHsahn SOObehtehwah eeKAHgahdehsooKAH?*

GUEST

Everything is fine, thank you.	*MEENNAH GEHnkeedehsoo, ahREEgahtoh.*
We need more chairs.	*MOHtoh eeSOOGAH eeREEMAHsoo.*
We need more coffee.	*MOHtoh KOHHEEgah eeREEMAHsoo.*
We need the ashtrays emptied.	*HAYEZAHrahoh SOHJEE sheeTEHkoodahsaye.*
We need more water.	*MOHtoh meeZOOGAH eeREEMAHsoo.*

ATTENDANT

I'll take care of it right away.	*TahDAYEmah eeTAHSHEE-MAHsoo.*
Is everything else satisfactory?	*SOObehteh yohROHSHEE-dehSHOHkah?*

GUEST

It's quite nice, but the room...	*EEndehsoogah, hehYAH gah...*
• needs more light.	• *MOHTOH ahKAHREEGAH heeTSOOYOH dehsoo.*
• is too bright.	• *mahBOOSHEESOOGEEroo.*
• needs more ventilation.	• *MOHTOH KAHNKEEGAH heeTSOOYOH dehsoo.*
• is too hot (cold).	• *ahTSOOSOOGEOOroo (sahMOOSOOGEEroo).*
• is a little noisy.	• *sooKOHshee ooROOSAYE dehsoo.*
• is crowded.	• *heeTOHDEH eePAYEdehsoo.*
Can you take care of it?	*NAHntohkah dehKEE-MAHsooKAH?*
Can we get another room?	*CHEEGAHOO hehYAHnee ooTSOOREHMAHsooKAH?*

ATTENDANT

Let me see what we can do.	*CHOHtoh MEEteh meeMAHSHOH.*

C. CATERING TO BUSINESS GUESTS

CONCIERGE

Good morning.	*OhHAHYOH gohZAYEMAHsoo.*
How may I help you?	*EeKAHGAH nahREHMAH-sheetahKAH?*

GUEST

Good morning. Where is breakfast for the _____ group?	*OhHAHYOH gohZAYEMAHsoo. _____ gooROOpoo noh CHOHSHOHKOO wah DOHkoh dehsooKAH?*
Where is the exhibits hall?	*TEHNJEEKAYE noh HOHroo-wah DOHkohdehsooKAH?*

CONCIERGE

There's a buffet set up outside your meeting room.	*OhTSOOKAYEnoh KAYEGEEsheetsoonoh SOHTOH noh BYOOwheh dehsoo.*
Just down the hall.	*HOHroo oh EETEHkoo-DAHSAYE.*
In the dining room.	*ShohKOODOH DEHsoo.*

GUEST

Thank you.	*AhREEgahtoh.*
I need a fax sent.	*WHAHkoosoo oh ohKOORAHNAHkehrehbah nahREEMAHSEHn.*
I need some typing done.	*TAYEpoo oh sheeAHGE-Hnahkehrehbah nahREEMAHSEHn.*
I need a hookup to the Internet.	*EENTAHNEHtoh neh sehTSOOZOHKOOgah heetsoo yoh dehsoo.*
I need a computer.	*KohmPYOOtah gah heeTSOO-YOH DEHsoo.*
I need a package sent overnight.	*KohDSOOtsoomee oh yohKOO-JEETSOO HYESOH shee-TAYENOHDEHsoogah.*
I need courier service.	*KOOREEEH SAHbeesoo gah eeREEMAHsoo.*

I need some letters mailed. *TehGAHMEEoh dahSAH-nahkehrehbah nahREEMAHSEHn.*

I need some copies made. *KOHpee oh tohRAHnahkehrehbah nahREEMAHSEHn.*

CONCIERGE

I'll take care of that right away. *TahDAYEMAH eeTAHSHEEMAHsoo.*

GUEST

Later, I'd like to host a small reception. *SohNOHAHtohdeh, CHEEsahnah rehSEHPOOSHOHN oh heeRAHKEETAYEnoh dehsoogah.*

Can you arrange that? *TEHhaye dehKEEMAHsooKAH?*

CONCIERGE

Certainly. What would you like? *KahSHEEKOHMAHREEMAH-sheetah./NAN NI gah heetsoo yoh DEHSOOkah?*

GUEST

We need a full bar and some hors d'oeuvres. *HooROOBAH toh OHdohbooroo gah eeREEMAHsoo.*

Make sure there are plenty of chilled shrimp. *RAYSAYE EHbeewah JOOBOOn YOY sheeTEH, kooDAHSAYE.*

Lots of champagne, please. *SHAHMPEHnmoh tahKOOSAHN, ohNEHGAYE sheeMAHsoo.*

CONCIERGE

I'll have Room Service put together a proposal right away, and get back to you. *TahDAYEmah ROOMOO-SAHbeesoonee TEHhayesahseh, gohREHNRAHKOO eeTAHSHEEMAHsoo.*

7. Checking Out

GUEST

At what time is checkout? *ChehKOOAHootohwah NAHnjee dehsooKAH?*

FRONT DESK CLERK

Checkout is at…	*ChehKOOAHootohwah…jeedeh gohZAYEMAHsoo.*
• 10 A.M.	• *GOHzehn JOOjee*
• noon.	• *SHOHgoh*
• 3 P.M.	• *GOHgoh SAHnjee*
You may audit your bill on channel ____ on your television.	*SEHKYOOSHOHnoh NAYEYOwah TEHrehbeenoh ____ CHAHnnehroodeh gohRAHNNEE nahREHMAHsoo.*
We provide an express checkout service.	*EhKOOSOOPOOrehsoo noh chehKOOAHootoh oh ohKOHNAHTEH ohREEMAHsoo.*
Your bill will be left outside your door the night before you check out.	*SEHKYOOSHOH wah ohKAHEHREENOH MAHehnoh YOHroonee ohHEHYAHnoh SOHtohnee OYTEIIohkeemahsoo.*
If you're satisfied with your bill, simply sign it,	*SEHKYOOSHOH nee MOHndayegah NAHkehrehbah shohMEHoh nahSAHtehKAHrah,*
and leave your key in your room.	*KAHGEEoh ohHEHYAHnee OYTEH EEteh, kooDAHSAYE.*
Any late charges such as breakfast or minibar will be added automatically.	*CHOHshohkooyah meeNEEBAH nahdohnoh RYOkeenwah jeeDOHTEHKEENEE TSOOEEKAH sahREHMAHsoo.*

GUEST

I'd like to check out, please.	*ChehKOOAHootoh, ohNEGAYESHEEMAHsoo.*

CLERK

May I have your luggage brought down?	*NEEmohtsoooh sheeTAHNEE ohHAHKOHBEE shee-MAHSHOHKAH?*

GUEST

Yes, please.	*OhNEHGAYESHEEMAHsoo.*

No, I brought (will bring) it myself.	*EEeh, jeeBOONDEH yahREEMAHsoo.*
CLERK	
How was everything?	*EeKAHgah dehsheetahKAH?*
GUEST	
It was very nice, thank you.	*TohTEHMOH KAYETEHKEE DEHsheetah, ahREEgahtoh.*
I want to speak with the manager.	*MahNEHJAHTOH hanNAHSHEETAYEnohdehsooga.*
CLERK	
Certainly. The manager on duty is ____. One moment, please.	*KAHSHEEKOHMAH-REEMAHsheetah. TAHnTOH noh mahNEHJAHwah ____ deh gohZAYEMAHsoo.*
GUEST	
Our experience was...	*KohKOHDEHnoh TAYEzayewah...*
• good.	• *YOHkahtahdehsoo.*
• excellent.	• *sooBAHRAHSHEEkahttah dehsoo.*
• poor.	• *ahMAHREE YOHkoo ahREEMAHSEHndehsheetah.*
• very bad.	• *tohTEHMOH heeDOHKAHtah dehsoo.*
MANAGER ON DUTY	
That's nice to hear.	*SohREHWAH KOHEHdehsoo.*
I'm sorry to hear that.*	*MOHshewahkeh gohzayemahsehn dehsheetah.*
Thank you. Please come again.	*AhREEgahtoh gohzayemahsheeta. MahTAH ohKOHSHEEKOOD-AHSAYEMAHseh.*

JAPANESE

*Please refer to "Guest Complaints in the Hotel" on page 264 for more on handling dissatisfied clients.

KOREAN

1. The Bare Essentials

A. PRONUNCIATION CHART

VOWELS

ROMANIZATION	PRONUNCIATION	ROMANIZATION	PRONUNCIATION
a	father	*yae*	yam
ya	yard, Yom Kippur	*e*	ten
eo	agree	*ye*	yes, yeah
yeo	onion, beyond	*oe*	way
o	raw	*wi*	we
yo	yolk, yore	*eui*	squeeze
u	sue	*wa*	wander, watt
yu	you	*wae*	wag
eu	broken	*weo*	wall, worry
i	seen, inn	*we*	wedding, wet
ae	pan, apple		

CONSONANTS

ROMANIZATION	PRONUNCIATION	ROMANIZATION	PRONUNCIATION
b	boom	*n*	no
ch'	church	*ng*	ring
d	do	*p*	puff
h	hello	*r/l*	ill
j	jump	*s*	sigh
k	kiss, guide	*t*	to
m	money		

DOUBLE CONSONANTS

ROMANIZATION	PRONUNCIATION
kk	s<u>ch</u>ool
tt	s<u>t</u>op
pp	s<u>p</u>ort
ss	<u>s</u>eed
jj	<u>j</u>eep
sh	<u>sh</u>eep

B. THE KOREAN LANGUAGE

Sentence Structure Although word order in Korean tends to be less rigid than in English, basic sentence structure follows the English pattern: subject-verb-object. Understood elements of a sentence, particularly subject pronouns, are often omitted in Korean.

Nouns Whereas English uses word order to demonstrate the grammatical function of a noun in a given sentence, Korean attaches postpositional particles, or suffixes, to nouns: *i-sa-ram-<u>EUN</u>* (this person, as the topic); *i-eum-sik-<u>I</u>* (this food, as the subject of a sentence); *i-ch'aek-<u>EUL</u>* (this book, as direct object); *Mary-<u>EGE</u>* (Mary, as indirect object); *ho-t'el-<u>RO</u>* (the hotel, as object of a directional preposition); *Mary-<u>EUI</u>* (Mary's, as a possessive).

Verbs Attached to a main Korean verb stem are particles that indicate the tense, the mood, and whether the sentence is a statement, a question, an order, or an exclamation. With some verbal particles, Korean verbs also indicate different levels of formality and respect. Relative differences in age, sex, social status, and length of acquaintanceship are some of the factors that indicate the appropriate level of speech. The following are all forms of the verb *go: ga-gess-seum-ni-da* (formal, polite); *ga-gess-eo-yo* (informal, polite); *ga-gess-eo* (intimate, with a younger person or a friend); *ga-gess-da* (neutral, to a child or a close friend); and *ga-gess-so* (authoritative, with subordinates).

KOREAN

C. THE KOREAN CULTURE

South Koreans enjoy a high standard of living and are proud of their country's recent economic success. The handshake is perfectly appropriate, although a Korean may bow slightly at the same time. If you exchange business cards with a Korean, present your card with both hands, and accept the guest's card the same way. You are then expected to thank that person sincerely. Koreans commonly push and crowd with one another and don't consider this behavior rude, so don't be alarmed if you see this.

You may find Korean men drinking a great deal of alcohol. This is customary among Korean businessmen as a way to break down some of their social reserve after business hours. Just be sure to monitor the situation to avoid American legal problems.

Koreans aren't used to tipping, as a service charge is customarily included in the bill in Korea. It's a good idea to include a service charge on the check.

2. Useful Expressions

A. GENERAL

Hello.	*An-nyeong-ha-se-yo.*
Good-bye.	*An-nyeong-hi-ga-se-yo.*
Yes.	*Ne./Ye.*
No.	*A-ni-o./A-ni-yo.*
Maybe.	*Geul-sse-yo.*
Please.	*Bu-t'ak-ham-ni-da.*
Thank you (very much).	*(Dae-dan-hi) Gam-sa-ham-ni-da.*
You're welcome.	*Ch'eon-man-e-yo.*
Excuse me.	*Sil-lye-ham-ni-da.*
I beg your pardon.	*Joe-song-ham-ni-da.*
I'm sorry.	*Mi-an-ham-ni-da.*
One moment, please.	*Jam-shi-man gi-da-ryeo ju-se-yo.*

Do you speak English?	*Yeong-eo-reul ha-shim-ni-kka?*
• Yes, I do.	• *Ne, ham-ni-da.*
• No, I don't.	• *A-ni-yo, mot-ham-ni-da.*
• A little.	• *Jo-geum ham-ni-da.*
• No, not at all.	• *A-ni-yo, jeon-hyeo mot-ham-ni-da.*
That's okay.	*Kwaen-ch'an-seum-ni-da.*
It doesn't matter.	*Sang-gwan eop-seum-ni-da.*
I don't speak Korean.	*Han-kook-mal mot-ham-ni-da.*
I can speak a little.	*Jo-geum mal-hal-su-iss-seum-ni-da.*
I understand a little.	*Jo-geum i-hae-ham-ni-da.*
I don't understand.	*Mot-a-ra deut-seum-ni-da.*
Please speak more slowly.	*Jom ch'eon-ch'eon-hi mal-sseum hae-ju-se-yo.*
Would you repeat that, please?	*Da-shi mal-sseum haeju-shi-gess-eo-yo?*
Yes, sir/ma'am.	*Ne, seon-saeng-nim/sa-mo-nim*
No problem.	*Munje eop-seum-ni-da.*
It's my pleasure.	*Yeong-kwang-im-ni-da.*

B. NEEDS

I'd like _____.	_____ *ko sip-seum-ni-da.*
I need _____.	_____ *p'i-ryo ham-ni-da.*
What would you like?	*Mu-eo-seul weon- ham-ni-kka?*
Please bring me _____.	_____ *jom-ga-jyeo-da-ju-se-yo.*
I'm looking for _____.	_____ *-(r)eul ch'at-seum-ni-da.*
I'm hungry.	*Bae-ga go-p'a-yo.*
I'm thirsty.	*Mog-i mal-la-yo.*
It's important.	*Jung-yo ham-ni-da.*
It's urgent.	*Geup ham-ni-da.*

C. QUESTION WORDS

How?	*Eo-tteo-k'e?*
How much?	*Eol-ma man-k'eum?*
How many?	*Myeot-kae?/Myeot-myeong?*
Which?	*Eo-neu?*
What?	*Mu-eot?*
What kind of?	*Eo-tteon jong-nyu?*
Who?	*Nu-gu?*
Where?	*Eo-di?*
When?	*Eon-je?*
What does this mean?	*I-geo-shi mu-seun tteus-im-ni-kka?*
What does that mean?	*Jeo-geo-shi mu-seun tteus-im-ni-kka?*
How do you say_____ in Korean?	_____ *-eul Han-kuk-mal-lo eo-tteo-k'e mal-ham-ni-kka?*

D. COLORS

black	*kka-man-saek*
blue	*p'a-ran-saek*
brown	*bam-saek*
gold	*keum-saek*
gray	*hoe-saek*
green	*nok-saek*
orange	*o-renji-sack*
pink	*bun-hong-saek*
purple	*ja-ju-saek*
red	*ppal-gan-saek*
silver	*eun-saek*
violet	*bo-ra-saek*
white	*heuin-saek*
yellow	*no-ran-saek*

E. CARDINAL NUMBERS

1	*il/hana*
2	*i/dul*
3	*sam/set*
4	*sa/net*
5	*o/da-seot*
6	*yuk/yeo-seot*
7	*ch'il/il-gop*
8	*p'al/yeo-deol*
9	*ku/a-hop*
10	*ship/yeol*
11	*ship-il/yeol-ha-na*
12	*ship-i/yeol-dul*
13	*ship-sam/yeol-set*
14	*ship-sa/yeol-net*
15	*ship-o/yeol-da-seot*
16	*ship-yuk/yeol-yeo-seot*
17	*ship-ch'il/yeol-il-gop*
18	*ship-p'al/yeol-yeo-deol*
19	*ship-gu/yeol-a-hop*
20	*i-ship/seu-mul*
21	*i-ship-il/seu-mul-hana*
22	*i-ship-i/seu-mul-tul*
23	*i-ship-sam/seu-mul-set*
24	*i-ship-sa/seu-mul-net*
25	*i-ship-o/seu-mul-ta-seot*
26	*i-ship-yuk/seu-mul-yeo-seot*
27	*i-ship-ch'il/seu-mul-il-gop*
28	*i-ship-p'al /seu-mul-yeo-deol*
29	*i-ship-gu/seu-mul-a-hop*

30	*sam-ship/seo-reun*
31	*sam-ship-il/seo-reun-ha-na*
32	*sam-ship-i/seo-reun-dul*
40	*se-ship/ma-heun*
50	*o-ship/shin*
60	*yuk-ship/ye-sun*
70	*ch'il-ship/il-heun*
80	*p'al-ship/yeo-deun*
90	*ku-ship/a-heun*
100	*baek*
101	*baek-il*
102	*baek-i*
110	*baek-ship*
120	*baek-i-ship*
200	*i-baek*
210	*i-baek-ship*
300	*sam-baek*
400	*sa-baek*
500	*o-baek*
600	*yuk-baek*
700	*ch'il-baek*
800	*p'al-baek*
900	*ku-baek*
1,000	*ch'eon*
1,100	*ch'eon-baek*
1,200	*ch'eon-i-baek*
2,000	*i-ch'eon*
10,000	*man*
50,000	*o-man*
100,000	*shim-man*

ao=ago yeo=yon eu=broken ae=at oe=way wi=we eui=squeeze r/l-ill

1,000,000	*baek-man*
1,000,000,000	*ship-eok*

F. ORDINAL NUMBERS

first	*ch'eot-jjae*
second	*dul-jjae*
third	*set-jjae*
fourth	*net-jjae*
fifth	*da-seot-jjae*
sixth	*yeo-seot-jjae*
seventh	*il-gop-jjae*
eighth	*yeo-deol-jjae*
ninth	*a-hop-jjae*
tenth	*yeol-jjae*
eleventh	*yeol-han-beon-jjae*
twelfth	*yeol-du-beon-jjae*
thirteenth	*yeol-se-beon-jjae*
fourteenth	*yeol-ne-beon-jjae*
fifteenth	*yeol-da-seot-beon-jjae*
sixteenth	*yeol-yeo-seot-beon-jjae*
seventeenth	*yeol-il-gop-beon-jjae*
eighteenth	*yeol-yeo-deol-beon-jjae*
nineteenth	*yeol-a-hop-beon-jjae*
twentieth	*seu-mu-beon-jjae*
twenty-first	*seu-mul-han-beon-jjae*
twenty-second	*seu-mul-du-beon-jjae*
thirtieth	*seo-reun-beon-jjae*
fortieth	*ma-heun-beon-jjae*
fiftieth	*o-ship-beon-jjae*
sixtieth	*ye-sun-beon-jjae*

seventieth	*il-reun-beon-jjae*
eightieth	*yeo-deun-beon-jjae*
ninetieth	*a-heun-beon-jjae*
hundredth	*baek-beon-jjae*
thousandth	*ch'eon-beon-jjae*

G. TIME OF DAY

1:00	*han-shi*
2:00	*du-shi*
3:00	*se-shi*
4:00	*ne-shi*
5:00	*da-seot-shi*
6:00	*yeo-seot-shi*
7:00	*il-gop-si*
8:00	*yeo-deol-shi*
9:00	*a-hop-si*
10:00	*yeol-si*
11:00	*yeol-han-si*
12:00	*yeol-du-si*
1:00 A.M.	*sae-byeok-han-si/o-jeon-han-si*
3:00 P.M.	*o-hu-se-si*
noon	*jeong-o*
midnight	*ja-jeong*
1:15	*han-si ship-o-bun*
12:45	*yeol-du-si sa-ship-o-bun / han-si ship-o-bun-jeon*
1:30	*han-si sam-ship-bun / han-si-ban*
7:05	*il-gop-si o-bun*
4:55	*Ne-si o-ship-o-bun/Da-seot-si o-bun-jeon*

H. DAYS OF THE WEEK

Monday *weol-yo-il*
Tuesday *hwa-yo-il*
Wednesday *su-yo-il*
Thursday *mog-yo-il*
Friday *keum-yo-il*
Saturday *t'o-yo-il*
Sunday *i-ryo-il*

I. MONTHS

January *il-weol*
February *i-weol*
March *sam-weol*
April *sa-weol*
May *o-weol*
June *yu-weol*
July *ch'il-weol*
August *p'al-weol*
September *gu-weol*
October *shi-weol*
November *ship-il-weol*
December *ship-i-weol*

J. DATES

1998 *ch'eon-gu-baek gu-ship-p'al-nyeon*
1999 *ch'eon-gu-baek gu-ship-gu-nyeon*
2000 *i-ch'eon-nyeon*
2001 *i-ch'eon-il-nyeon*
2002 *i-ch'eon-i-nyeon*
2003 *i-ch'eon-sam-nyeon*
2004 *i-ch'eon-sa-nyeon*

2005	*i-ch'eon-o-nyeon*
Today is Thursday, September 22.	*O-neul-eun gu-weol i-ship-i-il, mog-yo-il-im-ni-da.*
Yesterday was Wednesday, September 21.	*Eo-je-neun gu-weol i-ship-il-il, su-yo-il i-eoss-seum-ni-da.*
The day before yesterday was Tuesday, September 20.	*Geu-jeo-kke-neun gu-weol i-ship-il, hwa-yo-il i-eoss-seum-ni-da.*
Tomorrow is Friday, September 23.	*Nae-il-eun gu-weol i-ship-sam-il, keum-yo-il im-ni-da.*
The day after tomorrow is Saturday, September 24.	*Mo-re-neun gu-weol i-ship-sa-il, t'o-yo-il im-ni-da.*
Next Friday is September 30.	*Da-eum keum-yo-il-eun gu-weol sam-ship-il im-ni-da.*
Last Friday was September 16.	*Jeo-beon keum-yo-il-eun gu-weol shim yuk-il i-eoss-sum-ni-da.*

K. MEASUREMENTS: DISTANCE

inch	*in-ch'i*
foot	*p'u-t'eu*
yard	*ya-deu*
mile	*ma-il*
millimeter	*mi-li-mi-t'eo*
meter	*mi-t'eo*
kilometer	*ki-lo-mi-t'eo*

3. Common Hospitality Scenarios

A. GREETINGS AND INTRODUCTIONS

GREETING THE GUEST

EMPLOYEE

Good morning,...	***..., an-nyeong-hi chu-mu-shyeot-seum-ni-kka.***
• Mr. _____.	**• _____ *seon-saeng-nim***

• **Mrs. _____.**	• _____ ***sa-mo-nim***
• **Miss _____.**	• _____ ***yang***
• **sir.**	• ***Seon-saeng-nim/Sa-jang-nim***
• **ma'am.**	• ***Sa-mo-nim***
• **ladies and gentlemen.**	• ***Yeo-reo-bun***
• **everyone.**	• ***mo-du***
Good afternoon, Mr. _____.	***_____, seon-saeng-nim an-nyeong-ha-se-yo.***
Good evening, Mr._____.	***_____, seon-saeng-nim an-nyeong-ha-se-yo.***
Hello, Mr._____.	*_____, seon-saeng-nim an-nyeong-ha-se-yo.*
Welcome to...	***...-e o-shin-geot-seul hwa-nyeong-ham-ni-da.***
• **the hotel.**	• ***Ho-tel***
• **the restaurant.**	• ***Re-seu-t'o-rang/shik-dang***
• **our city.**	• ***Wu-ri-do-si***
• **the United States.**	• ***Mi-guk***

TIP! ••••

Most American employees are used to greeting guests jovially and asking them how they are. However, in any but the most informal settings, this behavior may actually be considered impolite. Asking guests how they are is stepping outside the bounds of your position and throws the burden onto the guest to answer you. Other cultures usually observe this principle to a much greater extent than we do.

If there is anything I can do to make your stay more pleasant, please let me know.	*P'yeon-hi chi-ne-shi-neun-de do-wa-deu-ril-geot-shi iss-seu-myeon, al-lyeo chu-ship-shi-yo.*
May I…	*…-deu-ril-kka-yo?*
• take your coat(s)?	• *K'o-teu geol-eo*
• carry your…for you?	• *…deul-reo*
• bags	• *Ga-bang*
• suitcase	• *Yeo-haeng-ga-bang*
How are you today?	*An-nyeong ha-se-yo?*
GUEST	
I am…	*Jeo-neun…*
• fine, thank you.	• *cho-a-yo, go-ma-wa-yo.*
• okay.	• *cho-a-yo.*
• so-so.	• *geu-jeo geu-rae-yo.*
• very tired.	• *a-ju p'i-gon-hae-yo.*
• not feeling well.	• *mom-i chom an-jo-a-yo.*
And you?	*Dang-shin-eun-yo?*

INTRODUCTIONS

TIP! ••••

It is typical of American employees to introduce themselves to the guest. This practice allows the guest to call an employee by name when s/he needs something. This is not a common practice in other countries, however, so the international guest may simply ignore your introduction.

EMPLOYEE

My name is _____.	*Je-i-reum-eun _____ im-ni-da.*
I am the…	*Jeo-neun tang-shin-eui…im-ni-da.*
• door attendant (doorman).	• *do-eo-maen*
• bell attendant (bellman).	• *bel-bo-i*
• valet-parking attendant.	• *ju-ch'a-ppo-i*
• driver.	• *un-jeon-gi-sa*
• captain.	• *k'aep-tin*
• concierge.	• *kwal-li-in*
• room attendant.	• *gaek-shil-dam-dang-weon*
• host.	• *ju-in/hos-t'eu*
• hostess.	• *yeo-ju-in/hos-t'e-seu*
• manager.	• *ji-bae-in*
• server (waiter/waitress).	• *we-i-teo/we-i-teu-re-seu*
• chef.	• *ju-bang-jang*
• activities director.	• *hwal-dong-dam-dang*
Mr. (Mrs., Miss) _____, this is Mr. (Mrs., Miss) _____, the manager.	*_____ seon-saeng-nim (sa-mo-nim, yang), i-bun-eun _____, ji-bae-in im-ni-da.*
Mr. (Mrs., Miss) _____, may I introduce our manager, Mr. (Mrs., Miss) _____?	*_____ seon-saeng-nim (sa-mo-nim, yang), _____ ji-bae-in-eul so-gae-ha-gess-seum-ni-da?*

B. RESERVATIONS

HOTEL RESERVATIONS

OPERATOR

Good morning, _____ Hotel.	*An-nyeong-ha-se-yo, _____ ho-tel im-ni-da.*
How may I direct your call?	*Eo-di-ro dae-deu-ril-kka-yo?*

GUEST

Hello. Do you speak Korean?	*Yeo-bo-seyo. Han-guk-eo ha-se-yo?*

KOREAN

OPERATOR

One moment, please.	*Jam-si-man-yo.*
I'll connect you with a bilingual operator.	*I-jung-eon-eo kyo-hwan-su-wa yeon-gyeol-hae-deu-ri-gess-seum-ni-da.*
I have a book here to help me.	*Yeo-gi-do-wa-jul-ch'aek-i iss-seum-ni-da.*
Please speak slowly.	*Ch'eon-ch'eon-hi mal-sseum-hae-ju-se-yo.*

GUEST

I would like to make a reservation, please.	*Ye-yak-eul ha-go-ship-seum-ni-da.*

OPERATOR

For a room or for one of the restaurants?	*Bang-i-yo, ani-myeon re-seu-t'o-rang-i-yo?*

GUEST

For a room, please.	*Bang-i-yo.*
For the _____ Restaurant, please.	_____ *re-seu-t'o-rang i-yo.*

OPERATOR

One moment, please. I will direct your call to Reservations.	*Jam-si-man-yo. Ye-yak-sil-ro yeon-gyeol hae-deu-ri -get-sseum-ni-da.*
One moment, please. I will direct your call to the restaurant.	*Jam-si-man-yo. Re-seu-t'o-rang-eu-ro yeon-kyeol hae-deu-ri-get-sseum-ni-da.*

CLERK

Hello. This is Reservations.	*Yeo-bo-se-yo. Ye-yak-sil-im-ni-da.*
What date would you like?	*Eo-neu-nal-eul weon-ha-shim-ni-kka?*

GUEST

May 27th.	*O-weol-i-sip-ch'il-il-i-yo.*

CLERK

For how many nights?	*Myeot-ch'il-gye-shil-geom-ni-kka?*

GUEST

For three nights, please.	*Sam-il-iss-eul-geom-ni-da.*
For a week.	*Il-ju-il-iss-eul-geom-ni-da.*
Just one night.	*Ha-rut-bam-ji-nael-geom-ni-da.*

CLERK

For how many people?	*Myeot-bun-i-shim-ni-kka?*

GUEST

For two people.	*Tu-myeong im-ni-da.*
For one person.	*Han-myeong im-ni-da.*
For two adults and a child.	*Eo-reun-dul-ha-go a-i-han-myeong im-ni-da.*

CLERK

Do you have....	*...iss-eum-ni-kka?*
• any special needs?	• *T'euk-byeol-yo-gu-ga*
• any special requests?	• *T'euk-beol-hi bu-t'ak-hal-keot-shi*

GUEST

No, thank you.	*A-ni-yo, gam-sa-ham-ni-da.*
Yes, I (we, my spouse) would like...	*Ne, jeo(uri, jeo-bu-in)-neun... ship-seum-ni-da.*
• to be near the stairs.	• *kye-dan-e ga-kka-i it-go*
• to be near an exit.	• *ch'ul-gu-e ga-kka-i it-go*
• a cot for our child.	• *uri-a-i ch'im-dae reul gat-go*
• a handicapped-accessible room.	• *sin-ch'ae-jang-ae-ja-reul-wi-han bang-eul gat-go*

CLERK

The rate is ____ per night.	*Bi-yong-eun ha-ru-bam-e ____ im-ni-da.*
Would you like to guarantee the reservation with a credit card?	*K'eu-re-dit-k'a-deu-ro ye-yak-ha-shi-gess-seum-ni-kka?*

GUEST

Yes, here is my ____ card.	*Ne, ____ k'a-deu yeo-gi iss-eo-yo.*

My credit card number is ____.	***K'eu-re-dit-k'a-deu-beon-ho-neun ____ im-ni-da.***
CLERK	
What is the expiration date?	***Man-lyo-nal-jja-neun-yo?***
Thank you.	***Gam-sa-ham-ni-da.***

RESTAURANT RESERVATIONS

RESTAURANT HOST	
Good morning (afternoon, evening), ____ Restaurant.	*An-nyeong-ha-shim-ni-kka, ____ re-seu-t'o-rang-im-ni-da.*
GUEST	
I'd like to reserve a table for…	*…ye-yak-eul ha-go-ship-seum-ni-da.*
• breakfast.	• *Ach'im*
• lunch.	• *Jeom-shim*
• dinner.	• *Jeo-nyeok*
HOST	
For what time?	*Myeot-shi-ro-ha-shi-gess-seum-ni-kka?*
GUEST	
For…o'clock.	*…shi-yo.*
• seven	• *Il-gop*
• eight	• *Yeo-deol*
• nine	• *A-hop*
For eight-thirty.	*Yeo-deol-shi-ban-i-yo.*
HOST	
For how many people?	*Myeot-bun-i-shim-ni-kka?*
GUEST	
For one person.	*Han-myeong im-ni-da.*
For…people.	*…myeong im-ni-da.*
• two	• *Du*
• four	• *Ne*

• six	• *Yeo-seot*
HOST	
And your name, please?	*Seong-ham-eun-yo?*
GUEST	
My name is _____.	_____ *im-ni-da.*
HOST	
And is there a phone number where we can reach you?	*Yeol-lak-ch'eo jeon-hwa beon-ho-neun-yo?*
GUEST	
Yes, the number is _____.	*Ne,* _____ *im-ni-da.*
By the way, do you have any…items on the menu?	*Geu-reon-de, me-nyu-e…eum-sik iss-seum-ni-kka?*
• vegetarian	• *ch'ae-shik-ju-eui*
• vegan	• *ch'eol-jeo-han ch'ae-sik-ju-eui*
• macrobiotic	• *geon-gang-shik*
• low-fat	• *jeo-ji-bang*
• low-sodium	• *so-geum-i jeok-eun*
HOST	
Would you like smoking or nonsmoking?	*Geum-yeon-seok-eul weon-ham-ni-kka?*
GUEST	
We would like….	*…-eul won-ham-ni-da.*
• smoking.	• *Heup-yeon-seok*
• nonsmoking.	• *Keum-yeon-seok*
HOST	
Thank you.	• *Kam-sa-ham-ni-da.*
That will be two people at eight o'clock.	*Yeo-deol-shi-e du-bun toe-shi-ket-seum-ni-da.*
That's a party of six at seven-thirty.	*Il-gop-shi-ban-e il-haeng-yeo-seot-bun im-ni-da.*

KOREAN

C. COURTESY AND COMPLAINTS

GENERAL EXPRESSIONS OF COURTESY

Please.	*Bu-t'ak-ham-ni-da.*
Thank you.	*Gam-sa-ham-ni-da.*
You're welcome.	*Ch'eon-man-e-yo.*
Excuse me.	*Shil-lye-ham-ni-da.*
I beg your pardon.	*Joe-song-ham-ni-da.*
I'm (terribly) sorry.	*(Jeong-mal) mi-an-ham-ni-da.*
That's okay.	*Gwaen-ch'an-seum-ni-da.*
No problem.	*Gwaen-ch'an-a-yo.*
It doesn't matter.	*Sang-kwan eop-seum-ni-da.*

COURTESY IN THE HOTEL

CONCIERGE

Good morning, sir, ma'am.	*An-nyeong ha-shim-ni-kka, seon-saeng nim, sa-mo-nim.*
May I help you with something today?	*Mu-eot-seul do-wa-deu-ril-kka-yo?*

GUEST

Yes, I need...	*a.) Ne,...p'il-yo-ham-ni-da.* *b.) Ne,...-go ship-seum-ni-da.*
• my room made up between now and _____.	• *ji-geum-ha-go _____ sa-i-e je-bang-eul ch'i-u-ge-ha (+b)*
• more towels, please.	• *t'a-ol-ideo (+a)*
• a rental car.	• *ren-teu-ch'a-ga (+a)*
• a taxi.	• *t'aek-si-ga (+a)*
• a fax sent.	• *p'aek-seu-reul bo-nae (+b)*
• some letters mailed.	• *p'yeon-ji-reul bo-nae (+b)*
• to make arrangements for a business meeting.	• *shil-mu-hoe-eui-reul jun-bi-ha (+b)*
• tickets to a concert.	• *eum-ak-hyoe ip-jang-gweon-i (+a)*

• tickets to a show.	• *ssyo-ip-jang-gweon-i (+a)*
• tickets to a game.	• *gu-kyeong-gi ip-jang-gweon-i (+a)*

GUEST COMPLAINTS IN THE HOTEL

CONCIERGE

Is everything satisfactory?	*Da-ma-eum-e deu-ship-ni-kka?*

GUEST

No, there is a problem.	*A-ni-yo, mun-je-ga ha-na iss-seum-ni-da.*
• The light	• *Cheon-deung*
• The toilet	• *Hwa-jang-shil*
• The television	• *Tel-le-bi-jon*
• The radio	• *Ra-di-o*
• The air-conditioning	• *E-eo-kon*
• The alarm clock	• *Cha-myeong-jong*
• The heat	• *Nan-bang*
• The key	• *Yeol-soe*
• The lock	• *Cha-mul-soe*
• The fan	• *Seon-p'ung-gi*
...doesn't work.	*...go-jang- im-ni-da.*

CLERK

I'll have Maintenance fix that right away.	*Ba-ro go-ch'eo deu-ri-get- sseum-ni-da.*
I apologize.	*Choe-song-ham-ni-da.*

GUEST

My room wasn't clean.	*Je-bang-i kkae-kkeut-ha-ji-an- ass-eo-yo.*
My room was noisy.	*Je-bang-i neo-mu shi-kkeu-reo-weot-seo-yo.*
My room stinks (smells).	*Je-bang-e-seo ak-ch'i-ga na-yo.*

The bed was uncomfortable.	*Ch'im-dae-ga b'ul-p'yeon hae-sseum-ni-da.*
The water wasn't hot.	*Mul-ri tteu-geob-ji a-na- sseum-ni-da.*
Room service was late.	*"Room service"-ga neu-jeo sseum-ni-da.*
The service was very poor.	*"Service"-ga neo-mu na-ppa-sseum-ni-da.*
The employees were...	*Jik-weon-deul-ri...*
• very good.	• *cho-a-sseum-ni-da.*
• excellent.	• *a-ju cho-a-sseum-ni-da.*
• rude.	• *keon-bang jeo-sseum-ni-da.*
• incompetent.	• *yu-neung-haji-mo-t'e- sseum-ni-da.*
• unfriendly.	• *ch'in-jeol-ha-ji-mo-t'e- sseum-ni-da.*
The room attendant is rude (incompetent).	*Gaek-shil ch'eong-so-bu-ga bul-son-hae-yo (il-eul mot-hae-yo).*
I didn't receive my wake-up call.	*Kkae-weo-ju-neun jeon-hwa-reul hae-ju-ji an-at-seo-yo.*
I'm very disappointed with the level of service in this hotel.	*I-ho-tel seo-bi-seu-e a-ju sil-mang-haet-seo-yo.*
This is the worst hotel I've ever seen.	*Yeo-t'e-kka-ji ga-bon-dejung-e ga-jang an-jo-eun ho-tel-im-ni-da.*

CONCIERGE

Please let me make the situation right.	*Shi-jeong ha-get-seum-ni-da.*
I'm certain we can straighten out the problem.	*Keu-mun-je-neun shi-jeong-ha-ket-seum-ni-da.*
You won't pay for anything that wasn't completely up to your standards.	*Go-gek-eui su-jun-e mot-mi-ch'in-keos-eun bi-yong-eul nae-ji an-a-do doem-ni-da.*
Please tell me what I can do to correct this terrible situation.	*Je-ga eo-tteot-k'e-ha-myeon i-na-ppeun-sang-hwang-eul si-jeong-hal-jji mal-sseum-hae-ju-se-yo.*

We'll take _____ percent off your bill.	*Ho-tel-bi-e-seo _____ p'eo-sen-t'eu-reul ppae-deu-ri-ket-seum-ni-da.*
We're going to give you _____ night(s), compliments of the hotel.	*Ho-tel-eui gam-sa-p'yo-shi-ro _____ bam-eul mu-ryo-ro ji-nae-ge-hae-deu-ri-gess-seum-ni-da.*
Your entire bill is compliments of the house.	*Dang-shin-eui jeon ho-tel-bi-reul i-ho-tel-i mu-ryo-ro hae-deu-ri-get-seum-ni-da.*

GUEST

Yes, that would be satisfactory.	*Ne, keu-reom man-jok-ham-ni-da.*
No, that would not be satisfactory.	*A-ni-o, keu-keo-seu-ron bu-jok-ham-ni-da.*
I appreciate all your efforts.	*Dang-shin-eui seong-eui-e gam-sa-deu-rim-ni-da.*
Thank you, that would be very nice.	*Keu-reot-k'e ha-shi-myeon, gam-sa-ha-get-seum-ni-da.*
I will never come here again.	*Yeo-ki-neun da-shi o-ji-an-eul-keom-ni-da.*

MANAGEMENT COMPLAINTS

MANAGER

We have had some complaints about the noise coming from your room.	*Son-nim-bang-e-seo-na-neun so-eum-ttae-mun-e bul-p'yeong-i it-sseot-seum-ni-da.*
You are disturbing…	*Son-nim-eun…e-ge p'ae-reul kki-ch'i-go iss-eum-ni-da.*
• the people in the room next door.	• *yeop-bang sa ram-deul*
• the people at the next table.	• *yeop-shik-t'ak sa-ram-deul*
• our other guests.	• *da-reun son-nim-deul*

GUEST

We're sorry.	*Mi-an-ham-ni-da.*
We understand.	*Al-get-seum-ni-da.*
We'll take care of it.	*Al-ra-seo ha-get-seum-ni-da.*

We'll keep it down from now on.	*I-je-bu-t'eo jo-yong-hi ha-get-seum-ni-da.*
Who cares!	*Sang-kwan eop-seo-yo!*
Leave us alone!	*Nae-beo-ryeo du-se-yo!*

MANAGER

If you don't cooperate, I'm afraid I'll have to...	*Hyeop-jo-hae-ju-shi-ji-an-eu-myeon,... su-ba-kke eop-seum-ni-da.*
• ask you to leave the hotel (restaurant).	• *ho-tel (re-seu-t'o-rang)-e-seo na-ga-dal-la-go-hal*
• call security.	• *kyeong-bi-won-eul bu-reul-*
• call the police.	• *kyeong-ch'al-eul bu-reul-*

D. EMERGENCIES AND SAFETY

EMPLOYEE

Please note the emergency exits on this card.	*I-k'a-deu-e-it-neun bis-ang-gu-reul ju-mok-hae-ju-ship-shi-yo.*
Please note the emergency escape route on the door.	*Mun-wi-e-it-neun bi-sang-t'al-ch'ul-gu-reul ju-mok-hae-ju-ship-shi-yo.*
Your room is equipped with smoke alarms.	*I-bang-eun yeon-gi-kyeong-po-gi-ga seol-ch'i-toe-eoiss-seum-ni-da.*
Here is the fire alarm.	*Yeo-gi-e hwa-jae-kyeong-bo-gi-ga iss-seum-ni-da.*
In an emergency, dial ____.	*Bi-sang-shi-e-neun, ____-eu-ro jeon-hwa-ha-ship-shi-yo.*

GUEST

Help!	*Do-wa-ju-se-yo!*
Fire!	*Bul-i-ya!*
I need a doctor.	*Eu-i-sa-reul bul-leo-ju-se-yo.*
I'm...	*Je-ga...*
My husband (wife) is...	*Je-nam-p'yeon (bu-in)-i...*
Someone is...	*Eo-tteon sa-ram-i...*
• very sick.	• *mae-u a-p'eum-ni-da.*

• having a heart attack.	• *shim-jang-ma-bi-im-ni-da.*
• nauseated.	• *gu-yeok-jil-eul ham-ni-da.*
• choking.	• *jil-sik-ha-go iss-seum-ni-da.*
• losing consciousness.	• *eui-sik-eul il-k'o-iss-seum-ni-da.*
• about to vomit.	• *t'o-ha-ryeo-go ham-ni-da.*
• having a seizure.	• *bal-jjak-eul ham-ni-da.*
• stuck.	• *bak-hyeo iss-seum-ni-da.*
I can't breathe.	*Sum-eul shil-su-eop-sseo-yo.*
MANAGER	
I'll call an ambulance.	*Gu-geup-ch'a-reul bu-reu-gess-seum-ni-da.*
Don't move.	*Um-jik-i-ji ma-ship-shi-yo.*
The doctor will be here very soon.	*Got eu-i-sa-ga ol-geot-ni-da.*
Are you hurt?	*Eo-di da-ch'eoss-seum-ni-kka?*
What happened?	*Mu-seun il-im-ni-kka?*
GUEST	
I tripped and fell.	*Geol-lyeo-seo neom-eo-jeot-seum-ni-da.*
I cut myself.	*Be-eot-seum-ni-da.*
I drank too much.	*Sul-eul neo-mu ma-ni ma-shyeot-seum-ni-da.*
I hit my head.	*Meo-ri-reul bu-di-ch'yeot-seum-ni-da.*
I don't know.	*Mo-reu-gess-seum-ni-da.*
I've injured my…	*…da-ch'eoss-seum-ni-da.*
• neck.	• *Mok-eul*
• back.	• *Deung-eul*
• arm.	• *P'al-eul*
• hand.	• *Son-eul*
• leg.	• *Da-ri-reul*
• foot.	• *Bal-eul*

• eye(s).	• *Nun-eul*

DOCTOR (MEDICAL TECHNICIAN)

You'll be fine; try to relax.	*An-shim-ha-se-yo; gwaen-ch'an-eul keom-ni-da.*
We're taking you to the hospital.	*Byeong-weon-eu-ro ga-ya-gess-seum-ni-da.*
Whom should we notify?	*Nu-gu-han-t'e yeol-lak-hal-kka-yo?*

GUEST

I've been robbed.	***Gang-do-reul dang-haet-seum-ni-da.***

MANAGER

What did they take?	***Mu-eos-eul ppaet-gyeot-seum-ni-kka?***
Let me call the police.	***Gyeong-ch'al-eul bu-reu-gess-seum-ni-da.***
Attention, ladies and gentlemen.	***Yeo-reo-bun, ju-mok-hae-ju-ship-shi-yo.***
May I have your attention, please?	***Ju-mok-hae-ju-ship-shi-yo.***
Please...	***...ju-ship-shi-yo.***
• remain calm.	***• Jin-jeong-hae***
• follow the instructions of the staff.	***• Jik-weon-deul-eui ji-shi-reul tta-ra***
• wait in your rooms.	***• Bang-e-seo gi-da-ryeo***
• get under a table or doorway.	***• T'e-i-beul-mit-i-na mun-gan-eu-ro ga-***
• follow the evacuation plan (route) **printed on your door** (in the hallways).	***• Mun*** *(t'ong-ro)*-***e bu-t'eo-it-neun-t'al-ch'ul-do-*** *(ro)*-***reul tta-ra.***
We'll have the situation under control as soon as possible.	***Toel-su-it-neun-han ppa-li sang-hwang-eul shi-jeong-hae-ga-gess-seup-ni-da.***
Thank you for your patience.	***Ch'am-a-ju-shyeo-seo gam-sa-ham-ni-da.***

4. Checking In

A. AT THE FRONT DESK

FRONT DESK CLERK

Good morning (afternoon, evening).	*An-nyeong-ha-se-yo.*
How may I help you?	*To-wa-deu-ril-kka-yo?*

GUEST

I have a reservation under the name _____.	_____ *(eu)ro ye-yak haet-sseum-ni-da.*
Do you have a room for one (two)?	*Il(i)-in-shil it-sseum-ni-kka?*

CLERK

Yes, we have your reservation.	*Ye, ye-yak-doe-it-sseum-ni-da.*
Yes, for how many nights?	*Ye, myeo-ch'il-bam won-ha-shim-ni-kka?*
No, I'm sorry, we're full.	*A-ni-yo, mi-an-ham-ni-da. P'ang-i eop-sseum-ni-da.*

GUEST

For _____ night(s), please.	_____ *bam im-ni-da.*
What are your rates?	*Yo-geum-eun eol-ma- im-ni-kka?*

CLERK

• For a single,	• *Il-in-shil-eun,*
• For a double,	• *I-in-shil-eun,*
• For adjoining rooms,	• *Yeop-bang-eun,*
• For a suite,	• *Seu-wi-teu-neun,*
...the rate is _____ per night.	*...il-bak-e* _____ *im-ni-da.*

GUEST

Are any meals included?	*Shik-bi-neun p'o-ham-doe-it-sseum-ni-kka?*
Is breakfast included?	*A-chim-eun p'o-ham-doe-it-sseum-ni-kka?*

CLERK

No, meals are extra.	*A-ni-o, shik-sa-neun tta-ro-chi-bul-hae-ya-ham-ni-da.*
Yes, breakfast is included.	*Ye, a-chim-eun p'o-ham-doe-it-sseum-ni-da.*
You can choose....	*...seon-taek-ha-shil-su-it-sseum-ni-da.*
• the American plan (all meals included).	• *(Mo-deun-shik-sa-ga-p'o-ham-doen) mi-guk-shik*
• the modified American plan (breakfast and dinner).	• *(A-chim-gwa cheo-nyeok-i-p'o-ham-doen) ban-mi-guk-shik*
• the European plan (no meals included).	• *(Shik-sa-ga-p'o-ham-doe-ji-an-eun) yu-reop-shik*

GUEST

I'd like a room...	*...bang-eu-ro chu-se-yo.*
• that faces the back (front).	• *Dwi(ap)-jjok*
• that faces the water (pool).	• *P'ul-jang-i bo-i-neun*
• with a private bath/toilet/shower.	• *Mok-yok-tang-i ttal-lin*
• with a handicapped-accessible bathroom.	• *Chang-ae-ja-yong wha-jang-shil-i in-neun*
• with air-conditioning.	• *E-eo-kon-i in-neun*
• with a TV.	• *Tel-le-bi-jon-i in-neun*
• with cable.	• *"Cable TV"-ga in-neun*
• with a fax machine.	• *Paek-seu-ga in-neun*
• with a phone.	• *Cheon-wha-ga in-neun*
• with a network hookup for my computer.	• *"Computer"-tong-shin-i ga-neung-han*
• with a view.	• *Cheon-mang cho-eun*
• with a whirlpool bath/Jacuzzi.	• *Cha-ku-ji-ga in-neun*
• with two double beds.	• *"Double beds"-tu-gae in-neun*
• with an extra bed.	• *Ch'u-ga ch'im-dae-ga in-neun*
• with a baby crib.	• *A-gi ch'im-dae-ga in-neun*

• with a balcony.	• *Bal-co-ni-ga in-neun*
• with a sitting area.	• *Eung-jeop se-teu-ga in-neun*
• with a bar.	• *Hom-ba-ga in-neun*
• with a kitchenette.	• *Bu-eog-i in-neun*
• away from the elevator.	• *"Elevator"-e-seo tteol-eo-jin*
• with no meals.	• *Shik-sa-ga eom-neun*

CLERK

No problem.	*Cho-sseum-ni-da.*
I'm sorry.	*Mi-an-ham-ni-da.*
There is none available.	*Eop-sseum-ni-da.*
We don't provide/offer that.	*Geu-ron seo-bi-seu-neun eop-sseum-ni-da.*

GUEST

Does the hotel have…	*…i-ho-tel-e it-sseum-ni-kka?*
• a restaurant?	• *Shik-dang-i*
• a bar?	• *Ba-ga*
• room service?	• *"Room service"-ga*
• a gym/health club?	• *"Health club"-i*
• a spa hot tub?	• *Ssa-u-na-ga*
• a swimming pool?	• *Su-yeong-jang-i*
• baby-sitting?	• *T'a-ga-shi-seol-i*
• tennis courts?	• *"Tennis court"-ga*
• laundry (dry-cleaning) service?	• *Se-tak seo-bi-seu-ga*
• a garage?	• *Ch'a-go-ga*
May I see the room?	*Pang-jom bo-yeo-ju-se-yo?*

CLERK

Yes, certainly. Here's the key.	*Ye, mul-lon-im-ni-da. Yeol-soe-ga yeo-gi it-sseum-ni-da.*
Would you like another room?	*Da-reun-bang-eu-ro deu-ril-kka-yo?*

GUEST	
I'd like something…	*…bang-eu-ro chu-se-yo.*
• smaller.	• *Deo chag-eun*
• larger.	• *Deo keun*
• quieter.	• *Deo cho-yong-han*
• better.	• *Deo cho-eun*
• cheaper.	• *Deo ssan*
• on another floor.	• *Da-reun ch'eung*
I'll take the room, please.	*I-bang-eu-ro ha-get-sseum-ni-da.*
CLERK	
Very well, how will you be *bul-* paying?	*Chot-seum-ni-da, eo-tteo-ke chi-* *ha-shi-get-sseum-ni-kka?*
GUEST	
I'll pay with…	*…chi-bul-ha-get-sseum-ni-da.*
• cash.	• *Hyeon-geum-eu-ro*
• a credit card.	• *Shin-yong-'card'-ro*
• traveler's checks.	• *Yeo-haeng-ja su-pyo-ro*
CLERK	
Thank you.	*Gam-sa-ham-ni-da.*
To charge meals and services to your room, I'll need a credit card.	*Gaek-shil-ro dal-a-no-ki wi-hae-seo, shin-yong-"card" chom bo-yeo-ju-se-yo.*
You may settle the bill with traveler's checks (cash).	*Yeo-haeng-ja su-pyo-ro (Hyeon-geum-eu-ro) gye-san-ha-shyeo-do doem-ni-da.*
If you would like to store valuables, we have a safe.	*Kwi-jung-pum bo-gwan keum-go-ga it-sseum-ni-da.*
Quiet hours are between _____ and _____.	_____ *si-e-seo* _____ *si sa-i-neun cho-yong-hi hae chu-se-yo.*
There are no pets allowed.	*Ae-wan dong-mul-eun sa-jeol-im-ni-da.*
Children under _____ stay free.	_____ *i-ha eo-rin-i-neun mu-ryo-im-ni-da.*

Smoking is allowed only in the bar.	*Heup-yeon-eun ba-e-seo-man heo-yong-doem-ni-da.*
We do not allow cooking in the rooms.	*Gaeg-sil-e-seo-neun yo-ri-ha-shil-su-eop-sseum-ni-da.*
GUEST	
Do I (we) have any messages?	*Jeo-han-te me-si-ji on-geot-it-sseum-ni-kka?*
I would like a wake-up call, please.	*Nae-il a-ch'im-e kkae-weo chu-se-yo.*
May we have…, please?	*…chom chu-se-yo?*
• extra blankets	• *Dam-nyo*
• extra towels	• *Su-geon*
• a hair dryer	• *Hae-eo-deu-ra-i-eo*
• an iron	• *Da-ri-mi*
• ice	• *Eo-reum*
CLERK	
I'll have that brought to your room right away.	*Ba-ro ga-tta-deu-ri-get- sseum-ni-da.*
GUEST	
Where is…	*…eo-di-e it-sseum-ni-kka?*
• the room attendant?	• *Ch'ong-so-bu-neun*
• the bellman (bell attendant)?	• *"Bellman"-neun*
• the manager?	• *Chi-bae-in-eun*
• the dining room?	• *Shik-dang-eun*
• the gift shop?	• *Gi-nyeom-p'um-jeom-eun*
• the newsstand?	• *Sin-mun p'an-mae-dae-neun*
CLERK	
Just over there.	*Ba-ro cheo-gi-e it-sseum-ni-da.*
GUEST	
How do I use the telephone?	*Cheon-hwa-neun eo-tteo-ke sseum-ni-kka?*

CLERK

The instructions are next to the phone.	*Sa-yong-beop-i cheon-hwa-gi yeo-p'e it-sseum-ni-da.*
Dial _____ for a local (long-distance) call,	*Shi-nae(shi-oe) cheon-hwa-neun _____ eul dol-li-se-yo,*
wait for the tone,	*shin-ho-eum-eul deut-go,*
then dial the number.	*beon-ho-reul dol-li-se-yo.*
Dial _____ for an operator.	*Kyo-hwan-eun _____ im-ni-da.*
To use a credit card, dial _____.	*Shin-yong-'card'-neun _____ im-ni-da.*

GUEST

Please have our luggage brought to our room.	*Chim-eul bang-eu-ro bo-nae-ju-se-yo.*
We'll need a wheelchair.	*"Wheelchair"-ga p'i-ryo-ham-ni-da.*

CLERK

Yes, right away.	*Keum-bang hae-deu-ri-get-sseum-ni-da.*

GUEST

We'd like to order a pizza, please.	*P'i-ja chom bo-nae-ju-se-yo.*

MANAGER

I'll be happy to call someone for you.	*Dae-sin cheon-hwa-reul geol-eo deu-ri-get-sseum-ni-da.*
We have room service, but we don't allow outside vendors into the hotel.	*"Room service"-ga it-sseum-ni-da. Oe-bu-p'an-mae-in-eun deu-reo-ol-su-eop-sseum-ni-da.*

GUEST

We'd like to entertain a few friends in our room.	*Ch'in-gu-reul ch'o-dae-ha-go ship-sseum-ni-da.*

MANAGER

We allow guests in the rooms until _____.	*_____ si kka-ji-man heo-yong-doem-ni-da.*

B. SHOWING GUESTS TO THEIR ROOMS

BELLMAN (BELL ATTENDANT)

My name is _____, and I'm your bell attendant.	*Che-i-reum-eun _____ im-ni-da. Cheo-neun "bellman" im-ni-da.*
May I show you to your room?	*Bang-eu-ro an-nae-hae deu-ril-kka-yo?*

GUEST

No, thanks. We'll find it ourselves.	*A-ni-yo. Cheo-hi-ga chig-jeop ga-get-sseum-ni-da.*
Yes, please.	*Ye, bu-t'ak-ham-ni-da.*

BELLMAN

This way, please.	*I-jjok im-ni-da.*
The elevator is over here.	*"Elevator"-neun yeo-gi im-ni-da.*
May I show you the features of your room?	*Gaeg-sil sa-yong-beop-eul mal-sseum-deu-ri-ge- sseum-ni-da?*
This is the key to the minibar.	*Mi-ni-ba yol-soe im-ni-da.*
• Any movie you select	• *Seon-taek-ha-sin yeong-hwa*
• Any long-distance calls you make	• *Sa-yong-han chang-geo-ri cheon-hwa*
• Any snack or beverage you take from the refrigerator	• *Naeng-jang-go-e-seo kkeo-nae chap-su-shin shig-eum-nyo*
...will be charged to your room.	*.... yo-geum-eun kwi-ha-eui bang-beon-ho-ro ch'eong-gu doem-ni-da.*

TIP! ••••

International guests in particular may have questions about using the telephone and will appreciate seeing how the television and pay movies work.

Here is the control for the heating (air-conditioning).	*Nan-bang(e-eo-kon) cho-jeol-gi im-ni-da.*
GUEST	
How do I call Room Service?	*"Room service"-reul eo-tteo-ke chu-mun-ham-ni-kka?*
BELLMAN	
Dial _____.	*_____ eul dol-li-se-yo.*
GUEST	
This room…	*I-bang-eun…*
• is too close to the elevator.	• *"elevator"-e-seo neo-mu ga-kka-weo-yo.*
• hasn't been made up.	• *ch'eong-so-ga an-doe-it-sseum-ni-da.*
• smells (like cigarettes).	• *(dambae) naem-se-ga na-yo.*
The toilet (bathtub, sink) is clogged.	*Hwa-jang-shil(yog-jo, sing-keu-dae)-i ma-kyeot-sseo-yo.*
May I (we) change rooms, please?	*Bang chom ba-kkwo-ju-se-yo?*
BELLMAN	
Please let me check our availability with the front desk.	*Do-wa-deu-ril-su in-neun-ji "front desk"-e al-a-bo-get-sseum-ni-da.*
Sure, I'll be happy to assist you.	*Mul-lon im-ni-da. Do-wa-deu-ri-ge-doe-seo gi-bbeum-ni-da.*
Please call if I can help you with anything else.	*Do-um-i p'i-ryo-ha-shi-myeon cheon-hwa ju-se-yo.*

VOCABULARY ••••

THE GUEST ROOM

air-conditioning	*e-eo-k'on*
balcony	*bal-ko-ni*
bath mat	*yok-shil mae-teu*
bathtub	*yok-jo*
bed	*ch'im-dae*
bedspread	*ch'im-dae k'eo-beo*
blanket	*dam-nyo*
blinds	*beul-la-in-deu*
carpet	*yang-t'an-ja*
ceiling	*ch'eon-jang*
chair	*eui-ja*
closet	*byeok-jang*
conditioner	*e-eo-k'on*
couch	*so-p'a*
crib	*a-gi ch'im-dae*
desk	*ch'aek-sang*
Do Not Disturb sign	*bang-hae-ha-ji ma-se-yo-ssa-in*
door	*mun*
drapes	*k'eo-t'en*
dresser	*hwa-jang-dae*
fan	*seon-p'ung-gi*
floor	*ma-ru*
glass(es)	*jan*
hair dryer	*he-eo-deu-ra-i-eo*
(coat) hanger	*ot-geo-ri*

(cont'd.)

KOREAN

The Guest Room *(cont'd.)*

heat	*nan-bang*
ice bucket	*eo-reum-t'ong*
iron	*da-ri-mi*
lamp	*cheon-deung*
light	*cho-myeong*
lock	*cha-mul-soe*
minibar	*mi-ni-ba*
mirror	*geo-ul*
nightstand	*jeon-deung*
pillow	*bae-gae*
radio	*ra-di-o*
razor	*myeon-do-gi*
sewing kit	*ba-neu-jil-se-t'eu*
shampoo	*shyam-p'u*
sheets	*shi-t'eu*
shower	*shya-weo*
shower cap	*shya-weo-yong k'aep*
sink	*sing-k'eu-dae*
soap	*bi-nu*
telephone	*cheon-hwa*
television	*t'el-le-bi-jeon*
thermostat	*on-do jo-jeol-jang-ch'i*
toilet	*hwa-jang-shil*
toilet paper	*hwa-jang-shil chong-i*
toothbrush	*ch'i-sol*
toothpaste	*ch'i-yak*
towel	*su-geon*
VCR	*bi-de-o*
wall	*byeok*
window	*ch'ang-mun*

5. Providing Assistance

A. GIVING DIRECTIONS

CONCIERGE

Good morning. May I help you? *An-nyeong-ha-se-yo. To-wa-deu-ril-kka-yo?*

GUEST

Yes, where is (are) the… *Ye,… eo-di-e it-sseum-ni-kka?*

- bathrooms? • *hwa-jang-shil-i*
- lounge/bar? • *ra-un-ji/ba-ga*
- restaurant? • *shik-dang-i*
- barbershop/hairdresser's? • *i-bal-so-ga/mi-jang-weon-i*
- gift shop? • *gi-nyeom-pum-jeom-i*
- health club/gym? • *"health club"-i*
- ballroom? • *mu-do-hoe-jang-i*
- elevator? • *seung-gang-gi-ga*
- pay phones? • *cheon-hwa-gi-ga*
- ice machine? • *eo-reum p'an-mae-gi-ga*

TIP! ••••

You can simply explain many directions, but when they're more complex, you should use either a map or written instructions (or both). Hotels should keep preprinted directions to major sites on hand. Also, many cultures don't speak of distance in terms of city blocks but will understand if you use the word "streets" instead. And remember that most international guests use the metric system and may have difficulties figuring a distance given in miles, yards, or feet.

KOREAN

CONCIERGE

Take…	…*i-yong-ha-se-yo.*
• the escalator.	• *Es-kal-e-i-teo-reul*
• the elevator.	• *Seung-gang-gi-reul*
• the stairs.	• *Kye-dan-eul*
Go…	…*ga-se-yo.*
• up.	• *Wi-ro*
• down.	• *A-rae-ro*
• left.	• *Oen-jjok-eu-ro*
• right.	• *O-reun-jjok-eu-ro*
• straight ahead.	• *Got-ba-ro a-p'eu-ro*
• around the corner.	• *Ko-neo-reul do-ra-seo*
• left, then right.	• *Oen-jjok-eu-ro don-da-eum, da-shi o-reun-jjok-eu-ro*
• past the elevators.	• *Seung-gang-gi-reul chi-na-seo*
• to the first (second, third, fourth) floor.	• *Il (i, sam, sa)-ch'eung-eu-ro*
• left (right) when you exit the elevator.	• *Seung-gang-gi-reul nae-ryeo-seo oen-jjok-eu-ro(o-reun-jjok-eu-ro)*
• in through the second set of doors.	• *Deu-beon-jjae mun-eu-ro deu-reo ga-se-yo*
It will be…	…*it-sseum-ni-da.*
• on your right.	• *Dang-shin-eui o-reun-jjok-e*
• on your left.	• *Dang-shin-eui oen jjok-e*
• right in front of you.	• *Dang-shin-eui a-p'e*

GUEST

How do I get…	…*eo-tteo-k'e ga-na-yo?*
• to the hospital?	• *Byeong-weon-eu-ro*
• to city hall?	• *Shi-ch'eong-eu-ro*
• to the ____ restaurant/hotel?	• ____ *shik-dang eu-ro/ho-t'el-lo*
• to the train station?	• *Gi-ch'a-yeok-eu-ro*
• to the bus station?	• *Ppeo-sseu cheong-nyu-jang-eu-ro*

• to the nearest bus stop?	• *Ga-jang ga-kka-un ppeo-sseu cheong-nyu-jang-eu-ro*
• to the mall?	• *Baek-hwa-jeom-eu-ro*
• to the post office?	• *U-ch'e-kuk-eu-ro*
• to the airport?	• *Kong-hang-eu-ro*
• downtown?	• *Si-nae-ro*
• to the car rental agency?	• *Cha-dong-ch'a bil-li-ryeo-myeon*
• to _____ Street/Avenue?	• _____ *keo-ri-ro*

CONCIERGE

When you exit the hotel, go…	*Ho-t'el-eul na-ga-seo,…ga-se-yo.*
• left.	• *oen-jjok-eu-ro*
• right.	• *o-reun-jjok-eu-ro*
• straight ahead.	• *got-ba-ro a-p'eu-ro*
• north.	• *buk-jjok-eu-ro*
• south.	• *nam-jjok-eu-ro*
• east.	• *dong-jjok-eu-ro*
• west.	• *seo-jjok-eu-ro*

GUEST

How far is it?	*Eol-ma-na meom-ni-kka?*

CONCIERGE

It's about _____…	*Yak _____…cheong-do im-ni-da.*
• blocks (streets).	• *beul-lok (keo-ri)*
• miles.	• *ma-il*
• kilometers.	• *ki-ro-mi-teo*
• minutes…	•…*bun*
• on foot.	• *keo-reo-seo*
• by car.	• *ch'a-ro*
• by bus.	• *ppeo-sseu-ro*
• by metro (subway).	• *chi-ha-ch'eol-ro*

GUEST

Can you show me on the map?	*Chi-do-reul bo-yeo-ju-se-yo?*

CONCIERGE

Sure, it's right here.	*Ye, ba-ro yeo-gi im-ni-da.*
Let me draw you a little map.	*Yak-do-reul geu-ryeo deu-ri-get-sseum-ni-da.*

GUEST

Can you tell me where I can…around here?	*I-geun-ch'eo eo-di-e-seo che-ga… su-in-na-yo?*
• take a walk	• *san-ch'ak-eul hal-*
• ride a bike	• *cha-cheon-geo-reul t'al-*
• jog	• *cho-ging-eul hal-*

CONCIERGE

Yes, we have maps of…trails right here.	*Ye, ba-ro yeo-gi-e…chi-do-ga it-sseum-ni-da.*
• jogging	• *cho-ging-k'o-seu*
• walking	• *san-ch'ak-ro*
• bike	• *cha-cheon-geo-do-ro*

B. RECOMMENDING PLACES OF INTEREST

GUEST

Can you recommend any places to visit?	*Ga-bol-man-han-got-seul ch'u-ch'eon-hae chu-shi-get-sseum-ni-kka?*

CONCIERGE

There are lots. Are you interested in…	*Man-sseum-ni-da.…-e kwan-shim-i it-sseum-ni-kka?*
• art?	• *Mi-sul*
• theater?	• *Keuk-jang*
• shopping?	• *Shyo-p'ing*
• museums?	• *Bang-mul-kwan*
• sports?	• *Un-dong*
• sight-seeing?	• *Kwan-kwang*
• music?	• *Eu-mak*

• outdoor activities?	• *Ya-oe hwal-ttong*
• children's activities?	• *A-i-deul-no-ri*
GUEST	
What do you recommend?	*Mu-eo-seul ch'u-ch'eon-hae chu-shi-get-sseum-ni-kka?*
CONCIERGE	
If you're interested in art, I'd suggest…	*Ye-sul-e kwan-shim-i it-sseu-shi-myeon,…-eul ch'u-ch'eon-ha-get-sseum-ni-da.*
• the _____ gallery.	• _____ *hwa-rang*
• the _____ art museum.	• _____ *ye-sul- bang-mul-kwan*
If you're interested in theater, I can get you tickets to…	*Keuk-jang-e kwan-shim-i it-sseu-shi-myeon,…p'yo-reul gu-hae-deu-ri-get-sseum-ni-da.*
• a show.	• *ssyo*
• an opera.	• *o-p'e-ra*
• a movie.	• *yeong-hwa*
For shopping, I'd recommend…	*Shyo-p'ing-eul ha-ryeo-myeon,…ch'u-ch'eon-ha-get-sseum-ni-da.*
• downtown.	• *shi-nae do-shim-ga-reul*
• the mall.	• *baek-hwa-jeom-eul*
• the discount outlets.	• *ha-rin mae-jang-eul*
GUEST	
Do they have…there?	*Geo-gi-e-neun…it-sseum-ni-kka?*
• clothes	• *ot-shi*
• furniture	• *ka-gu-ga*
• rugs (carpets)	• *yang-t'an-ja-ga*
• souvenirs	• *ki-nyeom-pum-i*
• books	• *ch'aek-i*
• sporting goods	• *seu-p'o-ch'eu yong-pum-i*
• candy	• *sa-t'ang-i*
• antiques	• *kol-dong-pum-i*

- electronics — • *ga-jeon-je-pum-i*
- computers — • *k'eom-p'yu-t'eo-ga*
- a farmers' market — • *nong-san-mul-si-jang-i*
- a supermarket — • *ssu-p'eo-ma-ket-shi*
- a flea market — • *byeo-ruk-shi-jang-i*

CONCIERGE

Perhaps you'd like a museum. — *A-ma bang-mul-kwan-eul cho-a-ha-shil-geo-shim-ni-da.*

A local favorite is the…museum. — *Yeo-gi sa-ram-deul-eun…bang-mul-kwan-eul jo-ha-ham-ni-da.*

- natural history — • *cha-yeon-sa*
- modern art — • *hyeon-dae ye-sul*
- science — • *kwa-hak*
- local history — • *chi-yeok-sa*

GUEST

We were thinking of sight-seeing. — *U-ri-neun kwan-kwang-eul ha-ryeo-goam-ni-da.*

CONCIERGE

I'd be happy to arrange a city tour. — *Shi-nae-kwan-kwang-eul-ye-yak-hae-deu-ril-kka-yo.*

GUEST

How about… — *…eo-tteo-shim-ni-kka?*

- interesting architecture? — • *Heung-mi-in-neun-keon-chuk-mul-eun*
- churches? — • *Kyo-hoe-neun*
- a vineyard? — • *P'o-do-bat-eun*
- the business district? — • *Shi-nae-jung-shim-ji-neun*
- the government buildings? — • *Kwan-gong-seo-keon-mul-eun*
- the university? — • *Dae-hak-kyo-neun*
- monuments? — • *Ki-nyeom-mul-eun*
- the countryside? — • *Kyo-oe-neun*

CONCIERGE	
There are many sports events.	*Seu-p'o-ch'eu kyeong-gi-ga mani yeol-lim-ni-da.*
Would you like tickets to...	*...p'yeo-reul weon-ha shim-ni-kka?*
• a baseball game?	• *Ya-gu*
• a basketball game?	• *Nong-gu*
• a football game?	• *Mi-shik-ch'uk-gu*
• a hockey game?	• *Ha-ki*
• a tennis match?	• *Te-ni-seu kyeong-gi*
GUEST	
Are there any musical events?	*Eum-ak haeng-sa-ga it-sseum-ni-kka?*
CONCIERGE	
There is a...concert tonight.	*O-neul-bam-e...eum-ak-hoe-ga-it-sseum-ni-da.*
• rock-and-roll	• *rak-en-rol*
• blues	• *beu-ru-seu*
• classical music	• *keul-lae-sik*
• jazz	• *jae-jeu*
There's musical entertainment at ____.	____ *e-seo eum-ak yon-ju-ga na-om-ni-da.*
GUEST	
Is there anything else going on tonight?	*O-neul-bam mu-seun-haeng-sa-ga it-sseum-ni-kka?*
CONCIERGE	
Other than the movies, I'd suggest...	*Yeong-hwa-i-oe-e-do,...it-sseum-ni-da.*
• bowling.	• *bol-ling-i*
• a nightclub.	• *na-i-teu-keul-leop-i*
• a video rental.	• *bi-de-o dae-yeo-ga*
GUEST	
What do you suggest for outdoor activities?	*Ya-oe-un-dong-eu-ro mu-eo-shi jo-sseum-ni-kka?*

CONCIERGE	
How about…	*…eo-tteo-se-yo?*
• hiking?	• *Ha-i-king*
• fishing?	• *Nak-shi*
• skiing?	• *Seu-ki*
• skating?	• *"Skating"*
• Rollerblading?	• *"Rollerblading"*
• swimming?	• *Su-yeong*
• surfing?	• *"Surfing"*
Or you might like to go…	*A-ni-myeon,…eo-tteo-se-yo.*
• to the river.	• *kang-eu-ro ka-neun-geot-shi*
• to the lake.	• *ho-su-ro ka-neun-geot-shi*
• to the mountains.	• *san-eu-ro ka-neun-geot-shi*
• for a drive.	• *"drive" ka-neun-geot-shi*
• to the beach.	• *hae-byeon-eu-ro ka-neun-geot-shi*
• to the forest.	• *su-peu-ro ka-neun-geot-shi*
GUEST	
Is there anything for children?	*Eo-rin-i-reul wi-hae-seo-neun eo-tteon-geot-shi-it-sseum-ni-kka?*
CONCIERGE	
Yes, there's…	*Ye,…i it-sseum-ni-da.*
• a zoo.	• *dong-mul-weon*
• a children's museum.	• *eo-rin-i bang-mul-gwan*
• an amusement park.	• *no-ri-gong-weon*
• a water park.	• *mul-no-ri-jang*
Would you like to rent…	*…bil-li-shi get-sseum-ni-kka?*
• a bicycle?	• *Ja-jeon-geo-reul*
• a car?	• *Ja-dong-ch'a-reul*
• some skis?	• *"Ski" reul*
• some Rollerblades?	• *"Rollerblade"-reul*
Would you like a tour guide who speaks Korean?	*Han-kuk-mal hal-kwan-kwang an-nae-weon-eul weon ha-shim-ni-kka?*

May I make a reservation for you?	*Ye-yak-hae deu-ril- kka-yo?*
GUEST	
Can you recommend a good restaurant?	*Jo-eun shik-dang-eul ga-reu-ch'eo ju-se-yo?*
CONCIERGE	
What type of cuisine would you like?	*Mu-seun jong-nyu- reul jo-a-ha-se-yo?*
GUEST	
We'd like a(n)...restaurant.	*...shik-dang-e ga-go-ship-seum-ni-da.*
• casual	• *Il-ban-jeok-in*
• elegant	• *Meot-jin*
• fast-food	• *"Fast food"-jeom*
• inexpensive	• *Jeo-ryeom-han*
• seafood	• *Hae-mul jeon-mun*
• vegetarian	• *Ya-ch'ae jeon-mun*
We'd like an authentic American steakhouse.	*Mi-guk-shik stei-keu jeon mun jeom.*
CONCIERGE	
You can get there by...	*...ga-shil-su it-sseum-ni-da.*
• bus.	• *Beo-seu-ro*
• train.	• *Ki-ch'a-ro*
• subway.	• *Ji-ha-ch'eol-lo*
Take the...bound for _____.	*..._____ ta-se-yo.*
• number _____ bus	• *_____ beon beo-s-reul*
• train	• *Ki-ch'a-reul*
• subway	• *Ji-ha-cheol-eul*
You'll need to transfer to... at _____.	*_____ e-seo...ro ga-ra-t'a-se-yo.*
• the _____ line	• *_____ seon-eu*
• the number _____ bus	• *_____ beon beo-seu*
Get off at _____.	*_____ e-seo nae-ri-se-yo.*

May I call you a taxi?	*Tek-si-reul bul-leo-deu-ril-kka-yo?*
We have a free shuttle bus service available to _____.	_____ *ro ga-neun shyeo-teul- beo-seu-ga it-sseum-ni-da.*
It leaves every _____ minutes.	*Mae* _____ *bun-ma-da it-sseum-ni-da.*
It leaves every hour.	*Mae shi-gan-ma-da it-sseum-ni-da.*

GUEST

What's the price range?	*Ga-gyeog-i eol-ma-im-ni-kka?*

6. Business Services and Clientele

A. BOOKING A BUSINESS MEETING

EMPLOYEE

Good morning.	*An-nyeong-ha-se-yo.*
How may I help you today?	*Eo-tteo-ke do-wa-deu-ril-kka-yo?*

GUEST

I'd like to make arrangements for a business meeting.	*Yeo-gi-seo hoe-eui-reul yeol-go shi-peun-de-yo.*

EMPLOYEE

For how many people?	*Myeot-myeong-i mo-im-ni-kka?*

GUEST

For _____ people on _____.	_____ *myeong-im-ni-da.*

TIP! ••••

Clients who do business from the hotel need a great deal of service from you. They tend to be seasoned travelers who don't want a lot of explanation from hotel employees, just competent action. Attending to their every need often yields substantial financial rewards!

EMPLOYEE

Fine.	*Jo-sseum-ni-da.*
We have space available.	*Hoe-eui-jang-so-ga it-sseum-ni-da.*
We can provide all your meals, as well as your meeting needs.	*Hoe-eui-e p'i-ryo-ha-shin-geo-bbun-a-ni-ra, shik-sa-do je-gong ha-get-sseum-ni-da.*

GUEST

That's good. We'd like…for each day.	*Jo-sseum-ni-da…hae-ju-se-yo.*
• a continental breakfast	• *keon-ti-nen-tal-lo*
• coffee breaks	• *keo-pi ma-shi-myeo shi-neun-shi-gan-eu-ro*
• a working lunch	• *jeom-shim meo-geu-myeon-seo-ha-neun-geol-lo*
• snacks	• *gan-shik-eu-ro*
• a cocktail reception	• *kak-te-il ri-sep-shyeon-eu-ro*
• dinner	• *jeo-nyeok-shik-sa-ro*
Also, we'll require…for the meeting room.	*Hoe-eui-shil-e…p'i-ryo-ham-ni-da.*
• a VCR with a large-screen monitor	• *dae-hyeong-mo-ni-teo-ga ttal-lin bi-de-o-ga*
• an overhead projector with transparencies and markers	• *t'u-myeong-ji wa pen, yeong-sa-gi-ga*
• a chalkboard	• *ch'il-pan-i*
• a flip chart	• *ch'a-teu-ga*
• a slide projector	• *seul-lai-deu yeong-sa-gi-ga*
• a computer with a large-screen monitor	• *dae-hyeong mo-ni-teo-ga ttal-lin keom-pu-teo-ga*
And please be sure to provide…	*…kkog jun-bi-hae-ju-se-yo.*
• water.	• *Mul-eul*
• pads with pencils.	• *Yeon-pil gwa me-mo-ji-reul*
• ashtrays.	• *Jae-tteo-ri-reul*

KOREAN

EMPLOYEE

Let's decide on what time you'd like everything, and we'll be all set. — *Mo-du eon-je p'i-ryo-ha-shin-ji mal-sseum-haeju-se-yo. Jun-bi-hae-no-ke-sseum-ni-da.*

GUEST

Okay. How will the room be set up? — *Hoe-eui-shil-eul eo-tteo-ke kku-mi-shi-get-sseum-ni-kka?*

EMPLOYEE

We can set up the room… — *…kku-mi-get-sseum-ni-da.*

- theater style. — *Keug-jjang shik-eu-ro*
- in a square. — *Sa-gak-eu-ro*
- horseshoe ("U") style. — *U-jja-hyeong-eu-ro*
- classroom style. — *Kyo-shil hyeong-t'e-ro*
- boardroom style. — *I-sa-hoe-eui-shil hyeong-t'e-ro*

We're looking forward to having your group here. — *Hoe-eui kae-ch'oe-reul ko-dae-ham-ni-da.*

B. AT THE MEETING

ATTENDANT

I'm _____, the meeting-room attendant. — *Jeo-neun mo-im-eul shi-jung-deul _____ im-ni-da.*

How is everything? — *Mo-deun-ge kwen-ch'an eu-shim-ni-kka?*

GUEST

Everything is fine, thank you. — *Man-jok-seu-reop-seum-ni-da.*

We need… — *…-p'i-ryo-ham-ni-da.*

- more chairs. — *Eui-ja-ga deo*
- more coffee. — *K'eo-p'i-ga*
- the ashtrays emptied. — *Sae jae-tteo-ri-ga*
- more water. — *Muljom*

ATTENDANT

I'll take care of it right away. — *Jeuk-shi hae-gyeol-hae deu-ri-get-sseum-ni-da.*

Is everything else satisfactory?	*Geu-oe-e-neun man-jok-ha-shim-ni-kka?*

GUEST

It's quite nice, but the room…	*Jo-sseum-ni-da, ha-ji-man bang…*
• needs more light.	• *i-deo bal-ga-sseu-myeon jo-k'e-sseum-ni-da.*
• is too bright.	• *i-neo-mu bal-sseum-ni-da.*
• needs more ventilation.	• *eul-hwan-gi-hal p'i-ryo-ga-it-sseum-ni-da.*
• is too hot (cold).	• *i-neo-mu deop(ch'up)-sseum-ni-da.*
• is a little noisy.	• *i-jom shi-kkeu-reop-sseum-ni-da.*
• is crowded.	• *e-sa-ra-mi neo-mu man-sseum-ni-da.*
Can you take care of it?	*Hae-gyol hae ju-shil su it-sseu-shim-ni-kka?*
Can we get another room?	*Bang-eul ba-kkweo-ju-shil su it-sseu-shim-ni-kka?*

ATTENDANT

Let me see what we can do.	*A-ra-bo-get-sseum-ni-da.*

C. CATERING TO BUSINESS GUESTS

CONCIERGE

Good morning.	*An-nyeong-ha-se-yo.*
How may I help you?	*Do-wa-deu-ril-kka-yo?*

GUEST

Where is breakfast for the _____ group?	_____ *reul wi-han a-ch'im-shik-sa-ga eo-di-e jun-bi doe-it-sseum-ni-kka?*
Where is the exhibits hall?	*Jeon-shi-shil-i eo-di-e i-sseum-ni-kka?*

CONCIERGE

There's a buffet set up outside your meeting room.	*Hoe-eui-shil bak-e bu-p'e-ga jun-bi-deo-it-sseum-ni-da.*

English	Korean
Just down the hall.	*Hol-a-rae jjo-ge.*
In the dining room.	*Shik-dang-e.*
GUEST	
Thank you.	*Gam-sa-ham-ni-da.*
I need a fax sent.	*Paek-seu-reul bo-nae-ya ham-ni-da.*
I need some typing done.	*Ta-i-ping ch'il kke it-sseum-ni-da.*
I need a hookup to the Internet.	*Internet tong-shin-eul hae-ya ham-ni-da.*
I need a computer.	*Keom-pu-teo ga-p'i-ryo-ham-ni-da.*
I need a package sent overnight.	*Ha-ru-bam jim-eul mat-gi-ge-sseum-ni-da.*
I need courier service.	*U-pyeon-mul seo-bi-seu-ga-p'i-ryo-ham-ni-da.*
I need some letters mailed.	*Pyeon-ji-reul bu-ch'eo ju-se-yo.*
I need some copies made.	*Bok-sa-ga p'i-ryo-ham-ni-da.*
CONCIERGE	
I'll take care of that right away.	*Jeuk-si hae-gyeol-ha-ge-sseum-ni-da.*
GUEST	
Later, I'd like to host a small reception.	*Ri-sep-shyeon-eul yeol-go ship-seum-ni-da.*
Can you arrange that?	*A-ra-bwa-ju-se-yo?*
CONCIERGE	
Certainly. What would you like?	*Mul-lon im-ni-da. Mu-eo-seul-weon ha-se-yo?*
GUEST	
We need a full bar and some hors d'oeuvres.	*Ba wa oreu-doe- bu-ru-ga p'i-ryo-ham-ni-da.*
Make sure there are plenty of chilled shrimp.	*Naeng-sae-u-reul ch'ung bun-hi jun-bi-hae-ju-se-yo.*
Lots of champagne, please.	*Sham-pe-in-do ch'ung-bun-hi jun-bi-hae-ju-se-yo.*

CONCIERGE

I'll have Room Service put together a proposal right away, and get back to you.
Rum-seo-bi-seu-reul jun-bi-ha-do-rok-ha-get-sseum-ni-da. Da-shi yeol-lak-deu-ri-get-ssem-ni-da.

7. Checking Out

GUEST

At what time is checkout?
Ch'ek-a-ut shi-ga-ni eon-je im-ni-kka?

FRONT DESK CLERK

Checkout is at…
Ch'ek-a-ut shi-gan-eun…im-ni-da.

- 10 A.M. — *yeol-shi*
- noon. — *jeong-o*
- 3 P.M. — *o-hu se-shi*

You may audit your bill on channel _____ on your television.
_____ beon tel-le-bi-jeon-e-seo ch'ong-gu-seo-reul geom-t'o-hae bo-se-yo.

We provide an express checkout service.
Shin-sok-han ch'ek-a-ut seo-bi-seu-reul je-gong ha-go it-sseum-ni-da.

Your bill will be left outside your door the night before you check out.
Ch'ek-a-ut ha-shi-gi jeon nal bam mun-bak-e ch'eong-gu-seo-reul gat-da-no-ke-sseum-ni-da.

If you're satisfied with your bill, simply sign it,
A-mu mun-je-ga eop-seu-shi-myeon sa-in-hae- ju-shi-go,

and leave your key in your room.
yeol-soe-neun bang-e nwa du-se-yo.

Any late charges such as breakfast or minibar will be added automatically.
A-ch'im-shik-sa-na mi-ni-ba yo-geum-eun ja-dong-jeog-eu-ro ch'u-ga doem-ni-da.

GUEST

I'd like to check out, please.
Ch'ek-a-ut ha-get-sseum-ni-da.

CLERK

May I have your luggage brought down?
Che-ga chim-eul deu-reo-deu-ril-kka-yo?

GUEST

Yes, please.	*Ye, bu-t'ak-ham-ni-da.*
No, I brought (will bring) it myself.	*A-ni-yo, che-ga chim-eul deul-get-sseum-ni-da.*

CLERK

How was everything?	*Meo-mu-neun dong-an eo-ttae-sseum-ni-kka?*

GUEST

It was very nice, thank you.	*A-ju cho-wass-sseum-ni-da. Gam-sa-ham-ni-da.*
I want to speak with the manager.	*Chi-bae-in-gwa i-ya-ki-reul ha-go-ship-sseum-ni-da.*

CLERK

Certainly. The manager on duty is _____. One moment, please.	*Ye. Chi-bae-in-eun _____ ip-ni-da. Cham-kkan-man gi-da-ryeo-ju-se-yo.*

GUEST

Our experience was…	*Meo-mu-neun dong-an…*
• good.	• *man-chok-seu-reo-weo-sseum-ni-da.*
• excellent.	• *a-ju man-chok-seu-reo-weo-sseum-ni-da.*
• poor.	• *byeol-lo man-chok-seu-reob-ji-mo-t'ae-sseum-ni-da.*
• very bad.	• *a-ju man-chok-seu-reob-ji-mo-t'ae-sseum-ni-da.*

MANAGER ON DUTY

That's nice to hear.	*Geu-reo-k'e mal-sseum-ha-shi-ni gi-bun-i-cho-sseum-ni-da.*
I'm sorry to hear that.*	*Mi-an-ham-ni-da.*
Thank you. Please come again.	*Kam-sa-ham-ni-da. Da-shi-o-ship-shi-yo.*

*Please refer to Guest Complaints in the Hotel on page 317 for more on handling dissatisfied clients.

SECTION G

PORTUGUESE

1. The Bare Essentials

A. THE PORTUGUESE ALPHABET

Aa	Ah	*Nn*	Eh-neh
Bb	Beh	*Oo*	Oh
Cc	Zeh	*Pp*	PEh
Dd	Dee	*Qq*	KAy
Ee	Eh	*Rr*	EH-hee
Ff	Ehf	*Ss*	EH-she
Gg	Gheh	*Tt*	THee
Hh	AHgah	*Uu*	OO
Ii	Ee	*Vv*	VEh
Jj	ZHOtah	*Xx*	SHees
Kk	KAh	*Ww*	DAH-bleh-oo
Ll	EH-lay	*Zz*	ZEh
Mm	Eh-meh		

B. PRONUNCIATION CHART

VOWELS

PORTUGUESE SPELLING	APPROXIMATE SOUND IN ENGLISH	EXAMPLE
a	p<u>ar</u>ty	*nadar*—(nah-DAHR) to swim
e	oth<u>er</u>	*pesado*—(pe-ZAH-doo) heavy
ê	l<u>a</u>te	*mês*—(meys) months

é	get	*café*—(kah-FEH) coffee
i	seed	*final*—(fi-NNAHL) end
o	boot	*caso*—(KAH-zoo) case
ô	note	*pôs*—(pohs) to put
u	soon	*número*—(NOO-me-roo) number

DIPHTHONGS

A diphthong is a double vowel combination that produces a single sound.

PORTUGUESE SPELLING	APPROXIMATE SOUND IN ENGLISH	EXAMPLE
ai	ripe	*pai*—(pahy) father
au	now	*auto*—(OW-too) car
ei	may	*cadeira*—(kah-DAY-rah) chair
eu	glue	*deu*—(DAY-oo) gave
ia	yacht	*diálogo*—(JYAH-loh-goo) dialogue
ie	yet	*piedade*—(pyeh-DAH-jee) compassion
io	Yolanda	*Yolanda*—(yoh-LAHN-dah)
iu	you	*viu*—(VEE-oo) saw
oi	soy	*noite*—(NOY-chee) night
ou	low	*outro*—(OH-troo) other
ua	watch	*água*—(AH-gwah) water
ue	wet	*suéter*—(SWEH-tehr) sweater
ui	we	*cuidar*—(kwee-DAHR) to care
uo	quota	*quota*—(KWOH-tah) quote

CONSONANTS

PORTUGUESE SPELLING	APPROXIMATE SOUND IN ENGLISH	EXAMPLE
b	similar to English	
c (before *e/i*)	*s* (as in save)	*cinema*—(see-NAY-mah) movie theater
c (before *a/o/u*)	*k* (as in key)	*casa*—(KAH-zah) house
ç (before *a/o/u*)	*s* (as in save)	*moço*—(MOH-soo) young man
ch	*sh* (as in shampoo)	*chuva*—(SHOO-vah) rain
d	similar to English except before *e* and *i;* then usually pronounced like *j*	*morde*—(MORH-jee) to bite *aprendido*—(ah-prehn-JEE-doo) learned
f	similar to English	
g (before *a/o/u*)	hard *g* (as in go)	*gato*—(GAH-too) cat
g (before *e/i*)	soft *g* (as in measure)	*geral*—(zheh-ROW) general
h	always silent, but sounds like *y* when following *n*	*senhor*—(sehn-YOHR) sir
j	(as in pleasure)	*José*—(zhoh-ZEH) name
l	same as English except in final position; then pronounced like *u*	*animal*—(ah-nee-MOW) animal
lh	*y* (as in yes)	*filho*—(FEEL-yoo) son
m	like English, but more nasal	
n	similar to English	
nh	*ny* (as in canyon)	*senhor*—(sehn-YOHR) sir
qu (before *a/o*)	*qu* (as in quote)	*quota*—(KWOH-tah) quota
qu (before *e/i*)	*k* (as kite)	*queixa*—(KAY-shah) complain

r and *rr*	a breathy *h* (as in hot) in initial and mid-positions; a breathy *h* in final positions; also sometimes trilled	*rosa*—(HOH-za) rose *carro*—(KAH-hoo) car *cantar*—(kahn-TAHR) to sing
s	*z* (as in zebra)	*rosa*—(HOH-zah) rose
ss	*s* (as in some)	*passo*—(PAH-soo) footstep
t	similar to English but often like *ch* (before *e* and *i*)	*noite*—(NOY-chee) night *gentil*—(zhehn-CHEE-oo) gentle
v	similar to English	
x	*sh* (as in sheet); *s* (as in see); or *x* (as in wax)	*caixa*—(KAHY-shah) box *táxi*—(TAHK-see) cab
z	similar to English	

NASAL VOWELS

Nasal vowels are pronounced through the mouth and through the nose at the same time, just as in the French nasal vowels (for example, the French *bon*), and their sound is quite similar to the nasal twang heard in some areas of America and England.

PORTUGUESE SPELLING	APPROXIMATE SOUND IN ENGLISH	EXAMPLE
ã, am, an	like *ung* in *lung* or like *an* in the French *dans*	*maçã*—(mah-SSAHN) apple *ancinho*—(an-SEE-noo) rake
em, en	something like *ing* in *sing*, but recalling also the long *a* in late	*centro*—(SAYNG-troo) center
im, in	a nasalized version of the *ee* in *feet*	*cinco*—(SEENG-koo) five
om, on	like *orn* in *corn* or like *on* in the French *bon*	*bom*—(bawng) good
um, un	a nasal version of the *oo* in *foot*	*um*—(oong) one

SEMI-NASALIZED DIPHTHONGS

In semi-nasalized dipththongs, the first sound is nasal, combined with a weak *i* sound (pronounced like the *y* in *yet*) or *u* (pronounced like the *w* in *was*).

PORTUGUESE SPELLING	APPROXIMATE SOUND IN ENGLISH	EXAMPLE
ãe, êm	final *ãe* pronounced as *n,* usually final *êm* pronounced as *ã,* followed by the *y* of *yet*	*mãe*—(mown) mother *sem*—(sehng) without
ão	final unstressed *ão* pronounced as *ã,* followed by the *w* of *was*	*mão*—(mahng) hand
õe	pronounced as *orn* in *corn* or on the French *bon,* followed by the *y* of *yet.*	*põe*—(powng) puts

C. THE PORTUGUESE LANGUAGE

Brazilian Portuguese differs from the Portuguese that is spoken in Portugal in many important respects. Brazilian speech is slower, and the words are not as linked together as they are in the speech of Portugal natives. Unstressed vowels sound clear when spoken by Brazilians, while in Portugal they are rapidly slurred over: In Brazil *s* and *z* at the end of a syllable tend to be pronounced like *s* in *sit* and the *z* in *razor* (rather than like *sh* in *shut* or the *s* in *pleasure,* as they are pronounced in Portugal).

Portuguese spelling is more consistent than English; once you learn the sounds, it will be easy to pronounce a word correctly just by reading it.

The vowels and vowel combinations require special attention. They are necessary to the proper pronunciation of words and to making oneself understood.

Portuguese uses several nasal sounds, which are made by allowing air to escape through the nose as well as the mouth. Vowels are often nasalized before *m* or *n,* as in *tem* or *homens.*

This is also true of vowels written with a tilde (~) such as *vão, lições,* and so on.

In Brazil, an initial *r* and double *rr* are usually pronounced like the English *h,* whereas in Portugal (and in some regions of Brazil that border Spanish-speaking areas) they are trilled, as in Spanish.

In Brazil, an initial *e* or *o* at the end of a word is pronounced as *ee* or *oo* respectively—for example, *breve* and *foto.* In Portugal (and some regions of Brazil), the final *s* is normally pronounced like *sh,* further distinguishing the Portuguese spoken in Portugal from Brazilian speech in São Paulo.

D. THE BRAZILIAN AND PORTUGUESE CULTURES

Portuguese speakers, either from Portugal or Brazil, are quite fashion conscious, and they will usually dress up when they go out. The Portuguese tend to dress in a conservative, European style, while Brazilians usually lean toward more modern fashions. Brazilians sometimes get people's attention with a "psiu." Do not take offense.

In both Brazil and Portugal, attitudes about time are very relaxed; if you need someone to be punctual, you should tell them ahead of time.

Brazil's national drinks are *caipirinha* (kahy-pee-REEN-yah), made of crushed line and sugar; and *pinga* (peen-gah) or *cachaça* (kah-SHAH-sah), a strong liquor made from sugar cane. When whipped with crushed ice and fruit juices and sometimes sweetened condensed milk, *pinga* is transformed into the popular *batida* (bah-chee-dah). But no drink is more Brazilian than coffee, *cafézinho* (ka-fey-ZEEN-yoo), which is served black, strong, and with plenty of sugar in small demitasse cups. Coffee is served in larger cups and with milk only at breakfast.

2. Useful Expressions

A. GENERAL

Hello.	*Como Vai?*	Kohmo-VHAee.
Good-bye.	*Adeus./Tchau.*	Ah-Day-oos./CHAW.

Yes.	*Sim.*	Seen.
No.	*Não.*	Nown.
Maybe.	*Talvez.*	Tow-VEHZ.
Please.	*Por favor.*	Poor fah-VOHR.
Thank you (very much).	*(Muito) Obrigado/a.*	(MWEE-too) ohbree-Gah-doo/dah.
You're welcome.	*De nada.*	Jee NAH-dah.
Excuse me.	*Com licença.*	Kahn lee-SEHN-sah.
I beg your pardon.	*Eu peço desculpas.*	Ehu peh-soo days-KOOL-phaas.
I'm sorry.	*Perdão.*	Pehr-DOWN.
One moment, please.	*Um momento, por favor.*	Oo-moh-men-toh, poor-fah-VOHR.
Do you speak English?	*O/A senhor/a fala inglês?*	Oh/ah sehn-YOHR/ ah fah-lah een-glays?
• Yes, I do.	• *Sim, eu falo.*	• Seen, ehu FAH-loh.
• No, I don't.	• *Não, eu não falo.*	• Nown, ehu nown FAH-loh.
• A little.	• *Um pouco.*	• Oon POH-koo.
• No, not at all.	• *Não, nada.*	• Nown, NAH-dah.
That's okay.	*Tudo bem.*	Too-doh-behn.
It doesn't matter.	*Não importa.*	Nown-eem-POHR-tah.
I don't speak Portuguese.	*Eu não falo Português.*	Eh-oo nown FAH-loo pohr too-GAYS.
I can speak a little.	*Posso falar um pouquinho.*	Poh-joo-Fah-lahr-oo-poh-KEEN-yoo.
I understand a little.	*Eu entendo um pouco.*	Ehu-enten-doo-OON-POH-koo.
I don't understand.	*Eu não entendo.*	Ehu-nown-ehn-TEHN-doo.
Please speak more slowly.	*Fale um pouco mais devagar, por favor.*	Fah-lee oon-POH-koo MAYS jee-vah-GAHR, poor-fah-VOHR.
Would you repeat that, please?	*Poderia repetir isso, por favor?*	Poh-jee-HRIA-hay-pee-thir ee-shoo, poor-fah-VOHR?

Yes, sir/ma'am.	*Sim, Senhor/a.*	Seen, sehn-YOHR/ah.
No problem.	*Não tem problema.*	Nown-tehn-proh-BLAY-mah.
It's my pleasure.	*O prazer é meu.*	Oo-prazayr-eh-MAY-o.

B. NEEDS

I'd like _____.	*Eu gostaria de _____.*	Eh-oo-gohs-tah-REE-ah jee _____.
I need _____.	*Eu necessito _____.*	Eh-oo-neh-she-SEE-too _____.
What would you like?	*O que você gostaria?*	Oo-keh-voh-say-gohs-tah-REE-ah?
Please bring me _____.	*Por favor, traga-me _____.*	Poor-fah-VOHR, TRAH-gah-mee _____.
I'm looking for _____.	*Estou procurando por _____.*	Ess-tohoo-proh-koo-RAHN-doo-poor _____.
I'm hungry.	*Estou com fome.*	Ess-TOH kahn FOM-meh.
I'm thirsty.	*Estou com sêde.*	Ess-TOH kahn SAY-deh.
It's important.	*Isto é importante.*	Ees-too eh eem-pohr-THAN-chee.
It's urgent.	*Isto é urgente.*	Ees-too eh oor-ZHAYN-chee.

C. QUESTION WORDS

How?	*Como?*	Koh-moo?
How much?	*Quanto?*	KWAHN-too?
How many?	*Quantos?/Quantas?*	KWAHN-tooz/KWAHN-taaz?
Which?	*Qual?*	Kwaw?
What?	*O que?*	Oo-kee?
What kind of?	*Que tipo de?*	Ke-TEE-phoh-deh?
Who?	*Quem?*	Kehn?
Where?	*Onde?*	Ohn-jee?

When?	*Quando?*	KWAHN-doo?
What does this mean?	*O que significa isto?*	Oo-ke-seeg-nee-FEE-kah-EES-too?
What does that mean?	*O que significa aquilo?*	Oo-ke-seeg-nee-FEE-ka-a-KE-loo?
How do you say _____ in Portuguese?	*Como você diz _____ em Português?*	Koh-moo-voh-say-JEEZ-_____ ehm pohr-too-GAYS?

D. COLORS

black	*preto*	pray-too
blue	*azul*	ah-ZOOL
brown	*marron*	mah-HOHN
gold	*dourado*	doa-RAH-doo
gray	*cinza*	SEEN-zah
green	*verde*	vehr-jee
orange	*laranja*	lah-RAHN-zhah
pink	*rosa*	HOH-zah
purple	*roxo*	ROA-shoo
red	*vermelho*	ver-MAYL-yoo
silver	*prateado*	praty-AH-doo
violet	*violeta*	vee-oh-LAY-tah
white	*branco*	BRAHN-koo
yellow	*amarelo*	ah-mah-REH-loo

E. CARDINAL NUMBERS

1	*um/uma*	oon/OO-mah
2	*dois/duas*	DOYS/DOO-ahs
3	*três*	trays
4	*quatro*	KWAH-troo
5	*cinco*	SEEN-koo
6	*seis*	SAYS
7	*sete*	SHE-chee
8	*oito*	OY-too

9	*nove*	NOH-vee
10	*dez*	deys
11	*onze*	OHN-zee
12	*doze*	DOH-zee
13	*treze*	TRAY-zee
14	*quatorze*	kah-TOHR-zee
15	*quinze*	KEEN-zee
16	*dezesseis*	deh-ZEE-SAYS
17	*dezessete*	deh-zee-SEH-chee
18	*dezoito*	dehz-OY-too
19	*dezenove*	deh-zee-NOH-vee
20	*vinte*	VEEN-chee
21	*vinte e um/uma*	VEEN-chee-ee-oon/OO-mah
22	*vinte e dois/duas*	VEEN-chee-ee-doys/DOO-ahs
23	*vinte e três*	VEEN-chee-ee-trays
24	*vinte e quatro*	VEEN-chee-ee-KWAH-troo
25	*vinte e cinco*	VEEN-chee-ee-SEEN-koo
26	*vinte e seis*	VEEN-chee-ee-SAYS
27	*vinte e sete*	VEEN-chee-ee-SHE-chee
28	*vinte e oito*	VEEN-chee-ee-OY-too
29	*vinte e nove*	VEEN-chee-ee-NOH-vee
30	*trinta*	TREEN-tah
31	*trinta e um/uma*	TREEN-tah-ee-oon/OO-mah
32	*trinta e dois/duas*	TREEN-tah-ee-doys/DOO-ahs
40	*quarenta*	kwah-REHN-tah
50	*cinqüenta*	seen-KWEHN-tah
60	*sessenta*	seh-SEHN-tah

70	*setenta*	seh-TEHN-tah
80	*oitenta*	oy-TEHN-tah
90	*noventa*	noh-VEHN-tah
100	*cem*	sehn
101	*cento e um/uma*	SEHN-too-ee-oon/OO-mah
102	*cento e dois/duas*	SEHN-too-ee-DOYS/DOO-ahs
110	*cento e dez*	SEHN-too-ee-days
120	*cento e vinte*	SEHN-too-ee-VEEN-chee
200	*duzentos/duzentas*	doo-ZEHN-toos/doo-ZEHN-tah
210	*duzentos e dez*	doo-ZEHN-toos-ee-days
300	*trezentos/trezentas*	tray-ZEHN-toos/tray-ZEHN-tahs
400	*quatrocentos/quarto-centas*	kwah-troo-SEHN-toos/kwah-troo-SEHN-tahs
500	*quinhentos/quin-hentas*	keen-YEHN-toos/keen-YEHN-tahs
600	*seiscentos/seiscentas*	says-SEHN-toos/says-SEHN-tahs
700	*setecentos/setecentas*	seh-chee-SEHN-toos/seh-chee-SEHN-tahs
800	*oitocentos/oitocentas*	oy-too-SEHN-toos/oy-too-SEHN-tahs
900	*novecentos/novecentas*	noh-vee-SEHN-toos/noh-vee-SEHN-tahs
1,000	*mil*	MEE-oo
1,100	*mil e cem*	MEE-oo-ee-SEHN
1,200	*mil e duzentos/duzentas*	MEE-oo-ee-doo-ZEHN-toos/doo-ZEHN-tahs
2,000	*dois mil*	doys-MEE-oo

10,000	*dez mil*	days-MEE-oo
50,000	*cinquenta mil*	seen-KWEHN-tah-MEE-oo
100,000	*cem mil*	SEHN-MEE-oo
1,000,000	*um milhão*	oon-meel-YOWN
1,000,000,000	*um bilhão*	oon-beel-YOWN

F. ORDINAL NUMBERS

first	*primeiro*	pree-MAY-roo
second	*segundo*	seh-GOON-doo
third	*terceiro*	tehr-SAY-roo
fourth	*quarto/quarta*	KWAHR-too/KWAHR-tah
fifth	*quinto/quinta*	KEEN-too/KEEN-tah
sixth	*sexto/sexta*	SEHKS-too/SEHKS-tah
seventh	*sétimo/sétima*	SEH-chee-moo/SEH-chee-mah
eighth	*oitavo/oitava*	oy-TAH-voo/oy-TAH-vah
ninth	*nono/nona*	NOH-noo/NOH-nah
tenth	*décimo/décima*	DEH-see-moo/DEH-see-mah
eleventh	*décimoprimeiro/ -primeira*	DEH-see-moo-pree-MAY-roo/ -pree-MAY-rah
twelfth	*décimosegundo/ -segunda*	DEH-see-moo-seh-GOON-doo/seh-GOON-dah
thirteenth	*décimoterceiro*	DEH-see-moo-tehr-SAY-roo
fourteenth	*décimoquarto*	DEH-see-moo-KWAHR-too
fifteenth	*décimoquinto*	DEH-see-moo-KEEN-too
sixteenth	*décimosexto*	DEH-see-moo-SEHKS-too

seventeenth	*décimosétimo*	DEH-see-moo-SEH-chee-moo
eighteenth	*décimooitavo*	DEH-see-moo-oy-TAH-voo
nineteenth	*décimonono*	DEH-see-moo-NOH-noo
twentieth	*vigésimo*	vee-JAY-see-moo
twenty-first	*vigésimo-primeiro*	vee-JAY-see-moo-pree-MAY-roo
twenty-second	*vigésimo-segundo*	vee-JAY-see-moo-she-GOON-doo
thirtieth	*trigésimo*	three-JAY-see-moo
fortieth	*quadragésimo*	kwa-dra-JAY-see-moo
fiftieth	*quinquagésimo*	kween-kwa-JAY-see-moo
sixtieth	*sexagésimo*	senk-sah-JAY-see-moo
seventieth	*septuagésimo*	sehp-thoo-ah-JAY-see-moo
eightieth	*octogésimo*	okee-tho-JAY-see-moo
ninetieth	*nonagésimo*	noh-nah-JAY-see-moo
hundredth	*centésimo*	sehn-TAY-see-moo
thousandth	*milésimo*	mee-LAY-see-moo

G. TIME OF DAY

1:00	*uma hora*	oo-mah-OH-rah
2:00	*duas horas*	doo-ahs-OH-rahs
3:00	*três horas*	trays-OH-rahs
4:00	*quatro horas*	KWAH-troo-OH-rahs
5:00	*cinco horas*	SEEN-koo-OH-rahs
6:00	*seis horas*	says-OH-rahs
7:00	*sete horas*	SEH-chee-OH-rahs
8:00	*oito horas*	OY-too-OH-rahs
9:00	*nove horas*	NOH-vee-OH-rahs
10:00	*dez horas*	days-OH-rahs
11:00	*onze horas*	OHN-zee-OH-rahs

12:00	*doze horas*	DOH-zee-OH-rahs
1:00 A.M.	*uma hora da manhã*	OO-mah-OH-rah-der-mahn-YAHNG
3:00 P.M.	*três horas da tarde*	trays-OH-rahs-der-TAHR-jee
noon	*meio-dia*	may-yoo-JEE-ah
midnight	*meia-noite*	may-yah-NOY-chee
1:15	*uma e quinze*	OO-mah-ee-KEEN-zee
12:45 P.M.	*meio-dia e quarenta e cinco.*	may-yoo-JEE-ah-ee-kwah-REHN-tah-ee-SEEN-koo
12:45 A.M.	*meia-noite e quarenta e cinco.*	may-yah-NOY-chee-ee-kwah-REHN-tah-ee-SEEN-koo
1:30	*uma e meia*	OO-mah-ee-MAY-yah
7:05	*sete e cinco*	SEH-chee-ee-SEEN-koo
4:55	*quatro e cinqüenta e cinco*	KWAH-troo-ee-seen-KWEHN-tah-ee-SEEN-koo

H. DAYS OF THE WEEK

Monday	*segunda-feira*	say-GOON-dah FAY-rah
Tuesday	*terça-feira*	TEHR-sah FAY-rah
Wednesday	*quarta-feira*	KWAHR-tah FAY-rah
Thursday	*quinta-feira*	KEEN-tah FAY-rah
Friday	*sexta-feira*	SEHS-tah FAY-rah
Saturday	*sábado*	SAH-bah-doo
Sunday	*domingo*	doh-MEEN-goo

I. MONTHS

January	*janeiro*	zhah-NAY-roo
February	*fevereiro*	feh-veh-RAY-roo
March	*março*	MAHR-soo
April	*abril*	ah-BREE-oo

May	*maio*	MAY-yoo
June	*junho*	ZHOON-yoo
July	*julho*	ZHOOL-yoo
August	*agôsto*	ah-GOHS-too
September	*setembro*	she-TEHM-broo
October	*outubro*	oh-TOO-broo
November	*novembro*	noh-VEHM-broo
December	*dezembro*	jee-ZEHM-broo

J. DATES

1998	*mil novecentos e noventa e oito*	MEE-oo noh-vay-SEHN-toos ee noh-VEHN-tah ee OY-too
1999	*mil novecentos e noventa e nove*	MEE-oo noh-vay-SEHN-tos ee noh-VEHN-tah ee NOH-vee
2000	*dois mil*	doys MEE-oo
2001	*dois mil e um*	doys MEE-oo-ee-oon
2002	*dois mil e dois*	doys-MEE-oo-ee-doys
2003	*dois mil e três*	doys-MEE-oo-ee-trays
2004	*dois mil e quatro*	doys MEE-oo-ee-KWAHN-troo
2005	*dois mil e cinco*	doys-MEE-oo-ee-SEEN-koo
Today is Thursday, September 22.	*Hoje é quinta-feira, vinte e dois de setembro.*	OH-zhee-eh-KEEN-tah-FAY-rah, VEEN-chee-ee-doys-jee-she-TEHM-broo.
Yesterday was Wednesday, September 21.	*Ontem foi quarta-feira, vinte e um de setembro.*	OHN-tehn-foh-ee-KWAHR-tah FAY-rah, VEEN-chee ee oon-jee she-TEHM-broo.
The day before yesterday was Tuesday, September 20.	*Anteontem foi terça-feira, vinte de setembro.*	Ahn-tay-OHN-tay foh-ee-tehr-sah-FAY-rah,VEEN-chee-jee-she-TEHM-broo.

Tomorrow is Friday, September 23.	*Amanhã é sexta-feira, vinte e três de setembro.*	Ah-mahn-YAHN eh SEHKS-tah FAY-rah, VEEN-chee ee trays jee she-TEHM-broo.
The day after tomorrow is Saturday, September 24.	*Depois de amanhã, é sábado, vinte e quatro de setembro.*	Dip-OH-ish jee ah-mahn-YAH eh SAH-bah-doo, VEEN-chee ee KWAH-troo jee she-TEHM-broo.
Next Friday is September 30.	*A próxima sexta-feira é trinta de setembro.*	Ah PROHK-see-maa SEHKS-tah FAY-rah eh TREEN-tah jee she-TEHM-broo.
Last Friday was September 6.	*Sexta-feira passada foi seis de setembro.*	SEHKS-tah FAY-rah pah-SA daa foh-ee says jee she-TEHM broo.

K. MEASUREMENTS: DISTANCE

inch	*polegada*	poo-lee-GAH-dah
foot	*pé*	peh
yard	*jarda*	ZHAHR-dah
millimeter	*milímetro*	mee-LEE-meh-troh
meter	*metro*	MEH-troh
kilometer	*quilômetro*	ki-LO-mee-troh

3. Common Hospitality Scenarios

A. GREETINGS AND INTRODUCTIONS

GREETING THE GUEST

EMPLOYEE

Good morning,...	***Bom dia,...***	Bohn-JEE-ah,...
• **Mr. _____.**	• ***Sr. _____.***	• Sehn-YOHR _____.
• **Mrs. _____.**	• ***Sra. _____.***	• Sehn-YOH-rah _____.
• **Miss _____.**	• ***Senhorita _____.***	• Sehn-yoh-REE-tah _____.
• **sir.**	• ***Senhor.***	• Sehn-YOHR.
• **madam.**	• ***Senhora.***	• Sehn-YOH-rah.

TIP! ••••

Most American employees are used to greeting guests jovially and asking them how they are. However, in any but the most informal settings, this behavior may actually be considered impolite. Asking guests how they are is stepping outside the bounds of your position and throws the burden onto the guest to answer you. Other cultures usually observe this principle to a much greater extent than we do.

• ladies and gentlemen.	• *Senhoras e Senhores.*	• Sehn-YOH-rahs-ee-Sehn-YOH-rehs.
• everyone.	• *todos.*	• TOH-doosh.
Good afternoon, Mr. _____.	*Boa tarde, Sr. _____.*	BOH-ah TAHR-jee, Sehn-YOHR _____.
Good evening, Mr. _____.	*Boa noite, Sr. _____.*	BOH-ah NOY-chee, Sehn-YOHR.
Hello, Mr. _____.	*Como vai, Sr. _____?*	KOH-moo-vahy-Sehn-YOHR _____?
Welcome…	*Bem-vindo…*	Behn-VEEN-doo…
• to the hotel.	• *ao hotel.*	• ah-oo-oh-TAY-oo.
• to the restaurant.	• *ao restaurante.*	• ah-oo-rehs-tow-RAHN-chee.
• to our city.	• *a nossa cidade.*	• ah NO-sash see-DAH-jee.
• to the United States.	• *aos Estados Unidos.*	• ah-oos-ehs-TAH-doos oo-NEE-doos.
If there is anything I can do to make your stay more pleasant, please let me know.	*Por favor, diga me se eu posso fazer alguna coisa para que a sua estadia seja mais agradável.*	Poor-fah-VOHR, JEE-gah me see eh-oo poo-soh fah-ZEHR ah-GOO-mah KWOY-zah pah-rah keh ah soo-ah ehs-tah-DEE-ah seh-jah mahys ah-grah-DAH-vay-oo.

May I…	*Eu posso…*	Ay-oo-POH-soo…
• take your coat(s)?	• *pegar o seu(s) casaco(s)?*	• peh-GAHR oh see-oo(s) kah-ZAH-koo(s)?
• carry your…for you?	• *carregar a sua… para você?*	• kah-ree-GAHNR ah soo-ah…PAH-rah-voh-SAY?
• bags	• *sacolas*	• sah-KOH-lahs
• suitcase	• *mala*	• MAH-lah
How are you today?	*Como está você hoje?*	KOH-moo ehs-TAH voh-SAY OH-zhee?

GUEST

I am…	*Eu estou…*	Ay-oo ehs-TOH…
• fine, thank you.	• *bem, obrigada/o.*	• behn oh-bree-GAH-doo/dah.
• okay.	• *okay.*	• O.K.
• so-so.	• *mais ou menos.*	• mahys-oh-MAY-noos.
• very tired.	• *muito cansado.*	• MWEE-too kahn-SAH-doo.
I'm not feeling well.	*Eu não me sinto bem.*	Eh-oo nown mee SEEN-oo behn.
And you?	*E você?*	Ee-voh-SAY?

INTRODUCTIONS

EMPLOYEE

My name is _____.	*Meu nome é _____.*	MAY-oo-NOH-mee-eh _____.

TIP! ••••

It is typical of American employees to introduce themselves to the guest. This practice allows the guest to call an employee by name when s/he needs something. This is not a common practice in other countries, however, so the international guest may simply ignore your introduction.

I am your...	*Eu sou o seu...*	Ay-oo-SOH-oo-SAY-oo...
• door attendant (doorman).	• *porteiro.*	• pohr-TAY-roo.
• bell attendant (bellman).	• *mensageiro.*	• mehn-sah-ZHAY-roo.
• driver.	• *motorista.*	• mo-to-RREZ-tah.
• captain.	• *capitaõ.*	• kah-pee-town.
• concierge.	• *recepcionista.*	• hay-say-pee-see-own-EES-tah.
• room attendant.	• *camareiro(a).*	• kah-mah-RAY-roo(rah).
• host.	• *funcionário.*	• foon-syoh-NAHR-ry-o.
• hostess.	• *funcionária.*	• foon-syoh-NAHR-ry-a.
• manager.	• *gerente.*	• zheh-RAYN-chee.
• waiter.	• *garçon.*	• gahr-SOHN.
• waitress.	• *garçonette.*	• gahr-soh-NAY-chee.
• chef.	• *chefe.*	• SHEH-fee.
• activities director.	• *diretor de atividades.*	• jee-reh-TOHR jee atee-veh-DAH-dees.
Mr. (Mrs., Miss) _____, this is Mr. (Mrs., Miss) _____, the manager.	*Sr. (Sra., Senhorita) _____, este/esta é o, Sr. (Sra., Senhorita) _____, o gerente.*	Seh-NYOHR (seh-NYOH-rah/seh-nyoh-REE-tah) _____ EHS-chee/EHS-cha-eh-oo(ah)-Sr. (Sra, seh-nyoh-REE-tah) _____, oo-je-RAYN-chee.
Mr. (Mrs., Miss) _____, may I introduce our manager, Mr. (Mrs., Miss) _____?	*Sr. (Sra., Sta.) _____, apresento-lhe nosso gerente, Sr. (Sra., Sta.) _____?*	Seh-NYOHR (seh-NYOH-rah/seh-nyoh-REE-tah) _____ ah-pray-zehn-too leh no-soo-je-RAYN-chee seh-NYOHR (seh-NYOH-rah/seh-nyoh-REE-tah) _____?

B. RESERVATIONS

HOTEL RESERVATIONS

OPERATOR

Good morning (afternoon, evening), ____ Hotel.	***Bom dia** (Boa tarde, Boa noite), **Hotel ____.***	Bohn JEE-ah (BOH-ah TAHR-jee, BOH-ah NOY-chee), oh-TAY-oo ____.
How may I direct your call?	***Como eu posso encaminar sua chamada?***	KOH-moo ay-oo POH-soo ehn-kah-mee-NAHR SWAH shah-MAH-dah?

GUEST

Hello. Do you speak Portuguese?	***Alô? Você fala Português?***	Ah-LOW? Voh-SAY FAH-lah pohr-TOO-gays?

OPERATOR

One moment, please.	***Um momento, por favor.***	Oon moh-MEN-too, poor-fah-VOHR.
I'll connect you with a bilingual operator.	***Passarei você para um operador bilingüe.***	Pah-sah-RAY voh-SAY pah-rah oon ope-hah-DOHR bay-LEEN-gweh.
I have a book here to help me.	***Eu tenho um livro aqui para me ajudar.***	Ay-oo tayn-yoo oon LEEV-roo ah-KEE PAH-rah meh ah-zhoo-DAHR.
Please speak slowly.	***Por favor, fale devagar.***	Poor-fah-VOHR, FAH-lee-jee-vah-GAHR.

GUEST

I would like to make a reservation, please.	***Eu gostaria de fazer uma reserva, por favor.***	Ay-oo gohs-tah-REE-ah jee fah-ZEHR OO-mah ray-ZEHR-vah, poor-fah-VOHR.

OPERATOR

For a room or for one of the restaurants?	***Para um quarto ou restaurante?***	PAH-rah oon KWAHR-too oh-go hehs-tow RAHR-chee?

GUEST

For a room, please.	***Para um quarto, por favor.***	PAH-rah oon KWAHR-too, poor-fah-VOHR.

English	Portuguese	Pronunciation
For the ____ Restaurant, please.	*Para o restaurante ____, por favor.*	PAH-rah oh hehs-tow-RAHR-chee, ____ poor-fah-VOHR.
OPERATOR		
One moment, please. I will direct your call to Reservations.	*Um momento, por favor. Passarei a sua ligaçaõ, para o departmamento de reservas.*	Oon moh-MEN-toh, poor-fah-VOHR. Pah-sahr-RAY ah swah-lee-gah-SOWN, PAH-rah oh day-pahr-tah-MEN-to jee hay-ZEHR-vahs.
One moment, please. I will direct your call to the restaurant.	*Um momento, por favor. Passarei a sua ligação, para o restaurante.*	Oo moh-MEN-toh, poor-fah-VOHR. Pah-sahr-RAY ah swah-lee-gah-SOWN PAH-rah oh hehs-tow-RAHR-chee.
CLERK		
Hello, this is Reservations.	*Alô, reserva.*	Ah-LOW, hay-ZEHR-vah.
What date would you like?	*Que data você gostaria?*	Keh dah-tah voh-SAY gohs-tah-REE-ah?
GUEST		
May 27th.	*27 de Maio.*	VEEN-chee ee SEH-chee dee MAY-yoo.
CLERK		
For how many nights?	*Para quantas noites?*	PAH-rah KWAHN-tahs NOY-chees?
GUEST		
For three nights, please.	*Para três noites, por favor.*	PAH-rah TRAYS NOY-chees, poor-fah-VOHR.
For a week.	*Para uma semana.*	PAH-rah OO-mah say-MAH-nah.
Just one night.	*Somente uma noite.*	Sohn-MEHN-tee OO-mah NOY-chee.
CLERK		
For how many people?	*Para quantas pessoas?*	PAH-rah KWAHN-tahs peh-SOH-ahs?

GUEST

For two people.	*Para duas pessoas.*	PAH-rah DOO-ahsh peh-SOH-ahs.
For one person.	*Para uma pessoa.*	PAH-rah OO-mah peh-SOH-ah.
For two adults and a child.	*Para dois adultos e uma criança.*	PAH-rah cloys ah-DOOL-toos eh oo-mah kree-AHN-sahs.

CLERK

Do you have any any special needs?	*Você necessita alguma coisa especial?*	Voh-SAY neh-se-SEE-tah ahl-GOO-mah KOH-ee-zah ehs-peh-SEE-ah?
Do have you any special requests?	*Você tem algum pedido especial?*	Voh-SAY tehm ahl-GOON- peh-JEE-doo ehs-peh-SEE-ahl?

GUEST

No, thank you.	*Não, obrigado/a.*	Nown, oh-bree-GAH-doo/oh-bree-GAH-doo/dah.
Yes, I would like…	*Sim, eu gostaria de…*	Seen, ay-oo gohs-tah-REE-ah jee…
• to be near the stairs.	• *ficar perto da escada.*	• fee-KAHR PEHR-too dah ehs-KAH-dah.
• to be near an exit.	• *ficar perto de uma saída.*	• fee-KAHR PEHR-too jee OO-mah sah-EE-dah.
• a cot for our child.	• *uma cama pequena para nosso filho/nossa filha.*	• OO-mah KAH-mah peh-KEH-naa PAH-rah nohs-soo FEEL-yoo/nohs-sah FEELyah.
• a handicapped-accessible room.	• *um quarto acessível para deficiente físico.*	• oon KWAHR-too aseh-SEE-veel PAH-rah deh-fee-see-EHN-tee FEE-say-koo.

CLERK

The rate is _____ per night.	*O preço é _____ por noite.*	Oh PRAY-soo eh _____ poor NOY-chee.

Would you like to guarantee the reservation with a credit card?	***Você gostaria de garantir a reserva com cartão de crédito?***	Voh-SAY gohs-tah-REE-ah jee gah-rahn-TEER a ray-ZEHR-vah kohn kahr-TOWN jee KREH-jee-too?
GUEST		
Yes, here is my ____ card.	***Sim, aqui está meu cartão ____.***	Seen, ah-KEE ehs-TAH MAY-oo kahr-TOWN ____.
My credit card number is ____.	***O número do meu cartão de crédito é ____.***	Oo NOO-meh-roo doo MAY-oo kahr-TOW jee KREH-jee-too eh ____.
CLERK		
What is the expiration date?	***Qual é a data de vencimento?***	Kwow eh ah DAH-tah jee vehn-see-MEN-too?
Thank you.	***Obrigado/a.***	Oh-bree-GAH-doo/ah.

RESTAURANT RESERVATIONS

RESTAURANT HOST		
Good morning (afternoon, evening), ____ Restaurant.	*Bom dia (Boa tarde, Boa noite), ____.*	Bohn-JEE-ah (BOH-ah-TAHR-jee, BOH-NOY-chee), ____.
RESTAURANT GUEST		
I'd like to reserve a a table for…	*Gostaria de reservar uma mesa para…*	Gohs-tah-REE-ah jee hay-zehr-VAHR OO-mah MAY-zah PAH-rah…
• breakfast.	• *o café da manhã.*	• oh kah-feh dah mahn-YAHN.
• lunch.	• *o almoço.*	• oh ahl-MOH-soo.
• dinner.	• *o jantar.*	• oh zhahn-TAHR.
HOST		
For what time?	*Para que horas?*	PAH-rah keh OH-rahs?
GUEST		
For…o'clock.	*Para…horas.*	PAH-rah…OH-rahs.
• seven	• *as sete*	• ahs SEH-chee

• eight	• *as oito*	• ahs OY-too
• nine	• *as nove*	• ahs NOH-vee
For eight-thirty.	*Para oito e meia.*	PAH-rah OY-too-ee-MAY-ah.
HOST		
For how many people?	*Para quantas pessoas?*	PAH-rah- KWAHN-taas pehs-SOH-ahs?
GUEST		
For one person.	*Para uma pessoa.*	PAH-rah OO-mah pehs-SOH-ah.
For...people.	*Para...pessoas.*	PAH-rah...pehs-SOH-ahs.
• two	• *duas*	• DOO-ahs
• four	• *quatro*	• KWAH-troo
• six	• *seis*	• says
HOST		
And your name, please?	*O seu nome, por favor?*	Oo SAY-oo NOH-mee, poor fah-VOHR?
GUEST		
My name is _____.	*Meu nome é _____.*	MAY-oo NOH-mee eh _____.
HOST		
And is there a phone number where we can reach you?	*E tem um telefone onde nós podemos encontrar você?*	Ee TEHM oon the-lay-FOH-nee OHN-jee nohs poh-DEH-moos ehn-kohn-TRAHR-voh-SAY?
GUEST		
Yes, the number is _____.	*Sim, o número é _____.*	Seen, oo NOO-meh-roo eh _____.
By the way, do you have any...items on the menu?	*A proposito, você tem algum prato...no menu?*	Ah proh-poh-see-too, voh-SAY TEHM ah-joom PRAH-too...noh mee-NEE?
• vegetarian	• *vegetariano*	• veh-jeh-tarhr-ya-AN-noo
• macrobiotic	• *macrobiótico*	• mah-kro-bee-OO-chee-koo

• low-fat	• *pouca gordura*	• POH-kaa gohr-DOO-ah
• low-sodium	• *pouco sal*	• POH-koo sow
HOST		
Would you like smoking or nonsmoking?	*Fumante ou não fumante?*	Foo-MAH-ahn-chee oh nown foo-MAH-ahn-chee?
GUEST		
We would like…	*Nós preferimos…*	Nohs pray-feh-REE-mohs…
• smoking.	• *fumante.*	• foo-MAH-ahn-chee.
• nonsmoking.	• *não fumante.*	• nown foo-MAH-ahn-chee.
HOST		
Thank you.	*Obrigado/a.*	Oh-bree-GAH-doo/dah.
That will be two people at eight o'clock.	*Serão duas pessoas às oito horas.*	See-ROWA DOO-ahs peh-SOH-ahs ahs OY-too OH-rahs.
That's a party of six at seven-thirty.	*É um gropo de seis a sete e meia.*	Eh-oom groo-poh jee says ah SEH-chee ee MAY-ah.

C. COURTESY AND COMPLAINTS

GENERAL EXPRESSIONS OF COURTESY

Please.	***Por favor.***	Poor-fah-VOHR.
Thank you.	***Obrigado/a.***	Oh-bree-GAH-doo/dah.
You're welcome.	***De nada.***	Jee-NAH-dah.
Excuse me.	***Com licença.***	Kahn-lee-SEHN-sah.
I beg your pardon.	***Eu peço desculpas.***	Ay-oo PEH-sho-days-KOOL-pahs.
I'm (terribly) sorry.	***Mil perdões.***	MEE-oo pehr-DOWNS.
That's okay.	***Tudo bem.***	TOO-doo-BEHN.
No problem.	***Não tem problema.***	Nown tehm proh-BLAY-mah.
It doesn't matter.	***Não importa.***	Nown eem-POHR-tah.

COURTESY IN THE HOTEL

CONCIERGE

Good morning, sir, ma'am.	*Bom dia, Sr., Sra.*	Bohn-JEE-ah, seh-NYOHR, seh-NYOH-rah.
May I help you with something today?	*Posso ajudar você em alguma coisa hoje?*	POH-soo ah-ZHOO-dahr voh-SAY ehn ah-GOO-mah KOH-ee-zah OH-zhee?

GUEST

Yes, I need…	*Sim, eu necessito…*	Seen, ay-oo neh-she-see-TOO…
• my room made up between now and ____.	• *que meu quarto esteje arrumado até ____.*	• keh may-go KWAHR-too ehs-TAY-zheh ah-hoo-MAH-doo ah-TEH ____.
• more towels, please.	• *mais toalhas, por favor.*	• mahys TWAHL-yah, poor-fah-VOHR.
• a rental car.	• *alugar um carro.*	• ah-loo-GAHR oon KAH-rroo.
• a taxi.	• *um taxi.*	• oon TAHK-see.
• a fax sent.	• *mandar um fax.*	• mahn-DAHR oon FAHKS.
• some letters mailed.	• *por algumas cartas no correio.*	• poor ahl-GOO-mahs KAHR-tahs noo koh-HAY-yoo.
• to make arrangements for a business meeting.	• *organizar uma reunião de trabalho.*	• ohr-gah-nee-ZAHR OO-mah hay-oo-nee-OWN jee trah-BAH-lyoo.
• tickets to a concert.	• *ingressos para um concerto.*	• een-GRAY-soos PAH-rah oom kohn-SAYR-too.
• tickets to a show.	• *ingressos para um show.*	• een-GRAY-soos PAH-rah oom show.
• tickets to a game.	• *ingressos para um jogo.*	• een-GRAY-soos PAH-rah oom ZHOH-goo.

GUEST COMPLAINTS IN THE HOTEL

CONCIERGE		
Is everything satisfactory?	***Está tudo satisfatorio?***	Ehs-TAH TOO-doo sah-teez-fah-TOH-ree-oo?
GUEST		
No, there is a problem.	***Não, tenho um problema.***	Nown, TEH-ny-oo oon proh-BLAY-mah.
• The light	• *A luz*	• Ah looz
• The toilet	• *O banheiro*	• Oo bahn-YAY-roo
• The television	• *A televisão*	• Ah the-lay-vee-ZOWN
• The radio	• *O rádio*	• Oo HAH-jyoo
• The air-conditioning	• *O ar acondicionado*	• Oo ahr ah-kohn-dee-syo-NAH-doo
• The alarm clock	• *O relógio despertador*	• Oo hay-LOH zhyoo deesh-pehr-tah-DOHR
• The heat	• *O aquecimento*	• Oo ah-keh-see-MEHN-too
• The key	• *A chave*	• Ah SHAH-vee
• The lock	• *A fechadura*	• Ah feh-shah-DOO-rah
• The fan	• *O ventilador*	• Oo vehn-chee-lah-DOHR
...doesn't work.	*...não funciona.*	...nown foon-SYOH-nah.
CLERK		
I'll have Maintenance fix that right away.	*O técnico já irá consertar.*	Oo TECK-nee-koo zhah ee-RAH kohn-sehr-tahr.
I apologize.	*Eu peço desculpas.*	AY-oo peh-soo days-KOOL-pahs.
GUEST		
My room...	***Meu quarto...***	MAY-oo KWAHR-too...
• wasn't clean.	***• não estava limpo.***	• nown ehs-TAH-vah LEEM-poo.

• was noisy.	• *era barulhento.*	• eh-rah bah-rool-YEHN-too.
• stinks (smells).	• *cheira mal.*	• SHAY-rah-mow.
The bed was uncomfortable.	*A cama estava desconfortável.*	Ah KAH-mah ehs-TAH-vah dehz-kohn-fohr-TAH-vewl.
The water wasn't hot.	*A água não estava quente.*	Ah-gwah nown ehs-TAH-vah KEHN-chee.
Room service was late.	*O serviço de quarto estava sempre atrasado.*	Oo sehr-VEE-soo jee KWAHR-too ehs-TAH-vah SEHM-pree ah-trah-ZAH-doo.
The service was very poor.	*O serviço estava ruim.*	Oo sehr-VEE-soo ehs-TAH-vah rooym.
The employees were…	*Os empregados foram…*	Oos ehm-pray-GAH-doos FOH-raw…
• very good.	• *ótimos.*	• OH-chee-moos.
• excellent.	• *excelentes.*	• ehs-seh-LEHN-chees.
• rude.	• *rudes.*	• HOO-jees.
• incompetent.	• *incompetentes.*	• een-kohm-peh-TEHN-jees.
• unfriendly.	• *descortêses.*	• days-kohr-TEHZ-ehs.
The room attendant is rude.	*O(A) camareiro(a) é grosseiro(a).*	Oh(Ah) kah-mah-RAY-roh(rah) eh gro-SAY-roh(rah).
I didn't receive my wake-up call.	*Não me acordaram.*	Nown mee ah-kohr-DAH-rown.
I'm very disappointed with the level of service in this hotel.	*Estou decepcionado como nível de serviço deste hotel.*	Ehs-TOH deh-say-PSEE-oh-nah-doo koom oh NEE-vehl jee sehr-VEE-soo dehs-chee oh-TAY-oo.
This is the worst hotel I've ever seen.	*Este é o pior hotel que eu já vi.*	EHS-chee eh oh pee-OHR oh-TAY-oo keh ay-oo ZHAH vee.

CONCIERGE

Please let me make the situation right.	*Por favor, deixe-me resolver a situação.*	Poor fah-VOHR, DAY-chee-mee hay-zohl-VEHR ah see-too-ah-SOWN.

I'm certain we can straighten out the problem.	*Estou certo que poderemos resolver o problema.*	Ees-TOH SEHR-too keh poo-deh-RAY-moos hay-zool-VEHR oh proh-BLAY-mah.
You won't pay for anything that wasn't completely up to your standards.	*Você não precisa pagar por nada que não estava ao seu gosto.*	Voh-SAY nown pray-SEE-zah pah-GAHR poor NAH-daa keh nown ehs-TAH-vah ah-oh SAY-oo GOHS-too.
Please tell me what I can do to correct this terrible situation.	*Por favor, diga me o que eu posso fazer para resolver esta terrível situação.*	Poor fah-VOHR, jee-gah mee oh keh AY-oo POH-soo fah-ZEER PAH-rah hay-zool-VEHR EHS-tah see-to-ah-SOWN.
We'll take ____ percent off your bill.	*Tiraremos ____ por cento da sua conta.*	Tee-rah-HAY-moos ____ poor SAYN-too jee swah KOWN-tah.
We're going to give you ____ night(s), compliments of the hotel.	*Daremos ao Senhor (a Senhora) ____ noite(s) como oferta do hotel.*	Dah-RAY-moos own see-nyohr (ah see-nyoh-rah) ____ NOY-chee(s) KOH-moo oh-FEHR-tah doo oh-TAY-oo.
Your entire bill is compliments of the house.	*O total da sua conta é ____ complemento da casa.*	Oh toh-TAHL dah swah KOHN-tah-eh ____ kom-play-MEEN-too dah KAH-zah.
GUEST		
Yes, that would be satisfactory.	*Sim, isto seria satisfatório.*	Seen, ees-toh seh-REE-ah sah-teez-fah-TOH-ree-oo.
No, that would not be satisfactory.	*Não, isto não seria satisfatório.*	Nown, ees-toh nown seh-REE-ah sah-teez-fah-TOH-ree-oo.
I appreciate all your efforts.	*Aprecio todo o seu esforço.*	Ah-pray-SEE-oo toh-doo oh say-oo ehs-FOHR-soo.
Thank you, that would be very nice.	*Obrigado/a, seria muito bom.*	Oh-bree-GAH-doo/dah, she-REE-ah MWEE-too bohn.
I will never come here again.	*Eu nunca mais volto aqui.*	AY-oo NOON-kaw mahys VOHL-toh ah-KEE.

MANAGEMENT COMPLAINTS

MANAGER

We have had some complaints about the noise coming form your room.	*Nós recebemos algumas reclamações de barulho vindo do seu quarto.*	NOHS reh-seh-beh-moos ahl-GOO-mahs ray-klah-mah-SOWEES jee bah-ROO-lyoo doo say-oo KWAHR-too.
You are disturbing…	*Você está perturbando…*	Voh-SAY ehs-TAH pehr-toor-BAWN-doo…
• the people in the room next door.	• *as pessoas do quarto ao lado.*	• ahs peh-SOH-ahs doo KWAHR-too ah-oo LAH-doo.
• the people at the next table.	• *as pessoas da mesa ao lado.*	• ahs peh-SOH-ahs dah MAY-zah ah-oo LAH-doo.
• our other guests.	• *nossos outros hóspedes.*	• NOH-sows OH-troos OHS-peh-jees.

GUEST

We're sorry.	*Desculpe-nos.*	Days-KOOL-peh-nohs.
We understand.	*Nós entendemos.*	NOHS ehn-tehn-DEH-moos.
We'll take care of it.	*Nós cuidaremos disto.*	NOHS kwee-dah-REE-moos JEES-too.
We'll keep it down from now on.	*Vamos diminuir.*	Vah-moos jee-mee-NWEER.
Who cares!	*Que me importa!*	Keh may eem-POHR-tah!
Leave us alone!	*Deixe-nos em paz!*	DAY-zhee-nohs ehm PAHS!

MANAGER

If you don't cooperate, I'm afraid I'll have to…	*Se você não cooperar, terei que…*	See voh-SAY nown koo-pay-RHAR, the-RAY keh…
• ask you to leave the hotel (restaurant).	• *pedir para que saia do hotel (do restaurante).*	• peh-JEER PAH-rah keh SAH-yah doo oh-TAY-oo (doo hehs-tawh-RAHN-tee).
• call security.	• *chamar a segurança.*	• shah-MAHR ah say-goo-RAN-sah.

• call the police.	• *chamar a polícia.*	• shah-MAHR ah poh-LEE-syah.

D. EMERGENCIES AND SAFETY

EMPLOYEE

Please note...	***Por favor, note a...***	Poor fah-VOHR, ah-NOH-chee ah...
• the emergency exits on this card.	***• saida de emergência neste cartão.***	• sah-EE-dah jee eh-mehr-ZHEN-see-ah NEHZ-tee kahr-TOWN.
• the emergency escape route on the door.	***• trajeto escapatorio na porta.***	• trah-ZHAY-too ehs-kah-pah-TOHR-ee-oo nah-POHR-tah.
Your room is equipped with smoke alarms.	***Seu quarto é equipado com alarme de fumaça.***	Sayoo KWAHR-too eh eh-kee-PAH-doo koom ah-LAHR-mee jee foo-MAH-sah.
Here is the fire alarm.	***Aqui está o alarme de fogo.***	Ah-KEE ehs-TAH oh ah-LAHR-mee jee FOH-goo.
In an emergency, dial ____.	***Numa emergência, ligue ____.***	NOO-mah eh-mehr-ZHEN-see-ah, LEE-gee ____.

GUEST

Help!	***Socorro!***	Soh-KOH-hoow!
Fire!	***Incéndio!***	Een-SEHN-jee-oo!
I need a doctor.	***Necessito um médico.***	Neh-she-SEE-too oon MEH-jee-koo.
I'm...	*Eu essou...*	AY-oo ehsh-soh...
My husband (wife) is...	*Meu marido (esposa) está...*	Meh-oo mah-REE-doo ehs-TAH...
Someone is...	*Alguém está...*	AHL-gehn- ehs-TAH...
• very sick.	• *muito doente.*	• MWEE-too DWEHN-chee.
• having a heart attack.	• *tendo um ataque de coração.*	• TEHN-doo oon ah-TAH-kee jee coh-rah-SOWN.
• nauseated.	• *com náuseas.*	• koom NAUHL-zee-ahs.

• choking.	• *asfixiando.*	• ahz-feek-see-AHN-doo.
• losing consciousness.	• *perdendo a consciência.*	• pehr-DAYN-doo ah kohn-see-AYN-see-ah.
• vomiting.	• *vomitando.*	• voh-mee-TANH-doo.
• having a seizure.	• *epilético.*	• eh-pee-LEE-tee-koo.
• stuck.	• *preso.*	• PRAY-soo.
I can't breathe.	*Não posso respirar.*	Nown POH-soo hays-pee-RAHR.
MANAGER		
I'll call an ambulance.	*Chamarei uma ambulância.*	Shah-mah-RAY-ee OO-mah ahm-boo-LAYN-see-ah.
Don't move.	*Não se mova.*	Nown see MOH-vah.
The doctor will be here very soon.	*O doutor chegará aqui logo.*	Oh doh-oo-TOHR chee-gah-RAH ah-KEE LOH-goo.
Are you hurt?	*Você está machucado?*	Voh-SAY ehs-TAH mah-shoo-KAH-doo?
What happened?	*O que aconteceu?*	Oh keh ah-kohn-tay-SAY-oo?
GUEST		
I tripped and fell.	*Eu tropecei e caí.*	AY-oo troh-peh-SAY eh kah-EE.
I cut myself.	*Eu me cortei.*	AY-oo may kohr-TAY.
I drank too much.	*Eu bebi muito.*	AY-oo beh-BEE MWEE-too.
I hit my head.	*Machuquei minha cabeça.*	Mah-shoo-KAY MEE-nya kah-BAY-sah.
I don't know.	*Não sei.*	Nown say.
I've injured…	*Machuquei…*	Mah-shoo-KAY…
• my neck.	• *meu pescoço.*	• MEH-oo pehs-KOH-soo.
• my back.	• *minhas costas.*	• MEE-nyahs KOHS-tahs.
• my arm.	• *meu braço.*	• MEH-oo BRAH-soo.

• my hand.	• *minha mão.*	• MEE-nyah mown.
• my leg.	• *minha perna.*	• MEE-nyah PEHR-nah.
• my foot.	• *meu pé.*	• MEH-oo peh.
• my eye(s).	• *meu(s) olho(s).*	• MEH-oo(s) OH-ly-oo(s).

DOCTOR (MEDICAL TECHNICIAN)

You'll be fine; try to relax.	*Você está bem; tente relaxar.*	Voh-SAY ehs-TAH behn; TEHN-chee hay-lah-SHAR.
We're taking you to the hospital.	*Levaremos você para o hospital.*	Lay-vah-RAY-moos voh-SAY PAH-rahoo ohs-pee-TOW.
Whom should we notify?	*À quem deveremos avisar?*	Ah kehn day-VERAY-moos ah-vee-ZAAHR?

GUEST

I've been robbed.	***Fui roubado.***	FOO-ee hoh-BAH-doo.

MANAGER

What did they take?	***O que eles levaram?***	Oh keh ay-lees lay-VAH-rawn?
Let me call the police.	***Deixe-me chamar a polícia.***	Day-shee may shah-MAHR ah poh-LEE-syah.
Attention, ladies and gentlemen.	***Atenção, senhoras e senhores.***	Ah-tayn-SOWN, sehn-YOH-rahs ee sehn-YOH-rehs.
May I have your attention, please?	***Posso ter a sua atenção, por favor?***	POH-sow tehr ah swah ah-tayn-SOWN poor fah-VOHR?
Please…	***Por favor…***	Poor fah-VOHR…
• remain calm.	***• fiquem calmos.***	• FEE-keem KAHL-moos.
• follow the instructions of the staff.	***• sigam as instruções dos funcionários.***	• SEE-gahm ahs eens-troo-SOWEES doos foon-syo-NAH-reos.
• wait in your rooms.	***• aguarde em seu quarto.***	• ah-GWAHR-dee ehm SAY-oo KWAHR-too.

• get under a table or doorway.	• *fiquem debaixo da mesa ou na entrada da porta.*	• FEE-keem day-BAY-zhoo dah MAY-zah ow- nah ehn-TRAH-dah dah POHR-tah.
• follow the evacuation plan printed on your door.	• *sigam as instruções de evacuação escritas na porta.*	• SEE-gahm ahs eens-troo-SOWEES jee eh-vah-koo-ah-SOWN, ehs-KREE-tahs nah POHR-tah.
We'll have the situation under control as soon as possible.	*A situação estará sob controle o mais rápido possivel.*	Ah see-too-ah-SOWN eez-tah-RAH sohb kon-TRO-lee oh mahys HAH-pee-doo poh-SEEvay-oo.
Thank you for your patience.	*Obrigado/a por sua paciência.*	Oh-bree-GAHdoo/dah poor SOOW-ah pah-see-AYN-see-ah.

4. Checking In

A. AT THE FRONT DESK

FRONT DESK CLERK

Good morning (afternoon, evening).	*Bom dia (Boa tarde, Boa noite).*	Bohn JEE-ah (BOH-ah TAHR-jee, BOH-ah NOY-chee).
How may I help you?	*No que eu poderia ajudar?*	Noh keh AY-oo poh-deh-REE-ah ah-zhoo-DAHR?

GUEST

I have a reservation under the name _____.	*Eu tenho uma reserva no nome de _____.*	Ay-oo TEHN-yoo OO-mah hay-ZEHR-vah noh NOH-mee jee _____.
Do you have a room for one (two)?	*Você tem um quarto para uma (duas) pessoa(s)?*	Voh-SAY TEHM oon KWAHR-too PAH-rah OO-mah (DOO-ahs) peh-SOH-ah(s)?

CLERK

Yes, we have your reservation.	*Sim, nós temos sua reserva.*	Seen, nohs TAY-moosh SOO-ah hay-ZEHR-vah.

Yes, for how many nights?	*Sim, para quantas noites?*	Seen, PAH-rah KWAHN-taas NOY-chees?
No, I'm sorry, we're full.	*Não, perdão, estamos lotados.*	Nown, pehr-DOWN, ehs-TAW-moos loh-TAH-doos.
GUEST		
For _____ night(s), please.	*Para _____ noite (s), por favor.*	PAH-rah _____ NOY-chee(s), poor fah-VOHR.
What are your rates?	*Qual é o preço?*	Kwow eh oo PRAY-so?
CLERK		
• For a single,	• *Para solteiro,*	• PAH-rah sohl-TAY-roo,
• For a double,	• *Para casal,*	• PAH-rah kah-ZAWL,
• For adjoining rooms,	• *Quartos juntos,*	• KWAHR-toos ZHOON-toos,
• For a suite,	• *Uma suíte,*	• OO-mah soo-EE-tee,
...the rate is _____ per night.	*...o preço por noite é _____.*	...oo PRAY-soo poor NOY-chee eh _____.
GUEST		
Are any meals included?	*A refeição está incluída?*	Ah hay-fay-SOWN ehs-TAH een-kloo-EE-dah?
Is breakfast included?	*O café da manhã está incluído?*	Oo kah-FEH dah mah-YAWN ehs-TAH een-kloo-EE-doh?
CLERK		
No, meals are extra.	*Não, as refeições são extra.*	Nown, ahs hay-fay-SOWNS SOWN EH-stra.
Yes, breakfast is included.	*Sim, o café da manhã está incluído.*	Seen, oh kah-FEH dah mah-YAWN ehs-TAH een-kloo-EE-doh.
You can choose...	*Você pode escolher...*	Voh-SAY poh-DEH ehs-kowl-YEHR...
• the American plan (all meals included).	• *plano americano (todas as refeições estão incluídas).*	• PLAH-noo ah-meh-ree-KAH-noo (TOH-daas ahs hay-fay-SOWNS ehs-TAWH een-kloo-EE-dahs).

• the modified American plan (breakfast and dinner).	• *plano americano modificado (o café da manhã e jantar).*	• PLAH-noo ah-meh-ree-KAH-noo moh-jee-fee-KAH-doo (oh kah-FEH dah mah-YAWN eh zhahn-TAHR).
• the European plan (no meals included).	• *plano europeu (as refeições não são incluídas).*	• PLAH-noo ayo-roh-PEH-oo (ahs hay-fay-SOWNS nown sown een-kloo-EE-dahs).

GUEST

I'd like a room…	*Eu gostaria de um quartò…*	Ay-oo gohs-tah-REE-ah jee oon KWAHR-too…
• that faces the back (front).	• *com as janelas atrás (na frente).*	• kohn zhah-NAY-lahs ah-TRAHS (nah FREHN-chee).
• that faces the pool.	• *as janelas para a piscina.*	• ahs zhah-NAY-lahs PAH-rah ah pees-SEE-nah.
• with a private bath/toilet/shower.	• *com banheiro privativo/toilet/chuveiro.*	• kown bah-NYAY-roh pree-vah-TEE-voh/twah-LEH-chee/shoo-VAY-roh.
• with a handicapped-accessible bathroom.	• *com banheiro accessível para pessoa com deficiencia física.*	• kown bahn-YAY-roo ack-say-SEE-vayl PAH-rah peh-SOH-ah kohm deh-fay-see-EHN-syah-FEE-see-kah.
• with air-conditioning.	• *com ar acondicionado.*	• kown ahr ah-kohn-dee-syo-NAH-doo.
• with a TV.	• *com uma TV.*	• kown OO-mah chee-veh.
• with cable.	• *com cabo.*	• kown CAH-boo.
• with a fax machine.	• *com uma máquina de fax.*	• kown OO-mah MAH-kee-nah jee fahx.
• with a phone.	• *com um telefone.*	• kown the-lay-FOH-nee.

• with a network hookup for my computer.	• *com um serviço de network para computador.*	• kown oon sehr-VEE-soo jee network PAH-rah kohm-poo-tah-DOHR.
• with a view.	• *com uma vista panorâmica.*	• kown OO-mah VEES-tah pah-noh-RAH-mee-kah.
• with a whirlpool bath/Jacuzzi.	• *com uma hidro-massagem.*	• kown OO-mah hee-drow-mah-SAH-zhehn.
• with two double beds.	• *com duas camas de casal.*	• kown doo-ash KAH-mahs jee kah-sah-oo.
• with a king-size bed.	• *com uma cama grande.*	• kown OO-mah KAH-mah GRAHN-jee.
• with an extra bed.	• *com uma cama extra.*	• kown OO-mah KAH-mah es-trah.
• with a baby crib.	• *com um berço.*	• kown oon BEHR-soo.
• with a balcony.	• *com um balcaõ.*	• kown oon bahl-KOWN.
• with a sitting area.	• *com uma sacada.*	• kown OO-mah sah-KAA-dah.
• with a bar.	• *com um bar.*	• kown oon bahr.
• with a kitchenette.	• *com uma cozinha.*	• kown OO-mah koh-ZEE-yah.
• away from the elevator.	• *longe do elevador.*	• LOHN-zbee doh eh-lay-vah-DOHR.
• with no meals.	• *sem refeições.*	• sehn hay-fay-SOWNS.

CLERK

No problem.	*Não tem problema.*	Nown tehm proh-BLAY-mah.
I'm sorry.	*Perdão./Desculpe.*	Pehr-DOWN./Deesh-KOOL-pee.
There is none available.	*Não temos nenhum disponivel.*	Nown tehn-moos nay-oon dees-poh-NAY-veel.
We don't provide/ offer that.	*Nós não fornecemos/ nós não oferecemos isto.*	Nohs nown for-nay-see-moos/nohs nown oh-feh-ray-see-moos eel-too.

GUEST

Does the hotel have…	*O hotel tem…*	Oo oh-TAY-oo tehm…
• a restaurant?	• *restaurante?*	• hehs-tow-RAHN-chee?
• a bar?	• *bar?*	• bahr?
• room service?	• *serviço de quarto?*	• sehr-VEE-soo jee KWAHR-too?
• a health club?	• *salão de exercicios?*	• sah-LOWN jee ehk-zeh-SEE-see-oos?
• a spa hot tub?	• *hidro-massagem?*	• hee-droo-mah-SAH-zhehm?
• a swimming pool?	• *piscina?*	• pee-SEE-nah?
• baby-sitting?	• *babá?*	• bah-BAH?
• tennis courts?	• *quadra de tênis?*	• KWAH-draa jee the-nees?
• laundry (dry-cleaning) service?	• *serviço de lavanderia (tinturaria)?*	• sehr-VEE-soo jee lah-vahn-deh-REE-ah (teen-too-rah-REE-ah)?
• a garage?	• *garagem?*	• gah-RAH-zhen?
May I see the room?	*Posso ver o quarto?*	Poh-soo vehr oo KWAHR-too?

CLERK

Yes, certainly. Here's the key.	*Sim, certamente. Aqui está a chave.*	Seen, sehr-tah-MAYN-jee. Ah-KEE ehs-TAH ah SHAH-vee.
Would you like another room?	*Você gostaria de outro quarto?*	Voh-SAY gohs-tah-REE-ah jee OH-troo KWAHR-too?

GUEST

I'd like something…	*Eu gostaria…*	AY-oo gohs-tah-REE-ah ahl-goo…
• smaller.	• *menor.*	• mee-NOHR.
• larger.	• *maior.*	• mah-YOHR.
• quieter.	• *mais quieto.*	• mah-ees kee-EH-too.
• better.	• *melhor.*	• mehl-YOHR.

• cheaper.	• *mais barato.*	• mah-ees bah-RAH-too.
• on another floor.	• *noutro andar.*	• NOH-troo ahn-DAHR.
I'll take the room, please.	*Eu quero o quarto, por favor.*	AY-oo KEH-roh oo KWAHR-too, poor fah-VOHR.
CLERK		
Very well, how will you be paying?	*Muito bem, como o(a) senhor(a) vai pagar?*	MWEE-too behn, KOH-moo oh(ah) seh-nyohr(rah) vahy pah-GAHR?
GUEST		
I'll pay with…	*Eu pagarei com…*	AY-oo pah-gah-RAY kohm…
• cash.	• *dinheiro.*	• jeen-YAY-roo.
• a credit card.	• *cartão de crédito.*	• kahr-TOWN jee KREH-jee-too.
• traveler's checks.	• *cheque de viagem.*	• SHEH-kee-jee VYAH-zhehn.
CLERK		
Thank you.	*Obrigado/a.*	Oh-bree-GAH-doo/dah.
To charge meals and services to your room, I'll need a credit card.	*Necessito um cartão de crédito para cobrar refeições e serviços para o quarto.*	Neh-she-SEE-too oon kahr-TOWN jee KREH-jee-too PAH-rah koh-BRAAR hay-fay-SOWNS eh sehr-VEE-soos PAH-rah oo KWAHR-too.
You may settle the bill with traveler's checks (cash).	*Você pode pagar a contá com cheque de viagem (dinheiro).*	Voh-SAY POH-deh pah-GAHR ah KOHN-tah kohn SHEH-kee jee VYAH-zhehn (-jeen-YAY-roo).
If you would like to store valuables, we have a safe.	*Se você quizer guardar objetos de valor, temos um cofre.*	See voh-SAY kee-ZERHR gwahr-DAHR oh-bee-JAY-toos jee vah-LOHR, teh-moos oon KO-free.

Please note that…	*Por favor, observe que…*	Poor fah-VOHR, oh-bee-SHER-vee-keh…
• quiet hours are between ____ and ____.	• *deve-se fazer silêncio entre ____ e ____.*	• DAY-vee-see fah-ZHEER see-LEHN-syoo EHN-tre ____ eh ____.
• there are no pets allowed.	• *não permitimos animais.*	• nown perhr-mee-TEE-moos ah-nee-MAH-eez.
• children under age ____ stay free.	• *criança menor de ____ anos tem estada grátis.*	• kree-AHN-sah may-NOHR jee ____ ah-nohs chem esh-TAH-dah GRAH-chees.
• smoking is allowed only in the bar.	• *é permitido fumar somente no bar.*	• eh perhr-mee-TEE-doo foo-MAHR soh-MAYN-chee noh bahr.
• we do not allow cooking in the rooms.	• *não permitimos cozinhar nos quartos.*	• nown pehr-mee-TEE-moos koh-zee-NYAR nohs KWAHR-toos.

GUEST

Do I (we) have any messages?	*Tem (temos) alguma mensagem?*	Tehn (TEH-moos) ahl-GOO-mah mehn-SAH-zhen?
I would like a wake-up call, please.	*Gostaria de ser acordado, por favor.*	Gohs-tah-REE-ah jee sehr ah-kohr-DAH-doo, poor fah-VOHR.
May we have…, please?	*Podemos ter…, por favor?*	Poh-DEH-moos tehr…, poor fah-VOHR?
• extra blankets	• *cobertores extras*	• koh-behr-TOHR-ehs ehs-trahs
• extra towels	• *toalhas extras*	• TWAHL-yahs ehs-trahs
• a hair dryer	• *secador de cabelo*	• she-kah-DOHR jee kah-BAY-loo
• an iron	• *um ferro*	• oon feh-HOO
• ice	• *gêlo*	• ZHEH-loo

CLERK

I'll have that brought to your room right away.	*Eu levarei isto logo em seguida para o seu quarto.*	AY-oo lay-vah-RAY eesh-too ehn she-GWEE-dah PAH-rah oo SAY-oo KWAHR-too.

GUEST

Where is…	*Onde está…*	OHN-jee ehsh-TAH…
• the room attendant?	• *o quarto de serviço?*	• oo KWAHR-too jee sehr-VEE-soo?
• the bellman (bell attendant)?	• *o mensageiro?*	• oo mehn-sah-ZHAY-roo?
Where is…	*Onde fica…*	OHN-jee FEE-kah…
• the manager?	• *o gerente?*	• oo jee-RAYN-chee?
• the dining room?	• *a sale de jantar?*	• ah SAH-la jee zhahn-TAHR?
• the gift shop?	• *a loja de souvenir?*	• ah LOH-zhah jee sourvenir?
• the newsstand?	• *a banca de revistas?*	• ah BAHN-kah jee ree-veesh-tahs?

CLERK

Just over there.	*Ali.*	Ah-LEE.

GUEST

How do I use the telephone?	*Como eu uso o telefone?*	KOH-moo AY-oo OO-zoo oo tek lay-FOH-nee?

CLERK

The instructions are next to the phone.	*As instruções estão ao lado do telefone.*	Ahs eens-throo-SOWN-ees esh-TAWN own lah-doo doh teh-lay-FOH-nee.
Dial ____ for a local (long-distance) call,	*Disque ____ para uma chamada local (interurbana),*	JEES-kee ____ PAH-rah OO-mah sha-MAH-dah loh-KAWL (een-tehr-roor-BAH-nah),
wait for the tone,	*espere pelo som,*	ehs-PEH-ree PEH-loo sohn,

and dial the number.	*e disque o numero.*	eh JEES-kee oo NOO-meh-roo.
Dial ____ for an operator.	*Disque ____ para a operadora.*	JEES-kee ____ PAH-rah ah oh-peh-RAH-doh-rah.
To use a credit card, dial ____.	*Para usar um cartão de crédito, disque ____.*	PAH-rah oo-ZAHR oon kahr-TOWN jee KREH-jee-too, JEES-kee ____.
GUEST		
Please have our luggage brought to our room.	*Por favor, leve a nossa bagagem para o quarto.*	Poor fah-VOHR, LAY-vee ah NOHS-sah bah-GAH-zhen PAH-rah oo KWAHR-too.
We'll need a wheelchair.	*Nós necessitamos uma cadeira de rodas.*	Nohs neh-she-see-TAH-moos OO-mah kah-DAY-rah jee HOH-dahs.
CLERK		
Yes, right away.	*Sim, em seguida.*	Seen, ehn she-GEE-dah.
GUEST		
We'd like to order a pizza, please.	*Gostariamos de ordenar uma pizza, por favor.*	Gohs-tah-REE-ah-moos jee ohr-deh-NAHR OO-mah pee-tzah, poor fah-VOHR.
MANAGER		
I'll be happy to call someone for you.	*Terei prazer em chamar alguém para você.*	The-RAY prah-ZEHR ehn sha-MAHR AHL-gehn PAH-rah voh-SAY.
We have room service, but we don't allow outside vendors into the hotel.	*Nós temos serviço de quarto, mas não permitimos vendedores no hotel.*	Nohs the-moos sehr-VEE-soo jee KWAHR-too, mahs nown pehr-mee-CHEE-moos vehn-day-DOH-rees noh oh-TAY-oo.

GUEST

We'd like to entertain a few friends in our room.	*Gostariamos de receber alguns amigos em nosso quarto.*	Gohs-tah-REE-ah-moos jee hay-say-BEHR ahl-GOONS ah-MEE-goos ehn noh-soo KWAHR-too.

MANAGER

We allow guests in the rooms until ____.	*Permitimos visitas nos quartos até ____.*	Pehr-mee-CHEE-moos vee-ZEE-tahs nohs KWAHR-toos ah-TEH ____.

B. SHOWING GUESTS TO THEIR ROOMS

BELLMAN (BELL ATTENDANT)

My name is ____, and I'm your bell attendant.	*Meu nome é ____, sou o mensageiro.*	MAY-oo NOH-mee eh ____, soh-oo oohmehn-sah-ZHAY-roo.
May I show you to your room?	*Posso levar-lhe para o quarto?*	POH-soo leh-VAHR-lhay pah-rah oo KWAHR-too?

GUEST

No, thanks. We'll find it ourselves.	*Não, obrigado/da. Nós iremos sozinhos.*	Nown, oh-bree-GAH-doo/dah. Nohs ee-RAY-moos soh-ZEE-nyoos.
Yes, please.	*Sim, por favor.*	Seen, poor fah-VOHR.

BELLMAN

This way, please.	*Por aqui, por favor.*	Poor ah-KEE, poor fah-VOHR.

TIP! ••••

International guests in particular may have questions about using the telephone and will appreciate seeing how the television and pay movies work.

The elevator is over here.	*O elevador está aqui.*	Oo eh-lay-vah-DOHR ehs-TAH ah-KEE.
May I show you the features of your room?	*Posso mostrar-lhe os recursos do seu quarto?*	Poh-soo mohs-TRAHR-lhay ohs heh-koor-sohs doh SAY-oo KWAHR-too?
This is the key to the minibar.	*Esta é a chave do mini-bar.*	ESH-tah eh ah SHAH-vee doh mee-nee-bahr.
• Any movie you select	• *Qualquer filme que você escolha*	• Kwow-KEHR FEEL-mee keh voh-SAY ehs-KOHL-yah.
• Any long-distance calls you make	• *Qualquer chamada interurbana que você faça*	• Kwow-KEHR sha-MAH-dah een-tehr-roor-BAH-nah keh voh-SAY FAH-sah
• Any snack or beverage you take from the refrigerator	• *Qualquer lanche ou bebida que você pegue da geladeira*	• Kwow-KEHR LAHN-shee ow beh-BEE-dah keh voh-SAY PEH-gwee dah zheh-lah-DAY-rah
...will be charged to your room.	*...será cobrado(a) na sua conta do quarto.*	...seh-RAH ko-BRAH-doo(dah) nah soo-ah KON-tah doo KWAHR-too.
Here is the control for the heating (air-conditioning).	*Aqui está o controle do aquecedor (ar acondicionado).*	Ah-KEE ehs-TAH oo kon-TROH-lee doo ah-keh-she-DOOR (ahr-ah-kohn-dee-syo-NAH-doo).
GUEST		
How do I call Room Service?	*Como eu posso chamar o-serviço de quarto?*	KOH-moo eh-oo POH-soo shah MAHR oo sehr-VEE-soo jee KWAHR-too?
BELLMAN		
Dial _____.	*Disque _____.*	JEES-kee _____.

GUEST

This room...	*Este quarto...*	EHS-chee KWAHR-too...
• is too close to the elevator(s).	• *está muito perto do elevador (elevadores).*	• ehs-TAH MWEE-too PEHR-too doo eh-lay-vah-DOOR.
• hasn't been made up.	• *naõ foi arrumado.*	• nown foy ahr-roo-MAH-doo.
• smells (like cigarettes).	• *cheira (à cigarros).*	• SHAY-raa (ah see-GAH-hohs).
The toilet (bathtub, sink) is clogged.	*A toilete (banheira, pia) está entupida.*	Ah toah-LEE-teh (bahn-YAY-rah, PEE-ah) ehs-TAH ehn-too-PEE-dah.
May (we) change rooms, please?	*Podemos mudar de quarto, por favor?*	Poh-DAY-moos moo-DAHR jee KWAHR-too, poor fah-VOHR?

BELLMAN

Please let me check our availability with the front desk.	*Por favor, deixe-me verificar a nossa disponibilidade com a recepção.*	Poor fah-VOHR, DAY-zheh-mee veh-ree-fee-KAR ah nohs-sah deez-poh-nee-bee-lee-DAH-deh kohn ah reh-sayp-SAWN.
Sure, I'll be happy to assist you.	*Certamente, será um prazer ajudar você.*	Sehr-tah-MAYN-chee, she-RAH oon prah-ZEHR ah-zhoo-DAHR voh-SAY.
Please call if I can help you with anything else.	*Chame se eu puder ajudá-lo em alguma coisa mais.*	SHAH-mee see AY-oopooh-DEHR ahjoo-DAH-loo ehn ahl-GOO-mah KOY-zah mahys.

VOCABULARY ••••

THE GUEST ROOM

air-conditioning	*ar acondicionado*	ahr ah-kohn-dee-syo-NAH-doo
balcony	*balcaõ*	bahl-KOWN
bath mat	*tapete de banheiro*	tah-PEH-chee jee bahn-YAY-rah
bathtub	*banheira*	bahn-YAY-rah
bed	*cama*	KAH-mah
bedspread	*colcha*	KOHL-shah
blanket	*cobertor*	koh-behr-TOHR
blinds	*cortinas*	kohr-CHEE-nahs
carpet	*carpete, tapête*	kahr-PEH-chee, tah-PEH-chee
ceiling	*teto*	TEH-too
chair	*cadeira*	kah-DAY-rah
closet	*armario*	ahr-MAH-ree-oo
conditioner	*condicionador*	kon-dee-seeo-nah-DOHR
couch	*poltrona*	pohl-TROH-nah
crib	*berço*	BEHR-soo
desk	*escrivaninha*	ezhs-chree-vayn-NEEN-ah
Do Not Disturb sign	*sinal: não perturbe*	see-NOW: nown pehr-TOOR-bee
door	*porta*	POHR-tah
drapes	*cortinas*	kohr-CHEE-nahs
dresser	*penteadeira*	pehn-chee-ah-DAY-rah
fan	*ventilador*	vehn-chee-lah-DOHR
floor	*chão/piso*	SHAWN/PEE-zoo
glass(es)	*copo(s)*	KOH-poo(s)
hair dryer	*secador de cabelo*	she-kah-DOHR jee kah-BAY-loo
(coat) hanger	*cabides*	kah-BEE-jee

(cont'd.)

The Guest Room *(cont'd.)*

heat	*aquecimento*	ah-keh-see-MEHN-too
ice bucket	*porta gêlo*	POHR-tah zheh-loo
iron	*ferro*	FEH-roh
lamp	*lâmpada*	LAHM-pah-dah
light	*luz*	looz
lock	*fechadura*	fay-sha-DOO-rah
minibar	*mini-bar*	mee-neebahr
mirror	*espelho*	ehs-PEHL-yoo
nightstand	*mesa de cabeceira*	MAY-sah jee kah-bay-SAY-raa
pillow	*travesseiro*	trah-vay-SAY-roo
radio	*rádio*	HAH-jyoo
razor	*barbeador*	bahr-byah-DOHR
sewing kit	*jogo para costura*	zhoh-goo PAH-rah kohs-TOO-rah
shampoo	*xampu*	SHAHM-poo
sheet	*lençol*	lehn-SOHL
shower	*chuveiro*	shoo-VAY-roo
shower cap	*tôca de banho*	toh-KAH jee BAHN-yoh
sink	*pia*	PEE-ah
soap	*sabão*	sah-BOWN
telephone	*telefone*	teh-lay-FOH-nee
television	*televisão*	teh-lay-vee-ZOWN
thermostat	*termostato*	tehr-mohs-TAH-too
toilet	*banheiro*	bahn-YAY-roo
toilet paper	*papel higiênico*	pah-PAY-oo ee-ZHEEAY-nee-koh
toothbrush	*escova de dentes*	ehs-KOH-vah jee DEHN-chees
toothpaste	*paste de dente*	PAHS-tah-jeeDEHN-chee
towel	*toalha*	TWAHL-yah
VCR	*VCR*	VCR
wall	*parede*	pah-REH-jee
window	*janela*	zhah-NAY-lah

5. Providing Assistance

A. GIVING DIRECTIONS

CONCIERGE		
Good morning. May I help you?	*Bom dia. Posso ajudá-lo?*	Bohn JEE-ah. POH-soo ah-joo-DAH-loo?
GUEST		
Yes, where is the...	*Sim, onde é o/a...*	Seen, OHN-jee eh oo/ah...
• bathroom?	• *banheiro?*	• bahn-YAY-roo?
• lounge/bar?	• *sala de espera/bar?*	• SAH-lah jee ehs-PEH-rah/bahr?
• coffee shop/ restaurant?	• o *café/restaurante?*	• oo ka-FEE/hehs-tow-RAHN-chee?
• barbershop/ hairdresser's?	• *barbearia/ cabelereiro?*	• bahr-bay-ah-REE-ah/ kah-beh-lay-RAY-roh?
• gift shop?	• *loja de souvenir?*	• LOH-jah jee soo-veh-neer?
• health club/gym?	• *salão de ginástica/ salão de jogos?*	• sah-LOWN jee jee-NAHS-chee-ka/sah-LOWN jee ZHOH-goos?

TIP! ••••

You can simply explain many directions, but when they're more complex, you should use either a map or written instructions (or both). Hotels should keep preprinted directions to major sites on hand. Also, many cultures don't speak of distance in terms of city blocks but will understand if you use the word "streets" instead. And remember that most international guests use the metric system and may have difficulties figuring a distance given in miles, yards, or feet.

• ballroom?	• *salão de festas?*	• sah-LAWN jee FEH-stahs?
• elevator?	• *elevador?*	• eh-lay-vah-DOHR?
• pay phones?	• *telefones público?*	• teh-lay-FOH-nee POO-blee-koo?
• ice machine?	• *máquina de gêlo?*	• MAH-kee-nah jee ZHEH-loo?

CONCIERGE

Take…	*Pegue…*	PEH-gwee…
• the escalator.	• *a escada rolante.*	• ah ehs-KAH-dah hoh-LAN-chee.
• the elevator.	• *o elevador.*	• oo eh-lay-vah-DOHR.
• the stairs.	• *a escada.*	• ah ehs-KAH-dah.
Go…	*Vá…*	VAH…
• up.	• *para cima.*	• pah-rah SEE-mah.
• down.	• *para baixo.*	• pah-rah BAHY-shoo.
• left.	• *para a esquerda.*	• pah-rah ah ehs-KEHR-dah.
• right.	• *para a direita.*	• pah-rah ah jee-RAY-tah.
• straight ahead.	• *em frente.*	• ehn FREHN-chee.
• left, then right.	• *para a esquerda e depois para a direita.*	• pah-rah ah ehs-KEHR-dah eh day-POH-eez pah-rah ah jee-RAY-tah.
• to the first (second, third, fourth) floor.	• *para o primeiro (segundo, terceiro, quarto) andar.*	• PAH-rah oo pree-MAY-roo (say-GOON-doo, tehr-SAY-roo) ahn-DAHR.
• left (right) when you exit the elevator.	• *para a esquerda (direita) quando sair do elevador.*	• pah-rah ah ehs-KEHR-dah (jee-RAY-tah) KWAHN-doo sa-EER doh eh-lay-vah-DOHR.
• in through the second set of doors.	• *passe a segunda porta.*	• pah-see ah say-GOON-daa POHR-tah.
Go around the corner.	*Vire a esquina.*	VEE-reh a ehs-KEE-nah.

Go past the elevators.	*Passe os elevadores.*	PAH-see ohs eh-lay-vah-DOHR-eez.
It will be…	*Estará…*	Ehs-tah-RAH…
• on your right.	• *na sua direita.*	• nah SOO-ah jee-RAY-tah.
• on your left.	• *na sua esquerda.*	• nah SOO-ah ehs-KEHR-dah.
• right in front of you.	• *bem na sua frente.*	• bein nah SOO-ah FREHN-chee.

GUEST

How do I get…	*Como eu chego…*	KOH-moo AY-oo SHAY-goo…
• to the hospital?	• *no hospital?*	• noh ohs-pee-TOW?
• to city hall?	• *na Prefeitura?*	• nah pray-fehay-TOO-rah?
• to the _____ restaurant/hotel?	• *no restaurante/hotel _____ ?*	• noh hehs-tow-RAHN-chee/oh-TAY-oo _____?
• to the train station?	• *na estação de trem?*	• nah ehs-tah-SOWN jee trehn?
• to the bus station?	• *no estaçaõ de ônibus?*	• noh esh-tah-sown jee OH-nee-boos?
• to the nearest bus stop?	• *no ponto de ônibus mais perto?*	• noh POHN-too je OH-pee-boos mahys PEHR-too?
• to the mall?	• *no "shopping center"?*	• noh SHOW-peen SAYN-tehr?
• to the post office?	• *no correio?*	• noh koh-HAY-oo?
• to the airport?	• *no aeroporto?*	• noh ah-her-oh-POHR-too?
• downtown?	• *no centro da cidade?*	• noh SAYN-troo dah see-DAH-jee?
• to the car rental agency?	• *na agência de aluguel de carro?*	• nah ah-JAYN-shee-ah jee ah-loo-GWEL jee KAH-roo?
• to _____ Street/Avenue?	• *na rua/avenida _____?*	• nah HOO-ah/ah-veh-NEE-dah _____?

CONCIERGE

When you exit the hotel, go…	*Quando você sair do hotel, vá…*	KWAHN-doo voh-SAY sah-EERdoooh-TAY-oo, VAH.…
• left.	• *à esquerda.*	• ah ehs-KEHR-dah.
• right.	• *à direita.*	• ah jee-RAY-tah.
• straight ahead.	• *em frente.*	• ehn FREHN-chee.
• north.	• *norte.*	• NOHR-chee.
• south.	• *sul.*	• sool.
• east.	• *leste.*	• LEHS-chee.
• west.	• *oeste.*	• oh-EHS-chee.

GUEST

How far is it?	*É longe?*	Eh LOHN-zhee?

CONCIERGE

It's about _____…	*Mais ou menos _____…*	Mahys ow MAY-noos _____…
• blocks (streets).	• *quadras*	• kwahd-rahs.
• miles.	• *milhas.*	• MEE-lhas.
• kilometers.	• *quilômetros.*	• kee-LOH-may-troos.
• minutes…	• *minutos…*	• mee-NOO-toos…
• on foot.	• *a pé.*	• ah peh.
• by car.	• *de carro.*	• jee KAH-roo.
• by bus.	• *de ônibus.*	• jee OH-nee-boos.
• by metro (subway).	• *de metrô.*	• jee meh-TROW.

GUEST

Can you show me on the map?	*Poderia me mostrar no mapa?*	Poh-deh-REE-ah mee mohs-TRAHR noo MAH-pah?

CONCIERGE

Sure, it's right here.	*Certamente, é aqui.*	Sehr-tah-MEHN-chee, eh ah-KEE.
Let me draw you a little map.	*Deixe-me desenhar um pequeno mapa para você.*	DAY-SHE-mee dee-senh-AHR oon pay-KEH-noo MAH pah PAH-rah voh-SAY.

GUEST

Can you tell me where I can... around here?	*Poderia me dizer onde eu posso... aqui perto?*	Poh-deh-REE-ah mee jee-ZEHR OHN-jee AY-oo POH-soo... ah-KEE PEHR-too?
• take a walk	• *caminhar*	• kah-meen-YAHR
• ride a bike	• *andar de bicicleta*	• ahn-DAHR jee bee-see-KLAY-tah
• jog	• *correr*	• koh-HEHR

CONCIERGE

Yes, we have maps of...trails right here.	*Sim, temos mapas para...aqui.*	Seen, TEH-moos MAH-pahs PAH-rah...ah-KEE.
• jogging	• *corrida*	• koh-HEE-dah
• walking	• *caminhada*	• kah-meen-YAH-dah
• bike	• *ciclismo*	• see-KLEES-moh

B. RECOMMENDING PLACES OF INTEREST

GUEST

Can you recommend any places to visit?	*Poderia recomendar-me algum lugar para visitar?*	Poh-deh-REE-ah hay-koh-mehn-DAHR-mee ahl-GOON loo-GAHR PAH-rah vee-zee-TAHR?

CONCIERGE

There are lots. Are you interested in...	*Têm vários. Você está interessado em...*	Tehn VAH-ryoos. Voh-SAY esh-TAH een-teh-ray-SAH-doo ehn...
• art?	• *arte?*	• AHR-chee?
• theater?	• *teatro?*	• teh-AH-troo?
• shopping?	• *compras?*	• KOHM-prahs?
• museums?	• *museus?*	• moo-ZAY-oos?
• sports?	• *esportes?*	• ehs-POHR-chees?
• sight-seeing?	• *pontos turísticos?*	• POHN-toos too-REEZ-chee-koos?
• music?	• *música?*	• MOO-zee-ka?
• outdoor activities?	• *atividades ao ar livre?*	• ah-chee-vee-DAH-jees own ahr LEEV-ray?

• children's activities?	• *atividades para crianças?*	• ah-chee-vee-DAH-jees PAH-rah kree-AH-sahs?

GUEST

What do you recommend?	*O que você recomenda?*	Oo keh voh-SAY hay-koh-MEHN-dah?

CONCIERGE

If you're interested in art, I'd suggest...	*Se você está interessado em arte, eu sugiro...*	See voh-SAY esh-TAH een-teh-ray-SAH-doo ehn AHR-chee, AY-oo soo-JEE-roh...
• the ____ gallery.	• *a galeria ____.*	• ah gah-lay-REE-ah ____.
• the ____ art museum.	• *o museu de arte ____.*	• oo moo-ZAY-oo jee AHR-chee ____.
If you're interested in theater, I can get you tickets to...	*Se você está interessado em teatro, eu posso conseguir ingressos para...*	See voh-SAY esh-TAH een-teh-ray-SAH-doo ehn teh-AH-troo, AY-oo POH-soo kohn-see-GWEER een-GREH-soos PAH-rah...
• a show.	• *um show.*	• oon SHOW.
• an opera.	• *uma ópera.*	• OO-mah OH-peh-rah.
• a movie.	• *um filme.*	• oon FEEL-mee.
For shopping, I'd recommend...	*Para compras, eu recomendo...*	PAH-rah KOHM-prahs, AY-oo hay-koh-MEHN-doo...
• downtown.	• *o centro da cidade.*	• oo SEHN-troo dah see-DAH-jee.
• the mall.	• *o shopping center.*	• oo SHOH-peen SEHN-tehr.
• the discount outlets.	• *as lojas de disconto.*	• ahs LOH-zhahs jee deesh-KOHN-too.

GUEST

Do they have...there?	*Eles têm...lá?*	AY-lees tehn...LAH?
• clothes	• *roupas*	• HOH-pahs
• furniture	• *móveis*	• MOH-vay-eez
• rugs (carpets)	• *tapetes (carpetes)*	• tah-PEH-chees (kahr-PEH-chees)

• souvenirs	• *souvenirs*	• soo-veh-NEERS
• books	• *livros*	• LEE-vroos
• sporting goods	• *artigos para esportivos*	• ahr-CHEE-goos PAH-rah ehs-pohr-CHEE-vohs
• candy	• *doces*	• DOH-sees
• antiques	• *antigüidades*	• ahn-chee-GWEE-dah-jees
• electronics	• *eletrônicos*	• eh-lay-TROH-nee-koos
• computers	• *computadores*	• kohm-poo-tah-DOHR-eez
• a farmers' market	• *mercado com produtos de comida*	• mehr-KAH-doo kohn proh-DOO-toos jee koh-MEE-dah
• a supermarket	• *supermercado*	• soo-pehr-mehr-KAH-doo
• a flea market	• *feira-livre*	• FAY-rah-LEE-vray

CONCIERGE

Perhaps you'd like a museum.	*Talvez você goste de museu.*	Tow-VEHZ voh-SAY GOHS-tah jee moo-ZAY-oo.
A local favorite is the…museum.	*O favorito é o Museu de…*	Oo fah-voh-REE-too eh oo moo-ZAY-oo jee…
• natural history	• *história natural*	• ees-TOH-ree-ah nah-too-RAW
• modern art	• *arte moderna*	• AHR-chee moh-DEHR-nah
• science	• *ciências*	• see-EHN-see-ahs
• local history	• *história local*	• ees-TOH-ree-ah loh-KAL

GUEST

We were thinking of sight-seeing.	*Nós estavamos pensando em visitar os pontos turísticos.*	Nohs ehs-TAH-vay-moos pehn-SAHN-doo ehn vee-zee-TAHR oos POHN-toostoo-REEZ-chee-koos.

CONCIERGE

I'd be happy to arrange a city tour.	*Será um prazer organizar um turismo pela cidade.*	She-RAH oon prah-ZEHRohr-gha-nee-ZHAR oon too-REEZ-moo PEH-lah see-DAH-jee.

GUEST

How about…	*Que tal…*	Keh TAHL…
• interesting architecture?	• *arquitetura interessante?*	• ahr-kee-teh-TOO-rah enn-teh-ray-SAH-jee?
• churches?	• *igrejas?*	• ee-GRAY-zhahs?
• a vineyard?	• *um vinhedo?*	• oon veen-AY-doo?
• the business district?	• *o setor comercial da cidade?*	• oo she-TOHR koh-mehr-SYOW daa see-DAH-jee?
• the government buildings?	• *edifícios do governo?*	• ay-dee-FEE-shee-oos doo goh-VEHR-noo?
• the university?	• *as universidades?*	• ahs oo-nee-vehr-see-DAH-jees?
• monuments?	• *monumentos?*	• moh-noo-MEHN-tos?
• the countryside?	• *a zona do campo?*	• ah SOH-noo doh KAHM-poo?

CONCIERGE

There are many sports events.	*Têm muitos eventos esportivos.*	Tehn MWEE-toos eh-VEHN-toos ehs-pohr-CHEE-voos.
Would you like tickets to…	*Gostaria de ingressos para…*	Gohs-tah-REE-ah jee een-GREH-soos PAH-rah…
• a baseball game?	• *um jogo de baseball?*	• oon ZHOH-goo jee baseball?
• a basketball game?	• *um jogo de basquete?*	• oon ZHOH-goo je bahs-KEH-chee?
• a football game?	• *um jogo de futebol?*	• oon ZHOH-goo jee foo chee-BOHL?
• a hockey game?	• *um jogo de "hockey"?*	• oon ZHOH-goo je "hockey"?

• a tennis match?	• *uma partida de tênis?*	• OO-mah pahr-CHEE-da jee THE-neez?
GUEST		
Are there any musical events?	*Têm algum evento musical?*	Tehn ahl-GOON eh-VAYN-too moo-zee KAHL?
CONCIERGE		
There is a...concert tonight.	*Têm um concerto de ...à noite.*	Tehn oon kohn-ZEHR-too jee...ah NOY-chee.
• rock-and-roll	• *rock and roll*	• rock een roll
• blues	• *"blues"*	• "blues"
• classical music	• *música classica*	• MOO-zee-kah KLAH-see-ka
• jazz	• *"jazz"*	• "jazz"
• folk	• *música folclórica*	• MOO-zee-kah fohlk-LOH-ree-kah
There's musical entertainment at _____.	*Hà um show musical no/na _____.*	Ah oon shoh MOO-zee-kahl noh/nah ___.
GUEST		
Is there anything else going on tonight?	*Têm também algum outro lugar para ir à noite?*	Tèhn than-BEHN ahl-GOON OH-troo loo GAHR PAH-rah eer aa NOY-chee?
CONCIERGE		
Other than the movies, I'd suggest...	*Têm filmes, posso sugerir...*	Tehn FEEL-mee, POH-soo soo-JEE-reehr...
• bowling.	• *boliche.*	• bowl-LEE-shee.
• a nightclub.	• *uma boate.*	• OO-mah boh-AH-chee.
• a video rental.	• *alugar um filme.*	• ah-loo-GAHR oon FEEL-mee.
GUEST		
What do you suggest for outdoor activities?	*O que você sugere como atividade ao ar livre?*	Oo keh voh-SAY soo-JEH-ree KOH-moo ah-chee-vee-DAH-jee aow ahr LEEV-ree?

CONCIERGE

How about…	*Que tal…*	Keh TAHL…
• hiking?	• *longa caminhada?*	• LOHN-gah kah-meen-YAH-dah?
• fishing?	• *pesca?*	• PEHZ-kah?
• skiing?	• *esquiar?*	• eehs-kee-AHR?
• skating?	• *patinar no gêlo?*	• pah-chee-NAHR noh ZHEH-loo?
• Rollerblading?	• *patinar?*	• pah-chee-NAHR?
• swimming?	• *nadar?*	• nah-DAHR?
• surfing?	• *surfar?*	• soohr-FAHR?
Or you might like to go…	*Ou você poderia ir…*	Ow voh-SAY poh-day-REE-ah eer…
• to the river.	• *no rio.*	• Noh HEE-oo.
• to the lake.	• *no lago.*	• noh LAH-goo.
• to the mountains.	• *nas montanhas.*	• nahs mohn-THAN-yahs.
• for a drive.	• *passear de carro.*	• pah-seh-AHR jee kahr-ROO.
• to the beach.	• *à praia.*	• ah PRAHY-yah.
• to the forest.	• *na floresta.*	• nah flow-REHS-tah.

GUEST

Is there anything for children?	*Têm alguma coisa para crianças?*	Tehn ahl-GOO-mah KOH-ee-zah PAH-rah ahs kree-AHN-sahs?

CONCIERGE

Yes, there's…	*Sim, têm…*	Seen, tehn…
• a zoo.	• *um zoológico.*	• oon zoh-LOH-jee-koo.
• a children's museum.	• *um museu infantil.*	• oon moo-ZAY-oo een-fayn-CHEEHL.
• an amusement park.	• *um parque de diversão.*	• oon PAHR-kee jee deeh-VEHR-SAWN.
• a water park.	• *um parque aquático.*	• oon PAHR-kee ah-GWAH-chee-koh.

Would you like to rent…	*Você gostaria de alugar…*	Voh-SAY gohs-tah-REE-ah jee ah-loo-GAHR…
• a bicycle?	• *uma bicicleta?*	• OO-mah bee-se-KLAY-tah?
• a car?	• *um carro?*	• oon kahr-ROO?
• a boat?	• *um barco?*	• oon BAHR-koo?
• some skis?	• *alguns esquis?*	• ahl-GOONS eehs-KEEZ?
• some Rollerblades?	• *alguns patins?*	• ahl-GOONS pah-cheens?
Would you like a tour guide who speaks Portuguese?	*Gostaria de um guia turístico que fale Português?*	Gohs-tah-REE-ah jee oon GWEE-ah too-REEZ-chee-koo keh FAH-lee pohr-TOO-gays?
May I make a reservation for you?	*Posso fazer uma reserva para você?*	POH-soo fah-ZEHR OO-mah hay-ZEHR-vah PAH-rah voh-SAY?

GUEST

Can you recommend a good restaurant?	*Você pode recomendar um bom restaurante?*	Voh-SAY POH-jee hay-koh-mehn-DAHR oon bohn hehs-tow-RAHN-chee?

CONCIERGE

What type of cuisine would you like?	*Que tipo de comida você prefere?*	Keh CHEE-poh jee koh-MEE-dah voh-SAY pray-FEH-ree?

GUEST

We'd like a(n)… restaurant.	*Nós gostaríamos de um restaurante…*	Nohs gohs-tah-REE-ah-moos jee oon hehs-tow-RAHN-chee…
• casual	• *comum.*	• koh-MOON.
• elegant	• *elegante.*	• eh-lay-GAHN-chee.
• fast-food	• *comida rápida.*	• koh-MEE-dah HAH-pee-dah.
• inexpensive	• *barato.*	• bah-RAH-too.
• kosher	• *judeu.*	• joo-DEE-oo.

• seafood	• *de frutos do mar.*	• jee froo-toos doh mahr.
• vegetarian	• *vegetariano.*	• veh-jeh-tah-REE-ya-noo.
We'd like a steakhouse.	*Nós gostaríamos de uma churrascaria.*	Nohs gohs-tah-REE-ah-moos jee OO-mah shoo-rrahss-kah-REE-ah.

CONCIERGE

You can get there by…	*Você pode chegar lá de…*	Voh-SAY POH-jee shay-GAHR LAH jee…
• bus.	• *ônibus.*	• OH-nee-boos.
• train.	• *trem.*	• trehn.
• subway.	• *metrô.*	• meh-TROW.
Take the…, bound for ____.	*Pegue o… ____ desça no.*	PEH-gwee oo… ____ days-SAH noh.
• number ____ bus	• *ônibus número ____*	• OH-nee-boos NOO-meh-roo ____
• train	• *o train*	• oo trehn
• subway	• *o metrô*	• oo meh-TROW
You'll need to transfer to… at ____.	*Troque pelo…na ____.*	TROH-kee peh-loo…nah ____.
• the ____ line	• *a linha ____*	• ah LEEN-yah ____
• the number ____ bus	• *o ônibus número ____*	• oo OH-nee-boos NOO-meh-roo ____
Get off at ____.	*Desça na ____.*	Days-SAH nah ____.
May I call you a taxi?	*Posso chamar um taxi para você?*	POH-soo shah-MAHR oon TAHK-see PAH-rah SAY?
We have a free shuttle bus service available to ____.	*Temos um serviço de transporte grátis para ____.*	Teh-moos oon sehr-VEE-soo jee trahns-POHR-chee GRAH-chees PAH-rah ____.
It leaves every ____ minutes.	*Ele sai a cada ____ minutos.*	AY-lee SAH-ee ah KAH-dah ____ mee-NOO-toos.

It leaves every hour.	*Ele sai de hora em hora.*	Ay-lee SAH-ee jee OH-rah ehn OH-rah.
GUEST		
What's the price range?	*Qual é o preço?*	Kwow eh oo PRAY-soo?

6. Business Services and Clientele

A. BOOKING A BUSINESS MEETING

EMPLOYEE		
Good morning.	*Bom dia.*	Bohn JEE-ah.
How may I help you today?	*No que eu posso ajudá-lo hoje?*	Noh keh AY-oo POH-soo ah-zhoo-DAH-loo OH-zhee?
GUEST		
I'd like to make arrangements for a business meeting.	*Gostaria de organizar uma reunião de negócios.*	Gohs-tah-REE-ah jee ohr-gah-nee-ZAHR OO-mah he-oo-nee-OWN jee GOH-syoos.
EMPLOYEE		
For how many people?	*Para quantas pessoas?*	PAH-rah KWAHN-ta peh-SOH-aas?
GUEST		
For ____ people on ____.	*Para ____ pessoas na ____.*	PAH-rah ____ peh-SOH-ahs nah ____.

TIP! ••••

Clients who do business from the hotel need a great deal of service from you. They tend to be seasoned travelers who don't want a lot of explanation from hotel employees, just competent action. Attending to their every need often yields substantial financial rewards!

EMPLOYEE

Fine.	*Muito bem.*	MWEE-too behn.
We have space available.	*Temos espaço disponível.*	TEH-moos ehs-PAH-soo jeehs-poh-NEE-vehw.
We can provide all your meals, as well as your meeting needs.	*Podemos providenciar tudo que necessitar, inclusive a comida.*	Poh-DEH-moos proh-vee-DEHN-see-ahr TOO-doo keh neh-she-SEE-tahr, ee kloo-ZEH-veh aa koh-MEE-dah.

GUEST

That's good. We'd like...for each day.	*Ótimo. Gostaríamos de...para cada dia.*	OH-chee-moo. Gohs-tah-REE-ah-moos jee...PAH-rah KAH-dah JEE-ah.
• a continental breakfast	• *café da manhã, estilo continental*	• kah-FEH dah mahn-YAHN, ehs-CHEE-lo kohn-chee-nehn-TAW
• coffee breaks	• *intervalos com café*	• een-tehr-VAH-loo kohn kah-FEH
• a working lunch	• *almoço enquanto trabalhamos*	• aw-MOH-soh ehn-KWAN-too trah-bahl-YAA-moos
• snacks	• *lanches*	• LAHN-shees
• a cocktail reception	• *uma recepçaô com coquetel*	• oo-nah reh-sehp-sown kohn kohk-TEWL
• dinner	• *jantar*	• zhah-TAHR
Also, we'll require...for the meeting room.	*Também queremos...na sala de reunião.*	Tahm-BEHN keh-RAY-moos...nah SAH-lah jee he-oo-nee-OWN.
• a VCR with a large-screen monitor	• *um VCR com uma televisão de tela grande*	• oon VCR kohn OO-mah teh-lay-vee-ZOWN jee TEH-laa GRAHN-jee
• an overhead projector with transparencies and markers	• *um projetor para transparências e marcadores*	• Ooon proh-zay-TOHR PAH-rah trahns-pah-RAYN-see-ahs ee mahr-kah-DOH-rehs.

• a chalkboard	• *uma lousa*	• OO-mah LOH-zhah
• a flip chart	• *um mapa*	• oon MAH-pah
• a slide projector	• *um projetor de slides*	• oon proh-jay-TOHR jee slay-jees
• a computer with a large-screen monitor	• *um computador com o monitor de tela grande*	• oon kohm-poo-tah-DOHR kohn oo moh-nee-TOHR jee TEH-lah GRAHN-jee
And please be sure to provide…	*E, por favor, providencie…*	Eh, poor fah-VOHR, proh-vee-DEHN-see-yeh…
• water.	• *água.*	• AH-gwah.
• pads with pencils.	• *pranchetas com lápis.*	• phran-SHAY-taas kohn LAH-pees.
• ashtrays.	• *cinzeiros.*	• seen-ZAY-roos.

EMPLOYEE

Let's decide on what time you'd like everything, and we'll be all set.	*Vamos marcar a hora que você quiser, para estar pronto no horário.*	VAH-moos mahr-KAHRah OH-rah keh voh-SAY kee-ZEHR, PAH-rah ehs-TAHR PROHN-too noh oh-RAH-ryoo.

GUEST

Okay. How will the room be set up?	*Muito bem. Como estará arrumada a sala?*	MWEE-too behn. KOH-moo ehs-tah-RAH ah-hoo-MAH-dah aa SAH-lah?

EMPLOYEE

We can set up the room…	*Poderemos arrumar a sala…*	POH-day-REH-moos ah-hoo-MAHR aa SAH-lah…
• theater style.	• *como um teatro.*	• KOH-moo oon teh-AH-troo.
• in a square.	• *quadrada.*	• kwah-DRAH-dah.
• horseshoe ("U") style.	• *em "U."*	• ehn "U" (oo).
• classroom style.	• *como uma sala de aula.*	• KOH-moo OO-manh SAH-lah jee OW-lah.

• boardroom style.	• *em volta da sala.*	• ehn VOHL-tah dah SAH-lah.
We're looking forward to having your group here.	*Estamos ansiosos por ter o seu grupo aqui.*	Ehs-TAH-moos ahn-see-OH-zoos poor tehr oo say-oo GROO-poo AH-kee.

B. AT THE MEETING

ATTENDANT

I'm _____, the meeting-room attendant.	*Sou _____, o garçon da reunião.*	SOH-oo _____, oo gahr-SOWN dah he-oo-nee-OWN.
How is everything?	*Como está tudo?*	KOH-moo ehs-TAH TOO-doo?

GUEST

Everything is fine, thank you.	*Tudo está bem, obrigado/a.*	TOO-doh ehs-TAH behn, oh-bree-GAH-doo/ah.
We need…	*Necessitamos…*	Neh-she-see-TAH-moos…
• more chairs.	• *mais cadeiras.*	• mahys kah-DAY-rahs.
• more coffee.	• *mais café.*	• mahys kah-FEH.
• the ashtrays emptied.	• *os cinzeiros limpos.*	• oos seen-ZAY-roos LEEM-poos.
• more water.	• *mais água.*	• mahys AH-gwah.

ATTENDANT

I'll take care of it right away.	*Providenciarei em seguida.*	Proh-vee-dehn-see-ah-RAY ehn she-GEE-dah.
Is everything else satisfactory?	*Está tudo satisfatório?*	Ehs-TAH TOO-doo sah-chees-fah-TOH-ree-oo?

GUEST

It's quite nice, but the room…	*Está tudo ótimo, mas a sala…*	Ehs-TAH TOO-doh OH-chee-moo, mahs ah SAH-lah…
• needs more light.	• *necessita mais luz.*	• neh-seh-SEE-tah mahys looz.

• is too bright.	• *está muito clara.*	• ehs-TAH MWEE-too KLAH-rah.
• needs more ventilation.	• *necessita mais ventilação.*	• neh-seh-SEE-tah mahys vehn-chee-lah-SOWN.
• is too hot (cold).	• *está muito quente (fria).*	• ehs-TAH MWEE-too KEHN-chee (FREE-ah).
• is a little noisy.	• *têm um pouco de barulho.*	• tehn oon POH-koo jee bah-ROOL-yoo.
• is crowded.	• *está muito cheia.*	• ehs-TAH MWEE-too SHAY-yah.
Can you take care of it?	*Você pode resolver isto?*	Voh-SAY POH-jee hay-zohl-VEHR EEZ-too?
Can we get another room?	*Podemos ir para outra sala?*	Poh-DEH-moos eer PAH-rah OH-traa SAH-lah?

ATTENDANT

Let me see what we can do.	*Deixe-me ver o que posso fazer.*	Day-SHEH-mee vehr oo keh POH-soo fah-ZEHR.

C. CATERING TO BUSINESS GUESTS

CONCIERGE

How may I help you?	*Posso ajudá-lo?*	POH-soo ah-zhoo-DAH-loo?

GUEST

Where is breakfast for the _____ group?	*Onde está o café da manhã para o grupo _____?*	OHN-jee ehs-TAH oo kah-FEH dah mahn-YAHN PAH-rah oo GROO-poo _____?
Where is the exhibits hall?	*Onde está a sala de exposiçaõ?*	OHN-jee ehs-TAH ah SAH-lah jee ehs-poo-see-SOWN?

CONCIERGE

There's a buffet set up outside your meeting room.	*O buffet está arrumado fora da sala dereunião.*	Oo boo-fey ehs-TAH ah-hoo-MAH-hoo-MAH-hoo-MAH-FOH-rah dah SAH-lah jee he-oo-nee-OWN.

Just down the hall.	*No fim do corredor.*	Noh feem doh koh-heh-DOHR.
In the dining room.	*Na sala de jantar.*	Nah SAH-lah jee zhahn-TAHR.

GUEST

Thank you.	*Obrigado/da.*	Oh-bree-GAH-doo/dah.
I need...	*Eu necessito...*	AY-oo neh-seh-SEE-too...
• a fax sent.	• *mandar um fax.*	• mahn-DAHR oon fax.
• some typing done.	• *alguns papéis datilografados.*	• ahl-GOONS pah-PAY-eez dah-chee-loh-grah-FAH-doos.
• a hookup to the Internet.	• *um cabo para "Internet."*	• Oon KAH-boo PAH-rah "Internet."
• a computer.	• *um computador.*	• oon kom-poo-tah-DOHR.
• a package sent overnight.	• *uma entrega rápida.*	• OO-mahn ehn-TRAY-gah HAH-pee-daa.
• courier service.	• *serviço de courrier.*	• sehr-VEE-soo jee koo-ree-ehr.
• some letters mailed.	• *colocar algumas cartas no correio.*	• koh-loh-KAHR ahl-GOO-mahns KAHR-tahs noh koh-HAY-yoo.
• some copies made.	• *algumas fotocópias.*	• ahl-GOO-mahns foh-toh-KOO-pee-ahs.

CONCIERGE

I'll take care of that right away.	*Cuidarei disto em seguida.*	Kwee-dah-RAY JEES-too ehn she-GWEE-dah.

GUEST

Later, I'd like to host a small reception.	*Mais tarde, gostaria de fazer uma pequena recepção.*	Mahys TAHR-jee, gohs-tah-REE-ah jee fah-ZEHR OO-mah peh-KEH-nah heh-seh-pee-SAWN.

Can you arrange that?	*Poderia providenciar isto?*	Poh-deh-REE-ah proh-vee-dehn-SEE-ahr EHS-too?
CONCIERGE		
Certainly. What would you like?	*Certamente. O que você gostaria?*	Sehr-tah-MEHN-chee. Oo keh voh-SAY gohs-tah-REE-ah?
GUEST		
We need a full bar and some hors d'oeuvres.	*Necessito bebidas e alguns tira-gôstos.*	Neh-she-SEE-too beh-BEE-dahs eh ahl-GOONS TEE-rah GOHS-toos.
Make sure there are plenty of chilled shrimp.	*Verifique se têm bastante coquetel de camarão.*	Veh-ree-FEE-kee see tehn bahs-THAN-chee kohk-TEH-oo jee kah-mah-ROWN.
Lots of champagne, please.	*Muita champagne, por favor.*	MWEE-taa sham-pah-gnee, poor fah-VOHR.
CONCIERGE		
I'll have Room Service put together a proposal right away.	*Farei o serviço de quarto organize isto.*	FAH-ray oo sehr-vee-soo jee KWAHR-too ohr-gah-nee-ZEE ees-too.

7. Checking Out

GUEST		
At what time is checkout?	*A que horas devo fechar a conta?*	Ah keh OH-rahs JEE-voh fay-CHAHR ah KOHN-tah?
FRONT DESK CLERK		
Checkout is at…	*Deve fechar a conta às…*	JEE-vee fay-CHAHR ah KOHN-tah ahs…
• 10 A.M.	• *dez horas da manhã.*	• days OH-rahs dah mahn-YAHN.
• noon.	• *ao meio-dia.*	• aow MAY-yoo-JEE-ah.
• 3 P.M.	• *às três horas da tarde.*	• ahs trays OH-rahs dah TAHR-jee.

You may audit your bill on channel _____ on your television.	*Você pode examiner sua conta no canal _____ de sua televisão.*	Voh-SAY POH-jee eh-zah-mee-NAHR SOO-ah KOHN-tahnoo kah-NAWL _____ jee SOO-ah teh-lay-vee-ZOWN.
We provide an express checkout service.	*Providenciaremos sua conta bem rápido.*	Proh-vee-dehn-see-ah-RAY-moos SOO-ah KOHN-tah behn HAH-pee-doo.
Your bill will be left outside your door the night before you check out.	*Sua conta vai estar na sua porta na noite anterior de sua saída.*	SOO-ah KOHN-tah vahy esh-TAHR nah SOO-ah POHR-tah nah NOY-chee ahn-the-ree-OHR deh SOO-ah sah-EE-dah.
If you're satisfied with your bill, simply sign it,	*Se você concorda com a conta, assine*	See voh-SAY kohn-KOHR-dah kohn aa KOHN-tah, ah-SEE-nee
and leave your key in your room.	*e deixe a chave em seu quarto.*	eh DAY-sheh ah SHAH-vee ehn SAY-oo KWAHR-too.
Any late charges, such as breakfast or minibar, will be added automatically.	*Qualquer gasto, que tiver do café da manhã ou do mini-bar, será adicionado automaticamente.*	Kwow-KEHR GAHS-too, keh chee-VEHR doo kah-FEH dah mahn-YAHN oo mee-nee barh, she-RAH ah-jee-see-oh-NAH-doo ow-toh-mahn-chee-kah-MEHN-chee.
GUEST		
I'd like to check out, please.	*Gostaria de fechar minha conta, por favor.*	Gohs-tah-REE-ah jee fay-SHAHRMEE-yahn KOHN-tah, poor fah-VOHR.
CLERK		
May I have your luggage brought down?	*Posso trazer sua bagagem para cai?*	POH-soo trah-ZEHR SOO-ah bah-GAH-zhehn PAH-rah kahy?
GUEST		
Yes, please.	*Sim, por favor.*	Seen, poor fah-VOHR.
No, I brought (will bring) it myself.	*Não, eu mesmo trago.*	Nown, AY-oo MAYZ-moo TRAH-goo.

CLERK

How was everything?	*Como estava tudo?*	KOH-moo ehs-TAH-vah TOO-doo?

GUEST

It was very nice, thank you.	*Estava ótimo, obrigado/da.*	Ehs-TAH-vah OH-chee-moo, oh-bree-GAH-doo/dah.
I want to speak with the manager.	*Eu quero falar com o gerente.*	AY-oo KEH-roo fah-LAHR kohn oo zheh-RAYN-chee.

CLERK

Certainly. The manager on duty is _____. One moment, please.	*Certamente. O gerente para este caso é _____. Um momento, por favor.*	Sehr-tah-MEHN-chee. Oo zheh-RAYN-chee PAH-rah ehs-chee KAH-soo eh _____. Oon moh-MEHN-too, poor fah-VOHR.

GUEST

Our experience was…	*Nossa experiência foi…*	Noh-sah ehs-peh-ree-EHN-see-ah foh-ee…
• good.	• *ótima.*	• OH-chee-maa.
• excellent.	• *excelente.*	• eh-seh-LEHN-chee.
• poor.	• *boa.*	• boh-ah.
• very bad.	• *péssima.*	• PAY-see-mah.

MANAGER ON DUTY

That's nice to hear.	*É bom escutar isto.*	Eh bohn ehs-koo-TAHR ehs-too.
I'm sorry to hear that.*	*Lamento escutar isto.*	Lah-mehn-too ehs-koo-TAHR ehs-too.
Thank you. Please come again.	*Muito obrigado/a. Por favor volte outra vez.*	MWEE-too oh-bree-GAH-doo/ah. Poor fah-VOHR VOHL-chee oot-rah vays.

*Please refer to "Guest Complaints in the Hotel" on page 375 for more on handling dissatisfied clients.

SECTION H

SPANISH

1. The Bare Essentials

A. THE SPANISH ALPHABET

a	ah	*ñ*	EH-nyeh
b	beh	*o*	oh
c	seh	*p*	peh
d	deh	*q*	koo
e	eh	*r*	EH-reh
f	EH-feh	*s*	EH-seh
g	heh	*t*	tehh
h	AH-cheh	*u*	oo
i	ee	*v*	veh
j	HOH-tah	*w*	doh-bleh-VEH
k	kah	*x*	EH-kees
l	EH-leh	*y*	ee-gree-EH-gah
m	EH-meh	*z*	SEH-tah
n	EH-neh		

B. PRONUNCIATION CHART

VOWELS

SPANISH SOUND	APPROXIMATE SOUND IN ENGLISH	EXAMPLE
a	(father)	*trabajar* (to work)
e	(ace, but cut off sharply)	*señor* (mister)
i	(fee)	*día* (day)
o	(note)	*pistola* (pistol)
u	(rule)	*mucho* (much)
y	(feet)	*y* (and) [only a vowel when standing alone]

DIPHTHONGS

SPANISH SOUND	APPROXIMATE SOUND IN ENGLISH	EXAMPLE
ai/ay	(aisle)	*bailar* (to dance) *hay* (there is, there are)
au	(now)	*auto* (car)
ei	(may)	*peine* (comb)
ia	(yarn)	*gracias* (thanks)
ie	(yet)	*siempre* (always)
io	(yodel)	*adiós* (bye)
iu	(you)	*ciudad* (city)
oi/oy	(oy)	*estoy* (I am)
ua	(wand)	*cuando* (when)
ue	(wet)	*bueno* (good)
ui/uy	(sweet)	*cuidado* (care) *muy* (very)

CONSONANTS

The letters *k* and *w* appear in Spanish in foreign words like *kilowatt, kilometer*. In some countries, the *k* is spelled with the Spanish equivalent, *qu: quilómetro*. The *w* in Spanish sounds like an English *v: kilowatt*.

SPANISH SOUND	APPROXIMATE SOUND IN ENGLISH	EXAMPLE
l/m/n/p/s/t	similar to English	
b	at the beginning of a word or after *m*, similar to English	*bueno* (good)
	elsewhere, similar to English, but softer, allowing air to pass between lips, like *v*	*cabeza* (head)
*c** (before *e/i*)	s (certain)	*cena* (dinner)
d	similar to English, but softer, allowing air to pass between lips, like th (the)	*verdad* (truth)
	after *n*, as in English: d (do)	*corriendo* (running)
c (before *a/o/u*)	k (catch)	*como* (how)
cc	cks (accent)	*acción* (action)

* In some regions of Latin America: *s* (vision).

ch	ch (church)	*mucho* (much)
g (before *a/o/u*)	hard g (go)	*gasolina* (gas)
g (before *e/i*)	hard h (he)	*gente* (people)
h	always silent	*alcohol* (alcohol)
j	hard h (he)	*jefe* (boss)
ll	In Latin America: * y (yet); in Spain: lli (million)	*llamar* (to call)
ñ	ny (canyon)	*niño* (child)
qu	k (kite)	*que* (that)
r	in middle of word, single trill (throw)	*pero* (but)

C. THE SPANISH LANGUAGE

Word Order The basic word order of Spanish is the same as in English: subject-verb-object:

El mesero	*lleva*	*la pizza.*	The waiter	brings	the pizza.
S	V	O	S	V	O

Nouns and Adjectives All nouns in Spanish have gender. *El* (the) and *un* (a/an) are used with masculine nouns, and *la* and *una* are used with feminine nouns. To form the plural, simply add an *-s* or an *-es* to the singular form. *Los* is the article used with plural masculine nouns, and *las* is used with plural feminine nouns. Adjectives in Spanish change to agree with the nouns they modify. Adjective endings follow the same pattern as with nouns: *el niño curioso* (the curious boy); *la niña curiosa* (the curious girl); *los niños curiosos* (the curious boys); and *las niñas curiosas* (the curious girls). Notice that most adjectives in Spanish come after the nouns they modify.

Verbs Spanish verbs undergo various changes to indicate subject, tense, or mood. *El mesero lleva la pizza.* (The waiter brings the pizza.) *Llevamos una botella.* (We bring a bottle.) *Llevaban unas flores.* (They were bringing some flowers.) *Llevaría el queso.*

* In certain Latin American countries, initial *ll* is pronounced with more friction, like *s* in vision, or *j* in judge.

(I would bring the cheese.) *¡Lleveme una cerveza!* (Bring me a beer!) *Señor Martinez llevará el dinero.* (Mr. Martinez will bring the money.)

Theses simple rules will help you communicate on a basic level in Spanish. The phrases and sentences in these Spanish sections are written so you can use them as printed. All you have to do is familiarize yourself with them, and you'll be ready to go. *¡Buena suerte!*

D. THE SPANISH CULTURE

Customs among Spanish speakers vary considerably. Generally more dressed up than Americans, the Spanish will tend toward conservative European fashions, and the Latin Americans toward either European or American styles. Respect and courtesy rank high with Spanish and Latin American guests, so service personnel are expected to show the utmost of traditional courtesy. When someone sneezes, there may or may not be a response expected, depending on the culture, so as a service person you would do best to ignore it. Gestures vary widely, but most will call the server with a raised index finger. It's important to remember that signaling someone in a service position isn't considered rude in most countries, so don't be offended when international guests do this.

Tipping customs vary widely. If you follow a policy of adding a service charge to international guests' bills, be sure this is clear to the Spanish speakers. Some might otherwise tip 15 percent or more, which would unfairly increase the cost of their meal. On the other hand, not adding a service charge to the check could result in a meager tip.

2. Useful Expressions

A. GENERAL

Hello.	*Hola.*	OH-lah.
Good-bye.	*Adiós.*	Ah-dee-OHS.

Yes.	*Sí.*	SEE.
No.	*No.*	NOH.
Maybe.	*Puede ser.*	PWEH-deh sehr.
Please.	*Por favor.*	Pohr fah-VOHR.
Thank you (very much).	*Gracias (Muchas gracias).*	GRAH-see-ahs (MOO-chahs GRAH-see-ahs).
You're welcome.	*De nada.*	Deh NAH-dah.
Excuse me.	*Disculpe.*	Dee-SKOOL-peh.
I beg your pardon.	*Le ruego me disculpe.*	Leh RWEH-goh meh dee-SKOOL-peh.
I'm sorry.	*Lo siento.*	Loh SEEHN-toh.
One moment, please.	*Un momento, por favor.*	Oon moh-MEHN-toh, pohr fah-VOHR.
Do you speak English?	*¿Habla inglés?*	¿Ah-blah een-GLEHS?
• Yes, I do.	• *Sí, hablo inglés.*	• SEEM, ah-bloh een-GLEHS.
• No, I don't.	• *No, no hablo inglés.*	• NOH, noh AH-bloh eenh-GLEHS.
• A little.	• *Un poquito.*	• Oon poh-KEEH-toh.
• No, not at all.	• *No, en absoluto.*	• NOH, ehn ahb-soh-LOO-toh.
That's okay.	*Está bien.*	Ehs-TAH BYEHN.
It doesn't matter.	*No importa.*	Noh eem-POHR-tah.
I don't speak Spanish.	*No hablo español.*	Noh AH-bloh ehs-pah-NYOHL.
I can speak a little.	*Puedo hablar un poquito.*	PWEH-doh ah-BLAHR oon poh-KEEH-toh.
I understand a little.	*Entiendo un poquito.*	Ehn-TYEHN-doh oon poh-KEE-toh.
I don't understand.	*No entiendo.*	Noh ehn-TYEHN-doh.
Please speak more slowly.	*Por favor, hable más despacio.*	Pohr fah-VOHR, AH-bleh MAHS deh-SPAH-syoh.
Would you repeat that, please?	*¿Podría repetir eso, por favor?*	¿Poh-DREE-ah reh-peh-TEER EH-soh, pohr fah-VOHR?

Yes, sir/ma'am.	*Sí señor/a.*	SEEH seh-NYORH/ah.
No problem.	*No hay problema.*	Noh ahy proh-BLEH-mah.
It's my pleasure.	*Es un placer.*	Ehs OON plah-SEHR.

B. NEEDS

I'd like _____.	*Me gustaría _____.*	Meh goo-stah-REE-ah _____.
I need _____.	*Necesito _____.*	Neh-seh-SEEH-toh _____.
What would you like?	*¿Qué le gustaría?*	¿KEH leh goo-stah-REE-ah?
Please bring me _____.	*Por favor tráigame _____.*	Pohr fah-VOHR TRAHY-gah-meh _____.
I'm looking for _____.	*Estoy buscando _____.*	Ehs-TOYH boohs-KAHN-doh _____.
I'm hungry.	*Tengo hambre.*	TEHN-goh AHM-breh.
I'm thirsty.	*Tengo sed.*	TEHN-goh SEHD.
It's important.	*Es importante.*	Ehs eem-pohr-TAHN-teh.
It's urgent.	*Es urgente.*	Ehs oor-HEHN-teh.

C. QUESTION WORDS

How?	*¿Cómo?*	¿KOH-moh?
How much?	*¿Cuánto?*	¿KWAHN-toh?
How many?	*¿Cuántos?*	¿KWAHN-tohs?
Which?	*¿Cuál?*	¿KWAHL?
What?	*¿Qué?*	¿KEH?
What kind of?	*¿Qué tipo de?*	¿KEH TEE-poh deh?
Who?	*¿Quién?*	¿KYEHN?
Where?	*¿Dónde?*	¿DOHN-deh?
When?	*¿Cuándo?*	¿KWAHN-doh?
What does this mean?	*¿Qué significa ésto?*	¿KEH seeg-nye-FEE-kah EHS-toh?

What does that mean?	*¿Qué significa éso?*	¿KEH seeg-nyee-FEE-kah EH-soh?
How do you say _____ in Spanish?	*¿Cómo se dice _____ en español?*	¿KOH-moh seh DEE-seh _____ ehn eh-spah-NYOHL?

D. COLORS

black	*negro*	NEH-groh
blue	*azul*	AH-sool
brown	*marrón*	mah-RROHN
gold	*dorado*	doh-RAH-doh
gray	*gris*	GREES
green	*verde*	VEHR-deh
orange	*naranja*	nah-RAHN-hah
pink	*rosa*	ROH-sah
purple	*púrpura*	POOR-poo-rah
red	*rojo*	ROH-hoh
silver	*plateado*	plah-TEH-ah-doh
violet	*violeta*	vee-oh-LEH-tah
white	*blanco*	BLAHN-koh
yellow	*amarillo*	ah-mah-REE-yoh

E. CARDINAL NUMBERS

1	*uno*	OO-noh
2	*dos*	DOHS
3	*tres*	TREHS
4	*cuatro*	KWAH-troh
5	*cinco*	SYEHN-koh
6	*seis*	SEH-ees
7	*siete*	SYEH-teh
8	*ocho*	OH-choh
9	*nueve*	NWEH-veh
10	*diez*	DYEHS

11	*once*	OHN-seh
12	*doce*	DOH-seh
13	*trece*	TREH-seh
14	*catorce*	kah-TOHR-seh
15	*quince*	KEEN-seh
16	*dieciséis*	dyeh-see-SEH-ees
17	*diecisiete*	dyeh-see-SYEH-teh
18	*dieciocho*	dyeh-see-OH-choh
19	*diecinueve*	dyeh-see-NWEH-veh
20	*veinte*	VEYNH-teh
21	*veintiuno*	veynh-tee-OO-noh
22	*veintidós*	veyhn-tee-DOHS
23	*veintitrés*	veyhn-tee-TREHS
24	*veinticuatro*	veyhn-tee-KWAH-troh
25	*veinticinco*	veyhn-tee-SEEN-koh
26	*veintiséis*	veyhn-tee-SEH-ees
27	*veintisiete*	veyhn-tee-SYEH-teh
28	*veintiocho*	veyhn-tee-OH-choh
29	*veintinueve*	veyhn-tee-NWEH-veh
30	*treinta*	TREYNH-tah
31	*treinta y uno*	TREYNH-tah eeh OO-noh
32	*treinta y dos*	TREYNH-tah eeh DOHS
40	*cuarenta*	kwah-REHN-tah
50	*cincuenta*	seen-KWEHN-tah
60	*sesenta*	seh-SEHN-tah
70	*setenta*	seh-TEHN-tah
80	*ochenta*	oh-CHEHN-tah
90	*noventa*	noh-VEHN-tah
100	*cien*	SYEHN
101	*cientouno*	SYEHN-toh-OO-noh
102	*ciento dos*	SYEHN-toh DOHS

110	*ciento diez*	SYEHN-toh DYEHS
120	*ciento veinte*	SYEHN-toh VEYHN-teh
200	*doscientos*	doh-SYEHN-tohs
210	*doscientos diez*	doh-SYEHN-tohs DYEHS
300	*trescientos*	treh-SYEHN-tohs
400	*cuatrocientos*	kwah-troh-SYEHN-tohs
500	*quinientos*	kee-NYEHN-tohs
600	*seiscientos*	say-SYEHN-tohs
700	*setecientos*	seh-teh-SYEHN-tohs
800	*ochocientos*	oh-choh-SYEHN-tohs
900	*novecientos*	noh-veh-SYEHN-tohs
1,000	*mil*	MEEL
1,100	*mil cien*	meel SYEHN
1,200	*mil doscientos*	meel doh-SYEHN-tohs
2,000	*dos mil*	dohs MEEL
10,000	*diez mil*	dyehs MEEL
50,000	*cincuenta mil*	seehn-KWEHN-tah MEEL
100,000	*cien mil*	syehn MEEL
1,000,000	*un millón*	oohn mee-LYOHN
1,000,000,000	*un billón*	oohn bee-LYHON

F. ORDINAL NUMBERS

first	*primero*	pree-MEH-roh
second	*segundo*	seh-GOON-doh
third	*tercero*	tehr-SEH-roh
fourth	*cuarto*	KWAHR-toh
fifth	*quinto*	KEEHN-toh
sixth	*sexto*	SEKS-toh
seventh	*séptimo*	SEP-tee-moh
eighth	*octavo*	ohk-TAH-voh

ninth	*noveno*	noh-VEH-noh
tenth	*décimo*	DEH-see-moh
eleventh	*onceavo*	ohn-seh-AH-voh
twelfth	*doceavo*	doh-seh-AH-voh
thirteenth	*treceavo*	treh-seh-AH-voh
fourteenth	*catorceavo*	kah-tohr-seh-AH-voh
fifteenth	*quinceavo*	keen-seh-AH-voh
sixteenth	*dieciseisavo*	dyeh-see-seyhs-AH-voh
seventeenth	*diecisieteavo*	dyeh-see-SYEH-teh-ah-voh
eighteenth	*dieciochouvo*	dyeh-see-OH-choh-AH-voh
nineteenth	*diecinueveavo*	dyeh-see-NWEH-veh-ah-voh
twentieth	*vigésimo*	vee-HEH-see-moh
twenty-first	*vigésimo primero*	vee-HEH-see-moh pree-MEH-roh
twenty-second	*vigésimo segundo*	vee-HEH-see-moh seh-GOON-doh
thirtieth	*trigésimo*	tree-HEH-see-moh
fortieth	*cuadragésimo*	kwah-drah-HEH-see-moh
fiftieth	*quincuagésimo*	keen-kwah-HEH-see-moh
sixtieth	*sexagésimo*	sek-sah-HEH-see-moh
seventieth	*septuagésimo*	sehp-twah-HEH-see-moh
eightieth	*octagésimo*	ohk-tah-HEH-see-moh
ninetieth	*nonagésimo*	noh-nah-HEH-see-moh
hundredth	*centésimo*	sehn-TEH-see-moh
thousandth	*milésimo*	mee-LEH-see-moh

G. TIME OF DAY

1:00	*la una*	lah OO-nah
2:00	*las dos*	lahs DOHS

3:00	*las tres*	lahs TREHS
4:00	*las cuatro*	lahs KWAH-troh
5:00	*las cinco*	lahs SEEN-koh
6:00	*las seis*	lahs SEYHS
7:00	*las siete*	lahs SYEH-teh
8:00	*las ocho*	lahs OH-choh
9:00	*las nueve*	lahs NWEH-veh
10:00	*las diez*	lahs DYEHS
11:00	*las once*	lahs OHN-seh
12:00	*las doce*	lahs DOH-seh
1:00 A.M.	*la una de la mañana*	lah OO-nah deh lah mah-NYAH-nah
3:00 P.M.	*las tres de la tarde*	lahs TREHS deh lah-TAHR-deh
noon	*mediodía*	meh-dyoh-DEE-ah
midnight	*medianoche*	meh-dyah-NOH-cheh
1:15	*una y cuarto*	OO-nah eeh KWAHR-toh
12:45	*una menos cuarto*	OO-nah MEH-nohs KWAHR-toh
1:30	*una y media*	OO-nah eeh MEH-dyah
7:05	*siete y cinco*	SYEH-teh ee SEEN-koh
4:55	*cinco menos cinco*	SEEN-koh MEH-nohs SEEN-koh

H. DAYS OF THE WEEK

Monday	*lunes*	LOO-nehs
Tuesday	*martes*	MAHR-tehs
Wednesday	*miércoles*	MYEHR-koh-lehs
Thursday	*jueves*	HWEH-vehs
Friday	*viernes*	VYEHR-nehs
Saturday	*sábado*	SAH-bah-doh
Sunday	*domingo*	doh-MEEN-goh

I. MONTHS

January	*enero*	eh-NEH-roh
February	*febrero*	feh-BREH-roh
March	*marzo*	MAHR-soh
April	*abril*	ah-BREEL
May	*mayo*	MAH-yoh
June	*junio*	HOO-nyoh
July	*julio*	HOO-lyoh
August	*agosto*	ah-GOHS-toh
September	*septiembre*	sehp-TYEHM-breh
October	*octubre*	okh-TOO-breh
November	*noviembre*	noh-VYEHM-breh
December	*diciembre*	dee-SYEHM-breh

J. DATES

1998	*mil novecientos noventa y ocho*	MEEL noh-veh-SYEHN-tohs noh-VEHN-tah ee OH-choh
1999	*mil novecientos noventa y nueve*	MEEL noh-veh-SYEHN-tohs noh-VEHN-tah ee NWEH-veh
2000	*dos mil*	dohs MEEL
2001	*dos mil uno*	dohs MEEL OO-noh
2002	*dos mil dos*	dohs MEEL DOHS
2003	*dos mil tres*	dohs MEEL TREHS
2004	*dos mil cuatro*	dohs MEEL KWAH-troh
2005	*dos mil cinco*	dohs MEEL SEEN-koh
Today is Thursday, September 22.	*Hoy es jueves, veintidós de septiembre.*	OY ehs HWEH-vehs, veyhn-tee-DOHS deh sehp-TYEHM-breh.

Yesterday was Wednesday, September 21.	*Ayer fue miércoles, veintiuno de septiembre.*	Ah-YEHR FOOEH meeh-EHR-koh-lehs, veyhn-tee-OO-noh deh sehp-TYEHM-breh.
The day before yesterday was Tuesday, September 20.	*El día anterior a ayer fue martes, veinte de septiembre.*	Ehl DEE-ah anh-teh-ree-OHR ah ah-YEHR FWEH MAHR-tehs, VEYN-teh deh sehp-TYEM-breh.
Tomorrow is Friday, September 23.	*Mañana es viernes, veintitrés de septiembre.*	Mah-NYAH-nah ehs VYEHR-nehs, veyn-tee-TREHS deh sehp-TYEHM-breh.
The day after tomorrow is Saturday, September 24.	*Pasado mañana es sábado, veinticuatro de septiembre.*	Pah-SAH-doh mah-NYAH-nah ehs SAH-bah-doh, veyn-tee-KWAH-troh deh sehp-TYEHM-breh.
Next Friday is September 30.	*El próximo viernes es treinta de septiembre.*	Ehl PROHK-see-moh VYER-nehs ehs TREYN-tah deh sehp-TYEM-breh.
Last Friday was September 16.	*El viernes pasado fue dieciseis de septiembre.*	Ehl VYER-nehs pah-SAH-doh FWEH dyes-ee-SEHS deh sehp-TYEM-breh.

K. MEASUREMENTS: DISTANCE

inch	*pulgada*	pool-GAH-dah
foot	*pie*	PYEH
yard	*yarda*	YAHR-dah
mile	*milla*	MEE-yah
millimeter	*milímetro*	mee-LEE-meh-troh
meter	*metro*	MEH-troh
kilometer	*kilómetro*	kee-LOH-meh-troh

3. Common Hospitality Scenarios

A. GREETINGS AND INTRODUCTIONS

GREETING THE GUEST

EMPLOYEE

Good morning,…	***Buenos días,…***	BWEH-nohs DYAHS,…
• Mr. ____.	***• Señor ____.***	• Seh-NYOHR ____.
• Mrs. ____.	***• Señora ____.***	• Seh-NYOH-rah ____.
• Miss ____.	***• Señorita ____.***	• Seh-nyoh-REE-tah ____.
• ladies and gentlemen.	***• damas y caballeros.***	• DAH-mahs ee kah-bah-YEH-rohs.
• everyone.	***• a todos.***	• ah TOH-dohs.
Good afternoon, Mr./Mrs. ____.	***Buenas tardes, Señor/a ____.***	BWEH-nahs TAHR-dehs, Seh-NYOHR/ah ____.
Good evening, Mr./Mrs. ____.	***Buenas noches, Señor/a ____.***	BWEH-nahs NOH-chehs, Seh-NYOHR/ah ____.
Hello, Mr. ____.	***Hola, Señor ____.***	OH-lah, Seh-NYOHR ____.

TIP! ••••

Most American employees are used to greeting guests jovially and asking them how they are. However, in any but the most informal settings, this behavior may actually be considered impolite. Asking guests how they are is stepping outside the bounds of your position and throws the burden onto the guest to answer you. Other cultures usually observe this principle to a much greater extent than we do.

Welcome to…	*Bienvenido a…*	Byen-veh-NEE-doh ah…
• the hotel.	• *el hotel.*	• ehl oh-TEHL.
• the restaurant.	• *el restaurante.*	• ehl rehs-tah-oo-RAHN-teh.
• our city.	• *nuestra ciudad.*	• NWEH-strah syoo-DAHD.
• the United States.	• *los Estados Unidos.*	• lohs Ehs-TAH-dohs Oo-NEE-dohs.
If there is anything I can do to make your stay more pleasant, please let me know.	*Si hay algo que yo pueda hacer para que su estancia sea más placentera, por favor déjenme saber.*	See ahy AHL-goh keh yoh PWEH-dah ah-SEHR PAH-rah keh SOO ehs-TAHN-seeah SEH-ah MAHS plah-sehn-TEH-rah, pohr FAH-vohr DEH-hehn-meh sah-BEHR.
May I…	*¿Podría yo…*	¿Poh-DREE-ah yoh…
• take your coat(s)?	• *llevar su(s) abrigo(s)?*	• yeh-VAHR soo(s) ah-BREE-goh(s)?
• carry your… for you?	• *cargar su… para usted?*	• kahr-GAHR soo… PAH-rah oo-STEHD?
• bags	• *bolsas*	• BOHL-sahs
• suitcase	• *maletas*	• mah-LEH-tahs
How are you today?	*¿Cómo está usted hoy?*	¿KOH-moh ehs-TAH ooh-STEHD oy?
GUEST		
I am…	*Estoy…*	Ehs-TOYH…
• fine, thank you.	• *bien, gracias.*	• BYEN, GRAH-syahs.
• okay.	• *O.K.*	• oh-KEHY.
• so-so.	• *más o menos.*	• MAHS oh MEH-nohs.
• very tired.	• *muy cansado(a).*	• MOOY-kahn-SAH-doh(dah).
I'm not feeling well.	*No me siento bien.*	Noh meh SYEHN-toh BYEHN.
And you?	*¿Y usted?*	¿Ee oo-STEHD?

INTRODUCTIONS

My name is _____.	*Mi nombre es _____.*	Mee NOHM-bre ehs _____.
I am your…	*Yo soy su…*	Yoh soy SOO…
• door attendant (doorman).	• *asistente de la puerta (portero).*	• ah-sees-TEHN-teh deh lah PWEHR-tah (pohr-TEH-roh).
• bell attendant (bellman).	• *paje del hotel (botones).*	• PAH-heh dehl oh-TEHL (boh-TOH-nehs).
• valet-parking attendant.	• *parqueador de autos.*	• pahr-kha-DOHR deh AOO-tohs.
• driver.	• *chofer.*	• choh-FEHR.
• captain.	• *capitán.*	• kah-pee-TAHN.
• concierge.	• *conserje.*	• kohn-SEHR-heh.
• room attendant.	• *asistente de habitación.*	• ah-sees-TEHN-teh deh ah-bee-tah-SYOHN.
• host.	• *anfitrión.*	• ahn-fee-tree-OHN.
• hostess.	• *anfitriona.*	• ahn-feeh-tree-OH-nah.
• manager.	• *gerente.*	• heh-REHN-teh.
• server (waiter/waitress).	• *mozo (camarero/camarera).*	• MOH-soh (kah-mah-REH-roh/kah-mah-REH-rah).

TIP! ••••

It is typical of American employees to introduce themselves to the guest. This practice allows the guest to call an employee by name when s/he needs something. This is not a common practice in other countries, however, so the international guest may simply ignore your introduction.

• activities director.	• *director de actividades.*	• dee-rek-TOHR deh ahk-tee-vee-DAH-dehs.
Mr. (Mrs., Miss) _____, **this is Mr.** (Mrs., Miss) _____, **the manager.**	***Señor*** *(Señora, Señorita)* _____, ***éste es el Señor*** *(Señora, Señorita)* _____, ***el (la) gerente.***	Seh-NYOHR (seh-NYOH-rah, seh-nyoh-REE-tah) _____, EHS-teh ehs ehl seh-NYOHR (seh-NYOH-rah, seh-nyoh-REE-tah) _____, ehl (lah) geh-REHN-teh.
May I introduce our manager, Mr. (Mrs., Miss) _____?	_____, ***¿Puedo presentarle al nuestrogerente, al Señor (Señora, Señorita) _____?***	¿PWEH-doh preh-sehn-TAHR-leh ahl NWEHS-troh heh-REHN-teh, ahl seh-NYOHR (seh-NYOH-rah, seh-nyoh-REE-tah) _____?

B. RESERVATIONS

HOTEL RESERVATIONS

OPERATOR

Good morning (afternoon, evening), _____ **Hotel.**	***Buenos días*** *(Buenas tardes, Buenas noches)* ***Hotel*** _____.	BWEH-nohs DYAHS (BWEH-nahs TAHR-dehs, BWEH-nahs NOH-chehs), oh-TEHL _____.
How may I direct your call?	***¿A dónde puedo transferir su llamada?***	¿Ah DOHN-deh poo-EH-doh tranhs-FEH-reer SOO yah-MAH-dah?

GUEST

Hello. Do you speak Spanish?	***Hola. ¿Usted habla español?***	OH-lah. ¿Oos-TEHD AH-blah ehs-pah-NYOHL?

OPERATOR

One moment, please.	***Un momento, por favor.***	Oon moh-MEHN-toh, pohr fah-VOHR.

English	Spanish	Pronunciation
I'll connect you with a bilingual operator.	*Le conectaré con un telefonista bilingüe.*	Leh koh-nehk-tah-REH kohn oon teh-leh-foh-NEE-stah bee-LEEN-gweh.
I have a book here to help me.	*Tengo aquí un libro para orientarme.*	TEHN-goh ah-KEE oon LEE-broh PAH-rah oh-ryehn-TAHR-meh.
Please speak slowly.	*Por favor, hable despacio.*	Pohr fah-VOHR, AH-bleh dehs-PAH-syoh.
GUEST		
I would like to make a reservation, please.	*Me gustaría hacer una reservación, por favor.*	Meh goos-tah-REE-ah ah-SEHR OO-nah reh-sehr-vah-SYOHN, pohr fah-VOHR.
OPERATOR		
For a room or for one of the restaurants?	*¿Para una habitación o para uno de los restaurantes?*	¿Pah-rah OO-nah ah-bee-tah-SYOHN oh pah-rah OO-noh deh lohs rehs-tah-oo-RAHN-tehs?
GUEST		
For a room, please.	*Para una habitación, por favor.*	PAH-rah OO-nah ah-bee-tah-SYOHN, pohr fah-VOHR.
For the ____ Restaurant, please.	*Para el restaurante ____, por favor.*	PAH-rah ehl rehs-tahoo-RAHN-teh ____, pohr fah-VOHR.
OPERATOR		
One moment, please.	*Un momento, por favor.*	Oon moh-MEHN-toh, pohr fah-VOHR.
I will direct your call to Reservations.	*Transferiré su llamada a Reservaciones.*	Trahns-feh-ree-REH soo yah-MAH-dah ah RE-sehr-vah-SYOH-nehs.
I will direct your call to the restaurant.	*Transferiré su llamada al restaurante.*	Trahns-feh-ree-REH soo yah-MAH-dah ahl rehs-tahoo-RAHN-teh.

CLERK

Hello. This is Reservations.	*Hola. Ésto es Reservaciones.*	OH-lah. EHS-toh ehs reh-sehr-vah-SYOH-nehs.
What date would you like?	*¿Para qué fecha desea?*	¿PAH-rah KEH FEH-chah deh-SEAH?

GUEST

May 27th.	*Veintisiete de mayo.*	Beyn-tee-SYEH-teh deh MAH-yoh.

CLERK

For how many nights?	*¿Para cuántas noches?*	¿PAH-rah KWAHN-tahs NOH-chehs?

GUEST

For three nights, please.	*Para tres noches, por favor.*	PAH-rah trehs NOH-chehs, pohr fah-VOHR.
For a week.	*Para una semana.*	PAH-rah OO-nah seh-MAH-nah.
Just one night.	*Sólo una noche.*	SOH-loh OO-nah NOH-cheh.

CLERK

For how many people?	*¿Para cuántas personas?*	¿PAH-rah KWAHN-tahs pehr-SOH-nahs?

GUEST

For two people.	*Para dos personas.*	PAH-rah DOHS pehr-SOH-nahs.
For one person.	*Para una persona.*	PAH-rah OO-nah pehr-SOH-nah.
For two adults and a child.	*Para dos adultos y un niño.*	PAH-rah DOHS ah-DOOL-tohs ee oon NEE-nyoh.

CLERK

Do you have…	*¿Tiene usted…*	¿TYEH-neh oos-TEHD…
• any special needs?	• *algunas necesidades especiales?*	• ahl-GOO-nahs neh-seh-see-DAH-dehs ehs-peh-SYAH-lehs?

• any special requests?	• *alguna solicitud especial?*	• ahl-GOO-nah soh-lee-seh-TOOD ehs-peh-SYAHL?

GUEST

No, thank you.	*No, gracias.*	NOH, GRAH-syahs.
Yes, I (we, my spouse) would like…	*Si, yo (nosotros, mi esposo) preferiría…*	SEE, yoh (noh-SOH-trohs, mee ehs-POH-soh) preh-feh-ree-REE-ah…
• to be near the stairs.	• *estar cerca de las escaleras.*	• ehs-TAHR SEHR-kah deh lahs ehs-kah-LEH-rahs.
• to be near an exit.	• *estar cerca de una salida.*	• ehs-TAHR SEHR-kah deh OO-nah sah-LEE-dah.
• a cot for our child.	• *un catre para nuestro niño.*	• oon KAH-treh PAH-rah NWEHS-troh NEE-nyoh.
• a handicapped-accessible room.	• *una habitación accesible para minusválidos.*	• oo-nah ah-bee-tah-SYOHN ahk-seh-SEE-blay PAH-rah mee-noos-VAH-lee-dohs.

CLERK

The rate is _____ per night.	*El precio es _____ por noche.*	Ehl PREH-syoh EHS _____ pohr NOH-cheh.
Would you like to guarantee the reservation with a credit card?	*¿Desea garantizar la reservación con una tarjeta de crédito?*	¿Deh-SEH-ah gah-rahn-tee-SAHR lah reh-sehr-vah-SYOHN kohn OO-nah tahr-HEH-tah deh KREH-dee-toh?

GUEST

Yes, here is my card.	*Si, aquí está mi tarjeta.*	SEE, ah-KEE ehs-TAH mee tahr-HEH-tah.
My credit card number is_____.	*El número de mi tarjeta es _____.*	Ehl NOO-meh-roh deh MEE tahr-HEH-tah EHS _____.

CLERK

What is the expiration date?	*¿Cuál es la fecha de expiración?*	¿KWAHL ehs lah FEH-chah deh eks-pee-rah-SYOHN?

Thank you.	*Gracias.*	GRAH-syahs.

RESTAURANT RESERVATIONS

RESTAURANT HOST

Good morning (afternoon, evening), _____ Restaurant.	*Buenos días (Buenas tardes, Buenas noches), restaurante _____.*	BWEH-nohs DEE-ahs (BWEH-nahs tahr-dehs, BWEH-nahs NOH-chehs), rehs-tah-oo-RAHN-teh _____.

GUEST

I'd like to reserve a table for…	*Quisiera reservar una mesa para…*	Keeh-see-EH-rah reh-sehr-VAHR OO-nah MEH-sah PAH-rah…
• breakfast.	• *el desayuno.*	• ehl deh-sah-YOO-noh.
• lunch.	• *el almuerzo.*	• ehl ahl-MWEHR-soh.
• dinner.	• *la cena.*	• lah SEH-nah.

HOST

For what time?	*¿Para qué hora?*	¿PAH-rah KEH OH-rah?

GUEST

For…o'clock.	*Para las…*	PAH-rah lahs…
• seven	• *siete.*	• SYEH-teh.
• eight	• *ocho.*	• OH-choh.
• nine	• *nueve.*	• NWEH-veh.
For eight-thirty.	*Para las ocho y media.*	PAH-rah lahs OH-choh ee MEH-dyah.

HOST

For how many people?	*¿Para cuántas personas?*	¿PAH-rah KWAHN-tahs pehr-SOH-nahs?

GUEST

For one person.	*Para una persona.*	PAH-rah OO-nah pehr-SOH-nah.
For…people.	*Para…personas.*	PAH-rah…pehr-SOH-nahs.
• two	• *dos*	• DOHS
• four	• *cuatro*	• KWAH-troh

• six	• *seis*	• SEYHS
HOST		
And your name, please?	*¿A nombre de quién, por favor?*	¿Ah NOHM-breh deh KYEHN, pohr fah-VOHR?
GUEST		
My name is ____.	*Mi nombre es ____.*	Mee NOHM-breh EHS ____.
HOST		
And is there a phone number where we can reach you?	*¿En qué número de teléfono podemos localizarlo(la)?*	¿Ehn keh NOO-meh-roh deh teh-LEH-foh-noh poh-DEH-mohs loh-kah-lee-SAHR-loh(lah)?
GUEST		
Yes, the number is ____.	*Si, mi número es ____.*	SEE, mee NOO-meh-roh EHS ____.
By the way, do you have any…items on the menu?	*A propósito, ¿ustedes tienen comida…en el menú?*	Ah pro-POH-see-toh, ¿oos-TEH-dehs TYEH-nehn koh-MEE-dah…ehn ehl meh-NOO?
• vegetarian	• *vegetariana*	• veh-heh-tah-RYAH-nah
• low-fat	• *baja en grasa*	• BAH-hah ehn GRAH-sah
• low-sodium	• *baja en sodio*	• BAH-hah ehn SOH-dyoh
HOST		
Would you like smoking or nonsmoking?	*¿Prefiere (el área para) fumadores o no fumadores?*	¿Preh-fee-EH-reh (ehl AH-reh-ah PAH-rah) foo-mah-DOH-rehs oh NOH foo-mah-DOH-rehs?
GUEST		
We would like…	*Nos gustaría…*	Nohs goos-tah-REE-ah…
• smoking.	• *fumadores.*	• foo-mah-DOH-rehs.
• nonsmoking.	• *no fumadores.*	• noh foo-mah-DOH-rehs.

HOST

Thank you.	*Gracias.*	GRAH-syahs.
That will be two people at eight o'clock.	*Serán dos personas a las ocho.*	Seh-RAHN DOHS pehr-SOH-nahs ah lahs OH-choh.
That's a party of six at seven-thirty.	*Hay un grupo de seis a las siete y media.*	AHY oon GROO-poh DEH SAYS ah lahs SYEH-teh EE MEH-dee-ah.

C. COURTESY AND COMPLAINTS

GENERAL EXPRESSIONS OF COURTESY

Please.	***Por favor.***	Pohr fah-VOHR.
Thank you.	***Gracias.***	GRAH-syahs.
You're welcome.	***De nada.***	Deh NAH-dah.
Excuse me.	***Discúlpeme.***	Dees-KOOL-peh-meh.
I beg your pardon.	***Perdón.***	Pehr-DOHN.
I'm (terribly) sorry.	***Lo siento (muchísimo).***	Loh SYEHN-toh (moo-CHEE-see-moh).
That's okay.	***Está bien.***	Ehs-TAH BYEHN.
No problem.	***No hay problema.***	Noh ahy proh-BLEH-mah.
It doesn't matter.	***No importa.***	Noh eehm-POHR-tah.

COURTESY IN THE HOTEL

CONCIERGE

Good morning, sir, ma'am.	***Buenos días, señor, señora.***	BWEH-nohs DEE-ahs, seh-NYOHR, seh-NYOH-rah.
May I help you with something today?	***¿Puedo ayudarlo(la) en algo hoy?***	¿PWEH-doh ah-yoo-DAHR-loh(lah) EHN AHL-goh OHY?

GUEST

Yes, I need...	***Sí, necesito...***	SEE, neh-seh-SEE-toh...
• my room made up between _____ and _____.	***• que hagan mi habitación entre las _____ y las _____.***	• keh AH-gahn mee ah-bee-tah-SYOHN EHN-treh lahs _____ EE lahs _____.

• more towels, please.	• *más toallas, por favor.*	• MAHS toh-AH-lyahs, pohr fah-VOHR.
• a rental car.	• *alquilar un auto.*	• ahl-KEE-lahr oon AHOO-toh.
• a taxi.	• *un taxi.*	• oon TAHK-see.
• a fax sent.	• *enviar un fax.*	• ehn-VEE-ar oon FAHKS.
• some letters mailed.	• *enviar unas cartas por correo.*	• ehn-VEE-ahr OO-nahs KAHR-tahs POHR koh-RREH-oh.
• to make arrangements for a business meeting.	• *hacer arreglos para una reunión de negocios.*	• ah-SEHR ah-RREH-glohs PAH-rah OO-nah reh-oo-NYOHN deh neh-GOH-syohs.
• tickets to a show.	• *boletos para un espectáculo.*	• boh-LEH-tohs pah-rah OHN ehs-pek-TAH-koo-loh.
• tickets to a concert.	• *boletos para un concierto.*	• boh-LEH-tohs PAH-rah oohn kohn-SYEHR-toh.
• tickets to a game.	• *boletos para un partido.*	• boh-LEH-tohs PAH-rah OON pahr-TEEH-doh.

GUEST COMPLAINTS IN THE HOTEL

CONCIERGE

Is everything satisfactory?	*¿Está todo bien?*	¿Ehs-TAH TOH-doh BYEHN?

GUEST

No, there is a problem.	*No, hay un problema.*	NOH, AHY oon proh-BLEH-mah.
• The light	• *La luz*	• Lah LOOS
• The toilet	• *El inodoro*	• Ehl ee-noh-DOH-roh
• The television	• *La televisión*	• Lah teh-leh-vee-SYOHN
• The radio	• *La radio*	• Lah RAH-dyoh

• The air-conditioning	• *El aire acondicionado*	• Ehl AHY-reh ah-kohn-dee-syoh-NAH-doh
• The alarm clock	• *El despertador*	• Ehl dehs-pehr-tah-DOHR
• The heat	• *La calefacción*	• Lah kah-leh-fak-SYOHN
• The key	• *La llave*	• Lah YAH-veh
• The lock	• *La cerradura*	• Lah seh-rrah-DOO-rah
• The fan	• *El ventilador*	• Ehl vehn-tee-lah-DOHR
...doesn't work.	*...no funciona.*	...noh foon-SYOH-nah.
CLERK		
I'll have Maintenance fix that right away.	*Haré que lo reparen ahora mismo.*	Ah-REH KEH loh reh-PAH-rehn ah-OH-rah MEES-moh.
I apologize.	*Me disculpo.*	Meh dee-SKOOL-poh.
GUEST		
My room...	***Mi habitación...***	Mee ah-bee-tah-SYOHN...
• wasn't clean.	***• no estaba limpia.***	• noh ehs-TAH-bah LEEM-pyah.
• was noisy.	***• era ruidosa.***	• EH-rah rooy-DOH-sah.
• smells.	***• huele.***	• WEH-leh.
The bed was uncomfortable.	***La cama era incómoda.***	Lah KHA-mah EH-rah een-KOH-moh-dah.
The water wasn't hot.	***El agua no estaba caliente.***	Ehl AH-gwah noh ehs-TAH-bah kah-LYEN-teh.
Room service was late.	***El servicio de habitación era lento.***	Ehl ser-VEE-syoh deh ah-bee-tah-SYOHN EH-rah LEHN-toh.
The service was very poor.	***El servicio fue regular.***	Ehl ser-VEE-syoh FWEH reh-goo-LAHR.

English	Spanish	Pronunciation
The employees were...	*Los empleados fueron...*	Lohs ehm-pleh-AH-dohs FWEH-rohn...
• very good.	• *muy buenos.*	• mooy BWEH-nohs.
• excellent.	• *excelentes.*	• ehk-seh-LEHN-tehs.
• rude.	• *maleducados.*	• mahl-eh-doo-KAH-dohs.
• incompetent.	• *incompetentes.*	• een-kohm-peh-TEHN-tehs.
• unfriendly.	• *antipáticos.*	• ahn-tee-PAH-tee-kohs.
The room attendant is incompetent.	*El asistente de la habitación es incompetente.*	Ehl ah-sees-TEHN-teh deh lah ah-bee-tah-SYOHN ehs een-kom-peh-TEHN-teh.
I didn't receive my wake-up call.	*No recibí mi llamada para despertarme.*	Noh reh-see-BEE mee yah-MAH-dah PAH-rah dehs-pehr-TAHR-meh.
I'm very disappointed with the level of service in this hotel.	*Estoy muy disgustado con el nivel de servicio de este hotel.*	Ehs-TOY MOOH dees-goos-TAH-doh kohn ehl nee-VEHL deh sehr-VEE-syoh deh EHS-teh oh-TEHL.
This is the worst hotel I've ever seen.	*Éste es el peor hotel que yo haya visto jamás.*	EHS-teh ehs ehl peh-OHR oh-TEHL keh yoh AH-yah VEE-stoh hah-MAHS.

CONCIERGE

English	Spanish	Pronunciation
Please let me make the situation right.	*Por favor, déjeme corregir la situación.*	Pohr fah-VOHR, DEH-heh-meh koh-rreh-HEER lah see-too-ah-SYOHN.
I'm certain we can straighten out the problem.	*Estoy seguro(a) que podemos arreglar el problema.*	Ehs-TOYH seh-GOO-roh(rah) deh keh poh-DEH-mohs ah-rreh-GLAHR ehl proh-BLEH-mah.
You won't pay for anything that wasn't completely up to your standards.	*Usted no pagará nada que no lo haya satisfecho por completo.*	Oos-TEHD noh pah-gah-RAH NAH-dah keh noh loh AH-yah sah-tees-FEH-choh pohr kohm-PLEH-toh.

Please tell me what I can do to correct this terrible situation.	*Por favor, dígame qué puedo hacer para corregir esta terrible situación.*	Pohr fah-VOHR, DEE-gah-meh KEH PWEH-doh ah-SEHR PAH-rah KOH-rreh-HEER EHS-tah teh-RREE-bleh see-too-ah-SYOHN.
We'll take ____ percent off your bill.	*Descontaremos el ____ por ciento de su cuenta.*	Dehs-kohn-tah-REH-mohs ehl ____ pohr SYEHN-toh deh soo KWEHN-tah.
We're going to give you ____ night(s), compliments of the hotel.	*Vamos a darle ____ noche(s) sin cargo, como cumplido.*	VAH-mohs ah DAHR-leh ____ NOH-cheh(s) SEEN KAHR-goh KOH-moh koom-PLEE-doh.
Your entire bill is compliments of the house.	*Su factura entera es un cumplido de la casa.*	SOO fak-TOO-rah ehn-TEH-rah ehs oon koom-PLEE-doh deh lah KAH-sah.

GUEST

Yes, that would be satisfactory.	*Sí, eso sería satisfactorio.*	SEE, EH-soh seh-RYAH sah-tees-fak-TOH-ryoh.
No, that would not be satisfactory.	*No, eso no sería satisfactorio.*	NOH, EH-soh noh seh-RYAH sah-tees-fak-TOH-ryoh.
I appreciate all your efforts.	*Aprecio todos sus esfuerzos.*	Ah-PREH-syoh TOH-dohs SOOS ehs-FWEHR-sohs.
Thank you, that would be very nice.	*Gracias, eso estaría muy bien.*	GRAH-syahs, EH-soh ehs-tah-REE-ah MOOY BYEN.
I will never come here again.	*Nunca volveré aquí.*	NOON-kah vohl-veh-REH ah-KEE.

MANAGEMENT COMPLAINTS

MANAGER

We have had some complaints about the noise coming from your room.	*Hemos oído algunas quejas sobre el ruido que viene de su habitación.*	EH-mohs oh-EE-doh ahl-GOO-nahs KEH-has SOH-breh EHL ROOY-doh keh VYEH-neh deh SOO ah-bee-tah-SYOHN.

You are disturbing…	*Usted está molestando…*	Oos-TEHD ehs-TAH moh-lehs-TAHN-doh…
• the people in the room next door.	• *a las personas de la habitación de al lado.*	• ah lahs pehr-SOH-nahs deh lah ah-bee-tah-SYOHN deh ahl LAH-doh.
• the people at the next table.	• *a las personas de la mesa de al lado.*	• ah lahs pohr-SOH-nahs deh lah MEH-sah deh ahl LAH-doh.
• our other guests.	• *a nuestros otros invitados.*	• ah NWEH-strohs OH-trohs een-vee-TAH-dohs.
GUEST		
We're sorry.	*Lo sentimos.*	Loh sehn-TEE-mohs.
We understand.	*Comprendemos.*	Kohm-prehn-DEH-mohs.
We'll take care of it.	*Nos ocuparemos de eso.*	Nohs oh-koo-pah-REH-mohs deh EH-soh.
We'll keep it down from now on.	*La mantendremos baja desde ahora.*	Lah mahn-tehn-DREH-mohs BAH-hah DEHS-deh ah-OH-rah.
Who cares!	*¡A quién le importa!*	¡Ah KYEHN leh eem-POHR-tah!
Leave us alone!	*¡Déjenos en paz!*	¡DEH-heh-nohs ehn PAHS!
MANAGER		
If you don't cooperate, I'm afraid I'll have to…	*Si usted no coopera, me temo que tendré que…*	See oos-TEHD noh koh-OH-peh-rah, meh TEH-moh KEH tehn-DREH keh…
• ask you to leave the hotel (restaurant).	• *pedirle que se vaya del hotel (restaurante).*	• peh-DEER-leh keh seh BAH-yah dehl oh-TEHL (rehs-taoo-RAHN-teh).
• call security.	• *llamar a seguridad.*	• yah-MAHR ah seh-goo-ree-DAHD.
• call the police.	• *llamar a la policía.*	• yah-MAHR ah lah poh-lee-SEE-ah.

D. EMERGENCIES AND SAFETY

EMPLOYEE

Please note the emergency exits on this card.	***Por favor, note las salidas de emergencia en esta tarjeta.***	Pohr fah-VOHR, NOH-teh lahs sah-LEE-dahs deh eh-mehr-HEHN-syah ehn EHS-tah tahr-HEH-tah.
Please note the emergency escape route on the door.	***Por favor, note la ruta de escape de emergencia en la puerta.***	Pohr fah-VOHR NOH-teh lah ROO-tah deh ehs-KAH-peh eh-mehr-HEN-syah ehn lah PWEHR-tah.
Your room is equipped with smoke alarms.	***Su habitación está equipada con alarmas de humo.***	Soo ah-bee-tah-SYOHN ehs-TAH eh-kee-PAH-da kohn ah-LAHR-mahs deh OO-moh.
Here is the fire alarm.	***Aquí está la alarma de fuego.***	Ah-KEE ehs-TAh lah ah-LAHR-mah deh FWEH-goh.
In an emergency, dial _____.	***En una emergencia, disque _____.***	Ehn OO-nah eh-mehr-HEN-syah DEES-keh _____.

GUEST

Help!	***¡Socorro!***	¡Soh-KOH-rroh!
Fire!	***¡Fuego!***	¡FWEH-goh!
I need a doctor.	***Necesito un doctor.***	Neh-seh-SEE-toh oon dok-TOHR.
I'm…	*Yo soy…*	Yoh SOY…
My husband (wife) is…	*Mi esposo (esposa) es…*	Mee ehs-POH-soh (ehs-POH-sah) ehs…
Someone is…	*Alguien está…*	AHL-gyen ehs-TAH…
• very sick.	• *muy enfermo/a.*	• MOOY ehn-FEHR-moh/mah.
• HAVING A HEART attack.	• *con un ataque al corazón.*	• kohn oon ah-TAH-keh ahl koh-rah-SOHN.
• nauseated.	• *con náuseas.*	• kohn NAH-oo-seh-ahs.
• choking.	• *ahogándose.*	• ah-oh-GAN-doh-seh.

• losing consciousness.	• *perdiendo el conocimiento.*	• pehr-DYEHN-doh ehl koh-noh-see-MYEHN-toh.
• about to vomit.	• *a punto de vomitar.*	• ah POON-toh deh voh-mee-TAHR.
• having a seizure.	• *con un ataque.*	• kohn oon ah-TAH-keh.
• stuck.	• *atrapado(a).*	• ah-trah-PAH-doh(dah).
I can't breathe.	*No puedo respirar.*	Noh PWEH-doh rehs-pee-RAHR.
MANAGER		
I'll call an ambulance.	*Llamaré a una ambulancia.*	Yah-mah-REH ah OO-nah ahm-boo-LAHN-syah.
Don't move.	*No se mueva.*	NOH seh MWEH-vah.
The doctor will be here very soon.	*El doctor estará aquí muy pronto.*	Ehl dohk-TOHR ehs-tah-RAH ah-KEE MOOY PROHN-toh.
Are you hurt?	*¿Está herido(a)?*	¿Ehs-TAH eh-REE-doh(dah)?
What happened?	*¿Qué pasó?*	¿KEH pah-SOH?
GUEST		
I tripped and fell.	*Tropecé y caí.*	Troh-peh-SEH ee kah-YEE.
I cut myself.	*Me corté.*	Meh kohr-TEH.
I drank too much.	*Bebí demasiado.*	Beh-BEE deh-mah-SYAH-doh.
I don't know.	*No sé.*	Noh SEH.
I've injured my…	*Me lesioné mi…*	Meh leh-syoh-NEH mee…
• HEAD.	• *cabeza.*	• kah-BEH-sah.
• neck.	• *cuello.*	• KWEH-yoh.
• back.	• *espalda.*	• ehs-PAHL-dah.
• arm.	• *brazo.*	• BRAH-soh.
• leg.	• *pierna.*	• PYEHR-nah.
• foot.	• *pies.*	• PYEHS.

• eye(s).	• *ojo(s).*	• OH-hoh(s).
DOCTOR (MEDICAL TECHNICIAN)		
You'll be fine; try to relax.	*Usted va a estar bien; trate de relajarse.*	Oos-TEHD VAH ah ehs-TAHR BYEHN; TRAH-teh DEH reh-lah-HAR-seh.
We're taking you to the hospital.	*Lo(La) estamos llevando al hospital.*	Loh(Lah) ehs-TAH-mohs yeh-VAHN-do ahl ohs-pee-TAHL.
Whom should we notify?	*¿A quién debemos notificar?*	¿Ah KYEHN deh-BEH-mohs noh-tee-fee-KAR?
GUEST		
I've been robbed.	***Me han robado.***	Meh ahn roh-BAH-doh.
MANAGER		
What did they take?	***¿Qué se llevaron?***	¿KEH seh yeh-VAH-rohn?
Let me call the police.	***Déjeme llamar a la policía.***	DEH-heh-meh yah-MAHR ah lah poh-lee-SEE-ah.
Attention, ladies and gentlemen.	***Atención, damas y caballeros.***	Ah-tehn-SYOHN, DAH-mahs ee kah-bah-YEH-rohs.
May I have your attention, please.	***Podrían prestarme atención, por favor.***	Poh-DREE-ahn prehs-TAHR-meh ah-tehn-SYOHN, pohr fah-VOHR.
Please…	***Por favor…***	Pohr fah-VOHR…
• remain calm.	***• manténgase en calma.***	• mahn-TEHN-gah-seh ehn KAHL-mah.
• follow the instructions of the staff.	***• siga las instrucciones del personal.***	• SEE-gah lahs een-strook-SYO-nehs dehl pehr-soh-NAHL.
• wait in your rooms.	***• espere en su habitación.***	• ehs-PEH-reh ehn SOO ah-bee-tah-SYOHN.
• get under a table or doorway.	***• póngase debajo de una mesa o del marco de la puerta.***	• POHN-gah-seh deh-BAH-hoh deh OO-nah MEH-sah oh dehl MAR-koh deh lah PWEHR-tah.

• **follow the evacuation plan** (route) **printed on your door** (in the hallways).	• ***siga el piano de evacuación*** *(ruta)* ***impreso en su puerta*** *(en los pasillos).*	• SEE-gah ehl PLAH-noh deh eh-vah-koo-ah-SYOHN (ROO-tah) eem-PREH-soh ehn soo PWEHR-tah (ehn lohs pah-SEE-yohs).
We'll have the situation under control as soon as possible.	***Tendremos la situación bajo control tan pronto como sea posible.***	Tehn-DREH-mohs lah see-too-ah-SYOHN BAH-hoh kohn-TROHL tahn PROHN-to KOH-moh SEH-yah poh-SEE-bleh.
Thank you for your patience.	***Gracias por su paciencia.***	GRAH-syahs pohr soo pah-SYEHN-syah.

4. Checking In

A. AT THE FRONT DESK

FRONT DESK CLERK

Good morning (afternoon, evening).	*Buenos días (Buenas tardes, Buenas noches).*	BWEH-nohs DEE-ahs (BWEH-nahs TAHR-dehs, BWEH-nahs NOH-chehs).
How may I help you?	*¿En qué puedo ayudarle?*	¿Ehn KEH PWEH-doh ah-yoo-DAHR-leh?

GUEST

I have a reservation under the name _____.	*Tengo una reserva a nombre de _____.*	TEHN-goh OO-nah reh-SEHR-vah ah NOHM-breh deh _____.
Do you have a room for one (two)?	*¿Tiene una habitación para uno (dos)?*	¿TYEH-neh OO-nah ah-bee-tah-SYOHN PAH-rah OO-noh (DOHS)?

CLERK

Yes, we have your reservation.	*Sí, tenemos su reserva.*	SEE, teh-NEH-mohs soo reh-SEHR-vah.

Yes, for how many nights?	*Sí, ¿para cuántas noches?*	SEE, ¿PAH-rah KWAHN-tahs NOH-chehs?
No, I'm sorry, we're full.	*No, lo siento, estamos llenos.*	NOH, loh SYEHN-to, ehs-TAH-mohs YEH-nohs.

GUEST

For ____ night(s), please.	*Para ____ noche(s), por favor.*	PAH-rah ____ NOH-cheh(s), pohr fah-VOHR.
What are your rates?	*¿Cuáles son sus tarifas?*	¿KWAH-lehs SOHN soos tah-REE-fahs?

CLERK

• For a single,	• *Por una simple…*	• Pohr OO-nah SEEM-pleh…
• For a double,	• *Por una doble…*	• Pohr OO-nah DOH-bleh…
• For adjoining rooms,	• *Por habitaciones adjuntas…*	• Pohr ah-bee-tah-SYOH-nehs ahd-HOON-tahs…
• For a suite,	• *Por una suite…*	• Pohr OO-nah "suite"…
…the rate is ____ per night.	*…la tarifa es ____ por noche.*	…lah tah-REE-fah ehs pohr NOH-cheh.

GUEST

Are any meals included?	*¿Las comidas están incluídas?*	¿Lahs ko-MEE-dahs ehs-TAHN een-kloo-EE-dahs?
Is breakfast included?	*¿El desayuno está incluído?*	¿Ehl deh-sah-YOO-noh ehs-TAH een-kloo-EE-doh?

CLERK

No, meals are extra.	*No, las comidas son aparte.*	NOH, lahs koh-MEE-dahs sohn ah-PAHR-teh.
Yes, breakfast is included.	*Sí, el desayuno está incluído.*	SEE, ehl deh-sah-YOO-noh ehs-TAH een-kloo-EE-doh.

You can choose…	*Usted puede elegir…*	OO-stehd PWEH-deh eh-leh-HEER…
• the American plan (all meals included).	• *el plan americano (todas las comidas incluídas).*	• ehl PLAHN ah-meh-ree-KAH-noh (TOH-dahs lahs ko-MEE-dahs een-kloo-EE-dahs).
• the modified American plan (breakfast and dinner).	• *el plan americano modificado (desayuno y cena).*	• ehl PLAHN ah-meh-ree-KAH-noh mo-dee-fee-KAH-doh (deh-sah-YOO-noh ee SEH-nah).
• the European plan (no meals included).	• *el plan europeo (las comidas no están incluídas).*	• ehl PLAHN eh-oo-roh-PEH-oh (lahs ko-MEE-dahs NOH ehs-THAN een-kloo-EE-dahs).

GUEST

I'd like a room…	*Desearía una habitación…*	Deh-eh-ah-REE-ah OO-nah ah-bee-tah-SYOHN…
• that faces the back (front).	• *que quede al fondo (alfrente).*	• keh KEH-deh ahl FON-doh (ahl FREHN-teh).
• that faces the water (pool).	• *que quede frente al mar (piscina).*	• keh KEH-deh FREHN-teh ahl MAHR (pee-SEE-nah).
• with a private bath/toilet/shower.	• *con baño privado/baño completo/ducha.*	• kohn BAH-nyoh pree-VAH-doh/BAH-nyoh kohm-PLEH-toh/DOOH-chah.
• with a handicapped-accessible bathroom.	• *con baño accesible a minusválidos.*	• kohn BAH-nyoh ahk-seh-SEE-bleh ah mee-noo-VAH-lee-dohs.
• with air-conditioning.	• *con aire acondicionado.*	• kohn AHY-reh ah-kohn-dee-syoh-NAH-doh.
• with a television.	• *con televísion*	• kohn teh-leh-vee-SYON.
• with cable.	• *con cable.*	• kohn KAH-bleh.

• with a fax machine.	• *con fax.*	• kohn "fax."
• with a phone.	• *con teléfono.*	• kohn teh-LEH-foh-noh.
• with a network hookup for my computer.	• *con un sistema de conexión para mi computadora.*	• kohn oon sees-TEH-mah deh koh-nehk-SYOHN PAH-rah MEE kohm-poo-tah-DOH-rah.
• with a view.	• *con vista.*	• kohn VEES-tah.
• with two double beds.	• *con dos camas dobles.*	• kohn DOHS KAH-mahs DOH-blehs.
• with a king-size bed.	• *con una cama tamaño "king."*	• kohn OO-nah KAH-mah ta-MAH-nyoh "king."
• with an extra bed.	• *con una cama extra.*	• kohn OO-nah KAH-mah EHK-strah.
• with a baby crib.	• *con una cunita.*	• kohn OO-nah koo-NEE-tah.
• with a balcony.	• *con balcón.*	• kohn bahl-KOHN.
• with a sitting area.	• *con un área de estar.*	• kohn oon AH-reh-ah deh ehs-TAHR.
• with a bar.	• *con un bar.*	• kohn oon BAHR.
• with a kitchenette.	• *con una cocinita.*	• kohn OO-na ko-see-NEE-tah.
• away from the elevator.	• *lejos del ascensor.*	• LEH-hohs dehl ah-SEHN-sohr.
• with no meals.	• *sin comidas.*	• SEEN koh-MEE-dahs.

CLERK

No problem.	*No hay problema.*	Noh AHY proh-BLEH-mah.
I'm sorry.	*Lo siento.*	Loh SYEHN-toh.
There is none available.	*No hay nada disponible.*	Noh AHY NAH-dah dees-poh-NEE-bleh.
We don't provide/ offer that.	*Nosotros no proveemos/ ofrecemos eso.*	Noh-SOH-trohs noh proh-veh-EH-mohs/ oh-fre-SEH-mohs EH-soh.

GUEST

Does the hotel have…	*¿El hotel tiene…*	¿Ehl oh-TEHL TYEH-neh…
• a restaurant?	• *un restaurante?*	• un rehs-tah-oo-RAHN-teh?
• a bar?	• *un bar?*	• oon BAHR?
• room service?	• *servicio de habitación?*	• sehr-VEE-syoh deh ah-bee-tah-SYOHN?
• a gym/health club?	• *gimnasio/club de salud?*	• heem-NAH-syoh/ KLOOB deh sa-LOOD?
• a spa hot tub?	• *baño "spa"?*	• BAH-nyoh "spa"?
• a swimming pool?	• *una pisicina para nadar?*	• OO-na pee-SEE-nah PAH-rah NAH-dahr?
• baby-sitting?	• *niñeras?*	• nee-NYEH-rahs?
• tennis courts?	• *campos de tennis?*	• kahm-pohs deh "tennis"?
• laundry (dry-cleaning) service?	• *servicio de lavandería (tintorería)?*	• ser-VEE-syoh deh lah-vahn-deh-REE-ah (teen-toh-reh-REE-ah)?
• a garage?	• *un garage?*	• oon gah-RAH-heh?
May I see the room?	*¿Podría ver la habitación?*	¿Poh-DRYAH vehr lah ah-bee-tah-SYOHN?

CLERK

Yes, certainly. Here's the key.	*Sí, por supuesto. Aquí está la llave.*	SEE, pohr soo-PWEHS-toh. Ah-KEE ehs-TAH lah YAH-veh.
Would you like another room?	*¿Desea otra habitación?*	¿De-SEH-ah OH-trah ah-bee-tah-SYOHN?

GUEST

I'd like something…	*Me gustaría algo…*	Meh goo-stah-REE-ah ahl-goh…
• smaller.	• *más pequeño.*	• MAHS peh-KEH-nyoh.
• larger.	• *más grande.*	• MAHS GRAHN-deh.
• quieter.	• *más tranquilo.*	• MAHS trahn-KEE-loh.

• better.	• *mejor.*	• meh-HOR.
• cheaper.	• *más barato.*	• MAHS bah-RAH-toh.
• on another floor.	• *en otro piso.*	• ehn OH-troh PEE-soh.
I'll take the room, please.	*Tomaré la habitación, por favor.*	Toh-mah-REH lah ah-bee-tah-SYOHN, pohr fah-VOHR.
CLERK		
Very well, how will you be paying?	*Muy bien, ¿cómo pagará?*	Mooy BYEHN, ¿KOH-moh pah-gah-RAH?
GUEST		
I'll pay with…	*Pagaré con…*	Pah-gha-REH kohn…
• cash.	• *efectivo.*	• eh-fek-TEE-voh.
• a credit card.	• *tarjeta de crédito.*	• tar-HEH-tah deh KREH-dee-toh.
• traveler's checks.	• *cheques de viajero.*	• CHEH-kehs deh vyah-HEH-roh.
CLERK		
Thank you.	*Gracias.*	GRAH-syahs.
To charge meals and services to your room, I'll need a credit card.	*Para cargar las comidas y los servicios a su habitación, necesitaré una tarjeta de crédito.*	PAH-rah kahr-GAHR lahs koh-MEE-dahs ee lohs ser-VEE-syohs ah bee-tah-SYOHN, ne-seh-see-tah-REH OO-nah tar-HEH-tah deh KREH-dee-toh.
You may settle the bill with traveler's checks (cash).	*Podría pagar la factura con cheques de viajero (efectivo).*	Poh-DREE-ah pah-GAHR lah fak-TOO-rah kohn CHEH-kehs deh vyah-HE-roh (eh-fek-TEE-voh).
If you would like to store valuables, we have a safe.	*Si desea guardar artículos de valor, tenemos una caja fuerte.*	See deh-SEH-yah gwahr-DAHR ahr-TEE-koo-lohs deh vah-LOHR, teh-NEH-mohs OO-nah KA-hah FWER-teh.
Please note that…	*Por favor, note que…*	Pohr fah-VOHR, NOH-teh keh…

• quiet hours are between _____ and _____.	• *las horas tranquilas son entre las _____ y las _____.*	• lahs OH-rahs trahn-KEE-lahs sohn EHN-trehl lahs _____ ee lahs _____.
• there are no pets allowed.	• *no se permiten animales.*	• noh seh pehr-MEE-ten ah-nee-MAH-lehs.
• children under _____ stay free.	• *los niños menores de _____ no pagan la estadía.*	• lohs NEE-nyohs meh-NOH-rehs deh _____ noh PAH-gahn lah ehs-tah-DEE-ah.
• smoking is allowed only in the bar.	• *sólo se puede fumar en el bar.*	• SOH-loh seh PWEH-deh foo-MAHR ehn ehl BAHR.
• we do not allow cooking in the rooms.	• *no permitimos que cocinen en las habitaciones.*	• noh pehr-mee-TEE-mohs keh koh-SEE-nehn ehn lahs ah-bee-tah-SYOH-nehs.

GUEST

Do I (we) have any messages?	*¿Tengo (Tenemos) algún mensaje?*	¿TEHN-goh (Teh-NEH-mohs) ahl-GOON mehn-SAH-heh?
I would like a wake-up call, please.	*Deseo que me llamen para despertarme.*	Deh-SEH-oh keh meh YAH-mehn PAH-rah dehs-pehr-TAHR-meh.
May we have…, please?	*¿Podríamos tener…, por favor?*	¿Po-DREE-ah-mohs teh-NEHR…, pohr fah-VOHR?
• extra blankets	• *mantas extras*	• MAHN-tahs EHK-strahs
• extra towels	• *toallas extras*	• toh-AH-yahs EHK-strahs
• a hair dryer	• *un secador de cabello*	• OON seh-kah-dohr de kah-BEH-yoh
• an iron	• *una plancha*	• OO-nah PLAHN-chah
• ice	• *hielo*	• YEH-loh

CLERK

I'll have that brought to your room right away.	*Haré que lleven esto a su habitación ahora mismo.*	Ah-REH keh YEH-vehn EHS-toh ah soo ah-bee-tah SYOHN ah OH-rah MEES-moh.

GUEST

Where is...	*¿Dónde está...*	¿DOHN-deh ehs-TAH...
• the room attendant?	• *el asistente de habitación?*	• ehl ah-seehs-TEHN-teh deh ah-bee-tah-SYOHN?
• the bellman (bell attendant)?	• *el botones?*	• ehl boh-TOH-nehs?
• the manager?	• *el gerente?*	• ehl heh-REHN-teh?
• the dining room?	• *el comedor?*	• ehl koh-meh-DOHR?
• the gift shop?	• *la tienda?*	• lah TYEHN-dah?
• the newsstand?	• *la tienda de periódicos?*	• lah TYEHN-dah deh peh-REE-oh-dee-kohs?

CLERK

Just over there.	*Por ahí.*	Pohr ah-EE.

GUEST

How do I use the telephone?	*¿Cómo se usa el teléfono?*	¿KOH-moh seh OO-sah ehl teh-LEH-foh-noh?

CLERK

The instructions are next to the phone.	*Las instrucciones están al lado del teléfono.*	Lahs eens-trook-SYOH-nehs ehs-TAHN ahl LAH-doh dehl teh-LEH-foh-noh.
Dial _____ for a local (long-distance) call,	*Marque el _____ para una llamada local (larga distancia),*	MAHR-keh ehl _____ PAH-ra OO-nah yah-MAH-dah loh-KAHL (LAHR-gha dees-TAHN-syah),
wait for the tone,	*espere al tono,*	ehs-PEH-reh ahl TOH-noh,

then dial the number.	*después marque el número.*	dehs-PWEHS MAHR-keh ehl NOO-meh-roh.
Dial _____ for an operator.	*Marque el _____ para un telefonista.*	MAHR-keh ehl _____ PAH-rah OON teh-leh-foh-NEES-tah.
To use a credit card, dial _____.	*Para usar su tarjeta de crédito, marque el _____.*	PAH-rah OO-sahr SOO tar-HEH-tah deh KREH-dee-toh, MAR-keh ehl _____.
GUEST		
Please have our luggage brought to our room.	*Por favor, llévenos el equipaje a nuestra habitación.*	Pohr fah-VOHR, YEH-veh-nohs ehl eh-kee-PAH-heh ah NWEHS-trah ah-bee-tah-SYOHN.
We'll need a wheelchair.	*Necesitaremos una silla de ruedas.*	Ne-seh-see-tah-REH-mos OO-nah see-yah deh RWEH-dahs.
CLERK		
Yes, right away.	*Sí, ahora mismo.*	SEE, ah-OH-rah MEES-moh.
GUEST		
We'd like to order a pizza, please.	*Nos gustaría ordenar una pizza, por favor.*	Nohs goos-tah-REE-ah ohr-deh-NAHR OO-nah PEE-tsah, pohr fah-VOHR.
MANAGER		
I'll be happy to call someone for you.	*Me complacerá llamar a alguien para usted.*	Meh kohm-plah-seh-RAH yah-MAHR ah AHL-gyen PAH-rah oos-TEHD.
We have room service, but we don't allow outside vendors into the hotel.	*Tenemos servicio de habitación, pero no permitimos vendedores de afuera en el hotel.*	Teh-NEH-mohs sehr-VEE-syoh deh ah-bee-tah-SYOHN, PEH-ro noh pehr-mee-TEE-mohs ven-deh-DOH-rehs deh ah-FWEH-rah ehn ehl oh-TEHL.

GUEST

We'd like to entertain a few friends in our room.
Nos gustaría invitar a unos amigos a nuestra habitación.
Nohs goos-tah-REE-ah een-bee-TAHR ah OO-nohs ah-MEE-gohs ah NWEH-strah ah-bee-tah-SYOHN.

MANAGER

We allow guests in the rooms until _____.
Permitimos invitados en las habitaciones hasta las _____.
Pehr-mee-TEE-mohs een-vee-TAH-dohs ehn lahs ah-bee-tah-SYOH-nehs AHS-tah lahs _____.

B. SHOWING GUESTS TO THEIR ROOMS

BELLMAN (BELL ATTENDANT)

My name is _____, and I'm your bell attendant.
Mi nombre es _____, y soy su botones.
Mee NOHM-breh ehs _____, ee soy soo boh-TOH-nehs.

May I show you to your room?
¿Puedo mostrarle su habitación?
¿PWEH-doh mohs-TRAHR-leh soo ah-bee-tah-SYHON?

GUEST

No, thanks. We'll find it ourselves.
No, gracias. La encontraremos nosotros mismos.
NOH, GRAH-syahs. Lah ehn-kohn-trah-REH-mohs noh-SOH-trohs MEES-mohs.

Yes, please.
Sí, por favor.
SEE, pohr fah-VOHR.

TIP! ••••

International guests in particular may have questions about using the telephone and will appreciate seeing how the television and pay movies work.

BELLMAN

This way, please.	*Por aquí, por favor.*	Pohr ah-KEE, pohr fah-VOHR.
The elevator is over here.	*El elevador está aquí.*	Ehl eh-leh-bah-DOHR ehs-TAH ah-KEE.
May I show you the features of your room?	*¿Puedo mostrarles las características de su habitación?*	¿PWEH-doh mohs-TRAHR-lehs lahs kah-rahk-teh-REES-tee-kahs deh soo ah-bee-tah-SYOHN?
This is the key to the minibar.	*Ésta es la llave del "minibar."*	EHS-tah EHS lah YAH-veh dehl "minibar."
• Any movie you select	• *Cualquier película que seleccione*	• Kwahl-KYEHR peh-LEE-koo-lah keh seh-lehk-SYOH-neh
• Any long-distance calls you make	• *Cualquier llamada de larga distancia que usted haga*	• Kwahl-KYEHR yah-MAH-dah deh LAHR-gah dee-STAHN-syah keh OOS-tehd AH-gah
• Any snack or beverage you take from the refrigerator	• *Cualquier merienda o bebida que tome del refrigerador*	• Kwahl-KYEHR meh-RYEHN-dah oh bee-BEE-dah keh TOH-meh dehl rreh-free-heh-rah-DOHR
...will be charged to your room.	*...será(n) cargada(s) a su habitación.*	...seh-RHA(N) kahr-GAH-dah(s) ah soo ah-bee-tah-SYOHN.
Here is the control for the heating (air-conditioning).	*Aquí está el control de la calefacción (del aire acondicionado).*	Ah-KEE ehs-TAH ehl kohn-TROHL DEHL lah kah-leh-fak-SYOHN (dehl AHY-reh ah-kohn-dee-syoh-NAH-doh).

GUEST

How do I call Room Service?	*¿Cómo llamo al servicio de habitación?*	¿KOH-moh YAH-moh ahl sehr-VEE-syoh deh ah-bee-tah-SYOHN?

BELLMAN

Dial ____.	*Marque el ____.*	MAHR-keh ehl ____.

GUEST

This room…	*Esta habitación…*	EHS-tah ah-bee-tah-SYOHN…
• is too close to the elevator(s).	• *está muy cerca del (de los) elevador(es).*	• ehs-TAH MOOY SEHR-kah dehl (deh lohs) eh-leh-bah-DOHR(ehs).
• hasn't been made up.	• *no ha sido arreglada.*	• noh ah SEE-doh ah-rreh-GLAH-dah.
• smells (like cigarettes).	• *huele (a cigarrillos).*	• WEH-leh (ah see-gah-REE-yohs).
The toilet (bathtub, sink) is clogged.	*El inodoro (bañera, lavamanos) está atascado(a).*	EHL ee-noh-DOH-roh (bah-NYEH-rah, lah-vah-MAH-nos) ehs-TAH ah-rahs-KAH-doh(dah).
May we change rooms, please?	*¿Podemos cambiar de habitación, por favor?*	¿Poh-DEH-mohs kahm-BYAHR deh ah-bee-tah-SYOHN, pohr fah-VOHR?

BELLMAN

Please let me check our availability with the front desk.	*Por favor, déjeme chequear nuestra disponibilidad con recepción.*	Pohr fah-VOHR, DEH-heh-meh cheh-keh-AHR NWEHS-trah dee-poh-nee-bee-lee-dahd khon reh-sehp SYOHN.
Sure, I'll be happy to assist you.	*Por supesto, me complace el ayudarle.*	Pohr soo-poo-EHS-toh, meh kohm-PLAH-seh ehl ah-yoo-DAHR-leh.
Please call if I can help you with anything else.	*Por favor, llámeme si puedo ayudarle en algo.*	Pohr fah-VOHR, YAH-meh-meh see PWEH-doh ah-yoo-DAHR-leh ehn AHL-gho.

VOCABULARY ••••

THE GUEST ROOM

air-conditioning	*aire acondicionado*	AHY-reh ah-kohn-dee-syoh-NAH-doh
balcony	*balcón*	bahl-KOHN
bath mat	*alfombra de baño*	ahl-FOHM-brah deh BAH-nyoh
bathtub	*bañera*	bah-NYEH-rah
bed	*cama*	KAH-mah
bedspread	*colcha*	KOHL-chah
blanket	*manta*	MAHN-tah
blinds	*cortina*	kohr-TEE-nah
carpet	*alfombra*	ahl-FOHM-brah
ceiling	*techo*	TEH-choh
chair	*silla*	SEE-yah
closet	*armario*	ahr-MAH-ryoh
conditioner	*acondicionador*	ah-kohn-dee-syoh-nah-DOHR
couch	*sofá*	soh-FAH
crib	*cama para niños*	KAH-mah PAH-rah NEE-nyohs
desk	*escritorio*	ehs-kree-TOH-ryoh
Do Not Disturb sign	*cartel de No Molestar*	kahr-TEHL deh Noh Moh-lehs-TAHR
door	*puerta*	PWEHR-tah
drapes	*cortina de tela*	kohr-TEE-nah deh TEH-lah
dresser	*cambiador*	kahm-byah-DOHR
fan	*ventilador*	vehn-tee-lah-DOHR
floor	*piso*	PEE-soh
glass(es)	*vidrio(s)*	VEE-dryoh(s)
hair dryer	*secador de cabello*	seh-kah-DOHR deh kah-BEH-yoh
(coat) hanger	*percha*	PEHR-chah

(cont'd.)

The Guest Room *(cont'd.)*

heat	*calefacción*	kah-leh-fahk-SYOHN
ice bucket	*cubetera*	koo-beh-TEH-rah
iron	*plancha*	PLAHN-chah
lamp	*lámpara*	LAHM-pah-rah
light	*luz*	LOOS
lock	*cerradura*	seh-rrah-DOO-rah
minibar	*"minibar"*	"minibar"
mirror	*espejo*	ehs-PEH-hoh
nightstand	*puesto nocturno*	PWEHS-toh nok-TOOR-noh
pillow	*almohada*	ahl-moh-HAH-dah
radio	*radio*	RRAH-dyoh
razor	*navaja*	nah-VAH-hah
sewing kit	*costurerito*	kohs-too-reh-REE-toh
shampoo	*champú*	chahm-POO
sheets	*sábanas*	SAH-bah-nahs
shower	*ducha*	DOO-chah
shower cap	*gorra para ducha*	GOHR-rah PAH-rah DOO-chah
sink	*lavamanos*	lah-vah-MAH-nohs
soap	*jabón*	ha-BOHN
telephone	*teléfono*	teh-LEH-foh-noh
television	*televisión*	teh-leh-vee-SYOHN
thermostat	*termostato*	tehr-mohs-TAH-toh
toilet	*inodoro*	ee-noh-DOH-roh
toilet paper	*paper higiénico*	pah-PEHL ee-HYEH-nee-koh
toothbrush	*cepillo de dientes*	seh-PEE-yoh deh DYEHN-tehs
toothpaste	*dentífrico*	dehn-TEE-freeh-koh
towel	*toalla*	toh-AH-yah
VCR	*video casetera*	vee-DEH-oh kah-seh-TEH-rah
wall	*pared*	PAH-rehd
window	*ventana*	vehn-TAH-nah

5. Providing Assistance

A. GIVING DIRECTIONS

CONCIERGE		
Good morning. May I help you?	*Buenos días. ¿Puedo ayudarle?*	BWEH-nohs DEE-ahs. ¿PWEH-doh ah-yoo-DAHR-leh?
GUEST		
Yes. Where is the…	*Sí. ¿Dónde está el/la…*	SEE. ¿DOHN-deh/ehs-TAH ehl/lah…
• bathroom?	• *baño?*	• BAH-nyoh?
• lounge/bar?	• *bar?*	• bahr?
• coffee shop/ restaurant?	• *cafetería/ restaurante?*	• kah-feh-teh-REE-ah/ rehs-tah-oo-RAHN-teh?
• barbershop/ hairdresser's?	• *barbería/ peluquería?*	• bahr-beh-REE-ah/ peh-loo-keh-REE-ah?
• gift shop?	• *tienda de regalos?*	• tee-EHN-dah deh reh-GAH-los?
• health club?	• *club de salud?*	• KLOOB deh sah-LOOD?

TIP! ••••

You can simply explain many directions, but when they're more complex, you should use either a map or written instructions (or both). Hotels should keep preprinted directions to major sites on hand. Also, many cultures don't speak of distance in terms of city blocks but will understand if you use the word "streets" instead. And remember that most international guests use the metric system and may have difficulties figuring a distance given in miles, yards, or feet.

• ballroom?	• *salón de baile?*	• sah-LOHN deh BAHY-leh?
• elevator?	• *elevador?*	• eh-leh-vah-DOHR?
• pay phone?	• *cabina telefónica?*	• kah-BEE-nah teh-leh-FOH-nee-kah?
• ice machine?	• *hielera?*	• yeh-LEH-rah?

CONCIERGE

Take…	*Tome…*	TOH-meh…
• the escalator.	• *la escalera eléctrica.*	• lah ehs-kah-LEH-rah eh-LEHK-tree-kah.
• the elevator.	• *el elevador.*	• ehl eh-leh-bah-DOHR.
• the stairs.	• *las escaleras.*	• lahs ehs-kah-LEH-rahs.
Go…	*Camine…*	Kah-MEE-neh…
• up.	• *hacia arriba.*	• AH-see-ah ahr-REE-bah.
• down.	• *hacia abajo.*	• AH-see-ah ah-BAH-hoh.
• left.	• *hacia la izquierda.*	• AH-see-ah lah ees-KYEHR-dah.
• right.	• *hacia la derecha.*	• AH-see-ah lah deh-REH-chah.
• straight ahead.	• *derecho.*	• deh-REH-choh.
• around the corner.	• *hacia allí y doble en la esquina.*	• AH-see-ah ah-EE ee DOH-bleh en lah ehs-KEE-nah.
• left, then right.	• *hacia la izquierda, después hacia la derecha.*	• AH-see-ah lah ees-KYEHR-dah, dehs-PWEHS, AH-see-ah lah deh-REH-chah.
• past the elevators.	• *pasando los elevadores.*	• pah-SAHN-doh LOHS eh-leh-bah-DOHR-ehs.
• to the first (second, third, fourth) floor.	• *al primer (segundo, tercero, cuarto) piso.*	• AHL PREE-mehr (seh-GOON-doh, tehr-SEH-roh, KWAHR-toh) PEE-soh.

• left (right) when you exit the elevator.	• *hacia la izquierda (derecha) cuando usted salga del elevador.*	• AH-see-ah lah ees-KYEHR-dah (deh-REH-chah) KWAHN-doh oos-TEHD sahl-gah DEHL eh-leh-bah-DOHR.
• in through the second set of doors.	• *a través del segundo juego de puertas.*	• ah trah-VEHS dehl seh-GOON-doh HWEH-goh deh PWEHR-tahs.
It will be…	*Estará…*	Ehs-tah-RAH…
• on your right.	• *a su derecha.*	• ah soo deh-REH-chah.
• on your left.	• *a su izquierda.*	• ah soo ees-KYEHR-dah.
• right in front of you.	• *justo frente a usted.*	• HOOS-toh FREHN-teh ah OOS-tehd.

GUEST

How do I get…	*¿Cómo se va…*	¿KOH-moh seh bah…
• to the hospital?	• *al hospital?*	• ahl ohs-pee-TAHL?
• to city hall?	• *a la municipalidad?*	• ah lah moo-nee-see-pah-lee-DAHD?
• to the _____ restaurant/hotel?	• *al restaurante/ hotel _____?*	• ahl rehs-tah-oo-RAHN-teh/oh-TEHL _____?
• to the train station?	• *a la estación de tren?*	• ah lah ehs-tah-SYOHN deh TREHN?
• to the bus station?	• *a la estación de bus?*	• ah lah ehs-tah-SYOHN deh BOOS?
• to the nearest bus stop?	• *a la parada de bus más cercana?*	• ah lah pah-RAH-dah deh BOOS MAHS sehr-KAH-nah?
• to the mall?	• *al centro comercial?*	• ahl SEHN-troh koh-mehr-SEE-ahl?
• to the post office?	• *al correo?*	• ahl kohr-REH-oh?
• to the airport?	• *al aeropuerto?*	• ahl ah-eh-roh-PWEHR-toh?

• downtown?	• *al centro de la ciudad?*	• ahl SEHN-troh DEH lah syoo-DAHD?
• to the car rental agency?	• *a la agencia de alquiler de autos?*	• ah lah ah-HEHN-syah deh ahl-kee-LEHR deh AHOO-tohs?
• to _____ Street/Avenue?	• *a calle/avenida _____?*	• ah KAH-yeh/ah-veh-NEE-dah _____?
CONCIERGE		
When you exit the hotel, go…	*Cuando salga del hotel, vaya…*	KWAHN-doh SAHL-gah dehl oh-TEHL, VAH-yah…
• left.	• *a la izquierda.*	• ah lah ees-KYEHR-dah.
• right.	• *a la derecha.*	• ah lah deh-REH-chah.
• straight ahead.	• *derecho.*	• deh-REH-choh.
• north.	• *al norte.*	• ahl NOHR-teh.
• south.	• *al sur.*	• ahl SOOR.
• east.	• *al este.*	• ahl EHS-teh.
• west.	• *al oeste.*	• ahl oh-EHS-teh.
GUEST		
How far is it?	*¿A qué distancia está?*	¿Ah KEH dee-STAHN syah ehs-TAH?
CONCIERGE		
It's about _____…	*Está alrededor de _____…*	Ehs-TAH ahl-reh-deh-DOHR deh _____…
• blocks (streets).	• *cuadras (calles).*	• KWAH-drahs (KAH-yehs).
• miles.	• *millas.*	• MEE-yahs.
• kilometers.	• *kilómetros.*	• kee-LOH-meh-trohs.
• minutes…	• *minutos…*	• mee-NOO-tohs…
• on foot.	• *a pie.*	• ah PYEH.
• by car.	• *en auto.*	• ehn AH-oo-toh.
• by bus.	• *en bus.*	• ehn BOOS.
• by metro (subway).	• *en metro (subterráneo).*	• ehn MEH-troh (soob-tehr-RAH-neh-oh).

GUEST

Can you show me on the map?	*¿Puede mostrármelo en un mapa?*	¿PWEH-deh mohs-TRAHR-meh-loh ehn oon MAH-pah?

CONCIERGE

Sure, it's right here.	*Por supesto, está aquí.*	Pohr soo-poo-EHS-toh, ehs-TAH ah-KEE.
Let me draw you a little map.	*Déjeme dibujarle un pequeño mapa.*	DEH-heh-meh dee-boo-HAHR-leh oon peh-KEH-nyoh MAH-pah.

GUEST

Can you tell me where I can… around here?	*¿Me puede decir dónde puedo… por aquí?*	¿Meh PWEH-deh deh-SEER DOHN-deh PWEH-doh…pohr ah-KEE?
• take a walk	• *caminar*	• kah-mee-NAHR
• ride a bike	• *montar en bicicleta*	• mohn-TAHR ehn bee-see-KLEH-tah
• jog	• *correr*	• koh-RREHR

CONCIERGE

Yes, we have maps of…trails right here.	*Sí, tenemos mapas de rutas…aquí.*	SEE, teh-NEH-mohs MAH pahs deh ROO-tahs…ah-KEE.
• jogging	• *para correr*	• PAH-rah koh-RREHR
• walking	• *para caminar*	• PAH-rah kah-mee-NAHR
• bike	• *para montar en bicicleta*	• PAH-rah mohn-TAHR ehn bee-see-KLEH-tah

B. RECOMMENDING PLACES OF INTEREST

GUEST

Can you recommend any places to visit?	*¿Me puede recomendar algún lugar para visitar?*	¿Meh PWEH-deh reh-koh-mehn-DAHR ahl-GOON loo-GAHR PAH-rah vee-see-TAHR?

CONCIERGE		
There are lots.	*Hay muchos.*	AHY MOO-chohs.
Are you interested in…	*¿Le interesa(n)…*	¿Le een-teh-REH-sah(n)…
• art?	• *el arte?*	• ehl AHR-teh?
• theater?	• *el teatro?*	• ehl teh-AH-troh?
• shopping?	• *ir de compras?*	• eer deh KOHM-prahs?
• museums?	• *museos?*	• moo-SEH-ohs?
• sports?	• *los deportes?*	• lohs deh-POHR-tehs?
• sight-seeing?	• *mirar el paisaje?*	• mee-RAHR ehl pahy-SAH-heh?
• music?	• *la música?*	• lah MOO-see-kah?
• outdoor activities?	• *las actividades al aire libre?*	• lahs ahk-tee-vee-DAH-dehs ahl AHY-reh LEE-breh?
• children's activities?	• *las actividades para niños?*	• lahs ahk-tee-vee-DAH-dehs PAH-rah NEE-nyohs?
GUEST		
What do you recommend?	*¿Qué recomienda?*	¿KEH reh-koh-MYEHN-dah?
CONCIERGE		
If you're interested in art, I'd suggest…	*Si a usted le interesa el arte, le sugiero…*	See ah OOS-tehd leh een-teh-REH-sah ehl AHR-teh, leh soo-HYEH-roh…
• the _____ gallery.	• *la galería _____.*	• lah gah-leh-REE-ah _____.
• the _____ art museum.	• *el museo de arte _____.*	• ehl moo-SEH-oh deh AHR-teh _____.
If you're interested in theater, I can get you tickets to…	*Si le interesa el teatro, puedo conseguirle boletos para…*	See leh een-teh-REH-sah ehl teh-AH-troh, PWEH-doh kohn-seh-GEER-leh boh-LEH-tohs PAH-rah…
• a show.	• *un espectáculo.*	• oon ehs-pehk-TAH-koo-loh.

• an opera.	• *una ópera.*	• OO-nah OH-peh-rah.
• a movie.	• *una película.*	• OO-nah peh-LEE-koo-lah.
For shopping, I'd recommend...	*Para comprar, le recomendaría...*	PAH-rah kohm-PRAHR, leh reh-koh-mehn-dah-REE-ah...
• downtown.	• *el centro de la ciudad.*	• ehl SEHN-troh deh lah syoo-DAHD.
• the mall.	• *el centro comercial.*	• ehl SEHN-troh koh-mehr-SYAHL.
• the discount outlets.	• *los lugares de descuentos.*	• lohs loo-GAH-rehs deh dehs-KWEHN-tohs.

GUEST

Do they have...there?	*¿Tendrán...allí?*	¿Tehn-DRAHN...ah-YEE?
• clothes	• *ropa*	• ROH-pah
• furniture	• *muebles*	• MWEH-blehs
• rugs (carpets)	• *alfombras*	• ahl-FOM-brahs
• souvenirs	• *souvenirs*	• souvenirs
• books	• *libros*	• LEE-brohs
• sporting goods	• *artículos deportivos*	• ahr-TEE-koo-lohs deh-pohr-TEE-vohs
• candy	• *caramelos*	• kah-rah-MEH-lohs
• antiques	• *antigüedades*	• ahn-tee-gweh-DAH-dehs
• electronics	• *aparatos electrónicos*	• ah-pah-RAH-tos eh-lehk-TROH-nee-kohs
• computers	• *computadoras*	• kohm-poo-tah-DOH-rahs
• a farmers' market	• *un mercado (de productos de granja)*	• oon mehr-KAH-doh (deh proh-DOOHK-tohs deh GRAHN-hah
• a supermarket	• *un supermercado*	• oon soo-pehr-mehr-KAH-doh
• a flea market	• *mercadillo*	• oon mehr-kah-DEE-yoh

CONCIERGE

Perhaps you'd like a museum.	*Quizás usted desearía ir a un museo.*	Kee-zahs oos-TEHD deh-seh-ah-REE-ah eer ah oon moo-SEH-oh.
A local favorite is the…museum.	*El museo local favorito es el museo…*	Ehl moo-SEH-oh loh-KAHL fah-voh-REE-toh ehs ehl moo-SEH-oh…
• natural history	• *de historia natural.*	• deh ees-TOH-ryah nah-too-RAHL.
• modern art	• *de arte moderno.*	• deh AHR-teh moh-DEHR-noh.
• science	• *de ciencia.*	• deh SYEHN-syah.
• local history	• *de historia local.*	• deh ees-TOH-ryah loh-KAHL.

GUEST

We were thinking of sight-seeing.	*Estamos pensando en recorrer el lugar.*	Ehs-TAH-mohs pehn-SAHN-doh ehn reh-kohr-REHR ehl loo-GAHR

CONCIERGE

I'd be happy to arrange a city tour.	*Les organizaré una gira por la ciudad.*	Leh ohr-gah-nee-sah-REH OO-nah HEE-rah pohr lah syoo-DAHD.

GUEST

How about…	*¿Qué les parece(n)…*	¿Keh lehs pah-REH-seh(n)…
• architecture?	• *la arquitectura?*	• lah ahr-kee-tehk-TOO-rah?
• churches?	• *las iglesias?*	• lahs ee-GLEH-syahs?
• a vineyard?	• *un viñedo?*	• oon vee-NYEH-doh?
• the business district?	• *el área financiera?*	• ehl AH-reh-ah fee-nahn-SYEH-rah?
• the government buildings?	• *los edificios del gobierno?*	• lohs eh-dee-FEE-syohs dehl goh-BYEHR-noh?
• the university?	• *la universidad?*	• lah oo-nee-vehr-see-DAHD?

• monuments?	• *los monumentos?*	• lohs moh-noo-MHEN-tohs?
• the countryside?	• *el campo?*	• ehl KAHM-poh?

CONCIERGE

There are many sports events.	*Hay muchos eventos deportivos.*	Ayh MOO-chohs eh-VEHN-tohs deh-pohr-TEE-vohs.
Would you like tickets to...	*¿Quiere boletos para...*	¿KYEH-reh boh-LEH-tohs PAH-rah...
• a baseball game?	• *un partido de béisbol?*	• oon pahr-TEE-doh deh BAYS-bohl?
• a basketball game?	• *un partido de baloncesto?*	• oon pahr-TEE-doh deh bah-lohn-SEHS-toh?
• a football game?	• *un partido de fútbol americano?*	• oon pahr-TEE-doh deh FOOT-bohl ah-meh-ree-KAH-noh?
• a hockey game?	• *un partido de "hockey"?*	• oon pahr-TEEH-doh deh "hockey"?
• a tennis match?	• *un partido de "tennis"?*	• oon pahr-TEEH-doh deh "tennis"?

GUEST

Are there any musical events?	*¿Hay algún evento musical?*	¿Ahy ahl-GOON eh-VEHN-toh moo-see-KHAL?

CONCIERGE

There is a...concert tonight.	*Hay un concierto de...esta noche.*	Ahy oon kohn-SYEHR-toh deh... EHS-tah NOH-cheh.
• rock-and-roll	• *"rock and roll"*	• "rock and roll"
• classical music	• *música clásica*	• MOO-see-kah KLAH-see-kah
• folk	• *música popular*	• MOO-see-kah poh-poo-LAHR
There's musical entertainment at _____.	*Hay un entretenimiento musical en _____.*	AHY oon ehn-treh-teh-nee-MYEHN-toh moo-see-KAHL ehn _____.

GUEST		
Is there anything else going on tonight?	*¿Hay algo más esta noche?*	¿Ahy AHL-goh MAHS EHS-tah NOH-cheh?
CONCIERGE		
Other than the movies, I'd suggest…	*A parte de los cines, le sugeriría…*	Ah PAHR-teh deh lohs SEE-nehs, leh soo-heh-ree-REE-ah…
• a nightclub.	• *una discoteca.*	• OO-nah dees-koh-TEH-kah.
• a video rental.	• *alquilar películas.*	• ahl-kee-LAHR peh-LEE-koo-lahs.
GUEST		
What do you suggest for outdoor activities?	*¿Qué actividades al aire libre sugiere?*	¿KEH ahk-tee-vee-DAH-dehs ahl AHY-reh LEE-breh soo-HYEH-reh?
CONCIERGE		
How about…	*¿Qué le parece…*	¿KEH leh pah-REH-seh…
• hiking?	• *alpinismo?*	• ahl-pee-NEES-moh?
• fishing?	• *la pesca?*	• lah PES-kah?
• skiing?	• *esquiar?*	• ehs-kee-AHR?
• skating?	• *patinar?*	• pah-tee-NAHR?
• swimming?	• *nadar?*	• nah-DAHR?
• surfing?	• *hacer surf?*	• ah-SEHR SOORF?
Or you might like to go…	*O quizás le gustaría ir…*	OH keeh-SAHS leh goos-tah-REE-ah eer…
• to the river.	• *al río.*	• ahl REE-oh.
• to the lake.	• *al lago.*	• ahl LAH-goh.
• to the mountains.	• *a las montañas.*	• ah lahs mohn-TAH-nyahs.
• for a drive.	• *a manejar.*	• ah mah-neh-HAR.
• to the beach.	• *a la playa.*	• ah lah PLAH-yah.
• to the forest.	• *al bosque.*	• ahl BOHS-keh.
GUEST		
Is there anything for children?	*¿Hay algo para los niños?*	¿AHY AHL-goh PAH-rah lohs NEE-nyohs?

CONCIERGE

Yes, there's…	*Sí, hay…*	SEE, ahy…
• a zoo.	• *un zoológico.*	• oon soh-oh-LOH-hee-koh.
• a children's museum.	• *un museo para niños.*	• oon moo-SEH-oh PAH-ra NEE-nyohs.
• an amusement park.	• *un parque de diversiones.*	• oon PAHR-keh deh dee-vehr-SYOH-nehs.
• a water park.	• *un parque acuático.*	• oon PAHR-keh ah-KWAH-tee-koh.
Would you like to rent…	*¿Le gustaría alquilar…*	¿Leh goos-tah-REE-ah ahl-kee-LAHR…
• a bicycle?	• *una bicicleta?*	• OO-nah bee-see-KLEH-tah?
• a car?	• *un auto?*	• oon AH-OO-toh?
• a boat?	• *un bote?*	• oon BOH-teh?
• some skis?	• *unos esquíes?*	• OO-nohs ehs-KEE-ehs?
• some Rollerblades?	• *unos patines?*	• OO-nohs pah-TEE-nehs?
Would you like a tour guide who speaks Spanish?	*¿Desea un guía turístico que hable español?*	¿Deh-SEH-ah oon GEE-ah too-REE-stee-koh KEH AH-bleh ehs-pah-NYOHL?
May I make a reservation for you?	*¿Le hago una reserva para usted?*	¿Leh AH-goh OO-nah re-SEHR-vah PAH-rah OOS-tehd?

GUEST

Can you recommend a good restaurant?	*¿Me puede recomendar un buen restaurante?*	¿Meh PWEH-deh reh-koh-mehn-DAHR oon BWEHN rrehs-tah-oo-RAHN-teh?

CONCIERGE

What type of cuisine would you like?	*¿Qué clase de comida le gusta?*	¿Keh KLAH-seh deh koh-MEE-dah leh GOOS-tah?

GUEST

We'd like a(n)... restaurant.	*Nos gustaría un restaurante...*	Nohs goos-tah-REE-ah oon rrehs-stah-oo-RHAN-teh...
• casual	• *casual.*	• kah-soo-AHL.
• elegant	• *elegante.*	• eh-leh-GAHN-teh.
• fast-food	• *de comida rápida.*	• deh koh-MEE-dah RAH-pee-dah.
• inexpensive	• *barato.*	• bah-RAH-toh.
• seafood	• *de mariscos.*	• deh mah-REES-kohs.
• vegetarian	• *vegetariano.*	• veh-heh-tah-RYAH-noh.

CONCIERGE

You can get there by...	*Usted puede ir en...*	OOS-tehd PWEH-deh eer ehn...
• bus.	• *bus.*	• BOOS.
• train.	• *tren.*	• TREHN.
• subway.	• *metro.*	• MEH-troh.
Take the...bound for ____.	*Tome el... hasta ____.*	TOH-meh ehl...AH-stah ____.
• number ____ bus	• *el bus número ____.*	• ehl BOOS NOO-meh-roh ____
• train	• *tren*	• TREHN
• subway	• *metro*	• MEH-troh
You'll need to transfer to... at ____.	*Necesitará cambiar al...en ____.*	Neh-seh-see-tah-RAH kahm-BYAHR al... ehn ____.
• the ____ line	• *la línea ____*	• lah LEEH-neh-ah ____
• the number ____ bus	• *el bus número ____*	• ehl BOOS NOO-meh-roh ____
Get off at ____.	*Bájese en ____.*	BAH-heh-seh ehn ____.
May I call you a taxi?	*¿Puedo llamarle un taxi?*	¿PWEH-doh yah-MAHR-leh oon TAHK-see?

We have a free shuttle bus service available to _____.	*Tenemos un servicio de bus gratis disponible a _____.*	Teh-NEH-mohs oon sehr-VEE-syoh deh BOOS GRAH-tees dees-poh-NEE-bleh ah _____.
It leaves every _____ minutes.	*Sale cada _____ minutos.*	SAH-leh KAH-dah _____ mee-NOO-tohs.
It leaves every hour.	*Sale cada hora.*	SAH-leh KAH-dah OH-rah.

GUEST

What's the price range?	*¿Cuál es el precio?*	¿KWAHL ehs ehl PREH-syoh?

6. Business Services and Clientele

A. BOOKING A BUSINESS MEETING

EMPLOYEE

Good morning.	*Buenos días.*	BWEH-nohs DEE-ahs.
How may I help you today?	*¿En qué puedo ayudarle hoy?*	¿Ehn KEH PWEH-doh ah-yoo-DAHR-leh ohy?

TIP! ••••

Clients who do business from the hotel need a great deal of service from you. They tend to be seasoned travelers who don't want a lot of explanation from hotel employees, just competent action. Attending to their every need often yields substantial financial rewards!

GUEST

I'd like to make arrangements for a business meeting.	*Me gustaría hacer los arreglos para una reunión de negocios.*	Meh goos-tah-REE-ah ah-SEHR lohs ahr-REH-glohs PAH-rah OO-nah ree-oo-NYOHN deh neh-GOH-syohs.

EMPLOYEE

For how many people?	*¿Para cuántas personas?*	¿PAH-rah KWAHN-tahs pehr-SOH-nahs?

GUEST

For ____ people on ____.	*Para ____ personas en ____.*	PAH-rah ____ pehr-SOH-nahs ehn ____.

EMPLOYEE

Fine.	*Está bien.*	Ehs-TAH BYEHN.
We have space available.	*Tenemos espacio disponible.*	Teh-NEH-mohs ehs-PAH-syoh dees-poh-NEE-bleh.
We can provide all your meals, as well as your meeting needs.	*Le podemos proveer con todas las comidas, así como satisfacer las necesidades de la reunión.*	Leh poh-DEH-mohs proh-VEH-ehr kohn TOH dahs lahs koh-MEE-dahs, ah-SEE KOH-moh sah-tees-fah-SEHR lahs neh-seh-see-DAH-dehs deh lah reh-oo-NYOHN.

GUEST

That's good.	*Me parece bien.*	Meh pah-REH-seh BYEHN.
We'd like…for each day.	*Nos gustaría… cada día.*	Nos goo-stah-REE-ah …KAH-dah DEE-ah.
• a continental breakfast	• *desayuno continental*	• deh-sah-YOO-noh kohn-tee-nehn-TAHL
• coffee breaks	• *descansos para el café*	• dehs-KAHN-sohs PAH-rah ehl kah-FEH
• a working lunch	• *almuerzo de trabajo*	• ahl-MWEHR-soh DEH trah-BAH-hoh
• snacks	• *picadas*	• pee-kah-dahs

• a cocktail reception	• *una recepción con cóctel*	• OO-nah reh-sehp-SYOHN kohn KOHK-tehl
• dinner	• *cena*	• SEH-nah
Also, we'll require… for the meeting room.	*También vamos a necesitar…para la sala de reuniones.*	Tahm-BYEHN VAH-mohs ah neh-seh-see-TAHR… PAH-rah lah SAH-lah deh reh-oo-NYOH-nehs.
• a VCR with a large-screen monitor	• *una video casetera con una pantalla grande*	• OO-nah vee-DEH-oh kah-seh-TEH-rah kohn OO-nah pahn-TAH-yah GRAHN-deh
• an overhead projector with transparencies and markers	• *un proyector de techo con transparencias y marcadores*	• OON proh-yehk-TOHR deh TEH-choh kohn trahns-pah-REHN-syahs ee mahr-kah-DOH-rehs
• a chalkboard	• *un pizarrón*	• oon pee-sah-rROHN
• a flip chart	• *un mapa movible*	• oon MAH-pah moh-VEE-bleh
• a slide projector	• *un proyector de diapositivas*	• oon proh-yehk-TOHR deh dee-ah-poh-see-TEE-bahs
• a computer with a large-screen monitor	• *una computadora con una pantalla grande*	• OO-nah kohm-poo-tah-DOH-rah kohn OO-nah pahn-TAH-yah GRAHN-deh
And please be sure to provide…	*Y por favor asegúrese de que tengamos…*	Ee pohr fah-VOHR ah-seh-GOO-reh-seh deh keh tehn-GAH-mohs…
• water.	• *agua.*	• AH-gwah.
• pads with pencils.	• *anotadores y lápices.*	• ah-noh-tah-DOH-rehs ee LAH-pee-sehs.
• ashtrays.	• *ceniceros.*	• seh-nee-SEH-rohs.

EMPLOYEE

Let's decide on what time you'd like everything, and we'll be all set.	*Decidamos a qué hora va a necesitar todo, y estará listo.*	Deh-see-DAH-mohs a KEH OH-rah vah ah neh-seh-see-TAHR TO-doh, ee tah-RAH LEES-toh.

GUEST

Okay. How will the room be set up?	*Okey. ¿Cómo estará arreglada la sala?*	Okey. ¿KOH-moh ehs-tah-RAH ahr-reh-GLAH-dah lah SAH-lah?

EMPLOYEE

We can set up the room…	*Podemos arreglar la sala…*	Poh-DEH-mohs ahr-reh-GLAHR lah SAH-lah…
• theater style.	• *estilo teatral.*	• ehs-TEE-loh teh-ah-TRAHL.
• in a square.	• *en cuadrado.*	• ehn kwah-DRAH-doh.
• horseshoe ("U") style.	• *en forma de herradura.*	• ehn FOHR-mah deh ehr-ra-DOO-rah.
• classroom style.	• *estilo escuela.*	• ehs-TEE-loh ehs-KWEH-lah.
• boardroom style.	• *estilo directorio.*	• ehs-TEE-loh dee-rehk-TOH-ryoh.
We're looking forward to having your group here.	*Nos alegra tener su grupo aquí.*	Nohs ah-LEH-grah TEH-nehr soo GROO-poh ah-KEE.

B. AT THE MEETING

ATTENDANT

I'm _____, the meeting-room attendant.	*Yo soy _____, y les serviré en la sala de reuniones.*	Yoh soyh _____, ee lehs sehr-bee-REH ehn lah SAH-lah DEH reh-oo-NYOH-nehs.
How is everything?	*¿Cómo está todo?*	¿KOH-moh ehs-TAH TOH-doh?

GUEST

Everything is fine, thank you.	*Está todo bien, gracias.*	Ehs-TAH TOH-doh BYEHN, GRAH-syahs.
We need…	*Necesitamos…*	Neh-seh-see-TAH-mohs…
• more chairs.	• *más sillas.*	• MAHS SEE-yahs.
• more coffee.	• *más café.*	• MAHS kah-FEH.

• the ashtrays emptied.	• *los ceniceros limpios.*	• lohs seh-nee-SEH-rohs LEEM-pyohs.
• more water.	• *más agua.*	• MAHS AH-gwah.
ATTENDANT		
I'll take care of it right away.	*Me haré cargo enseguida.*	Meh ah-REM kahr-goh ehn-seh-GEE-dah.
Is everything else satisfactory?	*¿Todo lo demás le satisface?*	¿TO-doh loh deh-MAHS leh sah-teehs-FAH-seh?
GUEST		
It's quite nice, but the room…	*Está bastante bien, pero la sala…*	Ehs-TAH bahs-TAHN-teh BYEHN, PEH-roh lah SAH-lah…
• needs more light.	• *necesita mas luz.*	• neh-seh-SEE-tah MAHS LOOS.
• is too bright.	• *es demasiado luminosa.*	• ehs deh-mah-SYAH-doh loo-mee-NOH-sah.
• needs more ventilation.	• *necesita más ventilación.*	• neh-seh-SEE-tah MAHS vehn-tee-lah-SYOHN.
• is a little noisy.	• *es un poco ruidosa.*	• ehs oon POH-koh rooy-DOH-sah.
• is crowded.	• *está muy llena.*	• ehs-TAH MOOY YEH-nah.
It's too hot (cold).	*Hace demasiado calor (frío).*	AH-seh deh-mah-see-AH-doh kah-LOHR (FREE-oh).
Can you take care of it?	*¿Se puede hacer cargo de eso?*	¿Seh PWEH-deh ah-SEHR KAHR-goh deh EH-soh?
Can we get another room?	*¿Podemos tomar otra sala?*	¿Poh-DEH-mohs toh-MAHR OH-trah SAH-lah?
ATTENDANT		
Let me see what we can do.	*Déjeme ver lo que podemos hacer.*	DEH-heh-meh loh vehr keh poh-DEH-mohs AH-sehr.

C. CATERING TO BUSINESS GUESTS

CONCIERGE

How may I help you?	*¿En qué puedo ayudarle?*	¿Ehn KEH PWEH-doh ah-yoo-DHAR-leh?

GUEST

Where is breakfast for the _____ group?	*¿Dónde está el desayuno para el grupo _____?*	¿DOHN-deh ehs-TAH ehl deh-sah-YOO-noh PAH-rah ehl GROO-poh _____?
Where is the exhibits hall?	*¿Dónde está la sala de exposiciones?*	¿DOHN-deh ehs-TAH lah SAH-lah deh ehk-spoh-see-SYOH-nehs?

CONCIERGE

There's a buffet set up outside your meeting room.	*Hay un buffet servido afuera de la sala de reuniones.*	Ahy OON boo-FEHT sehr-VEE-doh ah-FWEH-rah deh lah SAH-lah deh reh-oo-NYOH-nehs.
Just down the hall.	*Justo al final del pasillo.*	HOOS-toh ahl fee-NAHL dehl pah-SEE-yoh.
In the dining room.	*En el salón comedor.*	Ehn ehl sah-LOHN koh-meh-DOHR.

GUEST

Thank you.	*Gracias.*	GRAH-syahs.
I need...	*Necesito...*	Neh-seh-SEE-toh...
• a fax sent.	• *enviar un fax.*	• ehn-vee-AHR oon fax.
• some typing done.	• *un trabajo mecanográfico.*	• oon TRAH-BAH-hoh meh-kah-noh-GRAH-fee-koh.
• a hookup to the Internet.	• *conectarme con "Internet."*	• koh-nehk-TAHR-meh kohn"Internet."
• a computer.	• *una computadora.*	• OO-nah kohm-poo-tah-DOH-rah.
• a package sent overnight.	• *una entrega nocturna de paquetes.*	• OO-nah ehn-TREH-ghah nohk-TOOR-nah deh pah-KEH-dehs.

• courier service.	• *un servicio de correo rápido.*	• oon sehr-VEE-syoh deh kohr-REH-oh RAH-pee-doh.
• some letters mailed.	• *enviar unas cartas.*	• ehn-vee-AHR OO-nahs KAHR-tahs.
• some copies made.	• *unas copias.*	• OO-nahs KOH-pee-ahs.

CONCIERGE

I'll take care of that right away.	*Me encargaré de eso enseguida.*	Meh ehn-kahr-ghah-REH deh EH-soh ehn-seh-GEE-dah.

GUEST

Later, I'd like to host a small reception.	*Más tarde, me gustaría organizar una pequeña recepción.*	MAHS TAHR-deh, meh goo-stah-REE-ah ohr-gah-nee-SAHR OO-nah peh-KEH-nyah reh-sehp-SYOHN.
Can you arrange that?	*¿Puede arreglar eso?*	¿PWEH-deh ahr-reh-GLAHR EH-soh?

CONCIERGE

Certainly.	*Por supuesto.*	Pohr soo-PWEHS-toh.
What would you like?	*¿Qué desea usted?*	¿KEH deh-SEH-ah OOS-tehd?

GUEST

We need a full bar and some hors d'oeuvres.	*Necesitamos un bar completo y algunos aperitivos.*	Neh-seh-see-TAH-mohs OON bahr kohm-PLEH-toh ee ahl-GOO-nohs ah-peh-ree-TEE-vohs.
Make sure there are plenty of chilled shrimp.	*Asegúrese de que hayan muchos camarones frescos.*	Ah-seh-GOO-reh-seh deh keh AH-yahn MOO-chos kah-mah-ROH-nehs FREHS-kohs.
Lots of champagne, please.	*Bastante "champagne," por favor.*	Bah-STAHN-teh "champagne," pohr fah-VOHR.

CONCIERGE

I'll have Room Service put together a proposal right away, and get back to you.	*Haré que el Servicio de Habitación prepare una propuesta enseguida y le contesto.*	Ah-REH keh ehl sehr-VEE-syoh deh ah-bee-tah-SYOHN preh-PAH-reh OO-nah proh-PWEH-stah ehn-seh-GEE-dah ee leh kohn-TEHS-toh.

7. Checking Out

GUEST

At what time is checkout?	*¿A qué hora es la salida del hotel?*	¿Ah KEH OH-rah ehs lah sah-LEE-dah dehl oh-TEHL?

FRONT DESK CLERK

Checkout is…	*La salida es …*	Lah sah-LEE-dah ehs…
• at 10 A.M.	• *a las diez de la mañana.*	• ah lahs DYES deh lah mah-NYAH-nah.
• at noon.	• *al mediodía.*	• ahl meh-dyoh-DEE-ah.
• at 3 P.M.	• *a las tres de la tarde.*	• ah lahs TREHS deh la TAHR-deh.
You may audit your bill on channel _____ on your television.	*Usted puede controlar su cuenta a través del canal _____ de su T.V.*	Oo-STEHD PWEH-deh kohn-troh-LAHR soo KWEHN-tah ah trah-VEHS dehl kah-NAHL _____ deh soo TEH-VEH.
We provide an express checkout service.	*Le proveemos de un servicio de registración de salida muy rápido.*	Leh proh-veh-EH-mohs DEH OON sehr-VEE-syoh DEH reh-hee-strah-SYOHN deh sah-LEE-dah mooy RAH-pee-doh.
Your bill will be left outside your door the night before you check out.	*Le dejaremos su cuenta en la puerta la noche anterior a su partida.*	Leh deh-hah-REH-mohs soo KWEHN-tah ehn lah PWEHR-tah lah NOH-cheh ahn-teh-RYOHR ah soo pahr-TEE-dah.

If you're satisfied with your bill, simply sign it,	*Si usted está conforme con su cuenta, simplemente fírmela,*	See OOS-tehd ehs-TAH kohn-for-meh kohn soo KWEHN-tah, seem-pleh-MEHN-teh FEER-meh-lah,
and leave your key in your room.	*y deje la llave en su habitación.*	ee DEH-heh lah YAH-veh ehn soo ah-bee-tah-SYOHN.
Any late charges such as breakfast or mini-bar will be added automatically.	*Cualquier cargo de última hora será adicionado automáticamente.*	Kwahl-KYEHR KAHR-goh deh OOL-tee-mah OH-rah seh-RAH ah-dee-syoh-NAH-do ah-oo-toh-MAH-tee-kah-MEHN-teh.
GUEST		
I'd like to check out, please.	*Me gustaría firmar mi salida, por favor.*	Meh goo-stah-REE-ah feer-MAHR mee sah-LEE-dah, pohr fah-BOHR.
CLERK		
May I have your luggage brought down?	*¿Puedo hacer bajar su equipaje?*	¿PWEH-doh ah-SEHR bah-HAHR soo eh-kee-PAH-heh?
GUEST		
Yes, please.	*Sí, por favor.*	SEE, pohr fah-VOHR.
No, I brought (will bring) it myself.	*No, la bajé (la bajaré) yo mismo.*	NOH, lah bah-HEH (lah bah-hah-RHE) yoh MEES-moh.
CLERK		
How was everything?	*¿Cómo estuvo todo?*	¿KOH-moh ehs-TOO-voh TOH-doh?
GUEST		
It was very nice, thank you.	*Todo estuvo muy bien, gracias.*	TOH-doh ehs-TOO-voh MOOY BYEHN, GRAH-syahs.
I want to speak with the manager.	*Quiero hablar con el gerente.*	KYEH-roh ah-BLAHR kohn ehl heh-REHN-teh.

CLERK

Certainly. The manager on duty is ____.	*Por supuesto. El gerente en funciones es ____.*	Pohr soo-PWEHS-to. EHL heh-REHN-teh ehn foon-SYOH-nehs ehs ____.
One moment, please.	*Un momento, por favor.*	Oon moh-MEHN-toh, pohr fah-VOHR.

GUEST

Our experience was…	*Nuestra experiencia fue…*	NWEHS-trah ehk-speh-RYEHN-syah FWEH…
• good.	• *buena.*	• BWEH-nah.
• excellent.	• *excelente.*	• ehk-seh-LEHN-teh.
• poor.	• *regular.*	• re-goo-LAHR.

MANAGER ON DUTY

That's nice to hear.	*Me alegro mucho (de escuchar eso).*	Meh ah-LEH-groh MOO-choch (deh ehs-koo-CHAHR EH-soh).
I'm sorry to hear that.*	*Lamento escuchar eso.*	Lah-MEHN-toh ehs-koo-CHAHR EH-soh.
Thank you. Please come again.	*Gracias. Espero verle otra vez.*	GRAH-syahs. Ehs-PEH-roh BEHR-leh OH-trah BEHS.

*Please refer to "Guest Complaints in the Hotel" on page 440 for more on handling dissatisfied clients.